WORDSWORTH CLASSICS
OF WORLD LITERATURE

General Editor: Tom Griffith

REPUBLIC

Plato
Republic

*Translated by John Llewelyn Davies
and David James Vaughan*

With an Introduction by Stephen Watt

**WORDSWORTH CLASSICS
OF WORLD LITERATURE**

In loving memory of
MICHAEL TRAYLER
the founder of Wordsworth Editions

5

Readers who are interested in other titles from
Wordsworth Editions are invited to visit our website at
www.wordsworth-editions.com

For our latest list and a full mail-order service, contact
Bibliophile Books, 5 Thomas Road, London E14 7BN
TEL: +44 (0)20 7515 9222 FAX: +44 (0)20 7538 4115
E-MAIL: orders@bibliophilebooks.com

This edition published 1997 by Wordsworth Editions Limited
8B East Street, Ware, Hertfordshire SG12 9HJ

ISBN   978 1 85326 483 2

Typeset in Great Britain by Antony Gray
Printed and bound by Clays Ltd, St Ives plc

Contents

Introduction

1 Why read the *Republic*?

Many people will come to the *Republic* with some knowledge of its contents, and what they will usually know about the work is that it advocates a totalitarian society ruled by philosophers. Not even a professional academic is likely to find such a proposal attractive. So why bother to read the *Republic*?

One answer is that Plato has exerted an immense historical influence on world culture and that the *Republic,* because it contains accounts of many of the most important Platonic doctrines, is by far the best introduction to his thought. In the Christian West, the Platonism of Augustine of Hippo (354–430 AD) became a central influence on the development of church doctrine, an influence that persists in both the Roman Catholic and Reformed churches. At the Renaissance, Plato became championed by scholars such as Marsilio Ficino (1433–99) against a mediaeval style of philosophy predominantly influenced by Aristotle. More recently, a Platonic influence can be found in the works of philosophers such as Gottlob Frege (1848–1925), A.N.Whitehead (1861–1947) and G.E.Moore (1873–1958). Outside philosophy, aspects of the theories of Sigmund Freud (1856–1939) appear to owe much to Plato's psychology, whilst the novels *Brave New World* by Aldous Huxley (1894–1963) and *Nineteen Eighty-Four* by George Orwell (1903–50) both borrow and criticise features of the ideal society envisaged by Plato and set forth especially in the *Republic.*

Another, perhaps better, answer is that the ideas contained in the *Republic* continue to throw light on many issues that still trouble political scientists and philosophers. Before turning to consider some of these ideas, however, I shall first give a brief sketch of the historical background to the *Republic*'s creation. (In what follows, references to Plato's works are, as is customary, given by citing the pagination of the Stephanus edition of his complete works: this pagination is noted in the text.)

2 Historical background

Plato was born in Athens around 429 BC, the son of wealthy and well-connected parents. He thus grew up during the Peloponnesian War (431–404), a bitter conflict between Sparta and Athens which involved almost all the known civilised world. During the war and its aftermath, Athens experienced a number of revolutions and counter-revolutions in which democracy (government by the majority), the characteristic form of Athenian government, alternated with oligar-chy (government by a minority), the form of government character-istic of Sparta. Plato's family was heavily involved in the oligarchical regime of the Thirty which took power in 404, and it may well have been disgust at the ferocity of their rule which dissuaded Plato from pursuing a political career and led him into a private life devoted to the study of philosophy.

Whatever his motivation, around the age of twenty Plato joined the circle surrounding Socrates, and he remained there until Socrates' execution for irreligion by a democratic government in 399. As a consequence of the execution, Plato left Athens and travelled the Mediterranean world. Around 388 he returned to Athens, and established a philosophical community which became known as the Academy. Over the following years he drew pupils to the Academy from all over the Greek world, among whom was that other giant of classical philosophy, Aristotle. By the time of his death in Athens in 347, Plato had also written over twenty philosophical dialogues, in the majority of which Socrates plays the leading role. Among these dialogues is the *Republic*.

3 What sort of work is the *Republic*?

a. The Republic *as literature.* The *Republic* is ostensibly the record of an argument which takes place between Socrates and a number of other people, probably around the year 420 BC. That Socrates and the other characters in the dialogue actually existed is certain; that

Socrates taught by means of argument and conversation rather than by lectures or books is equally certain. A problem that has taxed scholars over the centuries is the so-called 'Socratic problem' – how much of the philosophy in the dialogues is a faithful reporting of Socrates' own arguments and how much is Plato's work. That is a question I shall ignore. But there is another related problem that I shall address: how important is it to understanding the *Republic* to remember that it is in the form of a dialogue rather than a treatise?

One thing that good philosophy should do is to consider objections to any argument. And to do philosophy well is to ensure that those objections are stated as clearly and forcibly as possible. Given this aspect of the subject, it is perfectly natural for philosophers to use different characters as mouthpieces for opposing arguments in a debate, and thus to write dialogues rather than treatises. But the point to be noticed here is that such a dialogue could easily be rewritten as a treatise and beyond a certain formal elegance, little would be lost. Most philosophical dialogues, including many of Plato's own, fall into this category.

Dialogues can also be used to embody literary rather than philosophical qualities, rather in the manner of a play. To what extent these aspects are to be found in the *Republic* is debatable; that they are to be found there to some extent is undeniable. The influence of character, for example, is particularly striking in Book 1. Cephalus, the spokesman for conventional morality, having spoken his piece, goes back to increasing his stock in heaven by sacrifices, thus avoiding further discussion (331d). Thrasymachus, a professional teacher of rhetoric whose pride and livelihood are threatened by Socrates' pre-eminence in conversation, tries to bully him into submission (336b). Later in the work, Polemarchus, young and rich, has his interest aroused by the sharing of women in the ideal city, and nudges his friend to get Socrates to tell more (449b). Other literary effects can be seen apart from the influence of character. A recurring theme in the *Republic* is the need for the philosopher to be compelled to act: Socrates is forced to go to Polemarchus' house (328b); he is (light-heartedly) threatened when he tries to deny the practical application of his theories (474a); the dweller in the Cave is forced into daylight (515e); the philosopher is compelled to return to political life (520a).

It is difficult to know what you should make of these literary rather than philosophical aspects of the *Republic*. In some cases they are doubtless mere ornament which can be ignored; in other cases, however, they do seem to be embodying meaning which could not easily be expressed in a more narrowly philosophical form. It has been said that to ignore Plato the poet is to ignore Plato the philosopher; it is in any case certain that much of the influence of Plato has resulted from these literary aspects of the dialogue and that any full assessment of the *Republic* has to take them into account. In what follows, I shall concentrate on the more strictly philosophical aspects of the work; by so doing, I emphasise the purely introductory nature of this essay.

b. Politics as psychology. The title, the *Republic,* comes from the Latin 'res publica' meaning 'public business', and stands for the Greek 'politeia' which means 'political system' or 'public and political life of the community'. Given this title, it might seem idle to ask whether the *Republic* actually is about politics. Nevertheless, it is an essential question to ask; for throughout the *Republic* there are clear statements that the real task of the dialogue is to understand the good individual. The point of discussing the good society is that, while its workings are analogous to those of a good mind, it is easier to understand because its parts, unlike those of the mind, are visible (e.g. 369a, 434d, 441c, 605b).

Are the descriptions of good societies then just extended analogies of the good individual? As I have already emphasised, Plato's work doesn't operate on just one level; and part of the attractiveness of the *Republic* is that it can be read as psychology as well as politics. Yet the link between individual and society isn't merely by analogy. Particular types of society will produce particular types of individual, and Plato discusses these links in Books 8 and 9. But even putting aside this causal connection between politics and psychology, it would still be wrong to claim that the only interest to be found in the politics of the *Republic* is as an analogy of the individual. Although the political structures put forward are of dubious practicality and are acknowledged as such in the dialogue itself (e.g. 472e), they certainly appear to have been intended in some sense to illuminate actual structures and to suggest improvements. Moreover, quite apart from Plato's intentions, his arguments have from the beginning been taken as politically directed and criticised accordingly.

Although you need to keep in mind the many-layered quality of the *Republic,* there is the danger that you become beguiled by the elusiveness of Plato, and stop asking the hard and clear questions that are needed to deal with the *Republic* as philosophical argument. If the *Republic* contains bad arguments on any one level, that needs to be said clearly, even while admitting and attempting to understand its other qualities. Failure to take the work seriously as straightforward philosophy diminishes its importance just as surely as the failure to be alive to the variety and complexity of other readings.

4 The structure of the *Republic*

It should be clear from the above that there is unlikely to be one description of the structure of the *Republic*. That said, beginners need some map to guide their exploration even if they are to abandon such guidance later on. In this section I shall therefore set out an understanding of the structure of the *Republic* commonly held among Anglo-American philosophers.

In general, the *Republic is* seen as an attack on the conventional assumption among Plato's contemporaries that living a good life is just a matter of performing certain actions (e.g. 331a–d), regardless of the sort of person you are and the spirit in which you perform those actions. Instead, Plato tries to move his audience to an understanding that a good life consists in being a certain sort of person rather than merely doing certain sorts of action: from an act-centred morality where the primary question is, 'What should I do?' to an agent-centred morality where the primary question is, 'What sort of person should I be?'

Book 1: Socrates asks: What is justice? He demonstrates the incompleteness of the conventional answer, proposed by Cephalus and Polemarchus, that it is simply doing just actions. He is attacked by Thrasymachus, who denies that it is in an agent's interests to act justly.

Books 2, 3 and 4: Glaucon and Adeimantus take up Thrasymachus' point and urge Socrates to show what reason an agent has to act justly. Socrates convinces them that an answer to this question may be arrived at by examining justice in a state. The ideally just state is sketched, and it is argued that its justice consists in the potentially competing classes within that state existing in harmony together under the leadership of the most rational. Analogously, it is concluded that a just individual is an individual whose potentially competing desires are in harmony under the rule of reason. As the absence of mental conflict is clearly desirable, an agent thus has a reason to be a just agent and therefore to be someone who acts justly.

Books 5, 6 and 7: a digression from the main argument. Prompted by Polemarchus and Adeimantus, Socrates describes the treatment of women, children and property in the ruling class in the ideal state. The rulers will be philosophers because only they can know what is truly good.

Books 8 and 9: resumption of the main argument from Book 4. The principal varieties of imperfect mental and political constitution are examined and the consequences of failing to be just are sketched.

Book 10: afterword. A discussion of poetry. The fate of the human soul after death is expounded in the Myth of Er.

Even this bare outline of a possible structure is likely to provoke questions. Why did Plato depart from the main line of argument in Books 5–7, and what is the explanation for the seemingly unconnected Book 10? Can examination of a just city really throw any light on a just individual? In what follows, I shall attempt to follow some major themes through the work and to suggest how the discussions remain of interest to contemporary philosophers.

5. Why be just?

Thrasymachus' attacks on Socrates in Book 1 are confused, and the analysis of them has received much attention from academics. But one of the challenges he sets Socrates is to explain why anyone should be just when just people tend to lose out to the unjust (343a–343c). Socrates sketches several solutions to this challenge, none of which is wholly satisfactory, and is forced to return to the question by Glaucon and Adeimantus (357a–367e).

Philosophers have traditionally distinguished between two sorts of answer to this kind of question. The deontological answer is broadly that if an act is right, it just should be done, an approach which typifies the work of Immanuel Kant (1724–1804). The alternative teleological or consequentialist answer is that you should only perform just actions if they produce good consequences, an approach adopted by utilitarians such as Jeremy Bentham (1748–1832) and John Stuart Mill (1806–1873). Both these styles of solution seem problematic. Deontology hardly seems to address the question at all; and while teleology may address the question, the answer has seemed to many either immoral – consequences shouldn't matter to a moral decision – or else liable only to postpone a deontological solution because, for any given consequence, the questioner will want to know: 'Why pursue this consequence?'

Socrates at the beginning of Book 2 seems to promise a third type of answer: that justice is to be valued both for its consequences and for itself (358a). Being just certainly has good consequences, at least on occasions. Telling the truth and keeping promises, for example, can lead to a reputation for probity and thereby encourage people to deal with you. But whatever the merit of this sort of consideration, Plato rigorously excludes such consequences from the argument (359b–361d; 367a–e) until Book 10 (612a ff.). The sort of consequences to which he initially restricts himself are what might be styled the natural consequences of just actions, and not ones, for example, dependent on other people's recognising and rewarding your justice (367e).

There are a number of distinctions that Plato might have made between various sorts of consequence, and didn't. Take intelligence, for example (357c). That being thought intelligent might lead to a good job would be excluded from consideration because it depended on other people's judgment of your qualities. But would the natural consequence of intelligence – that you were better at, say, finding food – be counted or not? Plato in fact doesn't answer the question, 'Why be just?' within the terms of the deontological/teleological debate. Instead he suggests that the terms of the debate, in the end, are misleading. For Plato, the importance of acting justly is that the failure to do so both leads to and is an instance of being a disordered personality (588b–592b).

The obvious rejoinder to this is to ask what's so bad about being disordered? One answer is to deny the force of this question: just as no one could seriously deny that being healthy is a good thing, so no one could deny that being disordered is a bad thing (445a–b). Emphasising this strand within the *Republic* makes it difficult to explain Books 5–7 as anything more than a digression (see section 4 above). Plato, however, in admitting the attractiveness of at least some sorts of disorder (eg 557c, 561e), obviously recognises that something more needs to be said. His response is to sketch in Books 5–7 the sort of person who would see the attractiveness of the ordered personality, even if others would not. To understand his answer, we have to turn to Plato's understanding of rationality.

6 The theory of Forms (Books 5–7)

The theory of Forms is perhaps Plato's best-known contribution to philosophy. Put very roughly, it is the theory that knowledge is gained not primarily by coming to know what is in the world of experience, but rather by coming to know the Forms which exist in some other world. Plato argues that the world of everyday objects imperfectly imitates the world of the Forms, in a way analogous to that in which a picture painter imperfectly imitates everyday objects (597a–e). Talk of another world may misleadingly suggest somewhere with a spatio-temporal location. This error may be more easily resisted if you remember that an alternative translation to 'Forms' is 'Ideas'. What Plato is saying, broadly, is that the most important truths are available through studying the world of ideas, entry to which is gained by reasoning, rather than by studying the world of experience, entry to which is gained by sense experience (eg 511b–c).

This general strategy is used through Plato's works to answer very many different types of philosophical question; moreover, the precise way in which the strategy is realised varies over Plato's career. As a result, the difficulties which such an account faces – and these are many – are also varied. In the *Republic* the theory of Forms is used primarily to address ethical questions, and it is on this area that I shall now concentrate.

There is a Form of the Good which is in some sense the most important Form (534). So Plato, in outline, is going to be saying that in order to see the point of having an ordered personality, you are going to have to see the Form of the Good. Before going any further, I need to make explicit a difference between the characteristic way in which Plato thought of bad people, and the way in which the Judaeo-Christian tradition regards them. A bad person in the Judaeo-Christian tradition is generally thought of as someone who knows what is good but refuses to act accordingly. For Plato, bad people are typically those who act in accordance with their understanding of what is good, but who have a false understanding. Now the former conception only makes sense if what is good is regarded as something fairly clear-cut and easily comprehended – the Ten Commandments, for instance. As soon as what is good is regarded as unclear and open to debate, Plato's conception begins to make more sense.

This difference is important because it serves to illuminate a problem that academics have long worried over in the *Republic:* the problem of the 'two worlds'. Plato seems to argue that knowledge is directed at the objects of one sort of world – that of the Forms – and that what is commonly called knowledge – and what Plato calls opinion – is directed at the objects of a completely separate world, that of everyday sense-experience (474b–480a; 509d–511e; 533e–534a). When you look at the famous myth of the cave (514a–518b), for example, the position of the prisoners in the Cave is not that of having imperfect knowledge of reality, but rather of having imperfect knowledge of a charade: what they see are not the shadows of the real world, but the shadows of statues.

All this makes it very hard to understand how knowledge of one world, the Forms, is supposed to have an impact on our understanding of an entirely separate world, that of sense-experience. Moreover, it renders problematic the commonsense view – a view seemingly implicit in the *Republic*'s own methodology – that true knowledge can be gained by starting out from everyday opinion and building on it through reasoning.

If knowledge and opinion are directed at different objects, then there is clearly a problem. Accordingly, some commentators deny that this is Plato's view in the *Republic,* instead interpreting his arguments as referring to different levels of understanding of the same objects. My own view is that Plato is confused on the question of the two worlds, and that his confusion is explicable given the primarily ethical concerns of the *Republic.*

To achieve knowledge, Plato prescribes the development of the habits of mind which allow a person to see the Form of the Good (521c ff.). Cut away from the details of Plato's account, the proposal – that a tough intellectual training in difficult subjects like mathematics develops virtues such as intelligence, concentration, memory and persistence which are essential either in further study or in living life well – whilst debatable, certainly isn't incredible. Only someone who has been trained in such virtues will be able to see what is good, because only such a person will be able to conduct the philosophical inquiry or dialectic required (532a–b).

If discerning what is good is very difficult and requires a good intellectual training, then what passes for morality in the absence of such training is likely to be a mess. Accordingly, the moralist is better off ignoring the present moral confusion, working out what actually is good, and then using that knowledge to abolish the mess. And indeed this call to clear away the confused nonsense of current beliefs and to start out afresh from principle has occurred rather frequently in human history. For people with such radically new moral knowledge, it would be reasonable to say that they are living in a completely different ethical world from those without that knowledge, in much the same way as it would be reasonable to say that nineteenth-century Christian missionaries did not share the cultural world of the peoples they tried to convert.

The two worlds problem arises because Plato thought that the truly good life was different from what passed for the good life in the Greece of his day: it accordingly became reasonable for him, in ethical matters, to think of two different worlds. None of this solves the problems for the two worlds view which I mentioned above; but it does explain why, in his rush for moral transcendence, Plato may have created those problems in the first place.

I turned to discuss Plato's theory of rationality because it serves to explain why only a certain sort of person – someone who is trained to be rational – can appreciate why it is not desirable to have a dis-ordered personality. There is nothing odd in the claim that only someone trained in a particular way can fully appreciate a particular activity. Thus it is probably true that only someone trained in classical music can fully appreciate a symphony. Where Plato goes beyond this is in the claim that a certain sort of character – the philosopher – is the only one who can make final judgments about the value of anything whatsoever. To understand this aspect of the *Republic,* I shall turn to consider Plato's views on art.

7 Art and the supremacy of philosophy (Books 2, 3 and 10)

According to Plato, there is an ancient quarrel between poetry and philosophy (607b). Wandering poets should therefore not be surprised if, when philosophy rules a state, they are politely but firmly excluded (398a). What is the justification for this hostility to art?

Modern Western societies prize artists. They are prized, not just because people enjoy their work, but because art is supposed to provide insights not available in other ways. The claim to provide insight is ambiguous. It might mean that artists put truths discerned by other disciplines in a form that is more readily assimilated by the public. So, for example, children learn songs about the alphabet because a song is more easily remembered than the mere list of letters. Alternatively, it might mean that some insights were only available through art. To hear a piece of music might show you an aspect of the world otherwise inaccessible, even if you would be hard put to express that aspect in words.

Plato is all in favour of the first understanding of the claim to provide insight. He acknowledges throughout the *Republic* the influence of art upon the mind (401d; 608ab). His aim in a good society is that this power should be employed in the service of truth (377a–c), that artists should take their direction from the rulers of a society who, ideally, would be philosophers.

What about the claim that art provides a unique insight, not expressible in other ways? The position in fourth-century BC Greece was that the works of poets, in particular those attributed to Homer, were central in the education of the young and that they were treated as authoritative in the good conduct of life. Note for example that Polemarchus claims the authority of the poet Simonides for his definition of justice (331d). The ancient quarrel between philosophy and poetry alluded to by Plato is accordingly over the question of authority: is the content of poetry subject to the tests set by philosophers, or is philosophy subject to poetry? It was this quarrel which cost Socrates his life; for the irreligion on which he was convicted was that involved in questioning the nature of the gods as set forth by the poets.

Plato of course argues that poetry should be subject to philosophy. As I have noted, he argues that only someone capable of rigorous intellectual enquiry is able to see what is truly good. Philosophy as practised by Socrates is a discipline that attempts to discern truth by the use of rational arguments or dialectic (533a–b). This doesn't mean that philosophy is a discipline that can discern all truths: it can't discern the sort of truths, say, that can only be dug up by archaeologists.

But what it does mean is that philosophy can discuss and assess why a separate discipline such as archaeology is required to discern certain types of truth and not others. Now this entails that philosophy is entitled to ask poets to put forward a case for their art and assess the poets' answers, whereas poetry is not similarly entitled to put philosophy to the question. To deny this runs the risk of denying any sort of check on the self-appointed authority of poetry. (The authority of philosophy is, on the other hand, always itself subject to the test of rational argument.)

When Plato tests the poets by the standards of rationality he finds that they are immoral and cause social unrest (379c; 424c). His prime argument against them is based on the fact that they imitate the world (392c–398b; 595a–608b). Is this a good argument?

Plato is surely right in his analysis that imitation is an important aspect of most literary art. Homer, who as the prime educator of Greece is the target Plato has chiefly in his sights, told stories about men fighting battles, sailing ships, falling in love. Unless his writing correctly mirrored these aspects of human life, we just wouldn't be interested in it. What human life is like is primary, and what Homer writes about it has to imitate that primary reality. This isn't to say that he mightn't be doing more than imitation; only that imitation has to play a large part in his art.

So imitation is an important part of the sort of art Plato is interested in – and probably of most literary art. Is this a bad thing? Plato thinks it is, for two reasons: firstly, because it imitates bad aspects of human life (603d–606d); secondly, because it only imitates life in a superficial way (595a–602b). On the not unreasonable – but debatable – assumption that constant acquaintance with wickedness tends to make someone wicked, Plato appears to have a case on the first point. His second claim is, on first sight, less plausible. Plato's point is this. Homer just needs to make, say, his generals in the Iliad *appear* to be satisfactory generals; that is, he just has to fit in with what the audience expect from generals rather than actually to imitate what real generals are like. Indeed, given a choice between flattering the preconceptions of an audience and setting out the truth, Homer will necessarily flatter the audience: military manuals make for dull reading and poor box-office (493a–d). This mightn't matter too much if the subject matter of poetry was fairly restricted: knowing little about the doings of the English rural clergy wouldn't be too much of a handicap. But the subject matter of poetry is the whole of human life (603c), and thus poetry flatters our preconceptions about the whole of human existence. This is a problem for Plato because he thinks that to gain knowledge, one has to become discontented with facile preconceptions. One needs to become discontented and restless with these in order to progress to knowledge (523a–524d): one needs to be forced to think and test by dialectic, whereas the imitativeness of art lulls the intellect into complacency. Plato therefore criticises artists for diverting an audience from reality. But he leaves it open to them to argue for their defence (607c). The argument against artists in the *Republic* amounts to an attack on their untested authority and a claim that they should be subject to the normal process of rational assessment to which all human activity ought to be subject – an assessment which Plato, full of regret (608a), thinks they will fail.

8 Cities in speech

Most of the interesting arguments in the *Republic* form part of Plato's description of the best city. For him, the best city is one where philosophers rule as the Guardians of the city, and where the rest of the population is divided into auxiliary guardians (soldiers) and workers. The classes are built up and maintained by a mixture of controlled breeding, education and selection. The justice of the city consists in the fact that each class does its own proper business without interfering with the other classes. The claim made by Thraymachus in Book 1, that justice is simply a matter of rulers ruling in their own interest, is dealt with by making the rulers live a communal life, a life where personal interests and those of the state are merged. This picture of an ordered stable society, ruled by the wise, has sunk deeply into Western culture and influenced politicians, philosophers and artists. In the twentieth century, the picture as a whole has been firmly criticised as totalitarian. Nonetheless, many specific aspects of the ideal city have remained attractive – for example, its egalitarian treatment of female Guardians (452a–457b). It mustn't be overlooked, however, that the ideal city is only one moment of a process of development that goes on throughout the *Republic*. Socrates in effect conducts a thought experiment, founding a city and watching it grow into maturity. The ideal city is the maturity of the city built in speech: it has been preceded by the city of necessity (369b ff) and the city of luxury (372d ff.). The city of luxury needs to acquire land and defend itself and thus needs soldiers or guardians. As the originally homogeneous population of artisans of the city of necessity has been split into soldiers and artisans, some sort of governing class is now required: the Guardians proper. But if the ideal city has a history, it also has a future. The Guardians run the city on the basis of reason, and have abandoned the traditions and conventions that lend stability to existing societies. But they get their reasoning wrong – inevitably, by dint of being human beings (546a b) – and the city spirals through the various stages of decline (543a–576b).

What are we to conclude from this? Are we to conclude that the *Republic* is ironical, that we are advised to pursue the just city, only to see it fall apart in our hands, revealing itself as a chimera? This seems unlikely. Socrates has been asked: what is justice? He argues that it is best exemplified in a city like this. Now, we might argue that it is a bad city because it isn't in fact just, and this has indeed been done, usually on the ground that it is totalitarian. But Plato argues that it is just. He also thinks that it is realisable, even though under rather particular conditions (499b–d). Again, we might disagree. On the assumptions, however, that the city is both just and realisable, that it cannot remain totally just is merely an unfortunate fact of life: that the justice of the best city is ephemeral does not alter the fact that it is the best, and that it can be achieved.

So the political theory of the *Republic* isn't just a fantasy or a joke: it has practical, though limited, application. It also serves as an ideal against which to judge actual social arrangements. Nevertheless, some commentators have regarded the reorientation of Glaucon away from a political life towards a philosophical one as the *Republic*'s central theme. Such an interpretation does at least capture something of the limitations of justice: that it will probably never be realised and even if it is, will be sustained for only a short time. Nor are its effects completely beneficial. There is at least a trace of Socratic irony in the portrayal of the life of the Guardians: originally philosophers, they end up living the communal life of a herd animal (457b–461e). The futility of public life can be seen again in the myth of Er, when Odysseus, King of Ithaca, a man renowned for his crafty manipulation of human affairs, picks a life of humdrum nonentity into which to be incarnated, and pronounces himself well pleased with his choice (620c–d). Whatever his hopes for the ideal society, Plato certainly thought that, given normal circumstances, the philosopher would do better to withdraw from public life (496c–e).

9 Conclusion

At the beginning of this essay I asked, why read the *Republic*. It is now time to reconsider that original question.

Firstly, there is the enormous richness of ideas in the work. As I have tried to make clear, the *Republic* contains not just several arguments, but numerous hints and fragments of arguments which are never fully developed. Disentangling these various strands provides an excellent training in philosophy. But as well as being a form of intellectual training, the wealth of arguments in the *Republic* continues to provide philosophers with insights on which to build in many areas.

Secondly, the *Republic* challenges the way in which academic philosophy is typically understood in the Anglo-American tradition. There are two aspects to this challenge. In the first place, many scholars have noted how the dialogue of Book 1 gives way in the remainder of the *Republic* to what is practically a lecture by Socrates. Among various explanations of this change in style, some have suggested that this is Plato's way of indicating the ineffectiveness of Socratic debate and the need to replace it with another form of philosophy. The other aspect – and this develops from the first point – is that Plato throughout the *Republic* relies on the form of the argument to persuade. Anglo–American philosophers have tended to aspire to an impersonal clarity of exposition, quite different from Plato's switching between dialogue, straightforward argument and myth. Yet it is clear that Plato would not have been so influential apart from his stylistic qualities. Thinkers such as Derrida (b. 1930), outside the tradition of Anglo-American analytical philosophy, have certainly considered the form of their writings to be an important part of their force; but even within that analytical tradition, perhaps the most influential twentieth century philosopher, Wittgenstein (1889–1951), wrote in a style both exciting and irritating in its suggestive incompleteness. In a world where philosophy has become a discipline with only a marginal influence outside universities, the implications of both points need to be pondered.

Finally, it must be acknowledged that wrestling with the *Republic* can sometimes be frustrating. Arguments start and stop abruptly.

Points applauded by the participants in the dialogue can seem thin and unconvincing to the reader. Nevertheless, there remains the feeling of having been given a glimpse of something rather wonderful. To read the *Republic* is to enjoy one of the great adventures of the mind, and such opportunities are too rare to be ignored.

STEPHEN WATT
The Open University

SUGGESTIONS FOR FURTHER READING

Introductions to the *Republic*

J. Annas, *An Introduction to Plato's Republic,* Oxford 1981

N. Pappas, *Plato and the Republic,* London 1995

Introductions to broader aspects of Plato's work

R. M. Hare, *Plato,* Oxford 1982

P. Huby, *Plato and Modern Morality,* London 1972

G. Klosko, *The Development of Plato's Political Theory,* London 1986

I. Murdoch, *The Fire and the Sun: Why Plato Banished the Artists,* Oxford 1977

C. J. Rowe, *Plato,* Brighton 1984

For the more advanced reader

T. Irwin, *Plato's Moral Theory,* Oxford 1977

Works on themes related to the *Republic*

G. E. Davie, *The Democratic Intellect,* Edinburgh 1961
A study of philosophy's role in university education.

T. Regan, *Bloomsbury's Prophet,* Philadelphia 1986
A study of the influence of G. E. Moore's moral Platonism.

Particularly good bibliographies are to be found in the first two titles listed above. Many themes in the *Republic* may be usefully pursued in Plato's other dialogues, references to which may be found throughout the introductory works mentioned above.

MAIN CHARACTERS IN THE DIALOGUE

SOCRATES: the narrator.

GLAUCON and ADEIMANTUS: elder brothers of Plato. With Socrates, the sole active participants in the dialogue after Book 1.

CEPHALUS: a rich foreign businessman. In real life, his wealth was later confiscated by the oligarchical regime known as the Thirty.

POLEMARCHUS: son of Cephalus and thus, by Athenian law, also a foreigner. It is his house in which the dialogue takes place. In real life, executed by the Thirty.

THRASYMACHUS: a foreign teacher of rhetoric.

The dialogue takes place in Piraeus, the port of Athens, and is narrated by Socrates to an audience on the following day.

NOTE ON THE TEXT

The translation printed here is that of Davies and Vaughan, 3rd edition, 1886. The punctuation has been revised to bring it closer to modern usage, and this edition has fewer capital letters and italics than the original. No other changes have been made.

BOOK ONE

I went yesterday to the Piraeus with Glaucon the son of Ariston, to offer up prayer to the goddess, and also from a wish to see how the festival,[1] then to be held for the first time, would be celebrated. I was very much pleased with the native Athenian procession; though that of the Thracians appeared to be no less brilliant. We had finished our prayers, and satisfied our curiosity, and were returning to the city, when Polemarchus the son of Cephalus caught sight of us at a distance, as we were on our way towards home, and told his servant to run and bid us wait for him. The servant came behind me, took hold of my cloak, and said, 'Polemarchus bids you wait.' I turned round and asked him where his master was. 'There he is,' he replied, 'coming on behind: pray wait for him.' ' We will wait,' answered Glaucon. Soon afterwards Polemarchus came up, with Adeimantus the brother of Glaucon, and Niceratus the son of Nicias, and a few other persons, apparently coming away from the procession.

Polemarchus instantly began: Socrates, if I am not deceived, you are taking your departure for the city.

You are not wrong in your conjecture, I replied.

Well, do you see what a large body we are?

Certainly I do.

Then either prove yourselves the stronger party, or else stay where you are.

No, I replied; there is still an alternative: suppose we persuade you that you ought to let us go.

Could you possibly persuade us, if we refused to listen?

Certainly not, replied Glaucon.

Make up your minds then that we shall refuse to listen.

Here Adeimantus interposed, and said, Are you not aware that towards evening there will be a torch-race on horseback in honour of the goddess?

On horseback! I exclaimed: that is a novelty. Will they carry torches, and pass them on to one another, while the horses are racing? or how do you mean?

As you say, replied Polemarchus: besides, there will be a night-festival, which it will be worth while to look at. We will rise after dinner, and go out to see this festival; and there we shall meet with many of our young men, with whom we can converse. Therefore stay, and do not refuse us.

Upon this Glaucon said, It seems we shall have to stay.

Well, said I, if you like, let us do so.

We went therefore home with Polemarchus, and found there his brothers Lysias and Euthydemus, and, along with them, Thrasymachus of Chalcedon, and Charmantides the Paeanian, and Cleitophon the son of Aristonymus. Polemarchus's father, Cephalus, was also in the house. I thought him looking very much aged; for it was long since I had seen him. He was sitting upon a cushioned chair, with a garland upon his head, as he happened to have been sacrificing in the court. We found seats placed round him, so we sat down there by his side. The moment Cephalus saw me, he greeted me, and said, It is seldom indeed, Socrates, that you pay us a visit at the Piraeus: you ought to come oftener. If I were still strong enough to walk with ease to the city, there would be no occasion for your coming here, because we should go to you. But as it is, you ought to come here more frequently. For I assure you that I find the decay of the mere bodily pleasures accompanied by a proportionate growth in my appetite for philosophical conversation and in the pleasure I derive from it. Therefore do not refuse my request, but let these young men have the benefit of your society, and come often to see us as thoroughly intimate friends.

To tell you the truth, Cephalus, I replied, I delight in conversing with very old persons. For as they have gone before us on the road over which perhaps we also shall have to travel, I think we ought to try to learn from them what the nature of that road is – whether it be rough and difficult, or smooth and easy. And now that you have arrived at that period of life, which poets call 'the threshold of Age', there is no one whose opinion I would more gladly ask. Is life painful at that age, or what report do you make of it?

I will certainly tell you, Socrates, what my own experience of it is. I and a few other people of my own age are in the habit of frequently meeting together, true to the old proverb. On these occasions, most of us give way to lamentations, and regret the pleasures of youth, and call up the memory of amours and drinking parties and banquets and similar proceedings. They are grievously discontented at the loss of what they consider great privileges, and describe themselves as living well in those days, whereas now, by their own account, they cannot be said to live at all. Some also complain of the manner in which their relations insult their infirmities, and make this a ground for reproaching old age with the many miseries it occasions them. But in my opinion, Socrates, these persons miss the true cause of their unhappiness. For if old age were the cause, the same discomforts would have been also felt by me, as an old man, and by every other person that has reached that period of life. But, as it is, I have before now met with several old men who expressed themselves quite in a different manner, and in particular I may mention Sophocles the poet, who was once asked in my presence, 'How do you feel about love, Sophocles? Are you still capable of it?' to which he replied, 'Hush! if you please: to my great delight I have escaped from it, and feel as if I had escaped from a frantic and savage master.' I thought then, as I do now, that he spoke wisely. For unquestionably old age brings us profound repose and freedom from this and other passions. When the appetites have abated, and their force is diminished, the description of Sophocles is perfectly realised. It is like being delivered from a multitude of furious masters. But the complaints on this score, as well as the troubles with relatives, may all be referred to one cause, and that is, not the age, Socrates, but the character, of the men. If they possess well-regulated minds and easy tempers, old age itself is no intolerable burden: if they are differently constituted, why in that case, Socrates, they find even youth as irksome to them as old age.

I admired these remarks of Cephalus, and wishing him to go on talking, I endeavoured to draw him out by saying: I fancy, Cephalus, that people do not generally acquiesce in these views of yours, because they think that it is not your character, but your great wealth, that enables you to bear with old age. For the rich, it is said, have many consolations.

True, he said, they will not believe me: and they are partly right, though not so right as they suppose. There is great truth in the reply of Themistocles to the Seriphian who tauntingly told him, that his reputation was due not to himself, but to his country – 'I should not have become famous, if I had been a native of Seriphus; neither would you, if you had been an Athenian.' And to those who, not being rich, are impatient under old age, it may be said with equal justice that while on the one hand, a good man cannot be altogether cheerful under old age and poverty combined, so on the other, no wealth can ever make a bad man at peace with himself.

But has your property, Cephalus, been chiefly inherited or acquired?

Have I acquired it, do you say, Socrates? Why, in the conduct of money matters, I stand midway between my grandfather and my father. My grandfather, whose name I bear, inherited nearly as much property as I now possess, and increased it till it was many times as large; while my father Lysanias brought it down even below what it now is. For my part, I shall be content to leave it to these my sons not less, but if anything rather larger, than it was when it came into my hands.

I asked the question, I said, because you seemed to me to be not very fond of money: which is generally the case with those who have not made it themselves; whereas those who have made it, are twice as much attached to it as other people. For just as poets love their own works, and fathers their own children, in the same way those who have created a fortune value their money, not merely for its uses, like other persons, but because it is their own production. This makes them moreover disagreeable companions, because they will praise nothing but riches.

It is true, he replied.

Indeed it is, said I. But let me ask you one more question. What do you think is the greatest advantage that you have derived from being wealthy?

If I mention it, he replied, I shall perhaps get few persons to agree with me. Be assured, Socrates, that when a man is nearly persuaded that he is going to die, he feels alarmed and concerned about things which never affected him before. Till then he has laughed at those stories about the departed, which tell us that he who has done wrong here must suffer for it in the other world; but now his mind is tormented with a fear that these stories may possibly be true. And either owing to the infirmity of old age, or because he is now nearer to the confines of the future state, he has a clearer insight into those mysteries. However that may be, he becomes full of misgiving and apprehension, and sets himself to the task of calculating and reflecting whether he has done any wrong to any one. Hereupon, if he finds his life full of unjust deeds, he is apt to start out of sleep in terror, as children do, and he lives haunted by gloomy anticipations. But if his conscience reproaches him with no injustice, he enjoys the abiding presence of sweet Hope, that 'kind nurse of old age', as Pindar calls it. For indeed, Socrates, those are beautiful words of his, in which he says of the man who has lived a just and holy life, 'Sweet Hope is his companion, cheering his heart, the nurse of age – Hope, which, more than aught else, steers the capricious will of mortal men.'[2] There is really a wonderful truth in this description. And it is this consideration, as I hold, that makes riches chiefly valuable, I do not say to everybody, but at any rate to the good. For they contribute greatly to our preservation from even unintentional deceit or falsehood, and from that alarm which would attend our departure to the other world, if we owed any sacrifices to a god, or any money to a man. They have also many other uses. But after weighing them all separately, Socrates, I am inclined to consider this service as anything but the least important which riches can render to a wise and sensible man.

You have spoken admirably, Cephalus. But what are we to understand by that very quality, justice, to which you refer? Are we to define it as neither more nor less than veracity and restitution of what one man has received from another, or is it possible for actions of this very nature to be sometimes just and sometimes unjust? For example, every one, I suppose, would admit that if a man, while in the possession of his senses, were to place dangerous weapons in the hands of a friend, and afterwards in a fit of madness to demand them back, such a deposit ought not to be restored, and that his friend would not be a just man if he either returned the weapons, or consented to tell the whole truth to one so circumstanced.

You are right, he replied.

Then it is no true definition of justice to say that it consists in speaking the truth and restoring what one has received.

Nay but it is, Socrates, said Polemarchus, interposing, at least if we are at all to believe Simonides.

Very well, said Cephalus, I will just leave the discussion to you. It is time for me to attend to the sacrifices.

Then Polemarchus inherits your share in it, does he not? I asked.

Certainly, he replied, with a smile; and immediately withdrew to the sacrifices.

Answer me then, I proceeded, you that are the heir to the discussion; What do you maintain to be the correct account of justice, as given by Simonides?

That to restore to each man what is his due, is just. To me it seems that Simonides is right in giving this account of the matter.

Well, certainly it is not an easy matter to disbelieve Simonides, for he is a wise and inspired man. But what he means by his words, you, Polemarchus, may perhaps understand, though I do not. It is clear that he does not mean what we were saying just now, namely that property given by one person in trust to another is to be returned to the donor, if he asks for it in a state of insanity. And yet I conclude that property given in trust is due to the truster. Is it not?

Yes, it is.

But when the person who asks for it is not in his senses, it must not be returned on any account, must it?

True, it must not.

Then it would seem that Simonides means something different from this, when he says that it is just to restore what is due.

Most certainly he does, he replied, for he declares that the debt of friend to friend is to do good to one another, and not harm.

I understand: the person who returns money to a depositor does not restore what is due, if the repayment on the one side, and the receipt on the other, prove to be injurious, and if the two parties are friends. Is not this, according to you, the meaning of Simonides?

Certainly it is.

Well: must we restore to our enemies whatever happens to be due to them?

Yes, no doubt – what is due to them: and the debt of enemy to enemy is, I imagine, harm; because harm is at the same time appropriate to such a relation.

So then it would seem that Simonides, after the manner of poets, employed a riddle to describe the nature of justice; for apparently he thought that justice consisted in rendering to each man that which is appropriate to him, which he called his due. But here let me entreat you to give me your opinion. Suppose that consequently some one had asked him the following question: 'That being the case, Simonides, what due and appropriate thing is rendered by the art called medicine, and what are the recipients?' What answer do you think he would have returned us?

Obviously he would have said that bodies are the recipients, and drugs, meats, and drinks the things rendered.

And what due and appropriate thing is rendered by the art called cookery, and what are the recipients?

Seasoning is the thing rendered; dishes are the recipients.

Good: then what is the thing rendered by the art that we are to call justice, and who are the recipients?

If we are to be at all guided by our previous statements, Socrates, assistance and harm are the things rendered, friends and enemies the recipients.

Then by justice Simonides means doing good to our friends, and harm to our enemies, does he?

I think so.

Now, in cases of illness, who is best able to do good to friends and harm to enemies, with reference to health and disease?

A physician.

And, on a voyage, who is best able to do good to friends and harm to enemies, with reference to the perils of the sea?

A pilot.

Well: in what transaction, and with reference to what object, is the just man best able to help his friends and injure his enemies?

In the transactions of war, I imagine – as the ally of the former, and the antagonist of the latter.

Good. You will grant, my dear Polemarchus, that a physician is useless to persons in sound health.

Certainly.

And a pilot to persons on shore.

Yes.

Is the just man, also, useless to those who are not at war?

I do not quite think that.

Then justice is useful in time of peace too, is it?

It is.

And so is agriculture, is it not?

Yes.

That is to say, as a means of acquiring the fruits of the earth.

Yes.

And further, the shoemaker's art is also useful, is it not?

Yes.

As a means of acquiring shoes, I suppose you will say.

Certainly.

Well then, of what does justice, according to you, promote the use or acquisition in time of peace?

Of covenants, Socrates.

And by covenants do you understand co-partnerships, or something different?

Co-partnerships, certainly.

Then is it the just man, or the skilful draught-player, that makes a good and useful partner in playing draughts?

The draught-player.

Well, in bricklaying and stonemasonry is the just man a more useful and a better partner than the regular builder?

By no means.

Well then, in what partnership is the just man superior to the harp-player, in the sense in which the harp-player is a better partner than the just man in playing music?

In a money-partnership, I think.

Excepting perhaps, Polemarchus, when the object is to lay out money; as when a horse is to be bought or sold by the partners, in which case, I imagine, the horse-dealer is better. Is he not?

Apparently he is.

And again, when a ship is to be bought or sold, the ship-wright or pilot is better.

It would seem so.

That being the case, when does the opportunity arrive for that joint use of silver or gold, in which the just man is more useful than any one else?

When you want to place your money in trust and have it safe, Socrates.

That is to say, when it is to be laid by, and not to be put to any use?

Just so.

So that justice can only be usefully applied to money when the money is useless?

It looks like it.

In the same way, when you want to keep a pruning-hook, justice is useful whether you be in partnership or not; but when you want to use it, justice gives place to the art of the vinedresser?

Apparently.

Do you also maintain that when you want to keep a shield or a lyre without using them, justice is useful; but when you want to use them, you require the art of the soldier or of the musician?

I must.

And so of everything else: justice is useless when a thing is in use, but useful when it is out of use?

So it would seem.

Then, my friend, justice cannot be a very valuable thing if it is only useful as applied to things useless. But let us continue the inquiry thus. Is not the man who is most expert in dealing blows in an encounter, whether pugilistic or otherwise, also most expert in parrying blows?

Certainly.

Is it not also true that whoever is expert in repelling a disease, and evading its attack, is also extremely expert in producing it in others?

I think so.

And undoubtedly a man is well able to guard an army, when he has also a talent for stealing the enemy's plans and all his other operations.

Certainly.

That is to say, a man can guard expertly whatever he can thieve expertly.

So it would seem.

Hence, if the just man is expert in guarding money, he is also expert in stealing it.

I confess the argument points that way.

Then, to all appearance, it turns out that the just man is a kind of thief, a doctrine which you have probably learnt from Homer, with whom Autolycus, the maternal grandfather of Odysseus, is a favourite, because, as the poet says, he outdid all men in thievishness and perjury. Justice therefore, according to you, Homer, and Simonides, appears to be a kind of art of stealing, whose object, however, is to help one's friends and injure one's enemies. Was not this your meaning?

Most certainly it was not, he replied, but I no longer know what I did mean. However, it is still my opinion that it is justice to help one's friends, and hurt one's enemies.

Should you describe a man's friends as those who *seem* to him to be, or those who really are, honest men, though they may not seem so? And do you define a man's enemies on the same principle?

I should certainly expect a man to love all whom he thinks honest, and hate all whom he thinks wicked.

But do not people make mistakes in this matter, and fancy many persons to be honest who are not really honest, and many wicked who are not really wicked?

They do.

Then to such persons the good are enemies, and the bad are friends, are they not?

Certainly they are.

And, notwithstanding this, it is just for such persons at such times to help the wicked and to injure the good.

Apparently it is.

Yet surely the good are just, and injustice is foreign to their nature.

True.

Then, according to your doctrine, it is just to do evil to those who commit no injustice.

Heaven forbid it, Socrates: for that looks like a wicked doctrine.

Then it is just, said I, to injure the unjust and to assist the just.

That is evidently a better theory than the former.

In that case, Polemarchus, the result will be that, in those numerous instances in which people have thoroughly mistaken their men, it is just for these mistaken persons to injure their friends, because in their eyes they are wicked; and to help their enemies, because they are good. And thus our statement will be in direct opposition to the meaning which we assigned to Simonides.

That consequence certainly follows, he replied. But let us change our positions; for very probably our definition of friend and enemy was incorrect.

What was our definition, Polemarchus?

That a friend is one who seems to be an honest man.

And what is to be our new definition?

That a friend is one who not only seems to be, but really is, an honest man; whereas the man who seems to be, but is not honest, is not really a friend, but only seems one. And I define an enemy on the same principle. Then, by this way of speaking, the good man will in all likelihood be a friend, and the wicked an enemy.

Yes.

Then you would have us attach to the idea of justice more than we at first included in it, when we called it just to do good to our friend and evil to our enemy. We are now, if I understand you, to make an addition to this, and render it thus – it is just to do good to our friend if he is a good man, and to hurt our enemy if he is a bad man.

Precisely so, he replied; I think that this would be a right statement.

Now is it the act of a just man, I asked, to hurt anybody?

Certainly it is, he replied; that is to say, it is his duty to hurt those who are both wicked and enemies of his.

Are horses made better or worse by being hurt?

Worse.

Worse with reference to the excellence of dogs, or that of horses?

That of horses.

Are dogs in the same way made worse by being hurt, with reference to the excellence of dogs and not of horses?

Unquestionably they are.

And must we not on the same principle assert, my friend, that men, by being hurt, are lowered in the scale of human excellence?

Indeed we must.

But is not justice a human excellence?

Undoubtedly it is.

And therefore, my friend, those men who are hurt must needs be rendered less just.

So it would seem.

Can musicians, by the art of music, make men unmusical?

They cannot.

Can riding-masters, by the art of riding, make men bad riders?

No.

But if so, can the just by justice make men unjust? In short, can the good by goodness make men bad?

No, it is impossible.

True; for, if I am not mistaken, it is the property, not of warmth, but of its opposite, to make things cold.

Yes.

And it is the property not of drought, but of its opposite, to make things wet.

Certainly.

Then it is the property not of good, but of its opposite, to hurt.

Apparently it is.

Well, is the just man good?

Certainly he is.

Then, Polemarchus, it is the property, not of the just man, but of his opposite, the unjust man, to hurt either friend or any other creature.

You seem to me to be perfectly right, Socrates.

Hence if any one asserts that it is just to render to every man his due, and if he understands by this that what is due on the part of the just man is injury to his enemies and assistance to his friends, the assertion is that of an unwise man. For the doctrine is untrue, because we have discovered that in no instance is it just to injure anybody.

I grant you are right.

Then you and I will make common cause against any one who shall attribute this doctrine to Simonides, or Bias, or Pittacus, or any other wise and highly-favoured man.

Very good, said he; I, for one, am quite ready to take my share of the fighting.

Pray do you know to whom I refer the authorship of this saying, that it is just to help our friends and hurt our enemies?

To whom?

I attribute it to Periander, or Perdiccas, or Xerxes, or Ismenias the Theban, or some other rich man who thought himself very powerful.

You are perfectly right.

Well, but as we have again failed to discover the true definition of justice and the just, what other definition can one propose?

While we were still in the middle of our discussion, Thrasymachus was, more than once, bent on interrupting the conversation with objections; but he was checked on each occasion by those who sat by, who wished to hear the argument out. However, when I had made this last remark and we had come to a pause, he could restrain himself no longer, but gathering himself up like a wild beast, he sprang upon us, as if he would tear us in pieces. I and Polemarchus were terrified and startled, while Thrasymachus raising his voice to the company, said, What nonsense has possessed you and Polemarchus all this time, Socrates? And why do you play the fool together with your mutual complaisance? No; if you really wish to understand what justice is, do not confine yourself to asking questions, and making a display of refuting the answers that are returned, (for you are aware that it is easier to ask questions than to answer them); but give us an answer also yourself, and tell us what you assert justice to be, and let me beg you to beware of defining it as the obligatory, or the advantageous, or the profitable, or the lucrative, or the expedient; but whatever your definition may be, let it be clear and precise: for I will not accept your answer if you talk such trash as that.

When I heard this speech, I was astounded, and gazed at the speaker in terror; and I think if I had not set eyes on him before he eyed me, I should have been struck dumb.[3] But, as it was, when he began to be exasperated by the conversation, I had looked him in the face first: so that I was enabled to reply to him, and said with a slight tremble; Thrasymachus, do not be hard upon us. If I and Polemarchus are making mistakes in our examination of the subject, be assured that the error is involuntary. You do not suppose that, if we were looking for a piece of gold, we should ever willingly be so complaisant to one another in the search as to spoil the chance of finding it; and therefore, pray do not suppose that in seeking for justice, which is a thing more precious than many pieces of gold, we should give way to one another so weakly as you describe, instead of doing our very best to bring it to light. You, my friend, may think so, if you choose: but my belief is that the subject is beyond our powers. Surely then we might very reasonably expect to be pitied, not harshly treated, by such clever men as you.

When he had heard my reply, he burst out laughing very scornfully, and said – O Hercules! Here is an instance of that mock-humility which Socrates affects. I knew how it would be, and warned the company that you would refuse to answer, and would feign ignorance, and do anything rather than reply, if any one asked you a question.

Yes, you are a wise man, Thrasymachus, I replied; and therefore you were well aware that if you asked a person what factors make the number 12, and at the same time warned him thus: 'Please to beware of telling me that 12 is twice 6, or 3 times 4, or 6 times 2, or 4 times 3; for I will not take such nonsense from you,' – you were well aware, I dare say, that no one would give an answer to such an inquirer. But suppose the person replied to you thus – 'Thrasymachus, explain yourself: am I to be precluded from all these answers which you have denounced? What, my good sir! Even if one of these is the real answer, am I still to be precluded from giving it, and am I to make a statement that is at variance with the truth? Or what is your meaning?' What reply should you make to this inquiry?

Oh, indeed! he exclaimed, as if the two cases were alike!

There is nothing to prevent their being so, I replied. However, suppose they are not alike; still if one of these answers seems the right one to the person questioned, do you think that our forbidding it, or not, will affect his determination to give the answer which he believes to be the correct one?

Do you not mean that this is what *you* are going to do? You will give one of the answers on which I have put a veto?

It would not surprise me if I did; supposing I thought right to do so, after reflection.

Then what if I produce another answer on the subject of justice, unlike those I denounced, and superior to them all? What punishment do you think you merit?

Simply the punishment which it is proper for the unenlightened to submit to; and that is, I conceive, to be instructed by the enlightened. This, then, is the punishment which I, among others, deserve to suffer.

Really you are a pleasant person, he replied. But besides being instructed, you must make me a payment.

I will, when I have any money, I replied.

But you have, said Glaucon. So as far as money is a consideration, speak on, Thrasymachus. We will all contribute for Socrates.

Oh, to be sure! said he; in order that Socrates, I suppose, may pursue his usual plan of refusing to propound an answer himself, while he criticises and refutes the answers given by other people.

My excellent friend, said I, how can an answer be given by a person who in the first place does not, and confesses he does not, know what to answer, and who in the next place, if he has any thoughts upon the subject, has been forbidden by a man of no common parts to give utterance to any of his fancies? No, it is more natural that you should be the speaker, because you profess to know the subject, and to have something to say. Therefore do not decline, but gratify me by answering, and do not grudge to instruct Glaucon and the rest of the company as well.

When I had said this, Glaucon and the others begged him to comply. Now it was evident that Thrasymachus was eager to speak, in order that he might gain glory, because he thought himself in possession of a very fine answer. But he affected to contend for my being the respondent. At last he gave in, and then said: This, forsooth, is the wisdom of Socrates! He will not give instruction himself, but he goes about and learns from others, without even showing gratitude for their lessons.

As for my learning from others, Thrasymachus, I replied, there you speak truth, but it is false of you to say that I pay no gratitude in return. I *do* pay all I can; and as I have no money, I can only give praise. How readily I do this, if in my judgment a person speaks well, you will very soon find, when you make your answer: for I expect *you* to speak well.

Then listen, said he. My doctrine is that justice is simply the interest of the stronger. Well: why do you not praise me? No, you refuse.

Not so, I replied, I am only waiting to understand your meaning, which at present I do not see. You say that the interest of the stronger is just. What in the world do you mean by this, Thrasymachus? You do not, I presume, mean anything like this – that if Polydamas, the athlete, is stronger than we are, and if it is for his interest to eat beef in order to strengthen his body, such food is for the interest of us weaker men, and therefore is just.

This is scandalous, Socrates: you understand my doctrine in the sense in which you can damage it most easily.

No, no, my excellent friend: but state your meaning more clearly.

So you are not aware, he continued, that some cities are governed by an autocrat, and others by a democracy, and others by an aristocracy?

Of course I am.

In every city does not superior strength reside in the ruling body?

Certainly it does

And further, each government has its laws framed to suit its own interests; a democracy making democratic laws, an autocrat despotic laws, and so on. Now by this procedure these governments have pronounced that what is for the interest of themselves is just for their subjects; and whoever deviates from this is chastised by them as guilty of illegality and injustice. Therefore, my good sir, my meaning is that in all cities the same thing, namely the interest of the established government, is just. And superior strength, I presume, is to be found on the side of government. So that the conclusion of right reasoning is that the same thing, namely the interest of the stronger, is everywhere just.

Now I understand your meaning, and I will endeavour to make out whether it is true or not. So then, Thrasymachus, you yourself in your answer have defined justice as interest, though you forbade my giving any such reply. To be sure, you have made an addition, and describe it as the interest of the stronger.

Yes; quite a trifling addition, perhaps.

It remains to be seen whether it is an important one. But this much is certain – that we are bound to examine into the correctness of your doctrine. For we both admit that justice is in harmony with interest: but you lengthen this into the assertion that justice is the interest of the stronger; to which I demur. Therefore we are certainly bound to study the subject.

Pray do so.

It shall be done. Be so good as to answer this question. You doubtless also maintain that it is just to obey the rulers?

I do.

Are the rulers infallible in each several city, or are they liable to make a few mistakes?

No doubt they are liable to make mistakes.

And therefore, when they undertake to frame laws, is their work sometimes rightly, and sometimes wrongly, done?

I should suppose so.

Do 'rightly' and 'wrongly' mean, respectively, legislating for, and against, their own interests? Or how do you state it?

Just as you do.

And do you maintain that whatever has been enacted by the rulers must be obeyed by their subjects, and that this is justice?

Unquestionably I do.

Then according to your argument, it is not only just to do what makes for the interest of the stronger, but also to do what runs counter to his interest – in other words, the opposite of the former.

What are you saying?

What *you* say, I believe. But let us examine the point more thoroughly. Has it not been admitted that when the rulers enjoin certain acts upon their subjects, they are sometimes thoroughly mistaken as to what is best for themselves, and that whatever is enjoined by them, it is just for their subjects to obey? Has not this been admitted?

Yes, I think so, he replied.

Then let me tell you that you have also admitted the justice of doing what runs counter to the interest of the ruling and stronger body on every occasion when this body unintentionally enjoins what is injurious to itself, so long as you maintain that it is just for the subjects to obey, in every instance, the injunctions of their rulers. In that case, O most wise Thrasymachus, must it not follow of course, that it is just to act in direct opposition to your theory? For obviously it is enjoined upon the weaker to do what is prejudicial to the interest of the stronger.

Yes, indeed, Socrates, said Polemarchus; that is perfectly clear.

No doubt, retorted Cleitophon, if you appear as a witness in Socrates' behalf.

Nay, what do we want witnesses for? said Polemarchus. Thrasymachus himself admits that the rulers sometimes enjoin what is bad for themselves, and that it is just for their subjects to obey such injunctions.

No, Polemarchus, Thrasymachus laid it down that to do what the rulers command is just.

Yes, Cleitophon, and he also laid it down that the interest of the stronger is just. And having laid down these two positions, he further admitted that the stronger party sometimes orders its weaker subjects to do what is prejudicial to its own interests. And the consequence of these admissions is that what is for the interest of the stronger will be not a bit more just than what is not for his interest.

But, said Cleitophon, by the interest of the stronger he meant what the stronger conceived to be for his own interest. His position was that this must be done by the weaker, and that this is the notion of justice.

That was not what he said, replied Polemarchus.

It does not matter, Polemarchus, said I: if Thrasymachus chooses to state his theory in that way now, let us make no objection to his doing so. Tell me, then, Thrasymachus: was this the definition you meant to give of justice, that it is what seems to the stronger to be the interest of the stronger, whether it be really for his interest or not? Shall we take that as your account of it?

Certainly not, he replied: do you think I should call a man who is mistaken, at the time of his mistake, the stronger?

Why, I thought that you said as much, when you admitted that rulers are not infallible, but do really commit some mistakes.

You are a quibbler, Socrates, in argument: do you call, now, that man a physician who is in error about the treatment of the sick, with strict reference to his error? Or do you call another an accountant, who makes a mistake in a calculation, at the time of his mistake, and with reference to that mistake? We say, to be sure, in so many words that the physician was in error, and the accountant or the writer was in error, but in fact each of these, I imagine, in so far as he is what we call him, never falls into error. So that, to speak with precise accuracy, since you require such preciseness of language, no craftsman errs. For it is through a failure of knowledge that a man errs, and to that extent he is no craftsman, so that whether as craftsman, or philosopher, or ruler, no one errs while he actually is what he professes to be: although it would be universally said that such a physician was in error, or such a ruler was in error. In this sense I would have you to understand my own recent answer. But the statement, if expressed with perfect accuracy, would be that a ruler, in so far as he is a ruler, never errs, and that so long as this is the case, he enacts what is best for himself, and that this is what the subject has to do. Therefore, as I began with saying, I call it just to do what is for the interest of the stronger.

Very good, Thrasymachus: you think me a quibbler, do you?

Yes, a thorough quibbler.

Do you think that I put you those questions with a mischievous intent to damage your position in the argument?

Nay, I am quite sure of it. However you shall gain nothing by it; for you shall neither injure me by taking me unawares, nor will you be able to overpower me by open argument.

I should not think of attempting it, my excellent friend! But that nothing of this kind may occur again, state whether you employ the words 'ruler' and 'stronger' in the popular sense of them, or in that strict signification of which you were speaking just now, when you say that it is just for the weaker to do what is for the interest of the ruler, as being the stronger.

I mean a ruler in the strictest sense of the word. So now try your powers of quibbling and mischief: I ask for no mercy. But your attempts will be ineffectual.

Why, do you suppose I should be so mad as to attempt to beard a lion, or play off quibbles on a Thrasymachus?

At any rate you tried it just now, though you failed utterly.

Enough of this banter, I replied. Tell me this: is the physician of whom you spoke as being strictly a physician, a maker of money or a healer of the sick? Take care you speak of the *genuine* physician.

A healer of the sick.

And what of a pilot? Is the true pilot a sailor or a commander of sailors?

A commander of sailors.

There is no need, I imagine, to take into the account his being on board the ship, nor should he be called a sailor: for it is not in virtue of his being on board that he has the name of pilot, but in virtue of his art and of his authority over the sailors.

True.

Has not each of these persons an interest of his own?

Certainly.

And is it not the proper end of their art to seek and procure what is for the interest of each of them?

It is.

Have the arts severally any other interest to pursue than their own highest perfection?

What does your question mean?

Why, if you were to ask me whether it is sufficient for a man's body to be a body, or whether it stands in need of something additional, I should say, Certainly it does. To this fact the discovery of the healing art is due, because the body is defective, and it is not enough for it to be a body. Therefore the art of healing has been put in requisition to procure what the interests of the body require. Should I be right, think you, in so expressing myself, or not?

You would be right.

Well then, is the art of healing itself defective, or does any art whatever require a certain additional virtue; as eyes require sight and ears hearing, so that these organs need a certain art which shall investigate and provide what is conducive to these ends – is there, I ask, any defectiveness in an art as such, so that every art should require another art to consider its interests, and this other provisional art a third, with a similar function, and so on without limit? Or will it investigate its own interest? Or is it unnecessary either for itself or for any other art to inquire into the appropriate remedy for its own defects because there are no defects or faults in any art, and because it is not the duty of an art to seek the interests of aught save that to which, as an art, it belongs, being itself free from hurt and blemish as a true art, so long as it continues strictly and in its integrity what it is? View the question according to the strict meaning of terms, as we agreed: is it so or otherwise?

Apparently it is so, he replied.

Then the art of healing does not consider the interest of the art of healing, but the interest of the body.

Yes.

Nor horsemanship what is good for horsemanship, but for horses: nor does any other art seek its own interest, (for it has no wants), but the good of that to which as an art it belongs.

Apparently it is so.

Well, but you will grant, Thrasymachus, that an art governs and is stronger than that of which it is the art.

He assented, with great reluctance, to this proposition.

Then no science investigates or enjoins the interest of the stronger, but the interest of the weaker, its subject.

To this also he at last assented, though he attempted to show fight about it. After gaining his admission, I proceeded: Then is it not also true that no physician, in so far as he is a physician, considers or enjoins what is for the physician's interest, but that all seek the good of their patients? For we have agreed that a physician strictly so called, is a ruler of bodies and not a maker of money; have we not?

He allowed that we had.

And that a pilot strictly so called is a commander of sailors and not a sailor?

We have.

Then this kind of pilot and commander will not seek and enjoin the pilot's interest, but that of the sailor and the subordinate.

He reluctantly gave his assent.

And thus, Thrasymachus, all who are in any place of command, in so far as they are rulers, neither consider nor enjoin their own interest, but that of the subjects for whom they exercise their craft: and in all that they do or say they act with an exclusive view to *them*, and to what is good and proper for *them*.

When we had arrived at this stage of the discussion, and it had become evident to all that the explanation of justice was completely reversed, Thrasymachus, instead of making any answer, said,

Tell me, Socrates, have you a nurse?

Why? I rejoined: had you not better answer my questions than make inquiries of that sort?

Why, because she leaves you to drivel, and omits to wipe your nose when you require it, so that in consequence of her neglect you cannot even distinguish between sheep and shepherd.

For what particular reason do you think so?

Because you think that shepherds and herdsmen regard the good of their sheep and of their oxen, and fatten them and take care of them with other views than to benefit their masters and themselves; and you actually imagine that the rulers in states, those I mean who are really rulers, are otherwise minded towards their subjects than as one would feel towards sheep, or that they think of anything else by night and by day than how they may secure their own advantage. And you are so far wrong in your notions respecting justice and injustice, the just and the unjust, that you do not know that the former is really the good of another, that is to say the interest of the stronger and of the ruler, but your own loss, where you are the subordinate and the servant; whereas injustice is the reverse, governing those that are really simple-minded and just, so that they, as subjects, do what is for the interest of the unjust man who is stronger than they, and promote his happiness by their services, but not their own in the least degree. You may see by the following considerations, my most simple Socrates, that a just man everywhere has the worst of it, compared with an unjust man. In the first place, in their mutual dealings, wherever a just man enters into partnership with an unjust man, you will find that at the dissolution of the partnership the just man never has more than the unjust man, but always less. Then again in their dealings with the state, when there is a property-tax to pay, the just man will pay more and the unjust less, on the same amount of property; and when there is anything to receive, the one gets nothing, while the other makes great gains. And whenever either of them holds any office of authority, if the just man suffers no other loss, at least his private affairs fall into disorder through want of attention to them, while his principles forbid his deriving any benefit from the public money; and besides this, it is his fate to offend his friends and acquaintances every time that he refuses to serve them at the expense of justice. But with the unjust man everything is reversed. I am speaking of the case I mentioned just now, of an unjust man who has the power to grasp on an extensive scale. To him you must direct your attention, if you wish to judge how much more profitable it is to a man's own self to be unjust than to be just. And you will learn this truth with the greatest ease if you turn your attention to the most consummate form of injustice, which, while it makes the wrong-doer most happy, makes those who are wronged, and will not retaliate, most miserable. This form is a despotism, which proceeds not by small degrees, but by wholesale, in its open or fraudulent appropriation of the property of others, whether it be sacred or profane, public or private; perpetrating offences which if a person commits in detail and is found out, he becomes liable to a penalty and incurs deep disgrace; for partial offenders in this class of crimes are called sacrilegious, men-stealers, burglars, thieves and robbers. But when a man not only seizes the property of his fellow-citizens but captures and enslaves their persons also, instead of those dishonourable titles he is called happy and highly favoured, not only by the men of his own city, but also by all others who hear of the comprehensive injustice which he has wrought. For when people abuse injustice, they do so because they are afraid, not of committing it, but of suffering it. Thus it is, Socrates, that injustice, realised on an adequate scale, is a stronger, a more liberal, and a more lordly thing than justice; and as I said at first, justice is the interest of the stronger; injustice, a thing profitable and advantageous to oneself.

When he had made this speech, Thrasymachus intended to take his departure, after deluging our ears like a bathingman with this copious and unbroken flood of words. Our companions however would not let him go, but obliged him to stay and answer for his doctrines. I myself also was especially urgent in my entreaties, exclaiming, Really, my good Thrasymachus, after flinging us such a speech as this, are you intending to take your leave before you have satisfactorily taught us, or learnt yourself, whether your theory is right or wrong? Do you think you are undertaking to settle some insignificant question, and not the principles on which each of us must conduct his life in order to lead the most profitable existence?

Why, that is not a true statement of the case, in my opinion, said Thrasymachus.

So it seems, I said, or else that you are quite indifferent about us, and feel no concern whether we shall live the better or the worse for our ignorance of what you profess to know. But pray vouchsafe, my good sir, to impart your knowledge to us also: any benefit you confer on such a large party as we are will surely be no bad investment. For I tell you plainly for my own part that I am not convinced, and that I do not believe that injustice is more profitable than justice, even if it be let alone and suffered to work its will unchecked. On the contrary, my good sir, let there be an unjust man, and let him have full power to practise injustice, either by evading detection or by overpowering opposition, still I am not convinced that such a course is more profitable than justice. This, perhaps, is the feeling of some others amongst us, as well as mine. Pray then convince us satisfactorily, my highly-gifted friend, that we are not well advised in valuing justice above injustice.

But how, said he, can I persuade you? If you are not convinced by my recent statements, what more can I do for you? Must I take the doctrine and thrust it into your mind?

Heaven forbid you should do that: but in the first place, abide by what you say, or if you change your ground, change it openly without deceiving us. As it is, Thrasymachus, (for we must not yet take leave of our former investigations,) you see that having first defined the meaning of the genuine physician, you did not think it necessary afterwards to adhere strictly to the genuine shepherd. On the contrary, you suppose him to feed his sheep, in so far as he is a shepherd, not with an eye to what is best for the flock, but like a votary of feasting who is going to give an entertainment, with an eye to the good cheer, or else to their sale, like a money-maker and not like a shepherd. Whereas the only concern of the shepherd's art is, I presume, how it shall procure what is best for *that* of which it is the appointed guardian; since as far as concerns its own perfection, sufficient provision is made, I suppose, for that, so long as it is all that is implied in its title: and so I confess I thought we were obliged just now to admit that every government, in so far as it is a government, looks solely to the advantage of that which is governed and tended by it, whether that government be of a public or a private nature. But what is your opinion? Do you think that the rulers in states, who really rule, do so willingly?

No, I do not *think* it, I am sure of it.

What, Thrasymachus, do you not observe that no one consents to take upon himself the common state-offices, if he can help it, but that they all ask to be paid on the assumption that the advantages of their government will not accrue to themselves, but to the governed? For answer me this question: do we not say without hesitation, that every art is distinguished from other arts by having a distinctive faculty? Be so good, my dear sir, as not to answer contrary to your opinion, or we shall make no progress.

Yes, that is what distinguishes it.

And does not each of them provide us with some special and peculiar benefit? The art of healing, for example, giving us health, that of piloting safety at sea, and so on?

Certainly.

Then is there not an art of wages which provides us with wages, this being its proper faculty? Or do you call the art of healing and that of piloting identical? Or if you choose to employ strict definitions as you engaged to do, the fact of a man's regaining his health while acting as a pilot, through the beneficial effects of the sea-voyage, would not make you call the art of the pilot a healing art, would it?

Certainly not.

Nor would you so describe the art of wages, I fancy, supposing a person to keep his health while in the receipt of wages.

No.

Well then, would you call the physician's art a mercenary art, if fees be taken for medical attendance?

No.

Did we not allow that the benefit of each art was peculiar to itself?

Be it so.

Then whatever benefit accrues in common to the professors of all arts, is clearly derived from a common use of some one and the same thing.

So it would seem.

And we further maintain that if these persons are benefited by earning wages, they owe it to their use of the art of wages in addition to that which they profess.

He reluctantly assented.

Then this advantage, the receipt of pay, does not come to each from his own art, but strictly considered, the art of healing produces health, and the art of wages pay; the art of house-building produces a house, while the art of wages follows it and produces pay; and so of all the rest; each works its own work, and benefits that which is its appointed object. If, however, an art be practised without pay, does the professor of it derive any benefit from his art?

Apparently not.

Does he also confer no benefit when he works gratuitously?

Nay, I suppose he does confer benefit.

So far then, Thrasymachus, we see clearly that an art or a

government never provides that which is profitable for itself, but as we said some time ago, it provides and enjoins what is profitable for the subject, looking to his interest who is the weaker, and not to the interest of the stronger. It was for these reasons that I said just now, my dear Thrasymachus, that no one will voluntarily take office, or assume the duty of correcting the disorders of others, but that all ask wages for the work, because one who is to prosper in his art never practises or prescribes what is best for himself, but only what is best for the subject, so long as he acts within the limits of his art: and on these grounds, apparently, wages must be given to make men willing to hold office, in the shape of money or honour, or of punishment in case of refusal.

What do you mean, Socrates? asked Glaucon. I understand two out of the three kinds of wages: but what the punishment is, and how you could describe it as playing the part of wages, I do not comprehend.

Then you do not comprehend, I said, the wages of the best men, which induce the most virtuous to hold office, when they consent to do so. Do you not know that to be ambitious and covetous is considered a disgrace, and really is a disgrace?

I do.

For this reason, then, good men will not consent to hold an office of power, either for the sake of money or for that of honour: for they neither wish to get the name of hirelings by openly exacting hire for their duties, nor of thieves by using their power to obtain it secretly, nor yet will they take office for the sake of honour, for they are not ambitious. Therefore compulsion and the fear of a penalty must be brought to bear upon them, to make them consent to hold office; which is probably the reason why it is thought dishonourable to accept power willingly without waiting to be compelled. Now the heaviest of all penalties is to be governed by a worse man, in case of one's own refusal to govern; and it is the fear of this, I believe, which induces virtuous men to take the posts of government; and when they do so, they enter upon their administration not with any idea of coming into a good thing, but as an unavoidable necessity – not expecting to enjoy themselves in it, but because they cannot find any person better or no worse than themselves to whom they can commit it. For the probability is that if there were a city composed of none but good men, it would be an object of competition to avoid the possession of power, just as now it is to obtain it, and then it would become clearly evident that it is not the nature of the genuine ruler to look to his own interest, but to that of the subject: so that every judicious man would choose to be the recipient of benefits, rather than to have the trouble of conferring them upon others. Therefore I will on no account concede to Thrasymachus that justice is the interest of the stronger. However we will resume this inquiry hereafter, for Thrasymachus now affirms that the life of the unjust man is better than the life of the just man; and this assertion seems to me of much greater importance than the other. Which side do *you* take, Glaucon? And which do you think the truer statement?

I for my part hold, he replied, that the life of the just man is the more advantageous.

Did you hear, I asked, what a long list of attractions Thrasymachus just now attributed to the life of the unjust man?

I did, but I am not convinced.

Should you then like us to convince him, if we can find any means of doing so, that what he says is not true?

Undoubtedly I should.

If then we adopt the plan of matching argument against argument – we enumerating all the advantages of being just, and Thrasymachus replying, and we again putting in a rejoinder – it will be necessary to count and measure the advantages which are claimed on both sides; and eventually we shall want a jury to give a verdict between us: but if we proceed in our inquiries, as we lately did, by the method of mutual admissions, we shall combine in our own persons the functions of jury and advocate.

Precisely so.

Which plan, then, do you prefer?

The latter, he said.

Come then, Thrasymachus, said I, let us start anew, and oblige us by answering: do you assert that a perfect injustice is more profitable than an equally perfect justice?

Most decidedly I do, and I have said why.

Pray, how do you describe them under another aspect? Probably you call one of them a virtue and the other a vice?

Undoubtedly.

That is, justice a virtue, and injustice a vice?

A likely thing, my facetious friend, when I assert that injustice is profitable, and justice the reverse.

Then what do you say?

Just the contrary.

Do you call justice a vice?

No: but I call it very egregious good nature.

Then do you call injustice ill nature?

No; I call it good policy.

Do you think, Thrasymachus, that the unjust are positively wise and good?

Yes, those who are able to practise injustice on the complete scale, having the power to reduce whole cities and nations of men to subjection. You, perhaps, imagine that I am speaking of the cut-purse tribe; and I certainly allow that even deeds like theirs are profitable if they escape detection: but they are not worthy to be considered in comparison with those I have just mentioned.

I quite understand what you mean: but I did wonder at your ranking injustice under the heads of virtue and wisdom, and justice under the opposites.

Well, I do so rank them, without hesitation.

You have now taken up a more stubborn position, my friend, and it is no longer easy to know what to say. If after laying down the position that injustice is profitable, you had still admitted it to be a vice and a baseness, as some others do, we should have had an answer to give, speaking according to generally received notions; but now it is plain enough that you will maintain it to be beautiful, and strong, and will ascribe to it all the qualities which we have been in the habit of ascribing to justice, seeing that you have actually ventured to rank it as a portion of virtue and of wisdom.

You divine most correctly, he said.

Nevertheless, I must not shrink from pursuing the inquiry and the argument, so long as I suppose that you are saying what you think: for if I am not mistaken, Thrasymachus, you are really not bantering now, but saying what you think to be the truth.

What difference does it make to you whether I think it true or not? Can you not assail the argument?

It makes none. But will you endeavour to answer me one more question? Do you think that a just man would wish to go beyond a just man in anything?

Certainly not: for then he would not be so charmingly simple as he is.

Would a just man go beyond a just line of conduct?

No, not beyond that either.

But would he go beyond an unjust man without scruple, and think it just to do so, or would he not think it just?

He would think it just, and would not scruple to do it, but he would not be able.

Nay, that was not my question; but whether a just man both resolves and desires to go beyond an unjust man, but not beyond a just man?

Well, it is so.

But how is it with the unjust man? Would he take upon himself to go beyond a just man and a just line of conduct?

Undoubtedly, when he takes upon himself to go beyond all and in every thing.

Then will not the unjust man also go beyond another unjust man and an unjust action, and struggle that he may himself obtain more than any one else?

He will.

Then let us put it in this form: the just man goes not beyond his like, but his unlike; the unjust man goes beyond both his like and his unlike?

Very well said.

And further, the unjust man is wise and good, the just man is neither.

Well spoken again.

Does not the unjust man further resemble the wise and the good, whereas the just man does not resemble them.

Why, of course, a man of a certain character must resemble others of that character, whereas one who is of a different character will not resemble them.

Very good: then the character of each is identical with that of those whom he resembles.

Why, what else would you have?

Very well, Thrasymachus: do you call one man musical and another unmusical?

I do.

Which of them do you call wise, and which unwise?

The musical man, of course, I call wise, and the unmusical, unwise.

Do you also say that wherein a man is wise, in that he is good, and wherein unwise, bad?

Yes.

Do you speak in the same manner of a medical man?

I do.

Do you think then, my excellent friend, that a musician, when he is tuning a lyre, would wish to go beyond a musician in the tightening or loosening of the strings, or would claim to have the advantage of him?

I do not.

Would he wish to have the advantage of an unmusical person?

Unquestionably he would.

How would a medical man act? Would he wish to go beyond a medical man or medical practice in a question of diet?

Certainly not.

But beyond an unprofessional man he would?

Yes.

Consider now, looking at every kind of knowledge and ignorance, whether you think that any scientific man whatever would, by his own consent, choose to do or say more than another scientific man, and not the same that one like himself would do in the same matter.

Well, perhaps the latter view is necessarily the true one.

But what do you say to the unscientific person? Would he not go beyond the scientific and the unscientific alike?

Perhaps.

And the scientific person is wise?

Yes.

And the wise man is good.

Yes.

Then a good and a wise man will not wish to go beyond his like, but his unlike and opposite?

So it would seem.

But a bad and an ignorant man will go beyond both his like and his opposite.

Apparently.

Well then, Thrasymachus, does not our unjust man go beyond both his like and his unlike? Was not that your statement?

It was.

But the just man will not go beyond his like, but only beyond his unlike?

Yes.

Consequently the just man resembles the wise and the good, whereas the unjust man resembles the bad and the ignorant.

So it would seem.

But we agreed, you know, that the character of each of them is identical with the character of those whom he resembles.

We did.

Consequently we have made the discovery that the just man is wise and good, and the unjust man ignorant and bad.

Thrasymachus had made all these admissions, not in the easy manner in which I now relate them, but reluctantly and after much resistance, in the course of which he perspired profusely, as it was hot weather to boot: on that occasion also I saw what I had never seen before – Thrasymachus blushing. But when we had thus mutually agreed that justice was a part of virtue and of wisdom, and injustice of vice and ignorance, I proceeded thus –

Very good: we will consider this point settled: but we said, you know, that injustice was also strong. Do you not remember it, Thrasymachus?

I do, he replied; but for my part I am not satisfied with your last conclusions, and I know what I could say on the subject. But if I were to express my thoughts, I am sure you would say that I was declaiming. Take your choice then; either allow me to say as much as I please, or if you prefer asking questions, do so: and I will do with you as we do with old women when they tell us stories: I will say 'Good,' and nod my head or shake it, as the occasion requires.

If so, pray do no violence to your own opinions.

Anything to please you, he said, as you will not allow me to speak. What else would you have?

Nothing, I assure you: but if you will do this, do so; and I will ask questions.

Proceed then.

Well then, I will repeat the question which I put to you just now, that our inquiry may be carried out continuously; namely, what sort of a thing justice is compared with injustice. It was said, I think, that injustice is more powerful and stronger than justice: but now, seeing that justice is both wisdom and virtue, and injustice is ignorance, it may easily be shown, I imagine, that justice is likewise stronger than injustice. No one can now fail to see this. But I do not wish to settle the question in that absolute way, Thrasymachus, but I would investigate it in the following manner: should you admit that a city may be unjust, and that it may unjustly attempt to enslave other cities, and so succeed in so doing, and hold many in such slavery to itself?

Undoubtedly I should: and this will be more frequently done by the best city, that is, the one that is most completely unjust, than by any other.

I understand, I said, that this is your position. But the question which I wish to consider is whether the city that becomes the mistress of another city will have this power without the aid of justice, or whether justice will be indispensable to it.

If, as you said just now, justice is wisdom, justice must lend her aid, but if it is as I said, injustice must lend hers.

I am quite delighted to find, Thrasymachus, that you are not content merely to nod and shake your head, but give exceedingly good answers.

I do it to indulge you.

You are very good: but pray indulge me so far as to say whether you think that either a city, or an army, or a band of thieves or robbers, or any other body of men, pursuing certain unjust ends in common, could succeed in any enterprise if they were to deal unjustly with one another?

Certainly not.

If they refrain from such conduct towards one another, will they not be more likely to succeed?

Yes, certainly.

Because, I presume, Thrasymachus, injustice breeds divisions and animosities and broils between man and man, while justice creates unanimity and friendship; does it not?

Be it so, he said, that I may not quarrel with you.

Truly I am very much obliged to you, my excellent friend: but pray tell me this; if the working of injustice is to implant hatred wherever it exists, will not the presence of it, whether among freemen or slaves, cause them to hate one another and to form parties, and disable them from acting together in concert?

Certainly.

Well, and if it exist in two persons, will they not quarrel and hate one another, and be enemies each to the other, and both to the just?

They will.

And supposing, my admirable friend, that injustice has taken up its residence in a single individual, will it lose its proper power, or retain it just the same?

We will say it retains it.

And does not its power appear to be of such a nature as to make any subject in which it resides, whether it be city, or family, or army, or anything else whatsoever, unable to act unitedly, because of the divisions and quarrels it excites, and moreover hostile both to itself and to everything that opposes it, and to the just? Is it not so?

Certainly it is.

Then if it appears in an individual also, it will produce all these its natural results: in the first place it will make him unable to act because of inward strife and division; in the next place, it will make him an enemy to himself and to the just, will it not?

It will.

And the gods, my friend, are just?

We will suppose they are.

Then to the gods also will the unjust man be an enemy, and the just a friend?

Feast on your argument, said he, to your heart's content: I will not oppose you, or I shall give offence to the company.

Be so good, said I, as to make my entertainment complete by continuing to answer as you have now been doing. I am aware, indeed, that the just are shown to be wiser, and better, and more able to act than the unjust, who are indeed, incapable of any combined action. Nay, we do not speak with entire accuracy when we say that any party of unjust men ever acted vigorously in concert together; for had they been thoroughly unjust, they could not have kept their hands off each other. But it is obvious that there was some justice at work in them, which made them refrain at any rate from injuring, at one and the same moment, both their comrades and the objects of their attacks, and which enabled them to achieve what they did achieve; and that their injustice partly disabled them, even in the pursuit of their unjust ends, since those who are complete villains, and thoroughly unjust, are also thoroughly unable to act. I learn that all this is true, and that the doctrine which you at first propounded is not true. But whether the just also live a better life, and are happier than the unjust, is a question which we proposed to consider next, and which we now have to investigate. Now for my part, I think it is already apparent, from what we have said, that they do: nevertheless, we must examine the point still more carefully. For we are debating no trivial question, but the manner in which a man ought to live.

Pray consider it.

I will. Tell me, do you think there is such a thing as a horse's function?

I do.

Would you, then, describe the function of a horse, or of anything else whatever, as that work for the accomplishment of which it is either the sole or the best instrument?

I do not understand.

Look at it this way. Can you see with anything besides eyes?

Certainly not.

Can you hear with anything besides ears?

No.

Then should we not justly say that seeing and hearing are the functions of these organs?

Yes, certainly.

Again, you might cut off a vine-shoot with a carving knife, or chisel, or many other tools?

Undoubtedly.

But with no tool, I imagine, so well as with the pruning knife made for the purpose.

True.

Then shall we not define pruning to be the function of the pruning knife?

By all means.

Now then, I think, you will better understand what I wished to learn from you just now, when I asked whether the function of a thing is not that work for the accomplishment of which it is either the sole or the best instrument?

I do understand, and I believe that this is in every case the function of a thing.

Very well: do you not also think that everything which has an appointed function has also a proper virtue? Let us revert to the same instances: we say that the eyes have a function?

They have.

Then have the eyes a virtue also?

They have.

And the ears: did we assign them a function?

Yes.

Then have they a virtue also?

They have.

And is it the same with all other things?

The same.

Attend then: do you suppose that the eyes could discharge their own function well if they had not their own proper virtue – that virtue being replaced by a vice?

How could they? You mean, probably, if sight is replaced by blindness.

I mean, whatever their virtue be, for I am not come to that question yet. At present I am asking whether it is through their own peculiar virtue that things perform their proper functions well, and through their own peculiar vice that they perform them ill?

You cannot be wrong in that.

Then if the ears lose their own virtue, will they execute their functions ill?

Certainly.

May we include all other things under the same proposition?

I think we may.

Come, then, consider this point next. Has the soul any function which could not be executed by means of anything else whatsoever? For example, could we in justice assign superintendence and government, deliberation and the like, to anything but the soul, or should we pronounce them to be peculiar to it?

We could ascribe them to nothing else.

Again, shall we declare life to be a function of the soul?

Decidedly.

Do we not also maintain that the soul has a virtue?

We do.

Then can it ever so happen, Thrasymachus, that the soul will perform its functions well when destitute of its own peculiar virtue, or is that impossible?

Impossible.

Then a bad soul must needs exercise authority and superintendence ill, and a good soul must do all these things well.

Unquestionably.

Now, did we not grant that justice was a virtue of the soul, and injustice a vice?

We did.

Consequently the just soul and the just man will live well, and the unjust man ill?

Apparently, according to your argument.

And you will allow that he who lives well is blessed and happy, and that he who lives otherwise is the reverse.

Unquestionably.

Consequently the just man is happy, and the unjust man miserable.

Let us suppose them to be so.

But surely it is not misery, but happiness, that is advantageous.

Undoubtedly.

Never then, my excellent Thrasymachus, is injustice more advantageous than justice.

Well, Socrates, let this be your entertainment for the feast of Bendis.[4]

I have to thank *you* for it, Thrasymachus, because you recovered your temper, and left off being angry with me. Nevertheless, I have not been well entertained; but that was my own fault, and not yours: for as your gourmands seize upon every new dish as it goes round, and taste its contents before they have had a reasonable enjoyment of its predecessor, so I seem to myself to have left the question which we were at first examining, concerning the real nature of justice, before we had found out the answer to it, in order to rush to the inquiry whether this unknown thing is a vice and an ignorance, or a virtue and a wisdom; and again, when a new theory, that injustice is more profitable than justice, was subsequently started, I could not refrain from passing from the other to this, so that at present the result of our conversation is that I know nothing: for while I do not know what justice is, I am little likely to know whether it is in fact a virtue or not, or whether its owner is happy or unhappy.

NOTES TO BOOK ONE

1 This festival, as we learn from a remark of Thrasymachus (354a), was in honour of Bendis, a Thracian goddess, generally identified with Artemis.

2 A fragment from a lost work of Pindar.

3 Socrates alludes to a popular belief that anyone meeting a wolf would be deprived of speech if the wolf happened to see him before he saw the wolf. Virgil refers to this superstition in a well-known passage, *Eclogues* ix, 53.

4 See note 1.

BOOK TWO

When I had made these remarks I thought we had done with discussing: whereas it seems it was only a prelude. For Glaucon, with that eminent courage which he displays on all occasions, would not acquiesce in the retreat of Thrasymachus, and began thus: Socrates, do you wish really to convince us that it is on every account better to be just than to be unjust, or only to seem to have convinced us?

If it were in my power, I replied, I should prefer convincing you really.

Then, he proceeded, you are not doing what you wish. Let me ask you: is there, in your opinion, a class of good things of such a kind that we are glad to possess them, not because we desire their consequences, but simply welcoming them for their own sake? Take for example the feelings of enjoyment and all those pleasures that are harmless, and that are followed by no result in the after time, beyond simple enjoyment in their possession.

Yes, I certainly think there is a class of this description.

Well, is there another class, do you think, of those which we value both for their own sake and for their results? Such as intelligence, and sight, and health, all of which are welcome, I apprehend, on both accounts.

Yes.

And do you further recognise a third class of good things, which would include gymnastic training and submission to medical treatment in illness, as well as the practice of medicine and all other means of making money? Things like these we should describe as irksome, and yet beneficial to us, and while we should reject them viewed simply in themselves, we accept them for the sake of the emoluments, and of the other consequences which result from them.

Yes, undoubtedly there is such a third class also: but what then?

In which of these classes do you place justice?

I should say in the highest, that is, among the good things which will be valued by one who is in the pursuit of true happiness, alike for their own sake and for their consequences.

Then your opinion is not that of the many, by whom justice is ranked in the irksome class, as a thing which in itself, and for its own sake, is disagreeable and repulsive, but which it is well to practise for the credit of it, with an eye to emolument and a good name.

I know it is so: and under this idea Thrasymachus has been for a long time disparaging justice and praising injustice. But apparently I am a dull scholar.

Pray then listen to my proposal, and tell me whether you agree to it. Thrasymachus appears to me to have yielded like a snake to your fascination sooner than he need have done; but for my part I am not satisfied as yet with the exposition that has been given of justice and injustice; for I long to be told what they respectively are, and what force they exert, taken simply by themselves, when residing in the soul, dismissing the consideration of their rewards and other consequences. This shall be my plan then, if you do not object: I will revive Thrasymachus's argument, and will first state the common view respecting the nature and origin of justice; in the second place, I will maintain that all who practise it do so against their will, because it is indispensable, not because it is a good thing; and thirdly, that they act reasonably in so doing, because the life of the unjust man is, as men say, far better than that of the just. Not that I think so myself, Socrates: only my ears are so dinned with what I hear from Thrasymachus and a thousand others, that I am puzzled. Now I have never heard the argument for the superiority of justice over injustice maintained to my satisfaction; for I should like to hear a panegyric upon it, considered simply in itself: and from you if from anyone I should expect such a treatment of the subject. Therefore I will speak as forcibly as I can in praise of an unjust life, and I shall thus give you a specimen of the manner in which I wish to hear you afterwards censure injustice and commend justice. See whether you approve of my plan.

Indeed I do; for on what other subject could a sensible man like better to talk and to hear others talk, again and again?

Admirably spoken! So now listen to me while I speak on my first theme, the nature and the origin of justice.

To commit injustice is, they say, in its nature a good thing, and to suffer it an evil thing; but the evil of the latter exceeds the good of the former; and so, after the twofold experience of both doing and suffering injustice, those who cannot avoid the latter and compass the former find it expedient to make a compact of mutual abstinence from injustice. Hence arose legislation and contracts between man and man, and hence it became the custom to call that which the law enjoined just, as well as lawful. Such, they tell us, is justice, and so it came into being; and it stands midway between that which is best, to commit injustice with impunity, and that which is worst, to suffer injustice without any power of retaliating. And being a mean between these two extremes, the principle of justice is regarded with satisfaction, not as a positive good, but because the inability to commit injustice has rendered it valuable; for they say that one who had it in his power to be unjust, and who deserved the name of a man, would never be so weak as to contract with any one that both the parties should abstain from injustice. Such is the current account, Socrates, of the nature of justice, and of the circumstances in which it originated.

The truth of my second statement – that men practise justice unwillingly, and because they lack the power to violate it, will be most readily perceived if we make a supposition like the following. Let us give full liberty to the just man and to the unjust alike, to do whatever they please, and then let us follow them and see whither the inclination of each will lead him. In that case we shall surprise the just man in the act of travelling in the same direction as the unjust, owing to that covetous desire, the gratification of which every creature naturally pursues as a good, only that it is forced out of its path by law, and constrained to respect the principle of equality. That full liberty of action would, perhaps, be most effectually realised if they were invested with a power which they say was in old time possessed by the ancestor of Gyges the Lydian. He was a shepherd, so the story runs, in the service of the reigning sovereign of Lydia, when one day a violent storm of rain fell, the ground was rent asunder by an earthquake, and a yawning gulf appeared on the spot where he was feeding his flocks. Seeing what had happened, and wondering at it, he went down into the gulf, and among other marvellous objects he saw, as the legend relates, a hollow brazen horse, with windows in its sides, through which he looked, and beheld in the interior a corpse, apparently of superhuman size; from which he took nothing but a golden ring off the hand, and therewith made his way out. Now when the usual meeting of the shepherds occurred, for the purpose of sending to the king their monthly report of the state of his flocks, this shepherd came with the rest, wearing the ring. And as he was seated with the company, he happened to turn the hoop of the ring round towards himself, till it came to the inside of his hand. Whereupon he became invisible to his neighbours, who fell to talking about him as if he were gone away. While he was marvelling at this, he again began playing with the ring, and turned the hoop to the outside, upon which he became once more visible. Having noticed this effect, he made experiments with the ring, to see whether it possessed this virtue; and so it was, that when he turned the hoop inwards he became invisible, and when he turned it outwards he was again visible. After this discovery, he immediately contrived to be appointed one of the messengers to carry the report to the king; and upon his arrival he seduced the queen and conspiring with her, slew the king, and took possession of the throne.

If then there were two such rings in existence, and if the just and the unjust man were each to put on one, it is to be thought that no one would be so steeled against temptation as to abide in the practice of justice, and resolutely to abstain from touching the property of his neighbours, when he had it in his power to help himself without fear to any thing he pleased in the market, or to go into private houses and have intercourse with whom he would, or to kill and release from prison according to his own pleasure, and in every thing else to act among men with the power of a god. And in thus following out his desires the just man will be doing precisely what the unjust man would do; and so they would both be pursuing the same path. Surely this will be allowed to be strong evidence that none are just willingly, but only by compulsion, because to be just is not a good to the individual; for all violate justice whenever they imagine that there is nothing to hinder them. And they do so because every one thinks that in the individual case injustice is much more profitable than justice; and they are right in so thinking, as the advocate of this doctrine will maintain. For if any one having this licence within his grasp were to refuse to do any injustice, or to touch the property of others, all who were aware of it would think him a most pitiful and irrational creature, though they would praise him before each other's faces, to impose on one another, through their fear of being treated with injustice. And so much for this topic.

But in actually deciding between the lives of the two persons in question, we shall be enabled to arrive at a correct conclusion by contrasting together the thoroughly just and the thoroughly unjust man – and only by so doing. Well then, how are we to contrast them? In this way. Let us make no deduction either from the injustice of the unjust, or from the justice of the just, but let us suppose each to be perfect in his own line of conduct. First of all then, the unjust man must act as skilful craftsmen do. For a first-rate pilot or physician perceives the difference between what is practicable and what is impracticable in his art, and while he attempts the former, he lets the latter alone; and moreover, should he happen to make a false step, he is able to recover himself. In the same way, if we are to form a conception of a consummately unjust man, we must suppose that he makes no mistake in the prosecution of his unjust enterprises, and that he escapes detection: but if he be found out, we must look upon him as a bungler, for it is the perfection of injustice to seem just without really being so. We must therefore grant to the perfectly unjust man, without any deduction, the most perfect injustice: and we must concede to him that while committing the grossest acts of injustice, he has won himself the highest reputation for justice, and that should he make a false step, he is able to recover himself, partly by a talent for speaking with effect, in case he be called in question for any of his misdeeds, and partly because his courage and strength, and his command of friends and money, enable him to employ force with success, whenever force is required. Such being our unjust man, let us, in pursuance of the argument, place the just man by his side, a man of true simplicity and nobleness, resolved, as Aeschylus[1] says, not to seem, but to be, good. We must certainly take away the seeming; for if he be thought to be a just man, he will have honours and gifts on the strength of this reputation, so that it will be uncertain whether it is for justice's sake, or for the sake of the gifts and honours, that he is what he is. Yes, we must strip him bare of everything but justice, and make his whole case the reverse of the former. Without being guilty of one unjust act, let him have the worst reputation for injustice, so that his virtue may be thoroughly tested, and shown to be proof against infamy and all its consequences; and let him go on till the day of his death, steadfast in his justice, but with a lifelong reputation for injustice, in order that, having brought both the men to the utmost limits of justice and of injustice respectively, we may then give judgment as to which of the two is the happier.

Good heavens! My dear Glaucon, said I, how vigorously you work, scouring the two characters clean for our judgment, like a pair of statues.

I do it as well as I can, he said. And after describing the men as we have done, there will be no further difficulty, I imagine, in proceeding to sketch the kind of life which awaits them respectively. Let me therefore describe it. And if the description be somewhat coarse, do not regard it as mine, Socrates, but as coming from those who commend injustice above justice. They will say that in such a situation the just man will be scourged, racked, fettered, will have his eyes burnt out, and at last, after suffering every kind of torture, will be crucified; and thus learn that it is best to resolve, not to be, but to seem, just. Indeed those words of Aeschylus are far more applicable to the unjust man than to the just. For it is in fact the unjust man, they will maintain, inasmuch as he devotes himself to a course which is allied to reality, and does not live with an eye to appearances, who 'is resolved not to seem, but to be,' unjust,

> Reaping a harvest of wise purposes,
> Sown in the fruitful furrows of his mind;

being enabled first of all to hold offices of state through his reputation for justice, and in the next place to choose a wife wherever he will, and marry his children into whatever family he pleases, to enter into contracts and join in partnership with any one he likes, and besides all this, to enrich himself by large profits, because he is not too nice to commit a fraud. Therefore, whenever he engages in a contest, whether public or private, he defeats and overreaches his enemies, and by so doing grows rich, and is enabled to benefit his friends and injure his enemies, and to offer sacrifices and dedicate gifts to the gods in magnificent abundance: and thus having greatly the advantage of the just man in the means of paying court to the gods, as well as to such men as he chooses, he is also more likely than the just man, as far as probabilities go, to enjoy the favour of heaven. And therefore they affirm, Socrates, that a better provision is made both by gods and men for the life of the unjust than for the life of the just.

When Glaucon had said this, before I could make the reply I was meditating, his brother Adeimantus exclaimed, You surely do not suppose, Socrates, that the doctrine has been satisfactorily expounded.

Why not, pray? said I.

The very point which it was most important to urge has been omitted.

Well then, according to the proverb, 'May a brother be present to help one', it is for you to supply his deficiencies, if there are any, by your assistance. But indeed, for my part, what Glaucon has said is enough to prostrate me, and put it out of my power to come up to the rescue of justice.

You are not in earnest, he said: pray listen to the following argument also, for we must now go through those representations which, reversing the declarations of Glaucon, commend justice and disparage injustice, in order to bring out more clearly what I take to be his meaning. Now I apprehend that when parents and others set forth the duty of being just, and impress it upon their children or those in whom they feel an interest, they do not praise justice in itself, but only the respectability which it gives, their object being that a reputation for justice may be gained, and that this reputation may bring in the preferment, the marriages, and the other good things which Glaucon has just told us are secured to the just man by his high character. And these persons carry the advantages of a good name still further; for by introducing the good opinion of the gods, they are enabled to describe innumerable blessings which the gods, they say, grant to the pious, as the excellent Hesiod tells us, and Homer too; the former saying that the gods cause the oak-trees of the just

> On their tops to bear acorns, and swarms of bees in the middle;
> Also their wool-laden sheep sink under the weight of their fleeces:[2]

with many other good things of the same sort: while the latter, in a similar passage, speaks of one

> Like to a blameless king, who godlike in virtue and wisdom,
> Justice ever maintains; whose rich land fruitfully yields him
> Harvests of barley and wheat, and his orchards are heavy with fruitage;
> Strong are the young of his flocks, and the sea gives him fish in
>   abundance.[3]

But the blessings which Musaeus and his son Eumolpus represent the gods as bestowing upon the just, are still more delectable than these; for they bring them to the abode of Hades, and describe them as reclining on couches at a banquet of the pious, and with garlands on their heads spending all eternity in wine-bibbing, the fairest reward of virtue being, in their estimation, an everlasting carousal. Others again do not stop even here in their enumeration of the rewards bestowed by the gods; for they tell us that the man who is pious and true to his oath leaves children's children and a posterity to follow him. Such, among others, are the commendations which they lavish upon justice. The ungodly, on the other hand, and the unjust, they plunge into a swamp in Hades, and condemn them to carry water in a sieve; and while they are still alive, they bring them into evil repute, and inflict upon the unjust precisely those punishments which Glaucon enumerated as the lot of the just who are reputed to be unjust – more they cannot. Such is their method of praising the one character and condemning the other.

Once more, Socrates, take into consideration another and a different mode of speaking with regard to justice and injustice, which we meet with both in common life and in the poets. All as with one mouth proclaim that to be temperate and just is an admirable thing certainly, but at the same time a hard and an irksome one; while intemperance and injustice are pleasant things and of easy acquisition, and only rendered base by law and public opinion. But they say that honesty is in general less profitable than dishonesty, and they do not hesitate to call wicked men happy, and to honour them both in public and in private when they are rich or possess other sources of power, and on the other hand to treat with dishonour and contempt those who are in any way feeble or poor, even while they admit that the latter are better men than the former. But of all their statements the most wonderful are those which relate to the gods and to virtue; according to which even the gods allot to many good men a calamitous and an evil life, and to men of the opposite character an opposite portion. And there are quacks and soothsayers who flock to the rich man's doors, and try to persuade him that they have a power at command, which they procure from heaven, and which enables them, by sacrifices and incantations performed amid feasting and indulgence, to make amends for any crime committed either by the individual himself or by his ancestors, and that should he desire to do a mischief to any one, it may be done at a trifling expense, whether the object of his hostility be a just or an unjust man, for they profess that by certain invocations and spells they can prevail upon the gods to do their bidding. And in support of all these assertions they produce the evidence of poets: some, to exhibit the facilities of vice, quoting the words –

Whoso wickedness seeks, may even in masses obtain it
Easily. Smooth is the way, and short, for nigh is her dwelling.
Virtue, Heav'n has ordained, shall be reached by the sweat of the
    forehead,[4]

and by a long and up-hill road; while others, to prove that the gods may be turned from their purpose by men, adduce the testimony of Homer,[5] who has said:

Yea, even the gods do yield to entreaty;
Therefore to them men offer both victims and meek supplications,
Incense and melting fat, and turn them from anger to mercy;
Sending up sorrowful prayers, when trespass and sin is committed.

And they produce a host of books written by Musaeus and Orpheus, children, as they say, of Selene and of the Muses, which form their ritual – persuading not individuals merely, but whole cities also, that men may be absolved and purified from crimes, both while they are still alive and even after their decease, by means of certain sacrifices and pleasurable amusements which they call mysteries: which deliver us from the torments of the other world, while the neglect of them is punished by an awful doom.

When views like these, he continued, my dear Socrates, are proclaimed and repeated with so much variety, concerning the honours in which virtue and vice are respectively held by gods and men, what can we suppose is the effect produced on the minds of all those young men of good natural parts who are able, after skimming like birds, as it were, over all that they hear, to draw conclusions from it, respecting the character which a man must possess, and the path in which he must walk, in order to live the best possible life? In all probability a young man would say to himself in the words of Pindar,[6] 'Shall I by justice or by crooked wiles climb to a loftier stronghold, and having thus fenced myself about, live my life?' For common opinion declares that to be just without being also thought just is no advantage to me, but only entails manifest trouble and loss, whereas if I am unjust and get myself a name for justice, an unspeakably happy life is promised me. Very well then; since the

outward semblance, as the wise inform me, overpowers the inward
reality, and is the sovereign dispenser of felicity, to this I must of
course wholly devote myself: I must draw round about me a picture
of virtue to serve as a frontage and exterior, but behind me I must
trail the fox, of which that most clever Archilochus tells us, with its
cunning and shiftiness.[7] Yes but, it will be objected, it is not an easy
matter always to conceal one's wickedness. No, we shall reply, nor
yet is anything else easy that is great: nevertheless, if happiness is to be
our goal, this must be our path, as the steps of the argument indicate.
To assist in keeping up the deception, we will form secret societies
and clubs. There are, moreover, teachers of persuasion who impart
skill in popular and forensic oratory; and so by fair means or by foul
we shall gain our ends, and carry on our dishonest proceedings with
impunity. Nay but, it is urged, neither evasion nor violence can
succeed with the gods. Well, but if they either do not exist, or do not
concern themselves with the affairs of men, why need *we* concern
ourselves to evade their observation? But if they do exist, and do pay
attention to us, we know nothing and have heard nothing of them
from any other quarter than the current traditions and the genealogies
of poets; and these very authorities state that the gods are beings who
may be wrought upon and diverted from their purpose by sacrifices
and meek supplications and votive offerings. Therefore we must
believe them in both statements or in neither. If we are to believe
them, we will act unjustly, and offer sacrifices from the proceeds of
our crimes. For if we are just, we shall, it is true, escape punishment at
the hands of the gods, but we renounce the profits which accrue
from injustice: but if we are unjust, we shall not only make these
gains, but also, by putting up prayers when we transgress and sin, we
shall prevail upon the gods to let us go unscathed. But then, it is again
objected, in Hades we shall pay the just penalty for the crimes
committed here, either in our own persons or in those of our
children's children. Nay but, my friend, the champion of the
argument will continue, the mystic rites, again, are very powerful,
and the absolving divinities, as we are told by the mightiest cities and
by the sons of the gods who have appeared as poets and inspired
prophets, who inform us that these things are so.

What consideration therefore remains which should induce us to
prefer justice to the greatest injustice? Since if we combine injustice
with a spurious decorum, we shall fare to our liking with the gods

and with men, in this life and the next, according to the most numerous and the highest authorities. Considering all that has been said, by what device, Socrates, can a man who has any advantages, either of high talent, or wealth, or personal appearance, or birth, bring himself to honour justice instead of smiling when he hears it praised? Indeed, if there is any one who is able to show the falsity of what we have said, and who is fully convinced that justice is best, far from being angry with the unjust, he doubtless makes great allowance for them, knowing that with the exception of those who may possibly refrain from injustice through the disgust of a godlike nature or from the acquisition of genuine knowledge, there is certainly no one else who is willingly just; but it is from cowardice, or age, or some other infirmity, that men condemn injustice, simply because they lack the power to commit it. And the truth of this is proved by the fact that the first of these people who comes to power is the first to commit injustice, to the extent of his ability.

And the cause of all this is simply that fact which my brother and I both stated at the very commencement of this address to you, Socrates, saying; With much respect be it spoken; you who profess to be admirers of justice, beginning with the heroes of old, of whom accounts have descended to the present generation, have every one of you, without exception, made the praise of justice and condemnation of injustice turn solely upon the reputation and honour and gifts resulting from them: but what each is in itself, by its own peculiar force as it resides in the soul of its possessor, unseen either by gods or men, has never in poetry or in prose been adequately discussed, so as to show that injustice is the greatest bane that a soul can receive into itself, and justice the greatest blessing. Had this been the language held by you all from the first, and had you tried to persuade us of this from our childhood, we should not be on the watch to check one another in the commission of injustice, because every one would be his own watchman, fearful lest by committing injustice he might attach to himself the greatest of evils

All this, Socrates, and perhaps still more than this, would be put forward respecting justice and injustice, by Thrasymachus and I dare say by others also; thus ignorantly reversing, in my opinion, the inherent efficacy of each. For my own part, I confess (for I do not want to hide anything from you) that I have a great desire to hear you defend the opposite view, and therefore I have exerted myself to speak as forcibly as I can. So do not limit your argument to the proposition that justice is superior to injustice, but show us what is that influence exerted by each of them on its possessor, whereby the one is in itself a blessing, and the other a bane; and deduct the estimation in which the two are held, as Glaucon urged you to do. For if you omit to withdraw from each quality its true reputation and to add the false, we shall declare that you are praising, not the reality but the semblance of justice, and blaming, not the reality but the semblance of injustice; that your advice, in fact, is to be unjust without being found out, and that you hold, with Thrasymachus, that justice is another man's good, being for the interest of the stronger; injustice a man's own interest and advantage, but against the interest of the weaker. Since then you have allowed that justice belongs to the highest class of good things, the possession of which is valuable both for the sake of their results and also in a higher degree for their own sake – such as sight, hearing, intelligence, health, and everything else which is genuinely good in its own nature and not merely reputed to be good – select for commendation this particular feature of justice, I mean the benefit which in itself it confers on its possessor, in contrast with the harm which injustice inflicts. The rewards and reputations leave to others to praise, because in others I can tolerate this mode of praising justice and condemning injustice, which consists in eulogising or reviling the reputations and the rewards which are connected with them; but in you I cannot, unless you require it, because you have spent your whole life in investigating such questions, and such only. Therefore do not content yourself with proving to us that justice is better than injustice; but show us what is that influence exerted by each on its possessor, by which, whether gods and men see it or not, the one is in itself a blessing and the other a bane.

Much as I had always admired the talents both of Glaucon and Adeimantus, I confess that on this occasion I was quite charmed with what I had heard; so I said: Fitly indeed did Glaucon's admirer address you, ye sons of the man there named, in the first line of his elegiac poem, after you had distinguished yourselves in the battle of Megara, saying:

Race of a famous man, ye godlike sons of Ariston.

There seems to me to be great truth in this epithet, my friends: for there is something truly god-like in the state of your minds, if you are not convinced that injustice is better than justice, when you can plead its cause so well. I do believe that you really are not convinced of it. But I infer it from your general character; for judging merely from your statements I should have distrusted you: but the more I place confidence in you, the more I am perplexed how to deal with the case; for though I do not know how I am to render assistance, having learnt how unequal I am to the task from your rejection of my answer to Thrasymachus, wherein I imagined that I had demonstrated that justice is better than injustice; yet, on the other hand, I dare not refuse my assistance: because I am afraid that it might be positively sinful in me, when I hear justice evil spoken of in my presence, to lose heart and desert her, so long as breath and utterance are left in me. My best plan, therefore, is to succour her in such fashion as I can.

Thereupon Glaucon, and all the rest with him, requested me by all means to give my assistance, and not to let the conversation drop, but thoroughly to investigate the real nature of justice and injustice, and which is the true doctrine with regard to their respective advantages. So I said what I really felt: The inquiry we are undertaking is no trivial one, but demands a keen sight, according to my notion of it. Therefore, since I am not a clever person, I think we had better adopt a mode of inquiry which may be thus illustrated. Suppose we had been ordered to read small writing at a distance, not having very good eye-sight, and that one of us discovered that the same writing was to be found somewhere else in larger letters, and upon a larger space, we should have looked upon it as a piece of luck, I imagine, that we could read the latter first, and then examine the smaller, and observe whether the two were alike.

Undoubtedly we should, said Adeimantus; but what parallel can you see to this, Socrates, in our inquiry after justice?

I will tell you, I replied. We speak of justice as residing in an individual mind, and as residing also in an entire city, do we not?

Certainly we do, he said.

Well, a city is larger than one man.

It is.

Perhaps, then, justice may exist in larger proportions in the greater subject, and thus be easier to discover: so, if you please, let us first investigate its character in cities; afterwards let us apply the same inquiry to the individual, looking for the counterpart of the greater as it exists in the form of the less.

Indeed, he said, I think your plan is a good one.

If then we were to trace in thought the gradual formation of a city, should we also see the growth of its justice or of its injustice?

Perhaps we should.

Then if this were done, might we not hope to see more easily the object of our search?

Yes, much more easily.

Is it your advice, then, that we should attempt to carry out our plan? It is no trifling task, I imagine; therefore consider it well.

We have considered it, said Adeimantus; yes, do so by all means.

Well then, I proceeded, the formation of a city is due, as I imagine, to this fact, that we are not individually independent, but have many wants. Or would you assign any other cause for the founding of cities?

No, I agree with you, he replied.

Thus it is, then, that owing to our many wants, and because each seeks the aid of others to supply his various requirements, we gather many associates and helpers into one dwelling-place, and give to this joint dwelling the name of city. Is it so?

Undoubtedly.

And everyone who gives or takes in exchange, whatever it be that he exchanges, does so from a belief that he is consulting his own interest.

Certainly.

Now then, let us construct our imaginary city from the beginning. It will owe its construction, it appears, to our natural wants.

Unquestionably.

Well, but the first and most pressing of all wants is that of sustenance to enable us to exist as living creatures.

Most decidedly.

Our second want would be that of a house, and our third that of clothing and the like.

True.

Then let us know what will render our city adequate to the supply of so many things. Must we not begin with a husbandman for one, and a house-builder, and besides these a weaver? Will these suffice, or shall we add to them a shoemaker, and perhaps one or two more of the class of people who minister to our bodily wants?

By all means.

Then the smallest possible city will consist of four or five men.

So we see.

To proceed then: ought each of these to place his own work at the disposal of the community, so that the single husbandman, for example, shall provide food for four, spending four times the amount of time and labour upon the preparation of food, and sharing it with others; or must he be regardless of them, and produce for his own consumption alone the fourth part of this quantity of food, in a fourth part of the time, spending the other three parts, one in making his house, another in procuring himself clothes, and the third in providing himself with shoes, saving himself the trouble of sharing with others, and doing his own business by himself and for himself?

To this Adeimantus replied, Well, Socrates, perhaps the former plan is the easier of the two.

Really, I said, it is not improbable; for I recollect myself, after your answer, that in the first place, no two persons are born exactly alike, but each differs from each in natural endowments, one being suited for one occupation, and another for another. Do you not think so?

I do.

Well; when is a man likely to succeed best? When he divides his exertions among many trades, or when he devotes himself exclusively to one?

When he devotes himself to one.

Again, it is also clear, I imagine, that if a person lets the right moment for any work go by, it never returns.

It is quite clear.

For the thing to be done does not choose, I imagine, to tarry the leisure of the doer, but the doer must be at the beck of the thing to be done, and not treat it as a secondary affair.

He must.

From these considerations it follows that all things will be produced in superior quantity and quality, and with greater ease, when each man works at a single occupation, in accordance with his natural gifts, and at the right moment, without meddling with anything else.

Unquestionably.

More than four citizens, then, Adeimantus, are needed to provide the requisites which we named. For the husbandman, it appears, will not make his own plough, if it is to be a good one, nor his mattock, nor any of the other tools employed in agriculture. No more will the builder make the numerous tools which he also requires: and so of the weaver and the shoemaker.

True.

Then we shall have carpenters and smiths, and many other artisans of the kind, who will become members of our little state, and create a population.

Certainly.

Still it will not yet be very large, supposing we add to them neatherds and shepherds, and the rest of that class, in order that the husbandmen may have oxen for ploughing, and the house-builders, as well as the husbandmen, beasts of burden for draught, and the weavers and shoemakers wool and leather.

It will not be a small state, either, if it contains all these.

Moreover, it is scarcely possible to plant the actual city in a place where it will have no need of imports.

No, it is impossible.

Then it will further require a new class of persons to bring from other cities all that it requires.

It will.

Well, but if the agent goes empty-handed, carrying with him none of the commodities in demand among those people from whom our state is to procure what it requires, he will also come empty-handed away: will he not?

I think so.

Then it must produce at home not only enough for itself, but also articles of the right kind and quantity to accommodate those whose services it needs.

It must.

Then our city requires larger numbers both of husbandmen and other craftsmen.

Yes, it does.

And among the rest it will need more of those agents also who are to export and import the several commodities: these are merchants, are they not?

Yes.

Then we shall require merchants also.

Certainly.

And if the traffic is carried on by sea, there will be a further demand for a considerable number of other persons, who are skilled in the practice of navigation.

A considerable number, undoubtedly.

But now tell me: in the city itself how are they to exchange their several productions? For it was to promote this exchange, you know, that we formed the community, and so founded our state.

Manifestly, by buying and selling.

Then this will give rise to a market and a currency, for the sake of exchange.

Undoubtedly.

Suppose then that the husbandman, or one of the other craftsmen, should come with some of his produce into the market, at a time when none of those who wish to make an exchange with him are there, is he to leave his occupation and sit idle in the market-place?

By no means: there are persons who, with an eye to this contingency, undertake the service required; and these in well-regulated states are, generally speaking, persons of excessive physical weakness, who are of no use in other kinds of labour. Their business is to remain on the spot in the market, and give money for goods to those who want to sell, and goods for money to those who want to buy.

This demand, then, causes a class of retail dealers to spring up in our city. For do we not give the name of retail dealers to those who station themselves in the market, to minister to buying and selling, applying the term merchants to those who go about from city to city?

Exactly so.

In addition to these, I imagine, there is also another class of operatives, consisting of those whose mental qualifications do not recommend them as associates, but whose bodily strength is equal to hard labour: these, selling the use of their strength and calling the price of it hire, are thence named, I believe, hired labourers. Is it not so?

Precisely.

Then hired labourers also form, as it seems, a complementary portion of a state.

I think so.

Shall we say then, Adeimantus, that our city has at length grown to its full stature?

Perhaps so.

Where then, I wonder, shall we find justice and injustice in it?

With which of these elements that we have contemplated has it simultaneously made its entrance?

I have no notion, Socrates, unless perhaps it be discoverable somewhere in the mutual relations of these same persons.

Well, perhaps you are right. We must investigate the matter, and not flinch from the task.

Let us consider then, in the first place, what kind of life will be led by persons thus provided. I presume they will produce corn and wine, and clothes and shoes, and build themselves houses; and in summer, no doubt, they will generally work without their coats and shoes, while in winter they will be suitably clothed and shod. And they will live, I suppose, on barley and wheat, baking cakes of the meal, and kneading loaves of the flour. And spreading these excellent cakes and loaves upon mats of straw or on clean leaves, and themselves reclining on rude beds of yew or myrtle-boughs, they will make merry, themselves and their children, drinking their wine, wearing garlands, and singing the praises of the gods, enjoying one another's society, and not begetting children beyond their means, through a prudent fear of poverty or war.

Glaucon here interrupted me, remarking, Apparently you describe your men as feasting without anything to relish their bread.

True, I said, I had forgotten – of course they will have something to relish their food; salt, no doubt, and olives and cheese, together with the country fare of boiled onions and cabbage. We shall also set before them a dessert, I imagine, of figs and pease and beans; and they may roast myrtle-berries and beech-nuts at the fire, taking wine with their fruit in moderation. And thus passing their days in tranquillity and sound health, they will in all probability live to an advanced age, and dying, bequeath to their children a life in which their own will be reproduced.

Upon this Glaucon exclaimed, Why Socrates, if you were founding a community of swine, this is just the style in which you would feed them up!

How then, said I, would you have them live, Glaucon?

In a civilised manner, he replied. They ought to recline on couches, I should think, if they are not to have a hard life of it, and dine off tables, and have the usual dishes and dessert of a modern dinner.

Very good; I understand. Apparently we are considering the growth not of a city merely, but of a luxurious city. I dare say it is not a bad plan: for by this extension of our inquiry we shall perhaps discover how it is that justice and injustice take root in cities. Now it appears to me that the city which we have described is the genuine and, so to speak, healthy city. But if you wish us also to contemplate a city that is suffering from inflammation, there is nothing to hinder us. Some people will not be satisfied, it seems, with the fare or the mode of life which we have described, but must have, in addition, couches and tables and every other article of furniture, as well as viands, and fragrant oils, and perfumes, and courtesans, and confectionery; and all these in plentiful variety. Moreover, we must not limit ourselves now to essentials in those articles which we specified at first, I mean houses and clothes and shoes, but we must set painting and embroidery to work, and acquire gold and ivory, and all similar valuables: must we not?

Yes.

Then we shall also have to enlarge our city, for our first or healthy city will not now be of sufficient size, but requires to be increased in bulk, and filled out with a multitude of callings which do not exist in cities to satisfy any natural want; for example, the whole class of hunters, and all who practise imitative arts, including many who use forms and colours, and many who use music; poets also, with those of whom the poet makes use, rhapsodists, actors, dancers, contractors; lastly, the manufacturers of all sorts of articles, and among others those which form part of a woman's dress. We shall similarly require more personal servants, shall we not? That is to say, tutors, wet-nurses, dry-nurses, tire-women, barbers, and cooks moreover and confectioners? Swineherds again are among the additions we shall require – a class of persons not to be found, because not wanted, in our former city, but needed among the rest in this. We shall also need great quantities of all kinds of cattle, for those who may wish to eat them; shall we not?

Of course we shall.

Then shall we not experience the need of medical men also, to a much greater extent under this than under the former regime?

Yes, indeed.

The country too, I presume, which was formerly adequate to the support of its then inhabitants will be now too small, and adequate no longer. Shall we say so?

Certainly.

Then must we not cut ourselves a slice of our neighbour's territory, if we are to have land enough both for pasture and tillage, while they will do the same to ours, if they, like us, permit themselves to overstep the limit of necessaries and plunge into the unbounded acquisition of wealth?

It must inevitably be so, Socrates.

Will our next step be to go to war, Glaucon, or how will it be?

As you say.

At this stage of our inquiry let us avoid asserting either that war does good or that it does harm, confining ourselves to this statement, that we have further traced the origin of war to causes which are the most fruitful sources of whatever evils befall a state, either in its corporate capacity, or in its individual members.

Exactly so.

Once more then, my friend, our state must receive an accession of no trifling extent, I mean that of a whole army, which must go forth and do battle with all invaders in defence of its entire property, and of the persons whom we were just now describing.

How? he asked; are not those persons sufficient of themselves?

They are not, if you and all the rest of us were right in the admissions which we made when we were modelling our state. We admitted, I think, if you remember, that it was impossible for one man to work well at many professions.

True.

Well then, is not the business of war looked upon as a profession in itself?

Undoubtedly.

And have we not as much reason to concern ourselves about the trade of war as about the trade of shoemaking?

Quite as much.

But we cautioned the shoemaker, you know, against attempting to be an agriculturist or a weaver or a builder besides, with a view to our shoemaking work being well done; and to every other artisan we assigned in like manner one occupation, namely that for which he was naturally fitted, and in which, if he let other things alone and wrought at it all his time without neglecting his opportunities, he was likely to prove a successful workman. Now is it not of the greatest moment that the work of war should be well done? Or is it so easy, that any one can succeed in it and be at the same time a husbandman or a shoemaker or a labourer at any other trade whatever, although there is no one in the world who could become a good draught-player or dice-player by merely taking up the game at unoccupied moments, instead of pursuing it as his especial study from his childhood? And will it be enough for a man merely to handle a shield or any other of the arms and implements of war, to be straightway competent to play his part well that very day in an engagement of heavy troops or in any other military service, although the mere handling of any other instrument will never make any one a true craftsman or athlete, nor will such instrument be even useful to one who has neither learnt its capabilities nor exercised himself sufficiently in its practical applications.

If it were so, these implements of war would be very valuable.

In proportion, then, to the importance of the work which these guardians have to do, will it require peculiar freedom from other engagements, as well as extraordinary skill and attention?

I quite think so.

Will it not also require natural endowments suited to this particular occupation?

Undoubtedly.

Then apparently it will belong to us to choose out, if we can, that especial order of natural endowments which qualifies its possessors for the guardianship of a state.

Certainly it belongs to us.

Then, I assure you, we have taken upon ourselves no trifling task; nevertheless there must be no flinching, so long as our strength holds out.

No, there must not.

Do you think then, I asked, that there is any difference, in the qualities required for keeping guard, between a well-bred dog and a gallant young man?

I do not quite understand you.

Why, I suppose, for instance, they ought both of them to be quick to discover an enemy, and swift to overtake him when discovered, and strong also, in case they have to fight when they have come up with him.

Certainly, all these qualities are required.

Moreover, they must be brave if they are to fight well.

Undoubtedly.

But will either a horse, or a dog, or any other animal, be likely to be brave if it is not spirited?[8] Or have you failed to observe what an irresistible and unconquerable thing spirit is, so that under its influence every creature will be fearless and unconquerable in the face of any danger?

I have observed it.

We know then what bodily qualities are required in our guardian.

We do.

And also what qualities of the mind, namely that he must be spirited.

Yes.

How then, Glaucon, if such be their natural disposition, are they to be kept from behaving fiercely to one another and to the rest of the citizens?

Really it will be difficult to obviate that.

Nevertheless, they certainly ought to be gentle to their friends, and dangerous only to their enemies: else they will not wait for others to destroy them, but will be the first to do it for themselves.

True.

What then shall we do? Where shall we find a character at once gentle and high-spirited? For I suppose a gentle nature is the opposite of a spirited one?

Apparently it is.

Nevertheless a man who is devoid of either gentleness or spirit cannot possibly make a good guardian. And as they seem to be incompatible, the result is that a good guardian is an impossibility.

It looks like it, he said.

Here then I was perplexed, but having reconsidered our conversation, I said, We deserve, my friend, to be puzzled, for we have deserted the illustration which we set before us.

How so?

It never struck us that after all there are natures, though we fancied there were none, which combine these opposite qualities.

Pray where is such a combination to be found?

You may see it in several animals, but particularly in the one which we ourselves compared to our guardian. For I suppose you know that it is the natural disposition of well-bred dogs to be perfectly gentle to their friends and acquaintance, but the reverse to strangers.

Certainly I do.

Therefore the thing is possible; and we are not contradicting nature in our endeavour to give such a character to our guardian.

So it would seem.

Then is it your opinion that in one who is to make a good guardian it is further required that his character should be philosophical as well as high-spirited?

How so? I do not understand you.

You will notice in dogs this other trait, which is really marvellous in the creature.

What is that?

Whenever they see a stranger, they are irritated before they have been provoked by any ill-usage; but when they see an acquaintance they welcome him, though they may never have experienced any kindness at his hands. Has this never excited your wonder?

I never paid any attention to it hitherto; but no doubt they do behave so.

Well, but this instinct is a very clever thing in the dog, and a genuine philosophic symptom.

How so, pray?

Why, because the only mark by which he distinguishes between the appearance of a friend and that of an enemy is that he knows the former and is ignorant of the latter. How, I ask, can the creature be other than fond of learning when it makes knowledge and ignorance the criteria of the familiar and the strange?

Beyond a question, it must be fond of learning.

Well, is not the love of learning identical with a philosophical disposition?

It is.

Shall we not then assert with confidence in the case of a man also, that if he is to show a gentle disposition towards his relatives and acquaintances, he must have a turn for learning and philosophy?

Be it so.

Then in our judgment the man whose natural gifts promise to make him a perfect guardian of the state will be philosophical, high-spirited, swift-footed and strong.

Undoubtedly he will.

This then will be the original character of our guardians. But in what way shall we rear and educate them? And will the investigation of this point help us on towards discovering that which is the object of all our speculations, namely the manner in which justice and injustice grow up in a state? For I wish us neither to omit anything useful, nor to occupy ourselves with anything redundant, in our inquiry.

Hereupon Glaucon's brother observed, Well, for my part I fully anticipate that this inquiry will promote our object.

If so, I said, we must certainly not give it up, my dear Adeimantus, even though it should prove somewhat long.

Indeed we must not.

Come then, like idle story-tellers in a story, let us describe the education of our men.

Yes, let us do so.

What then is the education to be? Perhaps we could hardly find a better than that which the experience of the past has already discovered, which consists, I believe, in gymnastic for the body, and music for the mind.

It does.

Shall we not then begin our course of education with music rather than with gymnastic?

Undoubtedly we shall.

Under the term music, do you include narratives, or not?

I do.

And of narratives there are two kinds, the true and the false.

Yes.

And must we instruct our pupils in both, but in the false first?

I do not understand what you mean.

Do you not understand that we begin with children by telling them fables? And these, I suppose, to speak generally, are false, though they contain some truths: and we employ such fables in the treatment of children at an earlier period than gymnastic exercises.

True.

That is what I meant when I said that music ought to be taken up before gymnastic.

You are right.

Then are you aware that in every work the beginning is the most important part, especially in dealing with anything young and tender? For that is the time when any impression which one may desire to communicate is most readily stamped and taken.

Precisely so.

Shall we then permit our children without scruple to hear any fables composed by any authors indifferently, and so to receive into their minds opinions generally the reverse of those which, when they are grown to manhood, we shall think they ought to entertain?

No, we shall not permit it on any account.

Then apparently our first duty will be to exercise a superintendence over the authors of fables, selecting their good productions and rejecting the bad. And the selected fables we shall advise our nurses and mothers to repeat to their children, that they may thus mould their minds with the fables even more than they shape their bodies with the hand. But we shall have to repudiate the greater part of those which are now in vogue.

Which do you mean? he asked.

In the greater fables, I answered, we shall also discern the less. For the general character and tendency of both the greater and the less must doubtless be identical. Do you not think so?

I do: but I am equally uncertain which you mean by the greater.

I mean the stories which Hesiod and Homer, and the other poets, tell us. For they, I imagine, have composed fictitious narratives which they told, and yet tell, to men.

Pray, what kind of fables do you mean, and what is the fault that you find with them?

A fault, I replied, which deserves the earliest and gravest condemnation, especially if the fiction has no beauty.

What is this fault?

It is whenever an author gives a bad representation of the characters of gods and heroes, like a painter whose picture should bear no resemblance to the objects he wishes to imitate.

Yes, it is quite right to condemn such faults: but pray explain further what we mean, and give some instances.

In the first place, the poet who conceived the boldest fiction on the highest subjects invented an ugly story, when he told how Ouranos acted as Hesiod[9] declares he did, and also how Kronos had his revenge upon him. And again, even if the deeds of Kronos[10] and his son's treatment of him were authentic facts, it would not have been right, I should have thought, to tell them without the least reserve to young and thoughtless persons: on the contrary, it would be best to suppress them altogether: or if for some reason they must be told, they should be imparted under the seal of secrecy to as few hearers as possible, and after the sacrifice, not of a pig[11] but of some rare and costly victim, which might aid to the utmost in restricting their number.

Certainly, these are offensive stories.

They are; and therefore, Adeimantus, they must not be repeated in our city. No, we must not tell a youthful listener that he will be doing nothing extraordinary if he commit the foulest crimes, nor yet if he chastise the crimes of a father in the most unscrupulous manner, but will simply be doing what the first and greatest of the gods have done before him.

I assure you, he said, I quite agree with you as to the impropriety of such stories.

Nor yet, I continued, is it proper to say in any case – what is indeed untrue – that gods wage war against gods, and intrigue and fight among themselves; that is, if the future guardians of our state are to deem it a most disgraceful thing to quarrel lightly with one another: far less ought we to select, as subjects for fiction and embroidery, the battles of the giants and numerous other feuds of all sorts, in which gods and heroes fight against their own kith and kin. But if there is any possibility of persuading them that to quarrel with one's fellow is a sin of which no member of a state was ever guilty, such ought rather to be the language told to our children from the first, by old men and old women, and all elderly persons: and such is the strain in which our poets must be compelled to write. But stories like the chaining of Hera by her son, and the flinging of Hephaestus out of heaven for trying to take his mother's part when his father was beating her, and all those battles of the gods which are to be found in Homer, must be refused admittance into our state, whether they be allegorical or not. For a child cannot discriminate between what is allegory and what is not; and whatever at that age is adopted as a matter of belief, has a tendency to become fixed and indelible; and therefore, perhaps, we ought to esteem it of the greatest importance that the fictions which children first hear should be adapted in the most perfect manner to the promotion of virtue.

There is certainly reason in this. But if any one were to proceed to ask us what these fictions are, and what the fables which convey them, how should we answer him?

To which I replied, My dear Adeimantus, you and I are not poets, on the present occasion, but founders of a state. And founders ought certainly to know the moulds in which their poets are to cast their fictions, and from which they must not be suffered to deviate; but they are not bound to compose tales themselves.

You are right; but to use your own words, what should these moulds be in the case of theology?

I think they may be described as follows: it is right, I presume, always to represent god as he really is, whether the poet describe him in an epic or a lyrical or a dramatic poem.

Yes, it is right.

Then surely god is good in reality, and is to be so represented?

Unquestionably.

Well, but nothing that is good is hurtful, is it?

I think not.

And does that which is not hurtful hurt?

By no means.

And does that which hurts not, do any evil?

I answer as before, no.

And that which does no evil cannot be the cause of any evil either?

How should it be?

Well: is that which is good beneficial?

Yes.

Then it is a cause of well-being?

Yes.

Then that which is good is not the cause of all things, but only of what is as it should be, being guiltless of originating evil.

Exactly so.

If that be so, then god, inasmuch as he is good, cannot be the cause of all things, according to the common doctrine. On the contrary, he is the author of only a small part of human affairs; of the larger part he is not the author, for our evil things far outnumber our good things: and the good things we must ascribe to no other than god, while we must seek elsewhere, and not in him, the causes of the evil things.

That seems to me the exact truth.

Then we must express our disapprobation, if Homer or any other poet is guilty of such a foolish blunder about the gods as to tell us that two jars

> By Zeus at his threshold are planted;
> All good fortunes the one, all evil the other containeth.[12]

And that he for whom Zeus mixes and gives of both,

> One day lighteth on evil, and one day meeteth with blessing:

but as for the man for whom there is no mixture, but who receives of one sort only,

> Him over god's wide earth fell ravenous hunger pursueth.

Nor must we admit that

> Zeus hath been made unto men both of weal and of woe the
> dispenser.

And if any one assert that the violation of oaths and treaties,[13] of which Pandarus was the author, was brought about by Athene and Zeus, we shall refuse our approbation: nor can we allow it to be said that the strife and trial of strength between the gods[14] was instigated by Themis and Zeus, nor, again, must we let our young people hear that, in the words of Aeschylus,

> When to destruction god will plague a house,
> He plants among its members guilt and sin.[15]

But if a poet writes about the sufferings of Niobe, as Aeschylus does in the play from which I have taken these lines, or the calamities of the house of Pelops, or the disasters at Troy, or any similar occurrences, either we must not allow him to call them the work of a god, or if they are to be so called, he must find out a theory to account for them, such as that for which we are now searching, and must say that what the god did was righteous and good, and the sufferers were chastened for their profit; but we cannot allow the poet to say that a god was the author of a punishment which made the objects of it miserable. No: if he should say that because the wicked are miserable, these men needed chastisement, and the infliction of it by the god was a benefit to them, we shall make no objection: but as to asserting that god, who is good, becomes the author of evil to any, we must do battle uncompromisingly for the principle that fictions conveying such a doctrine as this, whether in verse or in prose, shall neither be recited or heard in the city, by any member of it, young or old, if it is to be a well-regulated city; because such language may not be used without irreverence, and is moreover both injurious to us and self-contradictory.

I vote with you, he said, for this law, which pleases me.

Then one of those theological laws or moulds, in accordance with which we shall require our speakers to speak, and our authors to write, will be to this effect, that god is not the author of all things, but only of such as are good.

You have proved it quite satisfactorily, he replied.

Well, here is a second for you to consider. Do you think that god is a wizard, and likely to appear for special purposes in different forms at different times, sometimes actually assuming such forms, and altering his own person into a variety of shapes, and sometimes deceiving us and making us believe that such a transformation has taken place, or do you think that he is of a simple essence, and that it is the most unlikely thing that he should ever go out of his own proper form?

I cannot answer you all at once.

Then answer me this: if anything passes out of its proper form, must not the change be produced either by itself or some other thing?

It must.

And is it not the case that changes and motions communicated by any thing else affect least the things that are best? For instance, the body is changed by meat and drink and exertion, and every plant by sunshine and wind and similar influences, but is not the change slightest in the plant or the body which is healthiest and strongest?

Undoubtedly it is.

So of the mind, is it not the bravest and the wisest that will be the least disturbed and altered by any influence from without?

Yes.

Moreover, I conceive that the same principle applies to all manufactured things, such as furniture, houses and clothes: those that are well made and in good condition are least altered by time and other influences.

That is true.

So that everything which is good either by nature or by art, or by both, is least liable to be changed by another thing.

So it would seem.

But surely god and the things of god are in every way most excellent.

Unquestionably.

Then god will be very unlikely to assume many shapes through external influence.

Very unlikely indeed.

But will he change and alter himself?

Clearly he must, if he alters at all.

Does he then, by changing himself, attain to something better and fairer or to something worse and less beautiful than himself?

Something worse, necessarily, if he alters at all: for we shall not, I presume, affirm that there is any imperfection in the beauty or the goodness of god.

You are perfectly correct; and this being the case, do you think, Adeimantus, that any god or any man would voluntarily make himself worse than he is, in any respect?

It is impossible.

Then it is also impossible for a god to be willing to change himself, and therefore it would seem that every god, inasmuch as he is perfect to the utmost in beauty and goodness, abides ever simply and without variation in his own form.

The inference is inevitable, I think.

Then, my dear friend, let no poet tell us that

> gods in the likeness of wandering strangers
> Bodied in manifold forms, go roaming from city to city.[16]

And let no one slander Proteus and Thetis, or introduce in tragedies or any other poems, Hera transformed, collecting in the guise of a priestess,

> Alms for the life-giving children of Inachus, river of Argos.[17]

Not to mention many other similar falsehoods, which we must interdict. And once more, let not our mothers be persuaded by these poets into scaring their children by injudicious stories, telling them how certain gods go about by night in the likeness of strangers from every land; that they may not by one and the same act defame the gods and foster timidity in their children.

No, let that be forbidden.

But perhaps, I continued, though the gods have no tendency to change in themselves, they induce us, by deception and magic, to believe that they appear in various forms.

Perhaps they do.

Would a god consent to lie, think you, either in word or by an act, such as that of putting a phantom before our eyes?

I am not sure.

Are you not sure that a genuine lie, if I may be allowed the expression, is hated by all gods and by all men?

I do not know what you mean.

I mean that to lie with the highest part of himself, and concerning the highest subjects, is what no one voluntarily consents to do; on the contrary, every one fears above all things to harbour a lie in that quarter.

I do not even yet understand you.

Because you think I have some mysterious meaning, whereas what I mean is simply this: that to lie, or be the victim of a lie, and to be without knowledge, in the mind and concerning absolute realities, and in that quarter to harbour and possess the lie, is the last thing any man would consent to; for all men hold in especial abhorrence an untruth in a place like that.

Yes, in most especial abhorrence.

Well, but, as I was saying just now, this is what might most correctly be called a genuine lie, namely ignorance residing in the mind of the deluded person. For the spoken lie is a kind of imitation and embodiment of the anterior mental affection, and not a pure, unalloyed falsity; or am I wrong?

No, you are perfectly right.

Then a real lie is hated not only by gods, but likewise by men.

So I think.

Once more: when and to whom is the verbal falsehood useful, and therefore undeserving of hatred? Is it not when we are dealing with an enemy? Or when those that are called our friends attempt to do something mischievous in a fit of lunacy or madness of any kind, is it not then that a lie is useful, like a medicine, to turn them from their purpose? And in the legendary tales of which we were talking just now, is it not our ignorance of the true history of ancient times which renders falsehood useful to us, as the closest attainable copy of the truth?

Yes, that is exactly the case.

Then on which of these grounds is lying useful to god? Will he lie for the sake of approximation, because he knows not the things of old?

No; that would be indeed ridiculous.

Then there is no place in god for the poet's falsehood.

I think not.

Then will he lie through fear of his enemies?

Far from it.

Or because his friends are foolish or mad?

Nay, said he; no fool or madman is a friend of the gods.

Then there is no inducement for a god to lie.

There is not.

In every way, then, the nature of gods and godlike beings is incapable of falsehood.

Yes, wholly so.

God then is a being of perfect simplicity and truth, both in deed and word, and neither changes in himself nor imposes upon others, either by apparitions or by words or by sending signs, whether in dreams or in waking moments.

I believe it to be so myself, he said, after what you have stated.

Then do you grant that a second principle, in accordance with which all speaking and writing about the gods must be moulded, is this: that the gods neither metamorphose themselves like wizards, nor mislead us by falsehoods expressed either in word or act?

I do grant it.

Then while we commend much in Homer, we shall refuse to commend the story of the dream sent by Zeus to Agamemnon,[18] as well as that passage in Aeschylus[19] where Thetis says that Apollo singing at her marriage,

> Dwelt on my happy motherhood,
> The life from sickness free, and lengthened years.
> Then all-inclusively he blest my lot,
> Favoured of heaven, in strains that cheer'd my soul.
> And I too fondly deem'd those lips divine
> Sacred to truth fraught with prophetic skill;
> But he himself who sang, the marriage guest
> Himself, who spoke all this, 'twas even he
> That slew my son.

When a poet uses such language concerning the gods, we shall be angry with him and refuse him a chorus,[20] neither shall we allow our teachers to use his writings for the instruction of the young, if we would have our guardians grow up to be as godlike and godfearing as it is possible for man to be.

I entirely acquiesce, said he, in the propriety of these principles, and would adopt them as laws.

NOTES ON BOOK TWO

1 *Seven against Thebes* 574.

2 Hesiod, *Works and Days* 231.

3 *Odyssey* xix, 109.

4 Hesiod, *Works and Days* 287.

5 *Iliad* ix, 497.

6 This passage is not found in Pindar's extant works.

7 The difficulty of this passage, which appears to be fairly chargeable with confusion of metaphors, is increased by our ignorance of the fable of Archilochus, to which reference is made by other writers as well as Plato. It is probable, however, that the fox is here simply the emblem of selfish cunning, an application of which Archilochus set the first example in Greek literature.

8 The reader will gather from the context the true meaning of the important word θυμοειδής. We have adopted the word 'spirited', as the received and the least objectionable English rendering of it. This obliges us to translate θυμός, in the same sentence, 'spirit'; otherwise 'anger' would be a nearer English equivalent to it. A reference to any lexicon will show the difficulty of conveying the force of θυμοειδής in a single English word: but its meaning is sufficiently indicated by Plato himself.

9 Hesiod, *Theogony* 154.

10 Hesiod, *Theogony* 459.

11 A pig was the usual victim at the Mysteries.

12 *Iliad* xxiv, 527.

13 *Iliad* ii, 69.

14 *Iliad*, beginning of Book xx.

15 In a lost tragedy

16 *Odyssey* xvii, 485.

17 Supposed to be quoted from a lost play of Aeschylus.

18 *Iliad* ii, 1.

19 From a lost play.

20 'To give a chorus' was to authorise and supply the means of a stage representation, of which the chorus formed the most expensive element.

BOOK THREE

Concerning the gods, then, I continued, such, as it would appear, is the language to be held, and such the language to be forbidden, in the hearing of all, from childhood upwards, who are hereafter to honour the gods and their parents, and to set no small value on mutual friendship.

Yes, he said; and I think our views are correct.

To proceed then: if we intend our citizens to be brave, must we not add to this such lessons as are likely to preserve them most effectually from being afraid of death? Or do you think a man can ever become brave who is haunted by the fear of death?

No, indeed, I do not.

Well, do you imagine that a believer in Hades and its terrors will be free from all fear of death, and in the day of battle will prefer it to defeat and slavery?

Certainly not.

Then apparently we must assume a control over those who undertake to set forth these fables, as well as the others, requesting them not to revile the other world in that unqualified manner, but rather to speak well of it, because such language is neither true, nor beneficial to men who are intended to be warlike.

We certainly must.

Then we shall expunge the following passage, and with it all that are like it:

> I would e'en be a villein, and drudge on the lands of a master,
> Under a portionless wight, whose garner was scantily furnished,
> Sooner than reign supreme in the realm of the dead that have
>   perished.[1]

And this:

And those chambers be seen both by mortal men and immortals
Terrible, dank, and mouldering – even to gods an abhorrence.'[2]

And,

Well-a-day! Truly there are, yea e'en in the dwellings of Hades,
Souls and phantom forms, but no understanding is in them.[3]

And,

Wisdom is *his* alone, 'mid the flitting and shadowy phantoms.[4]

And,

Vanish'd the soul from the limbs, and flew to the nethermost
    Hades,
Sadly her destiny wailing, cut off in the ripeness of manhood.[5]

And,

Gibbering, under the ground his spirit fled, like a vapour.[6]

And,

As when bats, in the depth of a cavern's awful recesses,
Haply if one fall off from the rock where they hang in a cluster,
Squealing flutter about, and still cling fast to each other,
Thus did the ghosts move squealing together.[7]

These verses, and all that are like them, we shall entreat Homer and
the other poets not to be angry if we erase, not because they are
unpoetical, or otherwise than agreeable to the ear of most men; but
because, in proportion as they are more poetical, so much the less
ought they to be recited in the hearing of boys and men whom we
require to be freemen, fearing slavery more than death.

By all means let us do so.

Then we must likewise cast away all those terrible and alarming
names which belong to these subjects, the Cocytuses and Styxes[8] and
infernals and anatomies, and all other words coined after this stamp,
the mention of which makes men shudder to the last degree with
fear. I dare say that for some other purpose they may be useful: but
we are afraid for our guardians, lest the terrors in question should
render them more spiritless and effeminate than they ought to be.

And our fears are not groundless.

So then we are to discard those expressions, are we?

Yes.

And to speak and write after the model which is the reverse of this?

Clearly so.

Then shall we also strike out the weepings and the wailings of the heroes of renown?

Yes, we must, if we strike out the former.

Just consider, whether we shall be right or not in striking them out. What we maintain is that a good man will not look upon death as a dreadful thing for another good man, whose friend he also is, to undergo.

We do maintain it.

Then if so, he will not lament over such a person as if some dreadful disaster had befallen him.

Certainly not.

Moreover, we say this also, that such a man contains within himself, in the highest degree, whatever is necessary for a happy life, and is distinguished from the rest of the world by his peculiar independence of external resources.

True.

Then it is less dreadful to him than to any one to lose a son or a brother, or worldly wealth, or anything else of that kind.

Indeed it is.

If so, he is also less likely than any one to complain, and will rather bear it with all meekness, whenever any such calamity has overtaken him.

Yes, quite so.

Then we shall do well to strike out the dirges put in the mouths of famous men, and make them over to women (and those not the best of their sex) and to the baser sort of men, in order that those whom we profess to be training up to be the guardians of their country may scorn to act like such persons.

It will be well to do so.

Then once more we shall request Homer and the other poets not to represent Achilles, the son of a goddess, as 'tossing[9] now on his side, and now once more on his back, now on his face'; and then as rising up and 'pacing in frenzy the shore of the waste untameable ocean'; nor yet as taking in both hands black burnt-out ashes,[10] and pouring them over his head; nor as otherwise indulging in all that weeping and wailing which Homer has attributed to him: and not to describe

Priam, whose near ancestor was a god, as making supplication, and

> Rolling in dung, and by name to every man loudly appealing;[11]

and still more earnestly we shall beg them, whatever they do, not to represent the gods as complaining and saying,

> Wretch that I am! who bare to my sorrow the bravest of children,[12]

or if they will not so far respect all the gods, at least we shall entreat them not to presume to draw so unlike a picture of the highest of the gods as to make him say,

> Well-a-day! Him whom I love, pursued round the walls of the city,
> Thus with these eyes I behold, and my heart is troubled within me.[13]

And,

> Ah! woe's me for the doom, that the dearest of mortals Sarpedon,
> Must by Patroclus, Menoetius' son, be slain in the combat.[14]

For if, my dear Adeimantus, our young men were to listen seriously to such accounts, instead of laughing at them as unworthy descriptions, it would be very unlikely that any one of them should look upon himself, that is but a man, as above such behaviour, and rebuke himself if he were ever betrayed into it, either in word or act: nay rather, unchecked by shame or fortitude, he will chant a multitude of dirges and laments over even trivial misfortunes.

You speak with great truth.

But he ought not so to do, as we have just been taught by our argument; to which we must give heed, until some one can persuade us by another and a better one.

Certainly, he ought not.

Again, our guardians ought not to be given to laughter, for when any one indulges in violent laughter, such excess almost universally invites an equally violent reaction.

I think so.

Then if a poet represents even men of any consideration as overcome by laughter, our approval must be withheld; much more if gods are so described.

Much more indeed.

That being the case, we shall not allow Homer to speak of the gods in such terms as the following:

> Straight 'mid the blessed gods brake forth unquenchable laughter,
> When they beheld Hephaestus go bustling from chamber to
>   chamber.[15]

We must not sanction such language, according to your principles.

If you like to call them mine, he replied: no doubt we must not sanction them.

But again, a high value must be set also upon truth. For if we were right in what we said just now, and falsehood is really useless to the gods, and only useful to men in the way of a medicine, it is plain that such an agent must be kept in the hands of physicians, and that unprofessional men must not meddle with it.

Evidently.

To the rulers of the state then, if to any, it belongs of right to use falsehood, to deceive either enemies or their own citizens, for the good of the state: and no one else may meddle with this privilege. Nay, for a private person to tell a lie to such magistrates, we shall maintain to be at least as great a mistake as for a patient to deceive his physician, or a pupil his training-master, concerning the state of his own body, or for a sailor to tell an untruth to a pilot concerning the ship and the crew, in describing his own condition or that of any of his fellow sailors.

Most true.

If then the authorities find any one else guilty of lying in the city,

> Any of those that be craftsmen,
> Prophet and seer, or healer of hurts, or worker in timber,[16]

they will punish him for introducing a practice as pernicious and subversive in a state as in a ship.

Yes, he said, if performance follow upon profession.

Once more, will not our young men need to be temperate?

Undoubtedly they will.

And does not sobriety, as generally understood, imply the following principal elements: first, that men be obedient to their governors; and secondly, that they be themselves able to govern the pleasures which are gratified in eating, and drinking, and love?

I think so.

Then we shall approve, I imagine, of all language like that which Homer puts in the mouth of Diomedes:

> Friend, sit down in silence, and give good heed to my sayings,[17]

and of the lines that follow,

> Wrath breathing march'd the Achaeans,
> Silently dreading their captains:

and of every thing else of the same kind.

Yes, we shall.

But can we approve of such language as this,

> Drunken sot, who the face of a dog and the heart of a deer hast,[18]

and of what follows, and all the other insolent expressions which in prose or in poetry are put into the mouths of inferiors towards those in authority?

No, we cannot.

Because, I imagine, they do not tend to promote sobriety in youth. If on other accounts they give any gratification we need not be surprised. Is this your opinion?

It is.

But tell me: when the wisest of men is represented as saying that it appears to him the finest sight in the world when

> Tables are loaded
> Both with bread and with flesh, and the cup-bearers draw from
> the wine-bowl
> Sparkling draughts, which they carry around, and replenish the
> goblets;[19]

do you think that being told this will aid a young man in acquiring self-control? Or this –

> 'Tis most wretched by famine to die, and one's doom to encounter.[20]

Or what do you think of representing Zeus as so readily forgetting, in the eagerness of his desire, all that he had been meditating as he watched alone, while all others, gods and men, were asleep; and so smitten at the sight of Hera that he would not even defer the gratification of his passion till they should enter into their chamber, saying that he was possessed by a stronger passion than even then, when at first they met without the knowledge of their dear parents? And what say you to the story[21] how Ares and Aphrodite were bound in fetters by Hephaestus in consequence of a similar proceeding?

Upon my word, he replied, such stories strike me as very improper to be told.

But whatever acts of fortitude under all trials in deed and word are ascribed to men of renown, these we will contemplate and listen to, as for instance,

> Smiting his breast, to his heart thus spoke he in accents of
>   chiding,
> Patience, I pray thee, my heart: thou hast borne even worse
>   provocation.[22]

Yes, by all means.

Further, we must not permit our men, I presume, to be receivers of bribes or lovers of money?

Certainly not.

Then we must not sing to them that

> Gods are persuaded by gifts, by gifts dread kings are persuaded.[23]

Nor must we praise Phoenix, the tutor of Achilles, or allow that he spoke with wisdom when he advised him[24] to aid the Achaeans if he received presents from them, but without presents not to dismiss his anger. And we shall not believe or allow that Achilles himself was so avaricious as to take gifts from Agamemnon, and at another time to give up a dead body only on condition of receiving a price for it.

No, it is not right to commend such stories.

It is only my regard to Homer, I continued, that makes me slow to assert that it is a positive sin to say these things of Achilles, or to believe them when others say them: or again, to believe that he said to Apollo,

> Thou, far-worker, hast harmed me, no god so destructive as
>   thou art:
> Verily, had I the power, I would take vengeance upon thee;[25]

and that he behaved in so refractory a manner to the river,[26] who was a god, as to be prepared to fight with him; and that he said of the hair that was consecrated to the other river Spercheius,

> Fain would I offer this hair as a gift to the hero Patroclus,[27]

who was then a corpse, and that he fulfilled his purpose; all these tales are not to be believed. And again, all the stories[28] of his dragging

Hector round the tomb of Patroclus, and of his immolation of the captives on the funeral pile, we shall unhesitatingly declare untrue; and we shall not allow our young men to be persuaded that Achilles, the son of a goddess and of Peleus – who was a most discreet prince, and third in descent from Zeus – and the pupil of Cheiron, that wisest of teachers, was yet such a compound of confusions as to combine in himself two such opposite maladies as mean covetousness and arrogant contempt of gods and men.

You are right.

Then let us not believe, once more, or allow it to be said, that Theseus the son of Poseidon, and Peirithous the son of Zeus, went forth to commit so dire a rape; nor that any other god-sprung hero could have ventured to perpetrate such dreadful impieties as at the present day are falsely ascribed to them: rather let us oblige our poets to admit, either that the deeds in question were not their deeds, or else that they were not children of gods; but let them beware of combining the two assertions, and of attempting to make our young men believe that the gods are parents of evil, and that heroes are no better than common men: for, as we said above, these statements are at once irreverent and untrue; for we have proved, I believe, that evils cannot originate with the gods.

Undoubtedly we have.

And besides, such language is pernicious to the hearers: for every one will be indulgent to vice in himself, if he is convinced that such were and still are the practices of those who are

> Kinsfolk of gods, not far from Zeus himself,
> Whose is the altar to ancestral Zeus
> Upon the hill of Ida, in the sky;
> And still within their veins flows blood divine.[29]

On these accounts we must suppress such fables, lest they engender in our young men a great aptitude for wickedness.

I entirely agree with you.

What class then still remains, I continued, to complete our description of the kinds of narratives which may or may not be circulated? We have already stated what rules must be regarded in speaking of the gods, and the demigods, and heroes, and the souls of the departed.

We have.

Then the mode of speaking about men will be the remaining subject, will it not?

Yes, obviously.

It is quite impossible, my friend, to settle this at the present stage of our inquiry.

How so?

Because, I imagine, we shall assert that in fact poets and writers of prose are alike in error in the most important particulars, when they speak of men – making out that many are happy though unjust, and many just, yet miserable, and that injustice is profitable if it be not found out, whereas justice is a gain to your neighbour but a loss to yourself: and I imagine we shall forbid the use of such language, and lay our commands on all writers to express the very opposite sentiments in their songs and their legends. Do you not think so?

Nay, I am sure of it.

Then, as soon as you admit that I am right in that, shall I not fairly maintain that you have admitted the very proposition which is the subject of our inquiry?

Your assumption is correct, he replied.

Then must we not postpone coming to an agreement as to the terms to be employed in speaking of men, till we have first discovered the real nature of justice, and proved that it is naturally profitable to its possessor, whether he have the character of being just or not?

You are perfectly right.

Let us then here close our discussion of the subject-matter of narratives: our next task, I imagine, is to investigate the question of their form, and this done, we shall have thoroughly considered both what ought to be said and the mode of saying it.

Here Adeimantus remarked, I do not understand what you mean by that.

Well, but it is important that you should, said I. Perhaps you will see it better when I put it in this way. May not all the compositions of poets or legend-writers be described as narrations of past, present, or future events?

What else could they be?

Then does not the author obtain his object, either by narration simple, or by narration conveyed through the medium of imitation, or by a mixture of both?

This also, he said, still requires to be made more intelligible to me.

Apparently I am a ridiculously unintelligible teacher. I will therefore proceed like a man who has not the gift of making speeches; I will not attempt the general question, but I will detach a particular instance, and endeavour thereby to make my meaning clear to you. Tell me then, are you well acquainted with the beginning of the Iliad, in which the poet tells us that Chryses besought Agamemnon to release his daughter, and that Agamemnon was angry with him; whereupon Chryses, finding his suit denied, prayed to his god to avenge him on the Achaeans?

I am.

You know then that down to the lines,

> He petitioned all the Achaeans,
> Chiefly the twain that marshalled the host, the children
> of Atreus,

the poet speaks in his own person, and does not even attempt to divert our thoughts into supposing that the speaker is any other than himself: but in what follows he speaks in the person of Chryses, and endeavours, so far as he can, to make us believe that it is not Homer who is speaking, but the aged priest. And in this style, as nearly as may be, he has constructed all the rest of his narrative of the Trojan war, as well as of the events that took place in Ithaca and throughout the Odyssey.

Just so.

It is equally narration, is it not, whether the poet is reciting the occasional speeches or describing the intermediate events?

Undoubtedly it is.

But when he delivers a speech in the character of another man, shall we not say that on every such occasion he aims at the closest resemblance in style to the person introduced as the speaker?

We shall, of course.

And when one man assumes a resemblance to another, in voice or look, is not that imitation?

Undoubtedly it is.

Then in such a case it appears that both Homer and other poets carry on the narration through the medium of imitation.

Certainly they do.

But if the poet nowhere concealed his own personality, he would have completed his composition and narration wholly without imitation. That you may not say again that you do not understand how this would be, I will tell you. If Homer – after saying that Chryses came bringing his daughter's ransom, in the character of a suppliant to the Achaeans, and above all to the kings – had continued to speak, not as if he had become Chryses, but as if he were Homer still, that, you know, would have been not imitation, but simple narration. The story would have run in something like the following manner. I shall tell it in prose, for I am no poet. The priest came and prayed that the gods might grant to the Greeks the capture of Troy, and a safe return, if only they would release unto him his daughter, accepting the ransom, and reverencing his god. And when he had thus spoken, all the rest were moved with awe, and were willing to consent; but Agamemnon was wroth, and charged him to depart, and come again no more, lest the staff and the wreaths of the god should avail him nought; and ere his daughter should be set free, he said, she should grow old with him in Argos; so he bade him begone, and avoid provoking him, if he wished to reach home unhurt. And the old man, when he heard it, was afraid, and went away in silence, but when he was clear of the camp he prayed much to Apollo, calling upon the god by his titles, and putting him in remembrance, and asking to be repaid, if ever he had presented an acceptable offering to him in the building of temples or the sacrifice of oblations: in consideration of which things he prayed that he would avenge his tears upon the Achaeans, by shooting his arrows among them. In this, my friend, we have simple narration without imitation.

I understand, he said.

I would further have you understand that the opposite result ensues when you strike out the poet's own words that stand between the speeches, leaving only the alternate dialogue.

Yes, I understand: tragedies are a case of this sort.

You are perfectly right in your supposition. Now I think I can make you see clearly what before I could not, that one branch of poetry and legend-writing consists wholly of imitation – that is, as you say, tragedy and comedy – another branch employs the simple recital of the poet in his own person, and is chiefly to be found, I imagine, in dithyrambic poetry; while a third employs both recital and imitation, as is seen in the construction of epic poems, and in many other instances, if I make you understand me.

Yes, I quite comprehend now what you meant by that first remark.

Now then, recall what we said previously, which was that having settled the question of the matter of composition, it only remained for us to consider the manner.

I remember.

This then was precisely what I meant, that it was incumbent on us to come to an agreement whether we should allow our poets, in telling their story, to employ imitation exclusively, or partially (and if so, by what criterion they should be guided), or not at all.

I divine, said he, that you are speculating whether we shall admit tragedy and comedy into our city, or not.

It may be so, I replied: and it may be that other claims will be questioned besides those of tragedy and comedy: in fact, I do not yet know myself; but we must go where the argument carries us, as a vessel runs before the wind.

You are quite right.

Here then is a question for you to consider, Adeimantus: ought our guardians to be apt imitators, or not? Or does it follow from our previous admissions that any individual may pursue with success one calling, but not many; or if he attempts this, by his meddling with many he will fail in all, so far as to gain no distinction in any?

That would undoubtedly be the case.

Does not the same principle apply to imitation, or can the same person imitate many things as well as he can imitate one?

Certainly he cannot.

It is very improbable, then, that one who is engaged in any important calling will at the same time know how to imitate a variety of things, and be a successful imitator: for even two branches of imitation, which are thought to be closely allied, are more, I believe, than can be successfully pursued together by the same person; as, for instance, the writing of comedy and of tragedy, which you described just now as imitations, did you not?

I did; and you are right in saying that the same persons cannot succeed in both.

Nor yet can a man combine the professions of a reciter of epic poetry and an actor.

True.

Nay, the same actor cannot even play both tragedy and comedy; and all these are arts of imitation, are they not?

They are.

And human nature appears to me, Adeimantus, to be split up into yet more minute subdivisions than these, so that a man is unable to imitate many things well, or to do the things themselves of which the imitations are likenesses.

Most true.

If then we are to maintain our first view, that our guardians ought to be released from every other craft, that they may acquire consummate skill in the art of creating their country's freedom, and may follow no other occupation but such as tends to this result, it will not be desirable for them either to practise or to imitate anything else; or if they do imitate, let them imitate from very childhood whatever is proper to their profession – brave, sober, religious, honourable men, and the like – but meanness, and every other kind of baseness, let them neither practise nor be skilled to imitate, lest from the imitation they be infected with the reality. For have you not perceived that imitations, whether of bodily gestures, tones of voice, or modes of thought, if they be persevered in from an early age, are apt to grow into habits and a second nature?

Certainly I have.

Then we shall not permit those in whom we profess to take an interest, and whom we desire to become good men, to imitate a woman, being themselves men – whether she be young or old, either reviling a man, or striving and vaunting against the gods in the belief of her own felicity, or taken up with misfortunes and griefs and complaints: much more shall we forbid them to imitate one that is ill, or in love, or in labour.

Exactly so.

Again, they must not be permitted to imitate slaves, of either sex, engaged in the occupations of slaves.

No, they must not.

Nor yet bad men, it would seem, such as cowards, and generally those whose conduct is the reverse of what we described just now; men in the act of abusing and caricaturing one another, and uttering ribaldry, whether drunk or sober, or committing any of those offences against others, or amongst themselves, of which such men both in word and in deed are wont to be guilty. I think also that we must not accustom them to liken themselves to madmen, in word or in act. For though it is right they should know mad and wicked people of both sexes, they ought not to act like them, nor give imitations of them.

Most true.

Again, may they imitate smiths or any other craftsmen working at their trade, or rowers pulling at the oars in a galley, or their strokesmen, or anything else of the kind?

Impossible, he replied, since they are not to be permitted even to pay attention to any of these occupations.

Once more, shall they give imitations of horses neighing and bulls bellowing, or of roaring rivers and sounding seas, and claps of thunder, or of any such phenomena?

Nay, we have forbidden them either to be mad themselves, or to liken themselves to madmen.

If then I understand what you mean, there is a certain kind of style in narration which an honourable and accomplished man will adopt, whenever he is called upon to narrate anything; and another kind, unlike the former, to which a man who by nature and education is of the opposite character will on such occasions always adhere.

Pray, what are the two kinds? he asked.

The former, or the man of well-regulated character, when he comes in telling a story to a speech or action of a good man, will, I think, like to report it as if he were himself the subject of the narrative, and will not be ashamed of this kind of imitation, preferring to imitate the good man when his conduct is steady and sensible, and doing so less frequently and faithfully when he has been thrown off his balance by sickness or love, or it may be by intoxication or some other misfortune: but when he comes to a character that is unworthy of him, instead of being willing seriously to liken himself to his inferior, except perhaps for a short time, when the man is performing a good action, he will be ashamed to do it, partly because he has had no practice in imitating such characters, and partly because in his deliberate contempt for them he disdains to mould and cast himself after the models of baser men, unless it be for mere pastime.

So one would expect.

Then will he not use that style of narration which we described a little while since by referring to the poems of Homer, so that his style will partake both of imitation and of ordinary narration, the former however making but a small part of a long discourse? Or am I quite wrong?

Nay, you describe accurately what must be the model of such a speaker.

Then again, the man who is not of this character, the more contemptible he is, will be the more inclined to omit nothing in his narration, and to think nothing too low for him, so that he will attempt, seriously and in the presence of many hearers, to imitate everything without exception, even the phenomena we mentioned just now, claps of thunder and the noise of wind and of hail, and of wheels and pulleys and the sounds of trumpets and flutes and pipes and all manner of instruments, nay, even the barking of dogs, the bleating of sheep, and the notes of birds: and his style will either consist wholly of the imitation of sounds and forms, or will comprise but a small modicum of narration.

This must also inevitably be the case, he said.

These then are the two kinds of style which I meant.

True, there are two such styles.

Do you see then that the transitions which occur in one of the two are trifling; and if you can adapt a suitable harmony and rhythm to the style, it is nearly possible for correct recitation to proceed without change of style and in one harmony – the transitions being inconsiderable – and also in a similarly unchanging rhythm?

That is precisely the case.

Well, and does not the other kind require, on the contrary, all sorts of harmonies and rhythms, if in its turn it is to be appropriately recited, owing to the infinite variety of its transitions?

Most decidedly it does.

Then do all poets and all who narrate anything fall into one or other of these two types of style, or else into one which is formed by blending these two together?

They must.

What shall we do then? Shall we admit all the three types into our state, or only one of them – that is to say, either the composite type, or else one or other of the uncompounded?

If my judgment is to prevail, we shall admit only the pure and simple type which imitates the virtuous man.

Nevertheless, Adeimantus, there is an attraction about the composite type; while by far the most attractive of all to children and the attendants of children and to the vulgar mass, is the opposite of that which you prefer.

It is true.

But perhaps you will say that it is not in harmony with the genius of our commonwealth, because with us there is no twofold or manifold man, since every one has one single occupation.

You are quite right; it would not be in harmony.

And is not this the reason why in a state like ours, and in no other, we shall find the shoemaker a shoemaker, and not a pilot in addition, and the husbandman a husbandman, and not a juryman in addition, and the soldier a soldier, and not a tradesman in addition; and so on throughout?

True.

It is probable then, that if a man should arrive in our city, so clever as to be able to assume any character and imitate any object, and should propose to make a public display of his talents and his productions, we shall pay him reverence as a sacred, admirable, and charming personage, but we shall tell him that in our state there is no one like him, and that our law excludes such characters, and we shall send him away to another city after pouring perfumed oil upon his head, and crowning him with woollen fillets; but for ourselves, we shall employ, for the sake of our real good, that more austere and less fascinating poet and legend-writer, who will imitate for us the style of the virtuous man, and will cast his narratives in those moulds which we prescribed at the outset, when we were engaged with the training of our soldiers.

We shall certainly do so, if it be in our power.

Now then, my dear friend, it would seem that we have completely done with that branch of music which relates to fabulous and other narratives, for we have described both *what* is to be said, and *how* it is to be said.

I think so too.

Then our next subject, I continued, is that of melody and songs,[30] is it not?

Clearly it is.

Then can it be difficult now for any one to discover what we ought to say about them and their proper character, if we are to be consistent with our previous conclusions?

Here Glaucon smiled, and said, Then I am afraid that I, Socrates, do not come under the term 'any one': that is, I cannot this moment come to a satisfactory conclusion as to what kinds we must sanction, though I have my suspicions.

I presume, at all events, you feel quite able to affirm so much as this, that a song consists of three parts, the words, the harmony, and the rhythm.

Yes, I can affirm that.

Then I presume that between the words of a song and words not set to music there is no difference, so far as concerns the propriety of their being composed in accordance with the types which we lately appointed, and in the same manner.

True.

And you will grant that the harmony and the rhythm ought to follow the words.

Undoubtedly.

But we said, you know, that in the case of words we did not require dirges and complaints.

No, we do not.

Which then are the plaintive harmonies? Tell me, for you are musical.

Mixed Lydian and Hyperlydian, and such as are like these.

These then must be discarded: for they are useless even to women that are to be virtuously given, not to say to men.

Quite so.

And you will grant that drunkenness, effeminacy and idleness are most unbecoming things in guardians.

Undoubtedly they are.

Which of the harmonies then are effeminate and convivial?

The Ionian and the Lydian, which are called 'lax'.

Will you employ these then, my friend, in the training of men of war?

By no means: and if I mistake not, you have only the Dorian and the Phrygian left you.

I do not know the harmonies myself, I said; only see you leave me that particular harmony which will suitably represent the tones and accents of a brave man engaged in a feat of arms, or in any violent operation, who if he fails of success, or encounters wounds and death, or falls into any other calamity, in all such contingencies with unflinching endurance parries the blows of fortune; leave me also another harmony, expressive of the feelings of one who is engaged in an occupation not violent, but peaceful and unconstrained; it may be, using persuasion and entreaty, addressing either a prayer to a god or instruction and advice to a man; or on the other hand lending himself to the prayers or advice or persuasion of another, and after this succeeding to his wish; and not behaving arrogantly, but acting in all these circumstances with soberness and moderation, and in the same spirit acquiescing in every result. Leave me these two harmonies, the one violent, the other tranquil, such as shall best imitate the tones of men in adversity and in prosperity, in a temperate and in a courageous mood.

Well, said he, you are recommending me to leave precisely those which I just mentioned.

Then we shall not require for our songs and instrumental accompaniments a variety of strings, or an instrument embracing all harmonies.

I believe not.

Then we shall not maintain the makers of harps or dulcimers, or any instrument that has many strings and serves for many harmonies.

Apparently not.

But will you admit into your city flute-makers and flute-players? Or am I right in saying that the flute has more strings than any other instrument, and that the panharmonium itself is only an imitation of the flute?

Manifestly you are right.

Then you have the lyre and the guitar remaining, which will be of service in the town; while in the country the herdsmen will have some kind of pipe.

So at least the argument indicates to us.

Surely we are guilty of no innovation, my friend, in preferring Apollo and Apollo's instruments to Marsyas and *his* instruments.

No, I really think we are not.

Well, I protest, said I, we have been unconsciously purging the city, which we said just now was in too luxurious a condition.

And we have done wisely.

Come then, I continued, let us finish our purgation. Next after the harmonies will follow our law of rhythms, to the effect that we must not aim at a variety of them, or study all movements indiscriminately, but observe what are the natural rhythms of a well-regulated and manly life, and when we have discovered these we must compel the foot and the music to suit themselves to the sense of such a life, and not the sense to suit itself to the foot and the music. But what these rhythms may be, it is your business to explain, as you did the harmonies.

Nay, but in good faith, he said, I cannot tell. I certainly could say, from what I have observed, that there are three principal kinds into which all movements may be analysed, as in the case of sounds there are four kinds into which all harmonies may be resolved: but which kinds of rhythm express which kinds of life, I cannot say.

Well, said I, we will call in Damon to our counsels upon the question, what movements are akin to meanness and insolence, or to madness and other vices, and what rhythms are to be left as expressive of the opposite qualities. But I fancy that I have heard him indistinctly alluding to a certain complex warlike rhythm, and another that was dactylic, and a third heroic – arranging them I know not how, and showing that the rise and fall of each foot balance one another, by resolving them into short and long syllables; and he gave the name iambus to a certain foot, if I am not wrong, and trochee to another, affixing to them long and short marks. And in some of these, I think, he would blame or praise the march of the foot no less than the rhythm, or perhaps the two taken together: for I cannot speak positively. But let these questions, as I said before, be referred to Damon: for to settle them would require no short discussion; or do you think differently?

No, indeed I do not.

But this point at least you can settle, that grace and awkwardness accompany a good or a bad rhythm?

Of course they do.

And good and bad rhythm are, by a process of assimilation, results of a good style and its opposite respectively; and the same may be said of good and bad harmony; that is to say, if rhythm and harmony are to suit themselves to the words, as was asserted just now, and not the words to them.

No doubt they must suit themselves to the words.

But what do you say of the style and the words? Are they not determined by the moral disposition of the soul?

Undoubtedly they are.

And is all the rest determined by the style?

Yes.

Then good language and good harmony and grace and good rhythm all depend upon a good nature, by which I do not mean that silliness which by courtesy we call good nature, but a mind that is really well and nobly constituted in its moral character.

Precisely so.

Then must not our young men on all occasions pursue these qualities, if we intend them to perform their proper work?

Yes, they must,

And such qualities, I presume, enter largely into painting and all similar workmanship, into weaving and embroidery, into architecture, as well as the whole manufacture of utensils in general; nay, into the constitution of living bodies and of all plants: for in all these things gracefulness or ungracefulness finds place. And the absence of grace, and rhythm, and harmony, is closely allied to an evil style and an evil character: whereas their presence is allied to, and expressive of, the opposite character, which is brave and soberminded.

You are entirely right.

This being the case, ought we to confine ourselves to superintending our poets, and compelling them to impress on their productions the likeness of a good moral character, on pain of not composing among us; or ought we to extend our superintendence to the professors of every other craft as well, and forbid them to impress those signs of an evil nature, of dissoluteness, of meanness, and of ungracefulness, either on the likenesses of living creatures, or on buildings, or any other work of their hands, altogether interdicting such as cannot do otherwise from working in our city, that our guardians may not be reared amongst images of vice, as upon unwholesome pastures, culling much every day by little and little from many places, and feeding upon it until they insensibly accumulate a large mass of evil in their inmost souls? Ought we not, on the contrary, to seek out artists of another stamp, who by the power of genius can trace out the nature of the fair and the graceful, that our young men, dwelling as it were in a healthful region, may drink in good from every quarter, whence any emanation from noble works may strike upon their eye or their ear, like a gale wafting health from salubrious lands, and win them imperceptibly from their earliest childhood into resemblance, love, and harmony with the true beauty of reason?

Such a nurture, he replied, would be by far the best.

Is it then, Glaucon, on these accounts that we attach such supreme importance to a musical education, because rhythm and harmony sink most deeply into the recesses of the soul, and take most powerful hold of it, bringing gracefulness in their train, and making a man graceful if he be rightly nurtured, but if not, the reverse? And also because he that has been duly nurtured therein will have the keenest eye for defects, whether in the failures of art or the misgrowths of nature; and feeling a most just disdain for them, will commend beautiful objects, and gladly receive them into his soul, and feed upon them, and grow to be noble and good; whereas he will rightly censure and hate all repulsive objects, even in his childhood, before he is able to be reasoned with; and when reason comes, *he* will welcome her most cordially who can recognise her by the instinct of relationship, and because he has been thus nurtured?

I have no doubt, he said, that such are the reasons for a musical education.

You know, I continued, that in learning to read we were considered tolerably perfect as soon as we could be sure of recognising the few letters there are, scattered about in all existing words, and that we never treated them with disrespect in either a small word or a great, as if it did not signify to notice them, but were anxious to distinguish them everywhere, believing that we should be no scholars till we were thus qualified.

True.

Is it not also true that we shall not know the *images* of letters, as reflected either in still water or in a mirror, until we know the letters themselves, because the knowledge of both the reflections and the originals belongs to the same art and study?

It is perfectly true.

Tell me then, I pray you, to pass from my illustration to the things illustrated, shall we in like manner never become truly musical, neither ourselves nor the guardians whom we say we are to instruct, until we know the essential forms of temperance and courage and liberality and munificence, and all that are akin to these, and their opposites also, wherever they are scattered about, and discern them wherever they are to be found, themselves and their images, never slighting them either in small things or in great, but believing the knowledge of the forms and of their images to belong to the same art and study?

It must inevitably be so.

Surely, then, to him who has an eye to see, there can be no fairer spectacle than that of a man who combines the possession of moral beauty in his soul with outward beauty of form, corresponding and harmonising with the former, because the same great pattern enters into both.

There can be none so fair.

And you will grant that what is fairest is loveliest?

Undoubtedly it is.

Then the truly musical person will love those who combine most perfectly moral and physical beauty, but will not love any one in whom there is dissonance.

No, not if there be any defect in the soul, but if it is only a bodily blemish, he may so bear with it as to be willing to regard it with complacency.

I understand, I said, that you have now, or have had, a favourite of this kind; so I give way. But tell me this: has pleasure in excess any fellowship with temperance?

How can it have, when it unsettles the mind no less than pain?

Has it any with virtue generally?

Certainly not.

Well, has it anything in common with wantonness and licentiousness?

Most assuredly it has.

Can you mention any pleasure that is greater and more violent than that which accompanies the indulgence of the passion of love?

I cannot; nor yet one that is more akin to madness.

But is it not the nature of legitimate love to desire an orderly and beautiful object in a sober and harmonious temper?

Certainly it is.

Then nothing akin to madness or licentiousness must approach legitimate love?

It must not.

Then the pleasure in question must not approach it, nor must a lover and his beloved whose affections are rightly given and returned have anything to do with it.

They must not, indeed, Socrates.

Apparently then, in the state we are organising, you will legislate to this effect, that though a lover may be attached to a favourite, and frequent his society, and embrace him as a son, for his beauty's sake, if he can gain his consent; yet in other matters he shall so regulate his intercourse with the person he affects as that he shall never be suspected of extending his familiarity beyond this, on pain of being censured for vulgarity and want of taste, if he acts otherwise.

We shall do so.

Do you then think with me that our theory of music is now complete? At all events, it has ended where it ought to end: for music, I imagine, ought to end in the love of the beautiful.

I agree with you, he said.

Gymnastic will hold the next place to music in the education of our young men.

Certainly.

No doubt a careful training in gymnastic, as well as in music, ought to begin with their childhood, and go on through all their life. But the following is the true view of the case, in my opinion: see what you think of it. My belief is, not that a good body will by its own excellence make the soul good; but on the contrary, that a good soul will by *its* excellence render the body as perfect as it can be: but what is your view?

The same as yours.

Then if we were first to administer the requisite treatment to the mind, and then to charge it with the task of prescribing details with reference to the body, contenting ourselves with indicating no more than the general principles, in order to avoid prolixity, should we be doing right?

Quite so.

We have already said that the persons in question must refrain from drunkenness: for a guardian is the last person in the world, I should think, to be allowed to get drunk and not know where he is.

Truly it would be ridiculous for a guardian to require a guard.

But about eating: our men are combatants in a most important arena, are they not?

They are.

Then will the habit of body which is cultivated by the trained fighters of the palaestra be suitable to such persons?

Perhaps it will.

Well, but this is a sleepy kind of regimen, and produces a precarious state of health. For do you not observe that men in the regular training sleep their life away, and if they depart only slightly from the prescribed diet, are attacked by serious maladies in their worst form?

I do.

Then a better conceived regimen is required for our athletes of war, who must be wakeful like watch-dogs, and possess the utmost quickness both of eye and ear, and who are so exposed, when on service, to variations in the water they drink and the rest of their food, and to vicissitudes of sultry heats and wintry storms, that it will not do for them to be of precarious health.

I believe you are right.

Then will the best gymnastic be sister to the music which we described a little while ago?

How do you mean?

It will, I imagine, be a simple moderate system, especially that assigned to our fighting men.

What will it be like?

On these points we may take a lesson even from Homer. You know that at the repasts of his heroes, when they are in the field, he never sets fish before them, although they are upon the shore of the Hellespont, nor yet boiled meat, but only roast, which soldiers could of course procure most readily: for anywhere, one may say, there is less difficulty in using mere fire than in carrying about pots and pans.

Certainly.

Neither has Homer, if I remember right, ever said a word about sauces. However, this is as well known, I believe, to all that are in training, as to Homer, that a man who desires to be in good condition must abstain from all such indulgences: is it not?

They do know it, and are right in abstaining from them.

Then apparently, my good friend, you do not approve of a Syracusan table, and of a Sicilian variety of dishes, if you hold such abstinence to be right.

I think I do not.

Then you also disapprove of a taste for the damsels of Corinth, in men who are to be in good bodily condition.

Most assuredly I do.

Then do you also condemn those celebrated delicacies, our Athenian confectionery?

Of course I do.

In fact, it would not be amiss, I imagine, to compare this whole system of feeding and living to that kind of music and singing which is adapted to the panharmonium, and composed in every variety of rhythm.

Undoubtedly it would be a just comparison.

Is it not true, then, that as in music variety begat dissoluteness in the soul, so here it begets disease in the body, while simplicity in gymnastic is as productive of health, as in music it was productive of temperance?

Most true.

But when dissoluteness and diseases abound in a city, are not lawcourts and surgeries opened in abundance, and do not law and physic begin to hold their heads high, when numbers even of well-born persons devote themselves with eagerness to these professions?

What else can we expect?

But where can you find a more signal proof that a low and vicious education prevails in a state, than in the fact that first-rate physicians and jurymen are in request, not merely among base-born mechanics, but even among those who lay claim to the birth and breeding of gentlemen? Does it not seem to you a scandalous thing, and a strong proof of defective education, to be obliged to import justice from others, in the character of lords and judges, in consequence of the scanty supply at home?

Nothing can be more scandalous.

Do you think it at all less scandalous, when a man not only consumes the greater part of his life in courts of law as plaintiff or defendant, but actually has the vulgarity to plume himself upon this very fact, boasting of being an adept in crime, and such a master of tricks and turns, of manoeuvre and evasion, as always to be able to wriggle out of the grasp of justice and escape from punishment – and that for the sake of worthless trifles, not knowing how much nobler and better it were so to order his life as never to stand in need of a sleepy judge?

Nay, this is even a greater scandal than the other.

And do you not hold it disgraceful to require medical aid, unless it be for a wound or an attack of illness incidental to the time of year – to require it, I mean, owing to our laziness and the life we lead, and to get ourselves so stuffed with humours and wind, like quagmires, as to compel the clever sons of Asclepius to call diseases by such names as flatulence and catarrh.

To be sure these are very strange and newfangled names for disorders.

Such as did not exist, I imagine, in Asclepius' time. So I infer, because at Troy, when Eurypylus was wounded, his sons did not blame the woman who gave him a draught of Pramnian wine, with a plentiful sprinkling of barley-meal, and with cheese grated over it, which you know would be thought an inflammatory mixture, nor did they rebuke Patroclus who dressed his wounds.

Certainly, said he, it was a strange potion for a man in his state.

Not if you consider that formerly, till the time of Herodicus, as we are told, the disciples of Asclepius did not employ our present system of medicine, which waits upon diseases as the son of a rich man is waited on by his attendant. But Herodicus, who was a training-master and fell into bad health, made such a compound of physic and gymnastic that he first and chiefly worried out himself, and then many others after him.

How so?

By rendering his death a lingering one. For he followed his disease, which was a mortal one, step by step, and while he was unable, as I imagine, to cure himself, he devoted his whole time to the business of doctoring himself; living continually in torment, if ever he deviated from his usual diet; and thus struggling against death, was brought by his cleverness to old age.

A noble prize for his art to win him!

It is what one might expect, I continued, from a person ignorant that it was not because Asclepius did not know, or had not tried, this kind of medical treatment, that he never discovered it to his descendants; but because he was aware that in all well-regulated communities each has a work assigned to him in the state, which he must needs do, and that no one has leisure to spend his life as an invalid in the doctor's hands: a fact which we perceive in the case of the labouring population, but which, with ludicrous inconsistency, we fail to detect in the case of those who are reputed rich and happy.

How is that? he asked.

When a carpenter is ill, I replied, he expects to receive a draught from his doctor that will expel the disease by vomiting or purging, or else to get rid of it by cauterising, or a surgical operation; but if any one were to prescribe to him a long course of diet, and to order bandages for his head, with other treatment to correspond, he would soon tell such a medical adviser that he had no time to be ill, and that it was not worth his while to live in this way, devoting his mind to his malady and neglecting his proper occupation: and then wishing the physician a good morning, he would enter upon his usual course of life, and either regain his health and live in the performance of his business; or, should his constitution prove unable to bear up, death puts an end to his troubles.

Yes; and for a man in that station of life this is thought the proper use to make of medical assistance.

Is it because he had a work to do, which, if he failed to perform, it was not worth his while to live?

Manifestly.

But the rich man, as we say, has no appointed work of such a character, that if compelled to leave it undone, life is to him not worth having.

No, it is supposed he has not.

Then you do not listen to Phocylides, when he says that so soon as a man has got whereon to live, then he ought to practise virtue.

Yes, and before that too, I should think.

Let us have no quarrel with him on this subject, said I; but let us inform ourselves whether the rich have to practise virtue so that, if they do not, life is worthless to them; or, whether valetudinarianism, though an obstacle to mental application in carpentering and the other arts, forms no impediment to the fulfilment of the precept of Phocylides.

Nay, in very truth, I believe there is no greater impediment to it than that excessive care of the body which extends beyond gymnastic: for it is alike harassing to a man, whether he be engaged in domestic business, or serving in the field, or sitting as a magistrate at home.

But quite the worst of it is that it is a grievous hindrance to studies of all kinds, and reflection, and inward meditation, being ever apprehensive of some headache or dizziness, which it accuses philosophy of producing; and therefore in so far as virtue is practised and proved by intellectual study, it is a sheer obstacle to it; for it makes a man always fancy himself ill, and never lets him rest from the pangs of anxiety about his health.

Yes, that is the natural effect of it.

Then must we not maintain that Asclepius, knowing all this, revealed the healing art for the benefit of those whose constitutions were naturally sound, and had not been impaired by their habits of life, but who were suffering from some specific complaint, and that he used to expel their disorders by drugs and the use of the knife, without interrupting their customary avocations, that he might not damage the interests of the state; but that where the constitution was thoroughly diseased to the core, he would not attempt to protract a miserable existence by a studied regimen, drawing off from the system, and again pouring into it a little at a time, and suffer his patients to beget children in all probability as diseased as themselves; thinking medical treatment ill bestowed on one who could not live in his regular round of duties, since such a person is of no use either to himself or to the state?

You make out Asclepius to have been a profound statesman.

Clearly so: and because he was a man of that description, his sons, as you must have observed, proved themselves brave men in the battle before Troy, and also employed the healing art in the manner I have described. Or have you forgotten that when Menelaus had been wounded by the spear of Pandarus,

> Sucking the blood from the gash, they laid mild simples upon it.[31]

But what he was to eat or drink after this, they no more prescribed in his case than that of Eurypylus, knowing that the simples were sufficient to cure men who before receiving the wounds were healthy and regular in their mode of life, even if they happened to drink the next moment a compound of meal, wine, and cheese; but as for the constitutionally diseased and the intemperate, they thought the existence of such a man no gain either to himself or to others, believing that their art was not meant for persons of that sort, and that it would be wrong to attempt their cure, even if they were richer than Midas.

The sons of Asclepius were, by your account, very shrewd fellows.

And it was meet they should be. And yet the tragedians and Pindar dissent from us; and while they assert that Asclepius was the son of Apollo, declare that he was induced by a bribe of gold to raise to life a rich man who was already dead, which was indeed the cause of his being smitten by a thunderbolt. But we, agreeably to our principles, cannot believe both these statements of theirs: on the contrary, we shall maintain that if he was the son of a god, he was not covetous; if he was covetous, he was not the son of a god.

In that, he said, we shall be perfectly right. But what say you, Socrates, on this point? Ought we not to have good physicians in our city? Now the best physicians, I imagine, will be those who have had the largest practice both among the healthy and among the diseased; just as the best jurors in like manner will be those who have mixed with men of all varieties of character.

Decidedly, I replied, I am for having good ones: but do you know whom I consider such?

I shall if you inform me.

I will try to do so: but your question, I must premise, spoke of two dissimilar things in the same words.

How so?

Physicians, it is true, would acquire the greatest expertness if from their childhood upwards they not only studied their profession, but also came in contact with the greatest number of the worst cases, and had personal experience of every kind of malady, and were naturally not very healthy. For it is not the physician's body, I imagine, which cures the bodies of others – if it were, it could not be suffered at any time to be, or to become, diseased – but his mind, which cannot direct any treatment skilfully, if it has become, or always was, depraved.

You are right.

But a juror, my friend, governs mind by mind; his mind therefore cannot be suffered to be reared from a tender age among vicious minds, and to associate with them, and to run the whole round of crimes in its own experience, in order to be quick at inferring the guilt of others from its own self-knowledge, as is allowable in the case of bodily disorders: on the contrary, it ought from his early youth to have been free from all experience and taint of evil habits, if it is to be qualified by its own thorough excellence to administer sound justice. And this is the reason why good people, when young, appear to be simple and easy victims to the impositions of bad men, because they have not in their own consciousness examples of like passions with the wicked.

Yes, they are exceedingly liable to such imposition.

Therefore, to make a good juror a man must not be young, but old; and his knowledge of what injustice is should be acquired late in life, not by observing it as an inmate of his own soul, but by long practice in discerning its baneful nature as it exists out of himself in the souls of others; in other words, guided by knowledge, not by personal experience.

Certainly that would seem to be the noblest style of juror.

Yes, and a good one too, which is the point in question: for he that has a good soul is good. But your smart and suspicious juryman, who has been guilty himself of many crimes, and fancies himself knowing and clever, so long as he has to deal with men like himself, betrays astonishing wariness, thanks to those inward examples which he has ever in sight: but when he comes into communication with men of years and virtue, he shows himself to be no better than a fool, with his mistimed suspicions and his ignorance of a healthy character, which are the consequences of his not possessing any example of such a phenomenon. But as he falls in oftener with wicked than with good men, he seems both to himself and others to be rather clever than foolish.

That is most true.

It is not then in a man of this stamp that we must look for our good and wise juror, but in one of the former class. For vice can never know both itself and virtue; but virtue, in a well-instructed nature, will in time acquire a knowledge at once of itself and of vice. The virtuous man therefore, in my opinion, and not the vicious man, will make the wise judge.

I quite agree with you.

Then will you not establish in your city the two faculties, of medicine and of law, each having the character we have described, to bestow their services on those only of the citizens whose bodily and mental constitutions are sound and good, leaving those that are otherwise in body to die, and actually putting to death those who are naturally corrupt and incurable in soul?

Yes, he said: this has been proved to be the best course both for the patients themselves and for the state.

As for the young men, I continued, it is clear that they will be cautious how they incur any need of law, so long as they use that simple kind of music which, as we stated, generates sobriety in the soul.

Undoubtedly.

If then the accomplished student of music follow this same track in the pursuit of gymnastic, may he not, if he pleases, so far succeed as to be independent of the medical art except in extreme cases?

I think he may.

Moreover, in the exercises and toils which he imposes upon himself, his object will be rather to stimulate the spirited element of his nature than to gain strength; and he will not, like athletes in general, take the prescribed food and exercise merely for the sake of muscular power.

You are quite right.

Then, Glaucon, am I also right in saying that those who establish a system of education in music and gymnastic are not actuated by the purpose which some persons attribute to them, of applying the one to the improvement of the soul, the other to that of the body?

Why, what can be their object, if this is not?

Probably they introduce both mainly for the sake of the soul.

How so?

Do you not observe the characteristics which distinguish the minds of those who have been familiar with gymnastic all their lives, without any acquaintance with music? And again, of those whose condition is the reverse of this?

To what do you allude?

To the roughness and hardness which mark the one, and the softness and gentleness which mark the other.

Oh yes. Those who have devoted themselves to gymnastic exclusively become ruder than they ought to be: while those who have devoted themselves to music are made softer than is good for them.

We know, however, that rudeness is the natural product of the spirited element, which if rightly nurtured will be brave, but if strained to an improper pitch, will in all probability become harsh and disagreeable.

I think so.

Well, and will not gentleness be a property of the philosophic temperament? And a property which, if too much indulged, will produce in it an excess of softness; but which, rightly nurtured, will render it gentle and orderly?

True.

But we say that our guardians ought to combine both these temperaments.

They ought.

Then must they not be mutually harmonised?

Unquestionably.

And where this harmony exists, the soul is both temperate and brave?

Certainly.

And where it is wanting, the soul is cowardly and coarse?

Very much so.

Accordingly, when a man surrenders himself to music and flute-playing, and suffers his soul to be flooded through the funnel of his ears with those sweet and soft and plaintive harmonies of which we just spoke, and spends his whole life in warbling and delighting himself with song, such a man at the outset tempers like steel whatever portion of the spirited element he possesses, and makes it useful instead of brittle and useless: if, however, he relaxes not in his devotion, but yields to the enchantment, he then begins to liquefy and waste away, till the spirit is melted out of him, and the sinews of his soul are extirpated, and he is made 'a feeble wielder of the lance'.

Exactly so.

And if he has received a spiritless soul originally from the hand of nature, this result is soon brought to pass: but if the contrary, he so enfeebles his spirit as to render it easily swayed, quickly kindled and quickly slaked by trifling causes. Consequently, such persons, instead of being spirited, are made choleric and irritable, and the prey of morose tempers.

Precisely so.

Well, but if on the other hand he devotes himself to hard labour in gymnastic, and indulges to his heart's content in good living, while he keeps aloof from music and philosophy, does not the excellent condition of his body at first inspire him with self-confidence and spirit, and make him surpass himself in courage?

Yes, that it does.

But what is the consequence of thus engaging in this one occupation to the total exclusion of the Muse's influence? Even supposing him to have possessed at first some taste for learning, yet if that taste is never fed with knowledge or inquiry, and takes no part in rational discourse or any intellectual pursuits, does it not become weak and deaf and blind from the want of stimulus and nourishment, and because its senses are never thoroughly purged?

Just so.

Consequently such a man becomes a hater of discussion, I imagine, and an illiterate person, and abandoning the use of rational persuasion, he settles all his business like a wild beast by violence and roughness, and lives in ignorance and awkwardness, with no symmetry and no grace.

That is exactly the case.

To correct then, as it would appear, these two exclusive temperaments, the spirited and the philosophic, some god, as I for my part shall maintain, has given to men two arts, music and gymnastic, not for soul and body distinctively, except in a secondary way, but expressly for those two temperaments, in order that by the increase or relaxation of the tension to the due pitch they may be brought into mutual accord.

So it would appear.

Then whosoever can best blend gymnastic with music, and bring both to bear on the mind most judiciously, such a man we shall justly call perfect in music and a master of true harmony, much rather than the artist who tunes the strings of the lyre.

Yes, and with good reason, Socrates.

Then will not some such overseer be always needed in our state, Glaucon, if our commonwealth is designed to endure?

Yes, indeed, such an officer will be quite indispensable.

Such then will be the outlines of our system of education and training. For why should one enter into details respecting the dances which will be in vogue in a state like ours, the hunting and field-exercises, or the sports of the gymnasium and the race-course? It is tolerably clear that these must correspond with the foregoing outlines, and there will be no further difficulty in discovering them.

Perhaps not, he said.

Very good: then what will be the next point for us to settle? Is it not this? Which of the persons so educated are to be the rulers, and which the subjects?

Unquestionably it is.

There can be no doubt that the rulers must be the elderly men, and the subjects the younger.

True

And also that the rulers must be the best men among them.

True again.

Are not the best agriculturists those who are most agricultural?

Yes.

In the present case, as we require the best guardians, shall we not find them in those who are most capable of guarding a state?

Yes.

Then for this purpose must they not be intelligent and powerful, and, moreover, careful of the state?

They must.

And a man will be most careful of that which he loves?

Of course.

And assuredly he will love that most whose interests he regards as identical with his own, and in whose prosperity or adversity he believes his own fortunes to be involved.

Just so.

Then we must select from the whole body of guardians those individuals who appear to us, after due observation, to be remarkable above others for the zeal with which, through their whole life, they have done what they have thought advantageous to the state, and inflexibly refused to do what they thought the reverse.

Yes, these are the suitable persons, he said.

Then I think we must watch them at every stage of their life, to see if they are tenacious guardians of this conviction, and never bewitched or forced into a forgetful abandonment of the belief that they ought to do what is best for the state.

What is this abandonment you speak of?

I will tell you. Opinions appear to me to quit the mind either by a voluntary or involuntary act, a false opinion by a voluntary act, when the holder learns his error; but a true opinion invariably by an involuntary act.

I understand the notion of a voluntary abandonment, but I have yet to learn the meaning of the involuntary.

Well, then, do you not agree with me that men are deprived of good things against their will, of evil things with their will? And is it not an evil thing to be the victim of a lie, and a good thing to possess the truth? And do you not think that a man is in possession of the truth when his opinions represent things as they are?

Yes, you are right; and I believe that men are deprived of a true opinion against their will.

Then when this happens, must it not be owing either to theft, or witchcraft, or violence?

I do not even now understand.

I am afraid I use language as obscure as tragedy. By those who have a theft practised on them, I mean such as are argued out of or forget their belief, because in the one case argument, and in the other time, privily carries off their opinion. Now, I fancy, you understand?

Yes.

By those who have violence done to them I mean all whose opinions are changed by pain or grief.

That too I understand, and I think you are right.

And those who are bewitched, you would yourself, I believe, assert to be those who change their opinion either through the seductions of pleasure or under the pressure of fear.

Yes, everything that deceives may be said to bewitch.

Then as I said just now, we must inquire who are the best guardians of this inward conviction, that they may always do that which they think best for the state. We may watch them, I say, from their earliest childhood, giving them actions to perform in which people would be most likely to forget, or be beguiled of, such a belief, and then we must select those whose memory is tenacious, and who are proof against deceit, and exclude the rest. Must we not?

Yes.

We must also appoint them labours and vexations and contests, in which we must watch for the same symptoms of character.

Rightly so.

And as a third kind of test, we must try them with witchcraft, and observe their behaviour, and just as young horses are taken into the presence of noise and tumult, to see whether they are timid, so must we bring our men, while still young, into the midst of objects of terror, and presently transfer them to scenes of pleasure, trying them much more thoroughly than gold is tried in the fire, to find whether they show themselves under all circumstances inaccessible to witchcraft, and seemly in their bearing, good guardians of themselves and of the music which they have been taught, approving themselves on every occasion true to the laws of rhythm and harmony, and acting in such a way as would render them most useful to themselves and the state. And whoever from time to time, after being put to the proof, as a child, as a youth, and as a man, comes forth uninjured from the trial, must be appointed a ruler and guardian of the city, and must receive honours in life and in death, and be admitted to the highest privileges, in the way of funeral rites and other tributes to his memory. And all who are the reverse of this character must be rejected. Such appears to me, Glaucon, to be the true method of selecting and appointing our rulers and guardians, described simply in outline, without accuracy in detail.

I am pretty much of your mind.

Is it then really most correct to give to these the name of perfect guardians, as being qualified to take care that their friends at home shall not wish, and their enemies abroad not be able, to do any mischief; and to call the young men, whom up to this time we entitled guardians, auxiliaries whose office it is to support the resolutions of the rulers?

I quite think so, he said.

This being the case, I continued, can we contrive any ingenious mode of bringing into play one of those seasonable falsehoods of which we lately spoke, so that, propounding a single spirited fiction, we may bring even the rulers themselves, if possible, to believe it, or if not them, the rest of the city?

What kind of fiction?

Nothing new, but a Phoenician story, which has been realised often before now, as the poets tell and mankind believe, but which in our time has not been, nor, so far as I know, is likely to be realised, and for which it would require large powers of persuasion to obtain credit.

You seem very reluctant to tell it.

You will think my reluctance very natural when I have told it.

Speak out boldly and without fear.

Well, I will. And yet I hardly know where I shall find the courage or where the words to express myself. I shall try, I say, to persuade first the rulers themselves and the military class, and after them the rest of the city, that when we were training and instructing them, they only fancied, as in dreams, that all this was happening to them and about them, while in reality they were in course of formation and training in the bowels of the earth, where they themselves, their armour, and the rest of their equipments were manufactured, and from whence, as soon as they were thoroughly elaborated, the earth, their real mother, sent them up to its surface; and consequently, that they ought now to take thought for the land in which they dwell, as their mother and nurse, and repel all attacks upon it, and to feel towards their fellow-citizens as brother children of the soil.

It was not without reason that you were so long ashamed to tell us your fiction.

I dare say; nevertheless, hear the rest of the story. We shall tell our people, in mythical language: You are doubtless all brethren, as many as inhabit the city, but the god who created you mixed gold in the composition of such of you as are qualified to rule, which gives them the highest value; while in the auxiliaries he made silver an ingredient, assigning iron and copper to the cultivators of the soil and the other workmen. Therefore, inasmuch as you are all related to one another, although your children will generally resemble their parents, yet sometimes a golden parent will produce a silver child, and a silver parent a golden child, and so on, each producing any. The rulers therefore have received this in charge first and above all from the gods, to observe nothing more closely in their character of vigilant guardians, than the children that are born, to see which of these metals enters into the composition of their souls; and if a child be born in their class with an alloy of copper or iron, they are to have no manner of pity upon it, but giving it the value that belongs to its nature, they are to thrust it away into the class of artisans or agriculturists; and if again among these a child be born with any admixture of gold or silver, when they have assayed it, they are to raise it either to the class of guardians, or to that of auxiliaries: because there is an oracle which declares that the city shall then perish when it is guarded by iron or copper. Can you suggest any device by which we can make them believe this fiction?

None at all by which we could persuade the men with whom we begin our new state: but I think their sons, and the next generation, and all subsequent generations, might be taught to believe it.

Well, I said, even this might have a good effect towards making them care more for the city and for one another; for I think I understand what you mean. However, we will leave this fiction to its fate: but for our part, when we have armed these children of the soil, let us lead them forward under the command of their officers, till they arrive at the city: then let them look around them to discover the most eligible position for their camp, from which they may best coerce the inhabitants, if there be any disposition to refuse obedience to the laws, and repel foreigners, if an enemy should come down like a wolf on the fold. And when they have pitched their camp, and offered sacrifices to the proper divinities, let them arrange their sleeping-places. Is all this right?

It is.

And these sleeping-places must be such as will keep out the weather both in winter and summer, must they not?

Certainly: you mean dwelling-houses, if I am not mistaken.

I do; but the dwelling-houses of soldiers, not of moneyed men.

What is the difference which you imply?

I will endeavour to explain it to you, I replied. I presume it would be a most monstrous and scandalous proceeding in shepherds to keep for the protection of their flocks such a breed of dogs, or so to treat them, that owing to unruly tempers, or hunger, or any bad propensity whatever, the dogs themselves should begin to worry the sheep, and behave more like wolves than dogs.

It would be monstrous, undoubtedly.

Then must we not take every precaution that our auxiliary class, being stronger than the other citizens, may not act towards them in a similar fashion, and so resemble savage monsters rather than friendly allies?

We must.

And will they not be furnished with the best of safeguards if they are really well educated?

Nay, but they are *that* already, he exclaimed.

To which I replied, It is not worth while now to insist upon that point, my dear Glaucon: but it is most necessary to maintain what we said this minute, that they must have the right education, whatever it may be, if they are to have what will be most effectual in rendering them gentle to one another, and to those whom they guard.

True.

But besides this education a rational man would say that their dwellings and their circumstances generally should be arranged on such a scale as shall neither prevent them from being perfect guardians, nor provoke them to do mischief to the other citizens.

He will say so with truth.

Consider then, I continued, whether the following plan is the right one for their lives and their dwellings, if they I are to be of the character I have described. In the first place, no one should possess any private property, if it can possibly be avoided: secondly, no one should have a dwelling or storehouse into which all who please may not enter; whatever necessaries are required by temperate and courageous men who are trained to war, they should receive by regular appointment from their fellow-citizens, as wages for their services, and the amount should be such as to leave neither a surplus on the year's consumption nor a deficit; and they should attend common messes and live together as men do in a camp: as for gold and silver, we must tell them that they are in perpetual possession of a divine species of the precious metals, placed in their souls by the gods themselves, and therefore have no need of the earthly ore; that in fact it would be profanation to pollute their spiritual riches by mixing them with the possession of mortal gold, because the world's coinage has been the cause of countless impieties, whereas theirs is undefiled: therefore to them, as distinguished from the rest of the people, it is forbidden to handle or touch gold and silver, or enter under the same roof with them, or to wear them on their dresses, or to drink out of the precious metals. If they follow these rules, they will be safe themselves and the saviours of the city: but whenever they come to possess lands, and houses, and money of their own, they will be householders and cultivators instead of guardians, and will become hostile masters of their fellow-citizens rather than their allies; and so they will spend their whole lives, hating and hated, plotting and plotted against, standing in more frequent and intense alarm of their enemies at home than of their enemies abroad; by which time they and the rest of the city will be running on the very brink of ruin. On all these accounts, I asked, shall we say that the foregoing is the right arrangement of the houses and other concerns of our guardians, and shall we legislate accordingly; or not?

Yes, by all means, answered Glaucon.

NOTES TO BOOK THREE

1 *Odyssey* xi, 489.

2 *Iliad* xx, 64.

3 *Iliad* xxiii, 103.

4 *Odyssey* x, 495.

5 *Iliad* xvi, 856.

6 *Iliad* xxiii, 100.

7 *Odyssey* xxiv, 6.

8 The etymology of these words connects them with 'wailing' and 'hateful'.

9 *Iliad* xxiv, 10.

10 *Iliad* xviii, 23.

11 *Iliad* xxii, 168.

12 *Iliad* xviii, 54.

13 *Iliad* xxii, 168.

14 *Iliad* xvi, 433.

15 *Iliad* i, 599.

16 *Odyssey* xvii, 383.

17 *Iliad* iv, 412. The second clause of the next quotation is from the same book, line 431, but the first clause is now found in book iii, 3. Plato himself probably quotes from memory, as Socrates is supposed to be doing.

18 *Iliad* i, 225.

19 *Odyssey* ix, 8. This is said by Odysseus.

20 *Odyssey* xii, 342.

21 *Odyssey* viii, 266.

22 *Odyssey* xx, 17.

23 Supposed to be from Hesiod.

24 *Iliad* ix, 515.

25 *Iliad* xxii, 15.

26 *Iliad* xxi, 130.

27 *Iliad* xxiii, 151.

28 *Iliad* xxii, 394 and xxiii, 175.

29 From the *Niobe* of Aeschylus.

30 It has been found very difficult to interpret the terms of ancient music in those of the modern science. The word ἁρμονία has been rendered in the text by its English form 'harmony', but it will be seen that it does not strictly correspond in sense with the technical acceptation of the English word.

31 *Iliad* iv, 218.

BOOK FOUR

Here Adeimantus interposed, inquiring, Then what defence will you make, Socrates, if any one protests that you are not making the men of this class particularly happy – when it is their own fault, too, if they are not? For the city really belongs to them, and yet they derive no advantage from it, as others do, who own lands and build fine large houses, and furnish them in corresponding style, and perform private sacrifices to the gods, and entertain their friends, and in fact, as you said just now, possess gold and silver, and everything that is usually considered necessary to happiness; nay, they appear to be posted in the city, as it might be said, precisely like mercenary troops, wholly occupied in garrison duties.

Yes, I said, and for this they are only fed, and do not receive pay in addition to their rations, like the rest, so that it will be out of their power to take any journeys on their own account, should they wish to do so, or to make presents to mistresses, or to lay out money in the gratification of any other desire, after the plan of those who are considered happy. These and many similar counts you leave out of the indictment.

Well, said he, let us suppose these to be included in the charge.

What defence then shall we make, do you ask?

Yes.

By travelling the same road as before, we shall find, I think, what to say. We shall reply that though it would not surprise us if even this class in the given circumstances were very happy, yet that our object in the construction of our state is not to make any one class pre-eminently happy, but to make the whole state as happy as it can be made. For we thought that in such a state we should be most likely to discover justice, as, on the other hand, in the worst-regulated state we should be most likely to discover injustice, and that after having observed them we might decide the question we have been so long investigating. At present, we believe we are forming the happy state, not by selecting a few of its members and making them happy, but by making the whole so. Presently we shall examine a state of the opposite kind. Now, if some one came up to us while we were painting statues, and blamed us for not putting the most beautiful colours on the most beautiful parts of the body, because the eyes, being the most beautiful part, were not painted purple, but black, we should think it a sufficient defence to reply, Pray, sir, do not suppose that we ought to make the eyes so beautiful as not to look like eyes, nor the other parts in like manner, but observe whether, by giving to every part what properly belongs to it, we make the whole beautiful. In the same way do not, in the present instance, compel us to attach to our guardians such a species of happiness as shall make them anything but guardians. For we are well aware that we might, on the same principle, clothe our cultivators in long robes, and put golden coronets on their heads, and bid them till the land at their pleasure; and that we might stretch our potters at their ease on couches before the fire, to drink and make merry, placing the wheel by their side, with directions to ply their trade just so far as they should feel it agreeable; and that we might dispense this kind of bliss to all the rest, so that the entire city might thus be happy. But give not such advice to *us*: since, if we comply with your recommendation, the cultivator will be no cultivator, the potter no potter; nor will any of those professions which make up a state maintain its proper character. For the other occupations it matters less: for in cobblers, incompetency and degeneracy and pretence, without the reality, are not dangerous to a state: but when guardians of the laws and of the state are such in appearance only, and not in reality, you see that they radically destroy the whole state, as, on the other hand, they alone can create public prosperity and happiness. If then, while *we* aim at making genuine guardians, who shall be as far as possible from doing mischief to the state, the supposed objector makes a class who would be cultivators and as it were jovial feasters at a holiday gathering, rather than citizens of a state, he will be describing something which is not a state. We should examine then whether our object in constituting our guardians should be to secure to them the greatest possible amount of happiness, or whether our duty, as regards happiness, is to see if our state as a whole enjoys it, persuading or compelling these our auxiliaries and guardians to study only how to make themselves the best possible workmen at their own occupation, and treating all the rest in like manner, and thus, while the whole city grows and becomes prosperously organised, permitting each class to partake of as much happiness as the nature of the case allows to it.

I think, he replied, that what you say is quite right.

I wonder whether you will think the proposition that is sister to the last satisfactory also.

What may that be?

Consider whether the other craftsmen are similarly injured and spoiled by these agencies.

What agencies do you mean?

Wealth, I said, and poverty.

How so?

Thus: do you think that a potter after he has grown rich will care to attend to his trade any longer?

Certainly not.

But he will become more idle and careless than he was before?

Yes, much more.

Then does he not become a worse potter?

Yes, a much worse potter too.

On the other hand, if he is prevented by poverty from providing himself with tools or any other requisite of his trade, he will produce inferior articles, and his sons or apprentices will not be taught their trade so well.

Inevitably.

Then both these conditions, riches and poverty, deteriorate the productions of the artisans and the artisans themselves.

So it appears.

Then apparently we have found some other objects for the vigilance of our guardians, who must take every precaution that they may never evade their watch and steal into the city.

What are these?

Wealth, I replied, and poverty; because the former produces luxury and idleness and innovation, and the latter meanness and bad workmanship as well as innovation.

Exactly so. But on the other hand, consider, Socrates how our city will be able to go to war, if it possesses no wealth, especially in the case of its being compelled to take the field against a rich and populous state.

Obviously, I replied, against one such state it will be hard for it to carry on war, but against two it will be easier.

How so?

In the first place, if they are obliged to fight, will not their antagonists be rich men, while they themselves are trained soldiers?

Yes, that is true so far.

What then, Adeimantus? Do you not believe that one pugilist trained in the most perfect manner to his work would find it easy to fight with two rich and fat men, who do not understand boxing?

Not with both at once, perhaps.

What, not if he were able to give ground till one of his assailants was in advance of the other, and then to rally and attack him, repeating these tactics frequently under a burning sun? Could not such a combatant worst even more than two such antagonists?

Indeed, he replied, there would be nothing very surprising in it.

And do you not think that the rich are better acquainted, both theoretically and practically, with boxing than with the art of war?

I do.

Then in all probability our trained soldiers will find no difficulty in fighting double or treble their own number.

I shall give in to you; for I believe you are right.

But suppose they were to send an embassy to one of the two cities, and to say, what would be true, 'We make no use of gold and silver, nor is it allowed among us, though it is among you; therefore join your forces with ours, and let the property of the other people be yours;' do you think that any persons, after being told this, would choose to wage war against lean and wiry dogs, instead of making common cause with the dogs against fat and tender sheep?

I fancy not. But may not the accumulation of the wealth of the other party in one city be fraught with danger to the city which is not wealthy?

I congratulate you, I replied, on your idea that it is proper to describe as 'a city' any that is not the counterpart of that which we were organising.

Why, what would you have?

The others ought to be called by some grander name, for each of them is very many cities and not a city, as they say in the game.[1] In any case, there are two, hostile one to the other, the city of the poor and the city of the rich: and each of these contains very many cities;

and if you deal with them as one, you will find yourself thoroughly mistaken; but if you treat them as many, and give to one class the property and the power, or even the persons, of another, you will always have many allies and few enemies. And so long as your city is governed discreetly on the principles recently laid down, it will be very large; I do not mean that it will enjoy that reputation, but really and truly it will be very large, even if its army consists of no more than a thousand men. For you will not easily find one city as large as that, either among the Greeks or among the barbarians, though you may find many cities which seem to be several times as large. Do you think differently?

No, indeed, I do not.

This then, I continued, will also serve as the best standard for our governors to adopt in regulating the size of the state, and the amount of land which they should mark off for a state of the due size, leaving the rest alone.

What is the standard? he asked.

The following, I conceive; so long as the city can grow without abandoning its unity, up to that point it may be allowed to grow, but not beyond it.

A very good rule.

Then we shall lay this additional injunction upon our guardians, to take every precaution that the city be neither small nor in appearance large, but characterised by sufficiency and unity.

A trivial duty, perhaps, to impose upon them.

We will add, I continued, another yet more trivial than this, which we touched upon before, when we said that it would be right to send away any inferior child that might be born among the guardians, and place it in another class; and if a child of peculiar excellence were born in the other classes, to place him among the guardians. This was intended to intimate that the other citizens also ought to be set to the work for which nature has respectively qualified them, each to some one work, that so each practising his single occupation may become not many men, but one, and that thus the whole city may grow to be one city and not many cities.

Yes, he said, this is a smaller affair than the former.

Really, my good Adeimantus, these injunctions of ours are not, as one might suppose, a number of arduous tasks, but they will all be inconsiderable, if the guardians diligently observe the one great point, as the saying is, though it should rather be called sufficient than great.

What is that?

Education, I said, and rearing. For if by a good education they be made reasonable men, they will readily see through all these questions, as well as others which we pass by for the present, such as the relations between the sexes, marriage, and the procreation of children; in all which things they will see that the proverb ought as far as possible to be followed, which says that 'among friends everything is common property'.

Yes, that would be the most correct plan.

And indeed, if a state has once started well, it exhibits a kind of circular progress in its growth. Adherence to a good system of nurture and education creates good natures, and good natures, receiving the assistance of a good education, grow still better than they were, their breeding qualities improving among the rest, as is also seen in the lower animals.

Yes, naturally so. To speak briefly, therefore, the overseers of the state must hold fast to this principle, not allowing it to be impaired without their knowledge, but guarding it above everything; the principle, I mean, which forbids any innovation, in either gymnastic or music, upon the established order, requiring it, on the contrary, to be most strictly maintained, from a fear lest, when it is said that men care most for the song

Which being newest is sung, and its music encircleth the singers,[2]

it might perhaps be imagined that the poet is speaking not of new songs, but of a new style of music, and novelty should accordingly be commended. Whereas novelty ought not to be commended, nor ought the words to be so understood. For the introduction of a new kind of music must be shunned as imperilling the whole state; since styles of music are never disturbed without affecting the most important political institutions: at least so Damon affirms, and I believe him.

Pray include me too among the believers in this doctrine, said Adeimantus.

Then to all appearance, I continued, it is here in music that our guardians should erect their guard-house.

At any rate, said he, it is here that lawlessness easily creeps in unawares.

Yes, in the guise of amusement, and professing to do no mischief.

No, and it does none, except that gradually gaining a lodgement it quietly insinuates itself into manners and customs; and from these it issues in greater force, and makes its way into mutual compacts: and from compacts it goes on to attack laws and constitutions, displaying the utmost impudence, Socrates, until it ends by overturning everything both in public and in private.

Good, said I; is this so?

I think it is.

Then as we said in the beginning, must not our children from the very first be restricted to more lawful amusements, because when amusements are lawless, and children take after them, it is impossible for such children to grow into loyal and virtuous men?

Unquestionably.

Accordingly, when our children, beginning with right diversions, have received loyalty into their minds by the instrumentality of music, the result is the exact reverse of the former; for loyalty accompanies them into everything and promotes their progress, and raises up again any state institution which might happen to have been cast down.

Yes, that is true.

Consequently such persons make the discovery even of those trifling regulations, as they are held to be, which had all been lost by those whom we described before.

What regulations do you mean?

Those, for example, which require the young to maintain a decorous silence in the presence of their elders, stooping to them, and rising up at their entrance, and paying every attention to their parents; together with regulations as to the mode of wearing the hair, the style of dress and shoes and personal decoration in general, and everything else of the same kind. Is not this your opinion?

It is.

But to legislate on these matters would be foolish, I think: it is never done, I believe: nor could express verbal legislation on such points ever be permanent.

How could it be?

At any rate it is probable, Adeimantus, that the bent given by education will determine all that follows. For does not like always invite like?

Undoubtedly it does.

And so we should expect our system at last, I fancy, to end in some complete and grand result, whether this result be good or the reverse.

We certainly should.

On these grounds I should not attempt to extend our legislation to points like those.

With good reason.

But again, do tell me, as to those common business transactions between private individuals in the market, including if you please the contracts of artisans, libels, assaults, law-proceedings and the impanelling of juries, or again questions relating to tariffs, and the collection of such customs as may be necessary in the markets or in the harbours, and generally all regulations of the market, the police, the custom-house and the like; shall we condescend to legislate at all on such matters?

No, it is not worth while to give directions on these points to good and cultivated men: for in most cases they will have little difficulty in discovering all the legislation required.

Yes, my friend, if god enable them to maintain the laws which we have already discussed.

Otherwise, he said, they will spend their lives in continually enacting and amending numerous laws on such subjects, expecting to attain to perfection.

You mean that such persons will live as those do who are in bad health and yet, from their want of self-restraint, cannot make up their minds to relinquish a pernicious course of life.

Precisely so.

And truly such people lead a charming life! Always in the doctor's hands, they make no progress, but only complicate and aggravate their maladies, and yet they are always hoping that someone will recommend them a medicine which shall cure them.

Yes, that is just the case with invalids of this kind.

Again, is it not charming that they should regard as their greatest enemy any one who tells them the truth, and assures them that till they give up their drunkenness, gluttony and debauchery, and laziness, no drugs, nor any use of caustic or the knife, nor yet charms or amulets, or any thing of the kind, will do them any good?

It is not so very charming, he replied: for there is no charm in being angry with one who gives good advice.

You do not seem to approve of such people.

No, indeed, I do not.

Then, if so, should a whole city, as we were saying just now, act in a similar manner, it will not receive your approbation, and does it not appear to you that states do act like such individuals, when having a bad form of government they forewarn their citizens not to disturb the constitution, under pain of death to all who attempt to do so: while any one who can serve them most agreeably under their existing polity, and curry favour by fawning upon them and anticipating their wishes, being also clever in satisfying these wishes, he forsooth will be esteemed an excellent man, and full of profound wisdom, and will be honoured at their hands?

Yes, he replied, for my part I see no difference between the two cases, and I cannot in the least approve of such conduct.

On the other hand, do you not admire the courage and dexterity of those who are willing and anxious to serve such cities?

I do, except when they are deluded by them into fancying themselves real statesmen, because they are praised by the many.

What do you say? Do you not make allowances for them? Do you suppose it is possible for a man who knows nothing of measurement, when many other equally ignorant persons tell him that he is six feet high, not to believe it himself?

No, that is impossible.

Then be not angry with them: for indeed these are the most amusing people in the world, who imagine that with their everlasting enactments and amendments concerning the matters we lately described, they will find some way of putting down the knaveries that are practised in contracts, and those other embarrassments which I detailed just now, little thinking that they are in reality only cutting off the heads of a Hydra.

It is true, they are no better employed.

For my part, therefore, I should not have thought it incumbent upon the genuine legislator to trouble himself with these branches of law and government, whether his state be ill or well organised; in the former case because such regulations are useless, and do no good; and in the latter because some of them may be discovered by any person whatever, and others will follow spontaneously as a result of previous training.

What then, he asked, still remains for us as legislators to do?

And I replied, For us, nothing: but for the Delphian Apollo there will remain the most important, the noblest, and the highest acts of legislation.

What are these?

The erection of temples and the appointment of sacrifices and other ceremonies in honour of the gods and demigods and heroes, and likewise the mode of burning the dead, and all the observances which we must adopt in order to propitiate the inhabitants of the other world. These are subjects which we do not understand ourselves, and about which, in founding a state, we shall, if we are wise, listen to no other advice or exposition except that of our ancient national expositor. For it is this god, I apprehend, expounding from his seat on the Omphalos, at the earth's centre, who is the national expositor to all men on such subjects.

You are quite right: this is what we ought to do.

Then the organisation of our state is now complete, son of Ariston: and the next thing for you to do is to examine it, furnishing yourself with the necessary light from any quarter you can, and calling to your aid your brother and Polemarchus and the rest, in order to try if we can see where justice may be found in it, and where injustice, and wherein they differ the one from the other, and which of the two the man who desires to be happy ought to possess, whether all gods and men know it or not.

That will not do! exclaimed Glaucon; it was you that engaged to make the inquiry, on the ground that you would be guilty of a sin if you refused to justice all the aid in your power.

I recollect that it was as you say, I replied: and I must so do, but you also must assist me.

We will.

I am in hopes, then, that we may find the object of our search thus. I imagine that our state, being rightly organised, is a perfectly good state.

It must be.

Then obviously it is wise and brave and temperate and just.

Obviously.

Then if we can find some of these qualities in the state, there will be a remainder consisting of the undiscovered qualities.

Undoubtedly.

Suppose then that there were any other four things contained in any subject, and that we were in search of one of them. If we discovered this before the other three, we should be satisfied: but if we recognised the other three first, the thing sought for would by this very fact have been found; for it is plain that it could only be the remainder.

You are right.

Ought we not to adopt this mode of inquiry in the case before us, since the qualities in question are also four in number?

Clearly we ought.

To begin then: in the first place wisdom seems to be plainly discernible in our subject; and in connection with it a paradoxical fact presents itself.

What is that?

The state which we have described is really wise, if I am not mistaken, inasmuch as it is prudent in counsel, is it not?

It is.

And this very quality, prudence in counsel, is evidently a kind of knowledge: for it is not ignorance, I imagine, but knowledge, that makes men deliberate prudently.

Evidently.

But there are many different kinds of knowledge in the state.

Unquestionably there are.

Is it then in virtue of the knowledge of its carpenters that the state is to be described as wise, or prudent in counsel?

Certainly not; for in virtue of such knowledge it could only be called a city of good carpentry.

Then it is not the knowledge it employs in considering how vessels of wood may best be made that will justify us in calling our city wise.

Certainly not.

Well, is it the knowledge which has to do with vessels of brass, or any other of this kind?

No, none whatever.

Neither will a knowledge of the mode of raising produce from the soil give a state the claim to the title of wise, but only to that of a successful agricultural state.

So I think.

Tell me, then, does our newly-organised state contain any kind of knowledge, residing in any section of the citizens, which takes measures, not in behalf of anything *in* the state, but in behalf of the state as a whole, devising in what manner its internal and foreign relations may best be regulated?

Certainly it does.

What is this knowledge, and in whom does it reside?

It is our protective science, and it resides in that governing class whom we denominated just now perfect guardians.

Then in virtue of this knowledge what do you call the state?

I call it prudent in counsel and truly wise.

Which do you suppose will be the more numerous class in our state, the braziers or these genuine guardians?

The braziers will far outnumber the others.

Then will the guardians be the smallest of all the classes possessing this or that branch of knowledge, and bearing this or that name in consequence?

Yes, much the smallest.

Then it is the knowledge residing in its smallest class or section, that is to say, in the predominant and ruling body, which entitles a state, organised agreeably to nature, to be called wise as a whole: and that class whose right and duty it is to partake of the knowledge which alone of all kinds of knowledge is properly called wisdom, is naturally, as it appears, the least numerous body in the state.

Most true.

Here then we have made out, in some way or other, one of the four qualities, and the part of the state in which it is seated.

To my mind, said he, it has been made out satisfactorily.

Again, there can assuredly be no great difficulty in discerning the quality of courage and the class in which it resides, and which entitles the state to be called brave.

How so?

In pronouncing a city to be cowardly or brave, who would look to any but that portion of it which fights in its defence and takes the field in its behalf?

No one would look to anything else.

No; and for this reason, I imagine – that the cowardice or courage of the state itself is not necessarily implied in that of the other classes.

No, it is not.

Then a city is brave as well as wise in virtue of a certain portion of itself, because it has in that portion a power which can without intermission keep safe the right opinion concerning things to be feared, which teaches that they are such as the legislator has declared in the prescribed education. Is not this what you call courage?

I did not quite understand what you said; be so good as to repeat it.

I say that courage is a kind of safe keeping.

What kind of safe keeping?

The safe keeping of the opinion created by law through education, which teaches what things and what kind of things are to be feared. And when I spoke of keeping it safe without intermission, I meant that it was to be thoroughly preserved alike in moments of pain and of pleasure, of desire and of fear, and never to be cast away. And if you like, I will illustrate it by a comparison which seems to me an apt one.

I should like it.

Well then, you know that dyers, when they wish to dye wool so as to give it the true sea-purple, first select from the numerous colours one variety, that of white wool, and then subject it to much careful preparatory dressing, that it may take the colour as brilliantly as possible, after which they proceed to dye it. And when the wool has been dyed on this system, its colour is indelible, and no washing either with or without soap can rob it of its brilliancy, But when this course has not been pursued, you know the results, whether this or any other colour be dyed without previous preparation.

I know that the dye washes out in a ridiculous way.

You may understand from this what we were labouring, to the best of our ability, to bring about when we were selecting our soldiers and training them in music and gymnastic. Imagine that we were only contriving how they might be best wrought upon to take as it were the colour of the laws, in order that their opinion concerning things to be feared, and on all other subjects, might be indelible, owing to their congenial nature and appropriate training, and that their colour might not be washed out by such terribly efficacious detergents as pleasure, which works more powerfully than any potash or lye, and pain and fear and desire, which are more potent than any other solvent in the world. This power, therefore, to hold fast continually the right and lawful opinion concerning things to be feared and things not to be feared, I define to be courage, and call it by that name, if you do not object.

No, I do not: for when the right opinion on these matters is held without education, as by beasts and slaves, you would not, I think, regard it as altogether legitimate, and you would give it some other name than courage.

Most true.

Then I accept this account of courage.

Do so, at least as an account of the courage of citizens, and you will be right. On a future occasion, if you like, we will go into this question more fully: at present it is beside our inquiry, the object of which is justice: we have done enough therefore, I imagine, for the investigation of courage.

You are right.

Two things, I proceeded, now remain, that we must look for in the state – temperance, and that which is the cause of all these investigations, justice.

Exactly so.

Well, not to trouble ourselves any further about temperance, is there any way by which we can discover justice?

For my part, said he, I do not know, nor do I wish justice to be brought to light first, if we are to make no further inquiry after temperance; so if you wish to gratify me, examine into the latter before you proceed to the former.

Indeed, I do wish it, as I am an honest man,

Proceed then with the examination.

I will; and from our present point of view, temperance has more the appearance of a concord or harmony than the former qualities had.

How so?

Temperance is, I imagine, a kind of order and a mastery, as men say, over certain pleasures and desires. Thus we plainly hear people talking of a man's being master of himself, in some sense or other; and other similar expressions are used, in which we may trace a print of the thing. Is it not so?

Most certainly it is.

But is not the expression 'master of himself' a ridiculous one? For the man who is master of himself will also, I presume, be the slave of himself, and the slave will be the master. For the subject of all these phrases is the same person.

Undoubtedly.

Well, I continued, it appears to me that the meaning of the expression is that in the man himself, that is, in his soul, there resides a good principle and a bad, and when the naturally good principle is master of the bad, this state of things is described by the term 'master of himself'; certainly it is a term of praise – but when in consequence of evil training, or the influence of associates, the smaller force of the good principle is overpowered by the superior numbers of the bad, the person so situated is described in terms of reproach and condemnation, as a slave of self, and a dissolute person.

Yes, this seems a likely account of it.

Now turn your eyes towards our new state, and you will find one of these conditions realised in it: for you will allow that it may fairly be called 'master of itself', if temperance and self-mastery may be predicated of that in which the good principle governs the bad.

I am looking as you direct, and I acknowledge the truth of what you say.

It will further be admitted that those desires and pleasures and pains, which are many and various, will be chiefly found in children and women and servants; and in the vulgar mass also among nominal freemen.

Precisely so.

On the other hand, those simple and moderate desires which go hand in hand with intellect and right opinion, under the guidance of reasoning, will be found in a small number of men, that is, in those of the best natural endowments and the best education.

True.

Do you not see that the parallel to this exists in your state: in other words, that the desires of the vulgar many are there controlled by the desires and the wisdom of the cultivated few?

I do.

If any state then may be described as master of itself, its pleasures and its desires, ours may be so characterised.

Most certainly.

May we not then also call it temperate, on all these accounts?

Surely we may.

And again, if there is any city in which the governors and the governed are unanimous on the question who ought to govern, such unanimity will exist in ours. Do you not think so?

Most assuredly I do.

In which of the two classes of citizens will you say that temperance resides, when they are in this condition? In the rulers or in the subjects?

In both, I fancy.

Do you see, then, that we were not bad prophets when we divined just now that temperance resembled a kind of harmony?

Why, pray?

Because it does not operate like courage and wisdom, which by residing in particular sections of the state make it brave and wise respectively, but spreads throughout the whole in literal diapason, producing a unison between the weakest and the strongest and the middle class, whether you measure by the standard of intelligence, or bodily strength, or numbers, or wealth, or anything else of the kind: so that we shall be fully justified in pronouncing temperance to be that unanimity which we described as a concord between the naturally better element and the naturally worse, whether in a state or in a single person, as to which of the two has the right to govern.

I fully agree with you.

Very well, I continued: we have discerned in our state three out of the four principles; at least such is our present impression. Now, what will that remaining principle be through which the state will further participate in virtue? For this, we may be sure, is justice.

Evidently it is.

Now then, Glaucon, we must be like hunters surrounding a cover, and must give close attention that justice may nowhere escape us and disappear from our view: for it is manifest that she is somewhere here; so look for her, and strive to gain a sight of her, for perhaps you may discover her first, and give the alarm to me.

I wish I might, replied he; but you will use me quite well enough if instead of that you will treat me as one who is following your steps, and is able to see what is pointed out to him.

Follow me then, after joining your prayers with mine.

I will do so; only do you lead the way.

Truly, said I, the ground seems to be hard to traverse, and covered with wood: at all events it is dark and difficult to explore; but still we must on.

Yes, that we must.

Here I caught a glimpse, and exclaimed, Ho! ho! Glaucon, here is something that looks like a track, and I believe the game will not altogether escape us.

That is good news.

Upon my word, said I, we are in a most foolish predicament.

How so?

Why, my good sir, it appears that what we were looking for has been all this time rolling before our feet, and we never saw it, but did the most ridiculous thing. Just as people at times go about looking for something which they hold in their hands, so we, instead of fixing our eyes upon the thing itself, kept gazing at some point in the distance, and this was probably the reason why it eluded our search.

What do you mean?

This: that I believe we were conversing of it together, without understanding that we were in a manner describing it ourselves.

Your preface seems long to one who is anxious for the explanation.

Well then, listen, and judge whether I am right or not. What at the commencement we laid down as a universal rule of action, when we were founding our state, this, if I mistake not, or some modification of it, is justice. I think we affirmed, if you recollect, and frequently repeated, that every individual ought to have some one occupation in the state, which should be that to which his natural capacity was best adapted.

We did say so.

And again, we have often heard people say that to mind one's own business, and not be meddlesome, is justice; and we have often said the same thing ourselves.

We have said so.

Then it would seem, my friend, that to do one's own business, in some shape or other, is justice. Do you know whence I infer this?

No, be so good as to tell me.

I think that the remainder left in the state, after eliminating the qualities which we have considered, I mean temperance and courage and wisdom, must be that which made their entrance into it possible, and which preserves them there so long as they exist in it. Now we affirmed that the remaining quality, when three out of the four were found, would be justice.

Yes, unquestionably it would.

If however it were required to decide which of these qualities will have most influence in perfecting by its presence the virtue or our state, it would be difficult to determine whether it will be the harmony of opinion between the governors and the governed; or the faithful adherence on the part of the soldiers to the lawful belief concerning the things which are, and the things which are not, to be feared; or the existence of wisdom and watchfulness in the rulers; or whether the virtue of the state may not be chiefly traced to the presence of that fourth principle in every child and woman, in every slave, freeman, and artisan, in the ruler and in the subject, requiring each to do his own work, and not meddle with many things.

It would be a difficult point to settle, unquestionably.

Thus it appears that in promoting the virtue of a state, the power that makes each member of it do his own work may compete with its wisdom, and its temperance, and its courage.

Decidedly it may.

But if there is a principle which rivals these qualities in promoting the virtue of a state, will you not determine it to be justice?

Most assuredly.

Consider the question in another light, and see whether you will come to the same conclusion. Will you assign to the rulers of the state the adjudication of law-suits?

Certainly.

Will not their judgments be guided, above everything, by the desire that no one may appropriate what belongs to others, nor be deprived of what is his own?

Yes, that will be their main study.

Because that is just?

Yes.

Thus, according to this view also, it will be granted that to have and do what belongs to us and is our own, is justice.

True.

Now observe whether you hold the same opinion that I do. If a carpenter should undertake to execute the work of a shoemaker, or a shoemaker that of a carpenter, either by interchanging their tools and distinctions, or by the same person undertaking both trades, with all the changes involved in it, do you think it would greatly damage the state?

Not very greatly.

But when one whom nature has made an artisan, or a producer of any other kind, is so elated by wealth, or a large connection, or bodily strength, or any similar advantages, as to intrude himself into the class of the warriors; or when a warrior intrudes himself into the class of the senators and guardians, of which he is unworthy, and when these interchange their tools and their distinctions, or when one and the same person attempts to discharge all these duties at once, then, I imagine, you will agree with me that such change and meddling among these will be ruinous to the state.

Most assuredly they will.

Then any intermeddling in the three classes, or change from one to another, would inflict great damage on the state, and may with perfect propriety be described as in the strongest sense a doing of evil.

Quite so.

And will you not admit that evil-doing of the worst kind towards one's own state is injustice?

Unquestionably.

This then is injustice. On the other hand, let us state that, conversely, adherence to their own business on the part of the industrious, the military, and the guardian classes, each of these doing its own work in the state, is justice, and will render the state just.

I fully coincide, he said, in this view.

Let us not state it yet quite positively, but if we find, on applying this conception to the individual man, that there too it is admitted to constitute justice, we will then yield our assent – for what more can we say? But if not, in that case we will institute a new inquiry. At present, however, let us complete the investigation which we undertook in the belief that if we first endeavoured to contemplate justice in some larger subject which contains it, we should find it easier to discern its nature in the individual man. Such a subject we recognised in a state, and accordingly we organised the best we could, being sure that justice must reside in a good city. The view, therefore, which presented itself to us there, let us now apply to the individual: and if it be admitted, we shall be satisfied; but if we should find something different in the case of the individual, we will again go back to our city, and put our theory to the test. And perhaps by considering the two cases side by side, and rubbing them together, we may cause justice to flash out from the contact, like fire from dry bits of wood, and when it has become visible to us may settle it firmly in our own minds.

There is method in your proposal, he replied, and so let us do.

I proceeded therefore to ask: When two things, a greater and a less, are called by a common name, are they, in so far as the common name applies, unlike or like?

Like.

Then a just man will not differ from a just state, so far as the idea of justice is involved, but the two will be like.

They will.

Well, but we resolved that a state was just when the three classes of characters present in it were severally occupied in doing their proper work: and that it was temperate, and brave, and wise, in consequence of certain affections and conditions of these same classes.

True.

Then, my friend, we shall also adjudge, in the case of the individual man, that supposing him to possess in his soul the same generic parts, he is rightly entitled to the same names as the state, in virtue of affections of these parts identical with those of the classes in the state.

It must inevitably be so.

Once more then, my excellent friend, we have stumbled on an easy question concerning the nature of the soul, namely, whether it contains these three generic parts or not.

Not so very easy a question, I think: but perhaps, Socrates, the common saying is true, that the beautiful is difficult.

It would appear so; and I tell you plainly, Glaucon, that in my opinion we shall never attain to exact truth on this subject by such methods as we are employing in our present discussion. However, the path that leads to that goal is too long and toilsome; and I dare say we may arrive at the truth by our present methods, in a manner not unworthy of our former arguments and speculations.

Shall we not be content with that? For my part it would satisfy me for the present.

Well, certainly it will be quite enough for me.

Do not flag then, but proceed with the inquiry.

Tell me then, I continued, can we possibly refuse to admit that there exist in each of us the same generic parts and characteristics as are found in the state? For I presume the state has not received them from any other source. It would be ridiculous to imagine that the presence of the spirited element in cities is not to be traced to individuals, wherever this character is imputed to the people, as it is to the natives of Thrace and Scythia, and generally speaking of the northern countries, or the love of knowledge, which would be chiefly attributed to our own country; or the love of riches, which people would especially connect with the Phoenicians and the Egyptians.

Certainly.

This then is a fact so far, and one which it is not difficult to apprehend.

No, it is not.

But here begins a difficulty. Are all our actions alike performed by the one predominant faculty, or are there three faculties operating severally in our different actions? Do we learn with one internal faculty, and become angry with another, and with a third feel desire for all the pleasures connected with eating and drinking and the propagation of the species; or upon every impulse to action, do we perform these several operations with the whole soul? The difficulty will consist in settling these points in a satisfactory manner.

I think so too.

Let us try therefore the following plan, in order to ascertain whether the faculties engaged are distinct or identical.

What is your plan?

It is manifest that the same thing cannot do two opposite things, or be in two opposite states, in the same part of it, and with reference to the same object, so that where we find these phenomena occurring, we shall know that the subjects of them are not identical, but more than one.

Very well.

Now consider what I say.

Speak on.

Is it possible for the same thing to be at the same time, and in the same part of it, at rest and in motion?

Certainly not.

Let us come to a still more exact understanding, lest we should chance to differ as we proceed. If it were said of a man who is standing still, but moving his hands and his head, that the same individual is at the same time at rest and in motion, we should not, I imagine, allow this to be a correct way of speaking, but should say that part of the man is at rest, and part in motion: should we not?

We should.

And if the objector should indulge in yet further pleasantries, so far refining as to say that at any rate a top is wholly at rest and in motion at the same time, when it spins with its peg fixed on a given spot, or that anything else revolving in the same place is an instance of the same thing, we should reject his illustration, because in such cases the things are not both stationary and in motion in respect of the same parts of them, and we should reply that they contain an axis and a circumference, and that in respect of the axis they are stationary, inasmuch as they do not lean to any side; but in respect of the circumference they are moving round and round: but if, while the rotatory motion continues, the axis at the same time inclines to the right or to the left, forwards or backwards, then they cannot be said in any sense to be at rest.

That is true.

Then no objection of that kind will alarm us, or tend at all to convince us that it is ever possible for one and the same thing, at the same time, in the same part of it, and relatively to the same object, to be acted upon in two opposite ways, or to be two opposite things, or to produce two opposite effects.

I can answer for myself.

However, that we may not be compelled to spend time in discussing all such objections, and convincing ourselves that they are unsound, let us assume this to be the fact, and proceed forwards, with the understanding that if ever we take a different view of this matter, all the conclusions founded on this assumption will fall to the ground.

Yes, that will be the best way.

Well then, I continued, would you place assent and dissent, the seeking after an object and the refusal of it, attraction and repulsion, and the like, in the class of mutual opposites? Whether they be active or passive processes will not affect the question.

Yes I should.

Well, would you not, without exception, include hunger and thirst and the desires generally, and likewise willing and wishing, somewhere under the former of those general terms just mentioned? For instance, would you not say that the mind of a man under the influence of desire always either seeks after the object of desire, or attracts to itself that which it wishes to have; or again, so far as it wills the possession of anything, it assents inwardly thereto, as though it were asked a question, longing for the accomplishment of its wish?

I should.

Again: shall we not class disinclination, unwillingness and dislike under the head of mental rejection and repulsion, and of general terms wholly opposed to the former?

Unquestionably.

This being the case, shall we say that desires form a class, the most marked of which are what we call thirst and hunger?

We shall.

The one being a desire of drink, and the other of food?

Yes.

Can thirst then, so far as it is thirst, be an internal desire of anything more than drink? That is to say, is thirst, as such, a thirst for hot drink or cold, for much or little, or, in one word, for any particular kind of drink? Or will it not rather be true that if there be heat combined with the thirst, the desire of cold drink will be superadded to it, and if there be cold, of hot drink; and if owing to the presence of muchness the thirst be great, the desire of much will be added, and if little, the desire of little: but that thirst in itself cannot be a desire of anything else than its natural object, which is simple drink; or again, hunger, of anything but food?

You are right, he replied; every desire in itself has to do with its natural object in its simply abstract form, but the accessories of the desire determine the quality of the object.

Let not any one, I proceeded, for want of consideration on our part, disturb us by the objection that no one desires *drink* simply. but good drink, nor food simply, but good food, because, since all desire good things, if thirst is a desire, it must be a desire of something good, whether that something, which is its object, be drink or anything else; an argument which applies to all the desires.

True, there might seem to be something in the objection.

Recollect, however, that in the case of all essentially correlative terms, when the first member of the relation is qualified, the second is also qualified, if I am not mistaken. When the first is abstract, the second is also abstract.

I do not understand you.

Do you not understand that 'greater' is a relative term, implying another term?

Certainly.

It implies a 'less', does it not?

Yes.

And a much greater implies a much less, does it not?

Yes.

Does a once greater also imply a once less, and a future greater a future less?

Inevitably.

Does not the same reasoning apply to the correlative terms 'more' and 'fewer', 'double' and 'half', and all relations of quantity; also to the terms 'heavier' and 'lighter', 'quicker' and 'slower'; and likewise to 'cold' and 'hot', and all similar epithets?

Certainly it does.

But how is it with the various branches of scientific knowledge? Does not the same principle hold? That is, knowledge in the abstract is knowledge simply of the knowable, or of whatever that be called which is the object of knowledge, but a particular science, of a particular kind, has a particular object of a particular kind. To explain my meaning — as soon as a science of the construction of houses arose, was it not distinguished from other sciences, and therefore called the science of building?

Undoubtedly.

And is it not because it is of a particular character, which no other science possesses?

Yes.

And is not its particular character derived from the particular character of its object? And may we not say the same of all the other arts and sciences?

We may.

This, then, you are to regard as having been my meaning before; provided, that is, you now understand that in the case of all correlative terms, if the first member of the relation is abstract, the second is also abstract; if the second is qualified, the first is also qualified. I do not mean to say that the qualities of the two are identical, as for instance that the science of health is healthy, and the science of disease diseased, or that the science of evil things is evil, and of good things good: but as soon as science, instead of limiting itself to the abstract object of science, became related to a particular kind of object, namely, in the present case, the conditions of health and disease, the result was that the science also came to be qualified in a certain manner, so that it was no longer called simply science, but, by the addition of a qualifying epithet, medical science.

I understand, and I think what you say is true.

To recur to the case of thirst, I continued, do you not consider this to be one of the things whose nature it is to have an object correlative with themselves, assuming that there is such a thing as thirst?

I do, and its object is drink.

Then for any particular kind of drink there is a particular kind of thirst; but thirst in the abstract is neither for much drink, nor for little, neither for good drink nor for bad, nor, in one word, for any kind of drink, but simply and absolutely thirst for drink, is it not?

Most decidedly so.

Then the soul of a thirsty man, in so far as he is thirsty, has no other wish than to drink; but this it desires, and towards this it is impelled.

Clearly so.

Therefore, whenever anything pulls back a soul that is under the influence of thirst, it will be something in the soul distinct from the principle which thirsts, and which drives it like a beast to drink: for we hold it to be impossible that the same thing should, at the same time, with the same part of itself, in reference to the same object, be doing two opposite things.

Certainly it is.

Just as, I imagine, it would not be right to say of the bowman, that his hands are at the same time drawing the bow towards him, and pushing it from him, the fact being that one of his hands pushes it from him, and the other pulls it to him.

Precisely so.

Now, can we say that people sometimes are thirsty and yet do not wish to drink?

Yes, certainly; it often happens to many people.

What then can one say of them, except that their soul contains one principle which commands, and another which forbids, them to drink, the latter being distinct from and stronger than the former?

That is my opinion.

Whenever the authority which forbids such indulgences grows up in the soul, is it not engendered there by reasoning; while the powers which lead and draw the mind towards them, owe their presence to passive and morbid states?

It would appear so.

Then we shall have reasonable grounds for assuming that these are two principles distinct one from the other, and for giving to that part of the soul with which it reasons the title of the rational principle, and to that part with which it loves and hungers and thirsts, and experiences the flutter of the other desires, the title of the irrational and concupiscent principle, the ally of sundry indulgences and pleasures.

Yes, he replied: it will not be unreasonable to think so.

Let us consider it settled, then, that these two specific parts exist in the soul. But now, will spirit, or that by which we feel indignant, constitute a third distinct part? If not, with which of the two former has it a natural affinity?

Perhaps with the concupiscent principle.

But I was once told a story, which I can quite believe, to the effect that Leontius, the son of Aglaion, as he was walking up from the Piraeus and approaching the northern wall from the outside, observed some dead bodies on the ground, and the executioner standing by them. He immediately felt a desire to look at them, but at the same time loathing the thought he tried to divert himself from it. For some time he struggled with himself, and covered his eyes, till at length, over-mastered by the desire, he opened his eyes wide with his fingers, and running up to the bodies, exclaimed, 'There! you wretches! gaze your fill at the beautiful spectacle!'

I have heard the anecdote too.

This story, however, indicates that anger sometimes fights against the desires, which implies that they are two distinct principles.

True, it does indicate that.

And do we not often observe in other cases that when a man is overpowered by the desires against the dictates of his reason, he reviles himself, and resents the violence thus exerted within him, and that in this struggle of contending parties, the spirit sides with the reason? But that it should make common cause with the desires, when the reason pronounces that they ought not to act against itself, is a thing which I suppose you will not profess to have experienced yourself, nor yet, I imagine, have you ever noticed it in anyone else.

No, I am sure I have not.

Well, and when any one thinks he is in the wrong, is he not, in proportion to the nobleness of his character, so much the less able to be angry at being made to suffer hunger or cold or any similar pain at the hands of him whom he thinks justified in so treating him; his spirit, as I describe it, refusing to be roused against his punisher?

True.

On the other hand, when any one thinks he is wronged, does he not instantly boil and chafe, and enlist himself on the side of what he thinks to be justice; and whatever extremities of hunger and cold and the like he may have to suffer, does he not endure till he conquers, never ceasing from his noble efforts till he has either gained his point, or perished in the attempt, or been recalled and calmed by the voice of reason within, as a dog is called off by a shepherd?

Yes, he replied, the case answers very closely to your description; and in fact, in our city we made the auxiliaries, like sheep-dogs, subject to the rulers, who are as it were the shepherds of the state.

You rightly understand my meaning. But try whether you also apprehend my next observation.

What is it?

That our recent view of the spirited principle is exactly reversed. Then we thought it had something of the concupiscent character, but now we say that far from this being the case, it much more readily takes arms on the side of the rational principle in the party conflict of the soul.

Decidedly it does.

Is it then distinct from this principle also, or is it only a modification of it, thus making two instead of three distinct principles in the souls, namely the rational and the concupiscent? Or ought we to say that as the state was held together by three great classes, the producing class, the auxiliary and the deliberative, so also in the soul the spirited principle constitutes a third element, the natural ally of the rational principle, if it be not corrupted by evil training?

It must be a third, he replied.

Yes, I continued, if it shall appear to be distinct from the rational principle, as we found it different from the concupiscent.

Nay, that will easily appear. For even in little children any one may see this, that from their very birth they have plenty of spirit, whereas reason is a principle to which most men only attain after many years, and some, in my opinion, never.

Upon my word, you have well said. In brute beasts also one may see what you describe exemplified. And besides, that passage in Homer, which we quoted on a former occasion, will support our view:

> Smiting his breast, to his heart thus spoke he in accents of chiding.

For in this line Homer has distinctly made a difference between the two principles, representing that which had considered the good or the evil of the action as rebuking that which was indulging in unreflecting resentment.

You are perfectly right.

Here then, I proceeded, after a hard struggle, we have, though with difficulty, reached the land, and we are pretty well satisfied that there are corresponding divisions, equal in number, in a state and in the soul of every individual.

True.

Then does it not necessarily follow that as and whereby the state was wise, so and thereby the individual is wise?

Without doubt it does.

And that as and whereby the individual is brave, so and thereby is the state brave; and that everything conducing to virtue which is possessed by the one, finds its counterpart in the other?

It must be so.

Then we shall also assert, I imagine, Glaucon, that a man is just in the same way in which we found the state to be just.

This too is a necessary corollary.

But surely we have not allowed ourselves to forget that what makes the state just is the fact of each of the three classes therein doing its own work.

No, I think we have not forgotten this.

We must bear in mind, then, that each of us also, if his inward faculties do severally their proper work, will in virtue of that be a just man, and a doer of his proper work.

Certainly it must be borne in mind.

Is it not then essentially the province of the rational principle to command, inasmuch as it is wise, and has to exercise forethought in behalf of the entire soul, and the province of the spirited principle to be its subject and ally?

Yes, certainly.

And will not the combination of music and gymnastic bring them, as we said, into unison; elevating and fostering the one with lofty discourses and scientific teachings, and lowering the tone of the other by soothing address, till its wildness has been tamed by harmony and rhythm?

Yes, precisely so.

And so these two, having been thus trained, and having truly learnt their parts and received a real education, will exercise control over the concupiscent principle, which in every man forms the largest portion of the soul, and is by nature most insatiably covetous. And they will watch it narrowly, that it may not so batten upon what are called the pleasures of the body as to grow large and strong, and forthwith refuse to do its proper work, and even aspire to absolute dominion over the classes which it has no right according to its kind to govern, thus overturning fundamentally the life of all.

Certainly they will.

And would not these two principles be the best qualified to guard the entire soul and body against enemies from without, the one taking counsel, and the other fighting its battles, in obedience to the governing power, to whose designs it gives effect by its bravery?

True.

In like manner, I think, we call an individual brave in virtue of the spirited element of his nature, when this part of him holds fast, through pain and pleasure, the instructions of the reason as to what is to be feared and what is not.

Yes and rightly.

And we call him wise in virtue of that small part which reigns within him and issues these instructions, and which also in its turn contains within itself a true knowledge of what is advantageous for the whole community composed of these three principles, and for each member of it.

Exactly so.

Again, do we not call a man temperate in virtue of the friendship and harmony of these same principles, that is to say, when the two that are governed agree with that which governs in regarding the rational principle as the rightful sovereign, and set up no opposition to its authority?

Certainly, he replied, temperance is nothing else than this, whether in state or individual.

Lastly, a man will be just, in the way and by the means which we have repeatedly described.

Unquestionably he will.

Tell me then, I proceeded, do we find any indistinctness in our view of justice, which makes us regard it as something different from what we found it to be in the state?

I do not think so.

Because we might thoroughly confirm our opinion, if we have any lingering doubts in our minds, by applying commonplace examples to it.

What kind of examples do you mean?

For example, if in speaking of our ideal state, and of an individual who in nature and training resembles it, we were required to declare whether we think that such an individual would repudiate a deposit of gold or silver committed to his charge, do you suppose that anyone would think him more likely to do such a deed than other men who are not such as he is?

No one would think so.

And will he not also be clear of suspicion of sacrilege, and of theft, and of being either false to his friends or a traitor to his country?

He will.

Moreover, he will be wholly incapable of bad faith, in the case of an oath or of any other kind of compact.

Clearly he will.

Again, he is the last person in the world to be guilty of adultery, or neglect of parents, or indifference to the worship of the gods.

Certainly he is.

And is not all this attributable to the fact that each of his inward principles keeps to his own work in regard to the relations of ruler and subject?

Yes, it may be entirely attributed to this.

Do you still seek then for any other account of justice than that it is the power which creates such men and such states?

No, he replied, assuredly I do not.

Then our dream is completely realised, or that suspicion which we expressed, that at the very commencement of the work of constructing our state we were led by some divine intervention, as it would seem, to a kind of rudimentary type of justice.

Yes, it certainly is.

And so there really was, Glaucon, a rude outline of justice (and hence its utility) in the principle that it is right for a man whom nature intended for a shoemaker to confine himself to shoemaking, and for a man who has a turn for carpentering to do carpenter's work, and so on.

It appears so.

The truth being that justice is indeed, to all appearance, something of the kind, only that instead of dealing with a man's outward performance of his own work, it has to do with that inward performance of it which truly concerns the man himself and his own interests: so that the just man will not permit the several principles within him to do any work but their own, nor allow the distinct classes in his soul to interfere with each other, but will really set his house in order, and having gained the mastery over himself, will so regulate his own character as to be on good terms with himself, and to set those three principles in tune together, as if they were verily three chords of a harmony, a higher and a lower and a middle, and whatever may lie between these; and after he has bound all these together, and reduced the many elements of his nature to a real unity, as a temperate and duly harmonised man, he will then at length proceed to do whatever he may have to do, whether it involve the acquisition of property or attention to the wants of his body, whether it be a state affair or a business transaction of his own; in all which he will believe and profess that the just and honourable course is that which preserves and assists in creating the aforesaid habit of mind, and that the genuine knowledge which presides over such conduct is wisdom; while on the other hand he will hold that an unjust action is one which tends to destroy this habit, and that the mere opinion which presides over unjust conduct is folly.

What you say is thoroughly true, Socrates.

Very good: if we were to say we have discovered the just man and the just state, and what justice is as found in them, it would not be thought, I imagine, to be an altogether false statement.

No, indeed it would not.

Shall we say so then?

We will.

Be it so, I continued. In the next place we have to investigate, I imagine, what injustice is.

Evidently we have.

Must it not then, as the reverse of justice, be a state of strife between the three principles, and the disposition to meddle and interfere, and the insurrection of a part of the mind against the whole, this part aspiring to the supreme power within the mind, to which it has no right, its proper place and destination being, on the contrary, to do service to any member of the rightfully dominant class? Such doings as these, I imagine, and the confusion and bewilderment of the aforesaid principles, will in our opinion constitute injustice and licentiousness and cowardice and folly and, in one word, all vice.

Yes, precisely so.

And is it not now quite clear to us what it is to act unjustly and to be unjust, and, on the other hand, what it is to act justly, knowing as we do the nature of justice and injustice?

How so?

Because these phenomena in the soul are exactly like the phenomena of health and disease in the body.

In what way?

The conditions of health, I presume, produce health, and those of disease engender disease.

Yes.

In the same way, does not the practice of justice beget the habit of justice, and the practice of injustice the habit of injustice?

Inevitably.

Now to produce health is so to constitute the bodily forces as that they shall master and be mastered by one another in accordance with nature; and to produce disease is to make them govern and be governed by one another in a way which violates nature.

True.

Similarly, will it not be true that to beget justice is so to constitute the powers of the soul that they shall master and be mastered by one another in accordance with nature, and that to beget injustice is to make them govern and be governed by one another in a way which violates nature?

Quite so.

Then virtue, it appears, will be a kind of health and beauty, and good habit of the soul; and vice will be a disease and deformity, and sickness of it.

True.

And may we not add that all fair practices tend to the acquisition of virtue, and all foul practices to that of vice?

Undoubtedly they do.

What now remains for us, apparently, is to inquire whether it is also *profitable* to act justly, and to pursue honourable aims, and to be just, whether a man be known to be such or not – or to act unjustly, and to be unjust, if one suffer no punishment and be not made a better man by chastisement.

Nay, Socrates, to me, I confess, the inquiry begins to assume a ludicrous appearance, now that the real nature of justice and injustice has presented itself to us in the light described above. Do people think that when the constitution of the body is ruined, life is not worth having, though you may command all varieties of food and drink, and possess endless wealth and power; and shall we be told that when the constitution of that very principle whereby we live is going to rack and ruin, life is still worth having, let a man do what he will, if that is excepted which will enable him to get rid of vice and injustice, and to acquire virtue and justice?

Yes, it is ludicrous, I replied: still, as we have arrived at this point, we must not lose heart till we have ascertained, in the clearest possible manner, the correctness of our conclusions.

No, indeed, anything rather than lose heart.

Come with me, then, that you may see how many varieties of vice there are, according to my belief, looking only at those which are worth the survey.

I follow you: only tell me.

Well, I can see as it were from a watch-tower, now that we have ascended to this lofty stage in the argument, that while there is only one form of virtue, there are infinite varieties of vice, of which four in particular deserve to be noticed.

How do you mean?

It would seem that there are as many characters of mind as there are distinctive forms of government.

Pray, how many are they?

There are five forms of government, and five characters of mind.

Tell me what these are.

I will: one form of government will be that which we have been describing, and it may be called by two different names; should there arise among the governing body one man excelling the rest, it will be called a kingdom; if there be more than one of equal excellence, it will be entitled an aristocracy.

True.

This then I call one form: for whether the supreme power be in the hands of one or many, the important laws of the state will not be disturbed if their training and education be such as we have described.

So we may justly expect, he replied.

NOTES TO BOOK FOUR

1 We are told by commentators that there was a game called 'Cities', played with counters; but the rules of the game have not been preserved.

2 *Odyssey* i, 351.

BOOK FIVE

Such then is the state or constitution which I call good and right, and such is the good man: and if this one be right, I must call the rest bad and wrong, applying these terms both to the organisation of states and to the formation of individual character; and the vicious forms are reducible to four varieties.

Pray, what are these? he asked.

Hereupon I was proceeding to speak of them in order, as they appeared to me to pass severally into one another; when Polemarchus, who was seated a little further off than Adeimantus, put out his hand to take hold of his brother's dress high up near the shoulder, drew him towards himself, and leaning forwards whispered a few words into his ear, of which we only caught the following:

Shall we let him off then, or what shall we do?

Certainly not, said Adeimantus, beginning to speak aloud. Whereupon I said, Pray what may that be which you are not going to let off?

You, he replied.

And why, pray? I further inquired.

We have an idea that you are lagging, and stealing a whole section, and that a very important one, out of the subject, in order to avoid handling it; and we suppose you fancied that we should not notice your passing it over with the very slight remark that everyone would see that the rule 'among friends every thing is common property' would apply to the women and children.

Well, and was I not right, Adeimantus?

Yes: but this word 'right', like the rest, needs explanation. We must be told on what plan, among the many possible ones, this community of property is to be carried out. Do not therefore omit to tell us what plan you propose. For we have been long waiting in the expectation that you would specify the conditions under which children are to be begotten, and the manner of rearing them after they are born, and in fact that you would give a complete description of the community of women and children intended by you: for we are of opinion that the mode of carrying out this idea, according as it is right or wrong, will be a matter of great, or rather of vital, importance to a commonwealth. So finding that you are taking in hand another form of government before you have satisfactorily settled these points, we have come to the resolution which you overheard, not to let you go till you have discussed all these questions as fully as the others.

Add my vote also, said Glaucon, as a supporter of this motion.

In short, Socrates, said Thrasymachus, you may look upon us as unanimous in this resolution.

What a deed have you done, I exclaimed, in thus laying hands upon me! What a large question are you again raising, as if we were beginning anew, on the subject of our commonwealth! I was rejoicing in the idea of having already done with it, and was only too glad that those points should be let alone, and accepted as they were then delivered. You little know what a swarm of questions you are rousing by calling in these topics: but I saw at the time how the case stood, and therefore let the subject go by, lest it should occasion us endless trouble.

How? exclaimed Thrasymachus; do you suppose that we are come here on a gold-hunting errand, and not expressly to hear a philosophical discussion?[1]

Yes, one of reasonable length, I replied.

True, Socrates, said Glaucon, and in the eyes of sensible people their whole life is but a reasonable time for hearing such discussions. So never mind us, but pray do not grow tired yourself of stating your views on the subject about which we were asking. I mean, as to the nature of this community of wives and children which is to subsist among our guardians; and as to the training of the young in the interval between their birth and education, which is considered the most troublesome business of all. Try to explain to us on what principle this is to be conducted.

It is no easy matter, my gifted friend, to discuss this question; for it is beset by incredulity even more than our previous doctrines. In the first place, the practicability of our plans will not be believed; and in the next place, supposing them to be most completely carried out, their desirableness will be questioned. And that is why I feel a reluctance to grapple with the subject, lest I should be thought, my dear friend, to be indulging in a merely visionary speculation.

You need feel no reluctance, he replied: for your auditors are neither stupid, nor incredulous, nor unfriendly.

Upon which I asked, My excellent friend, did you wish to encourage me by your assurance?

I did.

Then let me tell you, you have done just the contrary. If I were confident of my own knowledge of the subject, your encouragement would have been well and good; for to speak on the most momentous and interesting topics in the company of intelligent friends is a thing that may be done with courage and safety, if one really knows the subject; but to broach a theory while one is still in the position of a doubting inquirer, as I am going to do, is a slippery course, and makes me afraid, not of being laughed at – that would be childish – but lest I should miss my footing upon the truth, and falling, drag my friends down with me, and that upon ground on which a false step is especially to be dreaded. I pray that the divine Nemesis may not overtake me, Glaucon, for what I am going to say; for I verily believe it is a more venial offence to be the involuntary cause of death to a man than to deceive him concerning noble and good and just institutions Such a risk it were better to run among enemies than among friends; so that you are happy in your choice of encouragement.

At this Glaucon laughed, and said, Well, Socrates, should your theory do us any harm, our blood shall not be upon your head; we absolve you from the guilt of deceiving us: therefore speak boldly.

To be sure, I replied, the law tells us that when a man has been absolved from an offence, he is clean even in the next world; and therefore, in all probability, in this world also.

Very well then, let not this fear hinder you from proceeding.

I must recur, then, to a portion of our subject which perhaps I ought to have discussed before in its proper place. But after all, the present order may be the best; the men having quite played out their piece, we proceed with the performance of the women; especially since this is the order of your challenge.

For men born and educated as we have described, the only right method, in my opinion, of acquiring and treating children and wives will be found in following out that original impulse which we communicated to them. The aim of our theory was, I believe, to make our men as it were guardians of a flock.

Yes.

Let us keep on the same track, and give corresponding rules for the propagation of the species, and for rearing the young; and let us observe whether we find them suitable or not.

How do you mean?

Thus. Do we think that the females of watch-dogs ought to guard the flock along with the males, and hunt with them, and share in all their other duties; or that the females ought to stay at home, because they are disabled by having to breed and rear the cubs, while the males are to labour and be charged with all the care of the flocks?

We expect them to share in whatever is to be done; only we treat the females as the weaker, and the males as the stronger.

Is it possible to use animals for the same work, if you do not give them the same training and education?

It is not.

If then we are to employ the women in the same duties as the men, we must give them the same instructions.

Yes.

To the men we gave music and gymnastic.

Yes.

Then we must train the women also in the same two arts, giving them besides a military education, and treating them in the same way as the men.

It follows naturally from what you say.

Perhaps many of the details of the question before us might appear unusually ridiculous, if carried out in the manner proposed.

No doubt they would.

Which of them do you find the most ridiculous? Is it not obviously the notion of the women exercising naked in the schools with the men, and not only the young women, but even those of an advanced age, just like those old men in the gymnasia who in spite of wrinkles and ugliness still keep up their fondness for active exercises?

Yes, indeed: at the present day that would appear truly ridiculous.

Well then, as we have started the subject, we must not be afraid of the numerous jests which worthy men may make upon the notion of carrying out such a change in reference to the gymnasia and music; and above all, in the wearing of armour and riding on horseback.

You are right.

On the contrary, as we have begun the discussion, we must travel on to the rougher ground of our law, entreating these witty men to leave off their usual practice, and try to be serious; and reminding them that not long since it was thought discreditable and ridiculous among the Greeks, as it is now among most barbarian nations, for men to be seen naked. And when the Cretans first, and after them the Lacedaemonians, began the practice of gymnastic exercises, the wits of the time had it in their power to make sport of those novelties. Do you not think so?

I do.

But when experience had shown that it was better to strip than to cover up the body, and when the ridiculous effect which this plan had to the eye had given way before the arguments establishing its superiority, it was at the same time, as I imagine, demonstrated that he is a fool who thinks anything ridiculous but that which is evil, and who attempts to raise a laugh by assuming any object to be ridiculous but that which is unwise and evil; or who chooses for the aim of his serious admiration any other mark save that which is good.

Most assuredly.

Must we not then first come to an agreement as to whether the regulations proposed are practicable or not, and give to any one, whether of a jocose or serious turn, an opportunity of raising the question whether the nature of the human female is such as to enable her to share in all the employments of the male, or whether she is wholly unequal to any, or equal to some and not to others; and if so, to which class military service belongs? Will not this be the way to make the best beginning, and in all probability the best ending also?

Yes, quite so.

Would you like, then, that we should argue against ourselves in behalf of an objector, that the adverse position may not be undefended against our attack?

There is no reason why we should not.

Then let us say in his behalf, 'Socrates and Glaucon, there is no need for others to advance anything against you: for you yourselves, at the beginning of your scheme for constructing a state, admitted that every individual therein ought, in accordance with nature, to do the one work which belongs to him.' 'We did admit this, I imagine: how could we do otherwise?' 'Can you deny that there is a very marked difference between the nature of woman and that of man?' 'Of course there is a difference.' 'Then is it not fitting to assign to each sex a different work, appropriate to its peculiar nature?' 'Undoubtedly.' 'Then if so, you must be in error now, and be contradicting yourselves when you go on to say that men and women ought to engage in the same occupations, when their natures are so widely diverse?' Shall you have any answer to make to that objection, my clever friend?

It is not so very easy to find one at a moment's notice: but I shall apply to you, and I do so now, to state what the arguments on our side are, and to expound them for us.

These objections, Glaucon, and many others like them, are what I anticipated all along; and that is why I was afraid and reluctant to meddle with the law that regulates the possession of the women and children, and the rearing of the latter.

To say the truth, it does seem no easy task.

Why no: but the fact is, that whether you fall into a small swimming-bath or into the middle of the great ocean, you have to swim all the same.

Exactly so.

Then is it not best for us, in the present instance, to strike out and endeavour to emerge in safety from the discussion, in the hope that either a dolphin[2] may take us on his back, or some other unlooked-for deliverance present itself?

It would seem so.

Come then, I continued, let us see if we can find the way out. We admitted, you say, that different natures ought to have different occupations, and that the natures of men and women are different; but now we maintain that these different natures ought to engage in the same occupations. Is this your charge against us?

Precisely.

Truly, Glaucon, the power of the art of controversy is a very extraordinary one.

Why so?

Because it seems to me that many fall into it even against their will, and fancy they are discussing, when they are merely debating, because they cannot distinguish the meanings of a term, in their investigation of any question, but carry on their opposition to what is stated by attacking the mere words, employing the art of debate and not that of philosophical discussion.

This is no doubt the case with many: does it apply to us at the present moment?

Most assuredly it does; at any rate there is every appearance of our having fallen unintentionally into a verbal controversy.

How so?

We are pressing hard upon the mere letter of the dogma that different natures ought not to engage in the same pursuits, in the most courageous style of verbal debate, but we have wholly forgotten to consider in what senses the words 'the same nature' and 'different natures' were employed, and what we had in view in our definition, when we assigned different pursuits to different natures, and the same pursuits to the same natures.

It is true we have not considered that.

That being the case, it is open to us apparently to ask ourselves whether bald men and long-haired men are of the same or of opposite natures, and after admitting the latter to be the case, we may say that if bald men make shoes, long-haired men must not be suffered to make them, or if the long-haired men make them, the others must be forbidden to do so.

Nay, that would be ridiculous.

Would it be ridiculous except for the reason that we were not then using the words 'the same' and 'different' in a universal sense, being engaged only with that particular species of likeness and difference which applied directly to the pursuits in question? For example, we said that two men who were mentally qualified for the medical profession, possessed the same nature. Do you not think so?

I do.

And that a man who would make a good physician had a different nature from one who would make a good carpenter.

Of course he has.

If, then, the male and the female sex appear to differ in reference to any art or other occupation, we shall say that such occupation must be appropriated to the one or the other: but if we find the difference between the sexes to consist simply in the parts they respectively bear in the propagation of the species, we shall assert that it has not yet been by any means demonstrated that the difference between man and woman touches our purpose; on the contrary, we shall still think it proper for our guardians and their wives to engage in the same pursuits.

And rightly.

Shall we not proceed to call upon our opponents to inform us what is that particular art or occupation connected with the organisation of a state, in reference to which the nature of a man and a woman are not the same, but diverse?

We certainly are entitled to do so.

Well, perhaps it might be pleaded by others, as it was a little while ago by you, that it is not easy to give a satisfactory answer at a moment's notice, but that with time for consideration it would not be difficult to do so.

True, it might.

Would you like us then to beg the author of such objections to accompany us, to see if we can show him that no occupation which belongs to the ordering of a state is peculiar to women?

By all means.

Well then, we will address him thus: Pray tell us whether, when you say that one man possesses talents for a particular study, and that another is without them, you mean that the former learns it easily, the latter with difficulty; and that the one with little instruction can find out much for himself in the subject he has studied, whereas the other after much teaching and practice cannot even retain what he has learnt; and that the mind of the one is duly aided, that of the other thwarted, by the bodily powers? Are not these the only marks by which you define the possession and the want of natural talents for any pursuit?

Every one will say yes.

Well then, do you know of any branch of human industry in which the female sex is not inferior in these respects to the male? Or need we go the length of specifying the art of weaving and the manufacture of pastry and preserves, in which women are thought to excel, and in which their discomfiture is most laughed at?

You are perfectly right that in almost every employment the one sex is vastly superior to the other. There are many women, no doubt, who are better in many things than many men; but speaking generally, it is as you say.

I conclude then, my friend, that none of the occupations which comprehend the ordering of a state belong to woman as woman, nor yet to man as man; but natural gifts are to be found here and there, in both sexes alike, and so far as her nature is concerned, the woman is admissible to all pursuits as well as the man, though in all of them the woman is weaker than the man.

Precisely so.

Shall we then appropriate all duties to men, and none to women?

How can we?

On the contrary, we shall hold, I imagine, that one woman may have talents for medicine, and another be without them; and that one may be musical, and another unmusical.

Undoubtedly.

And shall we not also say that one woman may have qualifications for gymnastic exercises and for war, and another be unwarlike and without a taste for gymnastics?

I think we shall.

Again, may there not be a love of knowledge in one, and a distaste for it in another? And may not one be spirited and another spiritless?

True again.

If that be so, there are some women who are fit, and others who are unfit, for the office of guardians. For were not those the qualities that we selected, in the case of the men, as marking their fitness for that office?

Yes, they were.

Then as far as the guardianship of a state is concerned, there is no difference between the natures of the man and of the woman, but only various degrees of weakness and strength.

Apparently there is none.

Then we shall have to select duly qualified women also, to share in the life and official labours of the duly qualified men; since we find that they are competent to the work, and of kindred nature with the men.

Just so.

And must we not assign the same pursuit to the same natures?

We must.

Then we are now brought round by a circuit to our former position, and we admit that it is no violation of nature to assign music and gymnastic to the wives of our guardians.

Precisely so.

Then our intended legislation was not impracticable, or visionary, since the proposed law was in accordance with nature: rather it is the existing usage, contravening this of ours, that to all appearance contravenes nature

So it appears.

Our inquiry was whether the proposed arrangement would be practicable, and whether it was the most desirable one, was it not?

It was.

Are we quite agreed that it is practicable?

Yes.

Then the next point to be settled is that it is also the most desirable arrangement?

Yes, obviously.

Very well, if the question is how to render a woman fit for the office of guardian, we shall not have one education for men and another for women, especially as the nature to be wrought upon is the same in both cases.

No, the education will be the same.

Well then, I should like to have your opinion on the following question.

Pray, what is it?

On what principle do you in your own mind estimate one man as better than another? Or do you look upon all as equal?

Certainly I do not.

Then in our ideal state, which of the two classes have, in your opinion, been made the better men – the guardians educated as we have described or the shoemakers brought up to shoemaking?

It is ridiculous to ask.

I understand you: but tell me, are not these the best of all the citizens?

Yes by far.

And will not these women be better than all the other women?

Yes, by far again.

Can there be anything better for a state than that it should contain the best possible men and women?

There cannot.

And this result will be brought about by music and gymnastic employed as we described?

Undoubtedly.

Then our intended regulation is not only practicable, but also one most desirable for the state.

It is.

Then the wives of our guardians must strip for their exercises, inasmuch as they will put on virtue instead of raiment, and must bear their part in war and the other duties comprised in the guardianship of the state, and must engage in no other occupations: though of these tasks the lighter parts must be given to the women rather than to the men, in consideration of the weakness of their sex. But as for the man who laughs at the idea of undressed women going through gymnastic exercises, as a means of realising what is most perfect, his ridicule is but 'unripe fruit plucked from the tree of wisdom',[3] and he knows not, to all appearance, what he is laughing at or what he is doing: for it is and ever will be a most excellent maxim, that the useful is noble, and the hurtful base.

Most assuredly it is.

Here then is one wave, as I may call it, which we may perhaps consider ourselves to have surmounted, in our discussion of the law relating to women; so that instead of our being altogether swamped by our assertion that it is the duty of our male and female guardians to have all their pursuits in common, our theory is found to be in a manner at one with itself as to the practicability and advisableness of its plan.

Yes indeed, he replied, it is no insignificant wave that you have surmounted.

You will not call it a large one, I continued, when you see the next.

Pray go on, and let me see it.

The last law and those which preceded it involve, as I conceive, another to this effect.

What is it?

That these women shall be, without exception, the common wives of these men, and that no one shall have a wife of his own: likewise that the children shall be common, and that the parent shall not know his child, nor the child his parent.

This law, he replied, is much more likely than the former to excite distrust both as to its practicability and as to its advisableness.

As to the latter, I said, I think no one could deny that it would be an immense advantage for the wives and children to be common to all, if it were possible: but I expect there would be most controversy about the practicability of the scheme.

Both points might very well be controverted.

Then there will be a junction of discussions. I thought I should run away and get off from one of them, if you agreed to the utility of the plan, so that I should only have to discuss its feasibility.

But you were found out in your attempt to escape: so please to render an account on both heads.

I must submit to justice. Grant me however this one favour: permit me to take a holiday, like one of those men of indolent minds, who are wont to feast themselves on their own thoughts, whenever they travel alone. Such persons, you know, before they have found out any means of effecting their wishes, pass that by, to avoid the fatigue of thinking whether such wishes are practicable or not, and assume that what they desire is already theirs; after which they proceed to arrange the remainder of the business, and please themselves with running over what they mean to do under the assumed circumstances, thus aggravating the indolence of an already indolent mind. So at this moment I too am yielding to laziness, and am desirous of putting off for subsequent investigation the question of possibility; and for the present assuming the possibility, I shall inquire, if you will give me leave, what arrangements the governing body will make when our rule is carried out, endeavouring also to show that in practice it would be the most advantageous of all things both to the state and to its guardians. These points I will first endeavour to examine thoroughly in company with you, and take the others afterwards, if you give me your leave.

You have my permission, he replied. So proceed with the inquiry.

I think then, I proceeded, that if our rulers shall prove worthy of the name, and their auxiliaries likewise, the latter will be willing to execute the orders they receive, and the former, in issuing those orders, will themselves yield implicit obedience to our laws; and in whatever cases we have left the details to them, will endeavour to carry out their spirit.

So we may expect.

It will be your duty, therefore, as their lawgiver, to select the women just as you selected the men, and to place them together, taking care, as far as possible, that they shall be of similar nature. Now inasmuch as the dwellings and mess-tables are all common, and no one possesses anything in the shape of private property, both sexes will live together, and in consequence of their indiscriminate association in active exercises, and in the rest of their daily life, they will be led, I imagine, by a constraining instinct to form alliances. Do you not think this will be inevitable?

The necessity truly will not be that of mathematical demonstration, but that of love, which perhaps is more constraining than the other in its power to persuade and draw after it the mass of men.

Quite so. But in the next place, Glaucon, irregular alliances, or indeed irregularity of any kind, would be a profanation among the members of a happy city, and will not be permitted by the magistrates.

And rightly so.

Manifestly then our next care will be to make the marriage-union as sacred a thing as we possibly can: and this sanctity will attach to the marriages which are most for the public good.

Precisely so.

Then tell me, Glaucon, how this end is to be attained. For I know you keep in your house both sporting dogs and a great number of game birds. I conjure you, therefore, to inform me whether you have paid any attention to the intercourse and the breeding of these animals.

In what respect?

In the first place, though all are well-bred, are there not some which are, or grow to be, superior to the rest?

There are.

Do you then breed from all alike, or are you anxious to breed as much as possible from the best?

From the best.

And at what age? When they are very young or very old, or when they are in their prime?

When they are in their prime.

And if you were to pursue a different course, do you think your breed of birds and dogs would degenerate very much?

I do.

Do you think it would be different with horses, or any other animals?

Certainly not; it would be absurd to suppose it.

Good heavens, my dear friend! I exclaimed. What very first-rate men our rulers ought to be, if the analogy hold with regard to the human race.

Well, it certainly does: but why first-rate?

Because they will be obliged to use medicine to a great extent. Now you know when invalids do not require medicine, but are willing to submit to a regimen, we think an ordinary doctor good enough for them; but when it is necessary to administer medicines, we know that a more able physician must be called in.

True; but how does this apply?

Thus. It is probable that our rulers will be compelled to have recourse to a good deal of falsehood and deceit for the benefit of their subjects. And, if you recollect, we said that all such practices were useful in the character of medicine.

Yes, and we were right.

Well then, it appears that this right principle applies particularly to the questions of marriage and propagation.

How so?

It follows from what has been already granted that the best of both sexes ought to be brought together as often as possible, and the worst as seldom as possible, and that the issue of the former unions ought to be reared, and that of the latter abandoned, if the flock is to attain to first-rate excellence; and these proceedings ought to be kept a secret from all but the magistrates themselves, if the herd of guardians is also to be as free as possible from internal strife.

You are perfectly right.

Then we shall have to ordain certain festivals, at which we shall bring together the brides and the bridegrooms, and we must have sacrifices performed, and hymns composed by our poets in strains appropriate to the occasion; but the number of marriages we shall place under the control of the magistrates, in order that they may, as far as they can, keep the population at the same point, taking into consideration the effects of war and disease, and all such agents, that our city may, to the best of our power, be prevented from becoming either too great or too small.

You are right.

We must therefore contrive an ingenious system of lots, I fancy, in order that those inferior persons, of whom I spoke, may impute the manner in which couples are united to chance, and not to the magistrates.

Certainly.

And those of our young men who distinguish themselves in the field or elsewhere, will receive, along with other privileges and rewards, more liberal permission to associate with the women, in order that under colour of this pretext the greatest number of children may be the issue of such parents.

You are right.

And, as fast as the children are born, they will be received by the officers appointed for the purpose, whether men or women, or both – for I presume that the state-offices also will be held in common both by men and women.

They will.

Well, these officers, I suppose, will take the children of good parents and place them in the general nursery under the charge of certain nurses, living apart in a particular quarter of the city: while the issue of inferior parents, and all imperfect children that are born to the others, will be concealed, as is fitting, in some mysterious and unknown hiding-place.

Yes, if the breed of the guardians is to be kept pure.

And will not these same officers have to superintend the rearing of the children, bringing the mothers to the nursery when their breasts are full, but taking every precaution that no mother shall know her own child, and providing other women that have milk, if the mothers have not enough; and must they not take care to limit the time during which the mothers are to suckle the children, committing the task of sitting up at night and the other troubles incident to infancy to nurses and attendants?

You make child-bearing a very easy business for the wives of the guardians.

Yes, and so it ought to be. Now, let us proceed to the next object of our interest. We said, you remember, that the children ought to be the issue of parents who are still in their prime.

True.

And do you agree with me that the prime of life may be reasonably reckoned at a period of twenty years for a woman, and thirty for a man?

Where do you place these years?

I should make it the rule for a woman to bear children to the state from her twentieth to her fortieth year: and for a man, after getting over the sharpest burst in the race of life, thenceforward to beget children to the state until he is fifty-five years old.

Doubtless, he said, in both sexes, this is the period of their prime, both of body and mind.

If then a man who is either above or under this age shall meddle with the business of begetting children for the commonwealth, we shall declare his act to be an offence against religion and justice, inasmuch as he is raising up a child for the state, how should detection be avoided, instead of having been begotten under the sanction of those sacrifices and prayers which are to be offered up at every marriage ceremonial by priests and priestesses, and the whole city, to the effect that the children to be born may ever be more virtuous and more useful than their virtuous and useful parents, will have been conceived under cover of darkness by the aid of dire incontinence.

You are right.

The same law will hold should a man who is still of an age to be a father meddle with a woman who is also of the proper age, without the introduction of the magistrate: for we shall accuse him of raising up to the state an illegitimate, unsponsored and unhallowed child.

You are perfectly right.

But as soon as the women and the men are past the prescribed age, we shall allow the latter, I imagine, to associate freely with whomsoever they please, so that it be not a daughter or mother or daughter's child or grandmother; and in like manner we shall permit the women to associate with any man except a son or a father, or one of their relations in the direct line, ascending or descending; but only after giving them strict orders to do their best, if possible, to prevent any child, haply so conceived, from seeing the light; but if that cannot sometimes be helped, to dispose of the infant on the understanding that the fruit of such a union is not to be reared.

That too is a reasonable plan; but how are they to distinguish fathers and daughters, and the relations you described just now?

Not at all, I replied; only, all the children that are born between the seventh and tenth month from the day on which one of their number was married, are to be called by him if male, his sons, if female, his daughters; and they shall call him father, and their children he shall call his grandchildren; these again shall call him and his fellow-bridegrooms and brides, grandfathers and grandmothers, likewise all shall regard as brothers and sisters those that were born in the period during which their own fathers and mothers were bringing them into the world, and as we said just now, all these shall refrain from touching one another. But the law will allow intercourse between brothers and sisters, if the lot chances to fall that way, and if the Delphian priestess also gives it her sanction.

That is quite right, said he.

Such will be the character, Glaucon, of the community of women and children that is to prevail among the guardians of your state. The argument must now go on to establish that the plan is in keeping with the rest of our polity, and quite the best conceivable arrangement. Or can you propose any other course?

Do as you say, by all means.

Will not the first step to an agreement on this point between us be to ask ourselves what we can name as the highest perfection in the constitution of a state, at which the legislator ought to aim in making his laws, and what as the greatest evil; and the next to inquire whether the plan we described just now fits into our outline of the perfection, and is out of keeping with our sketch of the evil?

Most decidedly.

Do we know then of any greater evil to the state than that which should tear it asunder, and make it into a multitude of states instead of one? Or of any higher perfection than that which should bind it together and make it one?

We do not.

Well, then, does not a community of feeling in pleasure and pain bind the citizens together, when they all, so far as is possible, rejoice and grieve alike at the same gains and the same losses?

Most assuredly it does.

And does not isolation in these feelings produce disunion, when some are much pleased and others equally grieved at the same events affecting the city and its inmates?

Of course it does.

And does not this state of things arise when the words 'mine' and 'not mine' are not pronounced by all simultaneously in the city? And when there is the same discrepancy in the use of the word 'another's'?

Precisely so.

That city then is best conducted in which the largest proportion of citizens apply the words 'mine' and 'not mine' similarly to the same objects.

Yes, much the best.

Or in other words, that city which comes nearest to the condition of an individual man. Thus, when one of our fingers is hurt, the whole fellowship that spreads through the body up to the soul, and there forms an organised unity under the governing principle, is sensible of the hurt, and there is a universal and simultaneous feeling of pain in sympathy with the wounded part; and therefore we say that the *man* has a pain in his finger: and in speaking of any part of our frame whatsoever, the same account may be given of the pain felt when it suffers, and the pleasure felt when it is easy.

The same, no doubt; and to return to your question, there is a very close analogy between such a case and the condition of the best-governed state.

Then I fancy that when any good or evil happens to one of the citizens, a state such as we are describing will be more likely than another to regard the affected member as a part of itself, and to sympathise as a whole with his pleasure or his pain.

It must do so, if it be well ordered.

It will now be time, I continued, for us to go back to our state, and to take notice whether it possesses in the highest degree the qualities to which our inquiry has unanimously brought us, or is surpassed therein by some other state.

We had better do so.

Well then, other states, and ours like the rest, contain magistrates and a commonalty, do they not?

They do.

And they will all address one another as citizens?

Of course.

But besides calling them citizens, how does the commonalty in other states style its magistrates?

In most cases it styles them masters, but in democracies simply magistrates.

But in our state, what name besides that of citizens does the commonalty bestow on the magistrates?

It calls them preservers and auxiliaries.

And what do *they* call the people?

Paymasters and maintainers.

And in other states the magistrates call the people – what?

Servants.

And what do the magistrates call one another?

Fellow-magistrates.

And ours?

Fellow-guardians.

Can you say whether in other states a magistrate, speaking of his fellow-magistrates, might describe one of them as a relative and another as a stranger?

Yes, many might.

And in so doing, does he not regard and speak of the former as belonging to himself, and the latter as not belonging to himself?

He does.

Well, could any of your guardians regard or describe one of his fellow-guardians as a stranger?

Certainly not: for they must look upon every one whom they meet as either a brother or a sister, or a father or a mother, or a son or a daughter, or one of the children or parents of these.

Excellently said; but answer me one more question; shall you be satisfied with instituting family names, or shall you further require them to act in every instance in accordance with the names – enjoining in the treatment of the fathers all that it is usual to enjoin towards fathers, as that a child shall honour, succour and be subject to his parents, otherwise it will be worse for him both before heaven and before men; inasmuch as his conduct, if he acts differently, will be an outrage upon religion and justice? Will you have these commandments, or any others, sounded from the first by all the citizens in the ears of the children, with reference to those who are pointed out to them as fathers, and to all other relations?

These, certainly: for it would be ridiculous if family names were merely uttered with the lips, without actions to correspond.

This then is the state, above all others, in which when good or evil betides an individual, every member will with one accord apply the expressions spoken of just now, saying, 'It is well with mine', or 'It is ill with mine.'

Most true.

And did we not say that a general sympathy in pleasure and in pain goes hand in hand with this mode of thinking and speaking?

Yes, and we said so rightly.

Then will not our citizens be remarkable for sharing in the same interest, which they will call 'mine', and having this common interest, thereby possess in a remarkable degree a community in pleasure and pain?

Yes, in a very remarkable degree.

Well, is not this owing, among the other features of our constitution, to the fact that our guardians hold their wives and children in common?

Yes, mainly to this.

But if you remember, we admitted this to be the highest perfection in a state, comparing the condition of a well-ordered state to the relation of a body to its members in the matter of pleasure and pain.

Yes; and we were right in our admission.

Then we have discovered that the highest perfection of the state is due to the community of wives and children, which is to prevail among our auxiliaries.

Exactly so.

And in this arrangement we were moreover consistent with our former conclusions, for I believe we said that all private property, whether in houses or lands or anything else, must be forbidden to our guardians, who are to receive a maintenance from the rest of the citizens as the wages of their office, and to lay it out in common, if they are destined to be guardians indeed.

True.

Well then, will not the regulations laid down before, and still more those we are now describing, make men genuine guardians, and prevent them from tearing the city asunder by applying the term 'mine' each to a different object, instead of all to the same, and by severally dragging to their several distinct abodes whatever they can acquire independently of the rest, and amongst other things, separate wives and children, thus creating exclusive pleasures and pains by their exclusive interests; causing them, on the contrary, to tend unitedly to a common centre by the fact of holding but one opinion concerning what is their own, and thus to be, as far as is possible, simultaneously affected by pleasure and pain?

Precisely so.

Further, will not all lawsuits and prosecutions disappear, so to speak, from among them, seeing that there is nothing which a man can call his own except his body, all other things being common property? And will not this deliver them from all those feuds which are occasioned among men by the separate possession of money and children and kindred?

They cannot fail to be rid of them.

Moreover, there will be, by rights, no actions for forcible seizure, or for assault and battery among them. For we shall probably maintain that to defend oneself against an assailant of one's own age is consistent both with honour and justice, recognising the necessity of taking care of the person.

Rightly so.

There is also this advantage, I continued, in such a law: if anyone should happen to fall into a passion with another, he would find a vent for his anger by a personal encounter, and thus the quarrel will be less likely to assume a more serious character.

Certainly.

An older person, however, will be authorised to command and chastise any that are younger than himself.

Clearly.

And surely it is to be expected that no younger man will presume either to strike or otherwise do violence to an elder, unless the magistrates commission him to do so. Nor yet, I think, will a young man insult his seniors in any other way; for there are two warders that will effectually interpose, namely fear and shame; shame restraining him from laying violent hands on one whom he regards as a parent, and fear lest the person attacked should be succoured by the rest, in the character of sons, brothers and fathers.

Yes, those will be the results of our regulations.

Then in every way the laws will secure mutual peace among our men.

Yes, in a high degree.

But if the men of this class be free from internal dissensions, there is no danger that the rest of the citizens will quarrel either with them or with one another.

No, there is not.

There are, moreover, evils of a very petty nature, and so mean that I scruple even to mention them, from which they will be exempt: I allude to the flatteries paid by the poor to the rich, and those embarrassments and vexations which beset men in rearing a family, and in the acquisition of the money that is needed for the bare maintenance of domestics – now borrowing and now repudiating, and by indiscriminate means procuring property which they place in the hands of their wives and servants, and entrust to their management;

all the troubles that these circumstances occasion, my dear friend, are obvious enough; and besides they are ignoble, and do not deserve to be described.

True, they are obvious even to the blind.

While they are free from all these evils, they will live a life more blessed than that blissful life which is the lot of conquerors at the Olympian games.

How so?

Why, the happiness ascribed to these comprehends but a small part of the blessings enjoyed by our men, whose victory is as much more glorious as their public maintenance is more complete. The victory they win is the preservation of the whole state, and while living they receive crowns and privileges from their country in the shape of maintenance and all that life requires, themselves and their children, and when they die they are admitted to an honourable interment.

Yes, indeed, these are glorious privileges.

Do you remember then, I continued, that some time back we were accused by some objector of not making our guardians happy because, with the power to take all that the citizens had, they possessed nothing of their own? To which we replied, I believe, that we would consider that point hereafter, if it should fall in our way, but that our object then was to make our guardians really guardians, and the state itself as happy as we could, without any idea of fixing our attention on any one class, and providing happiness for it?

I remember.

Well, but as we have now found that the life of the auxiliaries is much more glorious and more desirable than that of Olympian victors, can it be thought that the life of the shoemakers or any other artisans, or that of the agriculturists, is in any sense comparable to it?

I think not, he replied.

However, it is but right to repeat here what I said at the time, that if ever our guardians attempt to make themselves happy in such a way that they cease to be guardians, if instead of being satisfied with a life merely moderate and stable, such as we think the best, they become possessed with a silly and childish notion of happiness, impelling them to use their power to appropriate all the good things in the city, they will discover that Hesiod was truly wise when he said that in a certain sense 'the half is more than the whole'.[4]

If they take my advice they will abide by the life assigned to them.

Then you concede the principle that the women are to be put upon the same footing as the men, according to our description, in education, in bearing children and in watching over the other citizens, and that whether they remain at home or are sent into the field, they are to share the duties of guardianship with the men, and join with them in the chase like dogs, and have every thing in common with them so far as is at all possible, and that in so doing they will be following the most desirable course, and not violating the natural relation which ought to govern the mutual fellowship of the sexes?

I do concede all this, he replied.

Then does it not remain for us, I proceeded, to determine whether this community can possibly subsist among men, as it can among other animals, and what are the conditions of its possibility?

You have anticipated me in a suggestion I was about to make.

As for their warlike operations, I suppose it is easy to see how they will be conducted.

How? he asked.

Why, both sexes will take the field together, and they will also carry with them to the wars such of their children as are strong enough, in order that, like the children of all other craftsmen, they may be spectators of those occupations in which, when grown up, they will themselves be engaged: and they will require them, besides looking on, to act as servants and attendants in all the duties of war, and to wait upon their fathers and mothers. You have doubtless observed in the various trades, how the children of potters, for example, look on and fetch and carry for their parents, long before they put their own hand to the making of pots.

Certainly I have.

Shall potters then show more carefulness than our guardians in educating their children, by making then see and practise their proper duties?

No, that would be indeed ridiculous.

Then again, every creature will fight with peculiar courage in the presence of its offspring.

True: but there is considerable danger, Socrates, in case of one of those reverses which are common in war, that the children may be sacrificed with the parents, and so the rest of the city be weakened beyond the power of recovery.

That is quite true, I replied. But let me ask you, in the first place, whether you think we are bound to take measures to avoid every possible danger?

By no means.

Well, if danger is ever to be encountered, ought it not to be in a case in which success will be a means of improvement?

Manifestly it ought.

And do you regard it as a point too unimportant to justify the risk, whether those whose manhood is to be passed in the profession of arms see something of war in their childhood, or not?

Nay, it is certainly important for the purpose you describe.

Then it must be a fixed rule to make the children spectators of war, and also to contrive some plan for insuring their safety; and then all will be well, will it not?

It will.

Now, in the first place, will not their fathers be intelligent and sagacious judges, so far as men can be, as to what campaigns are likely to prove dangerous and what the reverse?

In all probability they will.

If so, they will carry their children to the latter, while they will be cautious about taking them to the former.

Rightly so.

And I presume they will set officers over them, not chosen for their worthlessness, but men qualified by experience and age to be their guides and tutors.

It is fit they should.

Still we must admit that many people have met with results contradicting their expectation.

Yes, very frequently.

Then to meet such emergencies, my dear friend, we must provide our children from the first with wings, to enable them, in case of necessity, to fly away and escape.

What do you mean?

We must put them on horseback at the earliest possible age, and when we have had them taught to ride, we must take them to see the fighting, mounted not on spirited animals or good chargers, but on horses selected for speed and docility. For by this plan they will obtain the best view of their future occupation, and at the same time will be most secure of making good their escape in case of need, following in the train of leaders of mature years.

I think your plan is the right one.

To come now to the rules of military service, I proceeded, on what footing are your soldiers to be, both among themselves and as regards the enemy? Tell me whether I am right in my views or not.

Let me know what they may be.

If one of the soldiers deserts his rank or throws away his arms, or is guilty of any such act of cowardice, must we not degrade him to the rank of an artisan or an agricultural labourer?

Decidedly.

And if a soldier falls alive into the hands of the enemy, ought we not to make a present of him to any one that will have him, to do what he pleases with his booty?

Yes, by all means.

But if a soldier highly distinguishes himself and gains himself credit, ought he not, think you, in the first place, while the army is still in the field, to be crowned with a garland by each of the youths and children in turn, among his comrades in arms?

Yes, I think so.

And shaken by the hand?

Yes, and shaken by the hand.

But I suppose you will hardly extend your approbation to my next proposition.

What is that?

That he should kiss and be kissed by them all.

Most certainly I do, and I would add to the law that during the continuance of the campaign no one whom he has a mind to kiss be permitted to refuse him the satisfaction, in order that if any soldier happens to entertain an admiration for either a male or a female comrade, he may be the more stimulated to carry off the meed of valour.

Good, I replied; and we have already said that a brave man will be allowed to enter into marriage-relations more frequently than others will, and to exercise more than the usual liberty of choice in such matters, so that as many children as possible may be obtained from a father of this character.

True, we did say so.

Again there are other honours with which, even according to Homer, it is just to reward those young men that distinguish themselves by good conduct. Homer says that Ajax, having won renown in the war, received by way of distinction 'whole chines of beef',[5] it being considered that an honour which, besides the glory of it, would augment his physical strength, was peculiarly appropriate to a brave man in the prime of his manhood.

A very just idea.

Then in this point at least we will follow the suggestion of Homer. We too, at our sacrificial feasts and all similar entertainments, will honour our meritorious soldiers according to the degree of merit they have displayed, not only with hymns and the privileges we have just stated, but also with 'goblets full to the brim, and meats and places of honour',[6] intending thereby not only to do honour to our brave men and women, but also to promote their training.

An excellent plan, he said.

Very good: and when there are any killed in a campaign, shall we not in the first place give out that those who fell with honour belong to the golden race?

Most assuredly we shall.

And shall we not believe in Hesiod's doctrine, that when any of this race die,

> They into spirits are changed, earth-haunting, beneficent, holy,
> Mighty to screen us from harm, and of speech-gifted men the
>   protectors?[7]

Yes, certainly we shall.

Shall we then inquire of the oracle how and with what distinctions we ought to inter men of superhuman and godlike mould, and then proceed to inter them in the manner and with the ceremonies that the oracle prescribes?

Of course we shall.

And for the future, shall we regard their sepulchres as those of superior beings, and pay them the due respect and worship? and shall we observe these same practices whenever any citizen who has been esteemed eminent for his bravery during his lifetime dies of old age or from any other cause?

Certainly it is but just to do so.

Again, what will be the conduct of our soldiers in dealing with their enemies?

In what respects?

In the first place, take the custom of making slaves. Does it seem just for Greeks to make slaves of the freemen of Grecian cities? Ought they not rather to do what they can to prevent the practice, and to introduce the custom of sparing their own race, from a prudent fear of being reduced to bondage by the barbarians?

The latter is the better course beyond all comparison.

Then it is better also not even to have Greek slaves in their possession, and to advise the other Greeks against the practice.

Decidedly so: their thoughts would then be more turned against the barbarians, and they would be less likely to molest one another.

Again, is it well to strip the slain, after a victory, of anything except their arms? Or does not the practice offer an excuse to cowards for not facing those who are still fighting, so long as they can pretend that they are in the way of their duty when they are stooping to rifle a dead body? And have not many armies before now been destroyed through this habit of pillaging?

No doubt of it.

And does it not seem a piece of ignoble avarice to plunder the dead, and is it not the sign of a womanish and petty mind to regard with hostile feelings the body of a dead man, when the real enemy has flown away, leaving only the instrument wherewith he fought? Are those who thus act any better, think you, than dogs which growl at the stones that have been thrown at them, but let the person who threw them alone?

No, not one bit better.

Then must we banish the practices of stripping the dead and interfering with the removal of the bodies?

Yes, we must indeed.

Neither, I presume, shall we carry the arms of our enemies to the temples, to dedicate them there, especially the arms of Greeks, if we care to cultivate a good understanding with the rest of the Greeks; on the contrary, we shall be fearful of desecrating a temple, if we carry to it such trophies won from our own brethren – that is to say, unless the god of the oracle shall pronounce a different judgment.

You are quite right.

Well, I continued, and how will your soldiers behave towards their enemies in the matter of ravaging the lands and burning the houses of Greeks?

I should like to hear your own opinion on the subject, he replied.

For my part, then, I confess I disapprove of both these practices, and should only allow the annual crop to be carried off. Would you like me to tell you my reasons?

I should.

It appears to me that as there are two names in use, war and sedition,[8] so there are two things representing two distinct kinds of disagreement. In the one case the parties are friends and relations, in the other aliens and foreigners. Now when hostility exists among the former, it is called sedition; when between strangers, it is called war.

There is nothing unreasonable in what you say.

Observe whether what I am going to add is equally reasonable: I affirm that all the members of the Greek race are brethren and kinsmen to one another, but aliens and foreigners to the barbarian world.

True.

Therefore when Greeks and barbarians fight together, we shall describe them as natural enemies warring against one another; and to this kind of hostility we shall give the name of war: but when Greeks are on this sort of footing with Greeks, we shall say that they are natural friends, but that in the case supposed Greece is in a morbid state of civil conflict; and to this kind of hostility we shall give the name of sedition.

I quite assent to this view.

Then bear in mind, I said, that in what is now confessedly called sedition, wherever this state of things arises and a city is divided, if each party ravage the lands and burn the houses of the other, the conflict is thought a sinful one, and both parties are looked upon as unpatriotic; for had they been patriotic, they would never have had the heart to mangle their nurse and mother. But it is thought that the victorious party cannot in fairness do more than carry off the crops of its adversaries, and ought to feel that they will one day be reconciled again, and not continue at war for ever.

Yes, he said, this feeling betokens a far more humanised condition than the other.

Very good; and is not the city you are founding to be a Grecian city?

It certainly should be.

Then will not its citizens be gentle and humane?

Certainly they will.

And will they not be patriotic Greeks, looking upon all Hellas as their own country, and sharing with their fellow-countrymen in the rites of a common religion?

Most certainly they will.

Thus regarding all the Greeks as their brethren, will they not look upon a quarrel with them in the light of a sedition, and refuse it the name of a war?

They will.

And therefore feel, throughout the quarrel, like persons who are presently to be reconciled?

Exactly so.

They will, therefore, correct them in a friendly spirit, and chastise them without any thought of enslaving or destroying them – simply as schoolmasters, not as enemies.

Just so.

Then being Greeks, they will not devastate Greece, nor burn houses, nor admit that all the men, women and children in a city are their foes, always confining this name to those few who were the authors of the quarrel. And on all these accounts they will refrain from laying waste the land or razing the houses, because the owners are in most cases their friends: and they will push the quarrel only thus far, till the innocent have done justice upon the guilty who plague them.

I readily admit, he said, that our citizens ought to adopt these rules in their conduct towards their adversaries; while I would have them behave to barbarians as the Greeks now behave to one another.

Then are we to add to our enactments a law forbidding our guardians either to ravage lands or set houses on fire?

Let us do so, he replied; and let us assume that both this and our former regulations are right.

But I really think, Socrates, he continued, that if you be permitted to go on in this way, you will never recollect what you put aside some time ago before you entered on all these questions, namely the task of showing that this constitution of things is possible, and how it might be realised. For in proof of the assertion that if it were realised, it would ensure all kinds of advantages to a city which was the seat of it, I can myself adduce facts which you have omitted, as that such soldiers would fight to perfection against their enemies, in consequence of the unwillingness to desert one another which would arise from their knowing one another as brothers, fathers or sons, and using these endearing names familiarly; and if the female sex were to serve in the army, whether in the same ranks with the men or posted as a reserve behind to strike terror into the enemy and render assistance at any point in case of need, I know that this would render them quite invincible: moreover, I see all the advantages, omitted by you, which they would enjoy at home. But as I fully admit the presence of all these merits and a thousand others in this constitution, if it were brought into existence, you need describe it no further. Rather let us try now to convince ourselves of this, that the thing *is* practicable, and *how* it is practicable, leaving all other questions to themselves.

What a sudden onslaught, I replied, you have made upon my argument! You have no compassion upon my uneasy loitering. Perhaps you do not know that after I have barely surmounted the first two waves, you are now bringing down upon me the third breaker, which is the most mountainous and formidable of the three; but when you have seen or rather heard it, you will think my conduct quite excusable, and you will allow that I had good reasons for hesitating and trembling to broach a theory so startling, and to undertake the investigation of it.

The more you talk in this strain, he said, the less likely shall we be to let you off from explaining how this constitution is possible. So proceed with your explanation, and let us have no more delay.

Well, then, I continued, in the first place we ought not to forget that we have been brought to this point by an inquiry into the nature of justice and injustice.

True: but what of that?

Why, nothing. But, if we find out what justice is, shall we expect the character of a just man not to differ in any point from that of justice itself, but to be its perfect counterpart? Or shall we be content provided he comes as near it as is possible, and partakes more largely of it than the rest of the world?

The latter – we shall be content.

Then the design of our investigations into the nature of justice in itself, and the character of the perfectly just man, as well as the possibility of his existence, and likewise into the nature of injustice and the character of the perfectly unjust man, was to use them as patterns, so that by looking upon the two men and observing how they stand in reference to happiness and its opposite, we might be compelled to admit in our own case that he who resembles them most closely in character will also have a lot most closely resembling theirs: but it was not our intention to demonstrate the possibility of these things in practice.

That is quite true, he said.

Do you think any the worse of the merits of an artist who has painted a beau ideal of human beauty, and has left nothing lacking in the picture, because he cannot prove that such a man as he has painted might possibly exist?

No, indeed, I do not.

Well, were not we likewise professing to construct in theory the pattern of a perfect state?

Yes, certainly.

Then will our theory suffer at all in your good opinion if we cannot prove that it is possible for a city to be organised in the manner proposed?

Certainly not.

This then is the true state of the case: but if for your gratification I am to exert myself also to show in what especial way and on what conditions our ideal might best be realised, I must ask you, with a view to this demonstration, to grant over again your former admissions.

Which do you mean?

In any case, can a theoretical sketch be perfectly realised in practice? Or is it a law of nature that performance can never hit the truth so closely as theory? Never mind if some think otherwise, but tell me whether you admit the fact or not.

I do admit it.

Then do not impose upon me the duty of exhibiting all our theory realised with precise accuracy in fact: but if we succeed in finding out how a state may be organised in very close accordance with our description, you must admit that we have discovered the possibility of realising the plan which you require me to consider. Shall you not be content if you gain thus much? For my own part I shall be.

So shall I.

Then our next step apparently must be to endeavour to search out and demonstrate what there is now amiss in the working of our states, preventing their being regulated in the manner described, and what is the smallest change that would enable a state to assume this form of constitution, confining ourselves, if possible, to a single change; if not, to two; or else to such as are fewest in number and least important in their influence.

Let us by all means endeavour so to do.

Well, I proceeded, there is one change by which, as I think we might show, the required revolution would be secured; but it is certainly neither a small nor an easy change, though it is a possible one.

What is it?

I am now on the point of confronting that very statement which we compared to the huge wave. Nevertheless it shall be spoken, even if it is to deluge me, literally like an exploding wave, with laughter and infamy. Pay attention to what I am going to say.

Say on, he replied.

Unless it happen either that philosophers acquire the kingly power in states, or that those who are now called kings and potentates be imbued with a sufficient measure of genuine philosophy – that is to say, unless political power and philosophy be united in the same person, most of those minds which at present pursue one to the exclusion of the other being peremptorily debarred from either – there will be no deliverance, my dear Glaucon, for cities, nor yet, I believe, for the human race; neither can the commonwealth which we have now sketched in theory, ever till then grow into a possibility, and see the light of day. But a consciousness how entirely this would contradict the common opinion made me all along so reluctant to give expression to it: for it is difficult to see that there is no other way by which happiness can be attained, by the state or by the individual.

Whereupon Glaucon remarked: The language and sentiments, Socrates, to which you have just given utterance are of such a nature that you may expect large numbers of by no means contemptible assailants to rush desperately upon you without a moment's delay, after throwing off their upper garments, as it were, and grasping, in that state, the first offensive weapon that comes in their way, to do signal execution upon you: so that if you fail to repel them with the weapons of argument, and make your escape, you will certainly suffer the penalty of being well jeered.

Well, I said, was it not you that brought all this upon me?

Yes and I did quite right. But I promise not to desert you: on the contrary, I will assist you with the weapons at my disposal, which are good-will and encouragement; and perhaps in my answers I may show more address than another. Therefore, relying on this assistance, endeavour to show to the incredulous that what you say is true.

I must make the attempt, I said, since you offer me such a valuable alliance. Now, if we are to have a chance of escaping from the assailants you speak of, I think it essential to give them our definition of 'philosophers', and show whom we mean when we venture to assert that such persons ought to govern; in order that, their character having been made thoroughly apparent, we may be able to defend ourselves by demonstrating that it is the natural province of these men to embrace philosophy, and take the lead in a state, and the province of all others to let philosophy alone, and follow the lead of the former.

Yes, it is a fit time, he said, to give this definition.

Come then, follow my steps, and let us try if we can in some way or other satisfactorily expound our notion.

Lead on.

Will it be necessary to remind you, or do you remember without it, that when we state that a man loves some object, we are bound to show if the statement be correct that he does not love one part of that object to the exclusion of another, but that he takes delight in the whole?

I require to be reminded, it seems: for I do not quite understand you.

Such a confession, Glaucon, would have been more appropriate in another person. A man of your amorous nature ought not to forget that a boy-loving, susceptible person is in some way or other attracted and excited by the charms of all who are in their bloom, and thinks they all deserve his attentions and addresses. Is not this the manner in which you behave to your favourites? You will praise a boy with a turned-up nose as having a winning look; the hooked nose of another you consider kinglike; while a third, whose nose is between the two extremes, has a beautifully-proportioned face: the dark, you say, have a manly look, the fair are children of the gods: and who do you suppose coined the phrase 'olive-pale' but a lover who could palliate and easily put up with paleness when he found it on the cheek of youth? In one word, you invent all kinds of excuses, and employ every variety of expression, sooner than reject any that are in the flower and prime of life.

If you wish, replied Glaucon, to found on my case an assertion that the amatively disposed thus act, I will allow you to do so for the argument's sake.

To take another illustration, do you not observe that those who are fond of wine behave in a precisely similar manner, finding some excuse or other to admire every sort of wine?

Yes, certainly.

And you doubtless have seen how persons who love honour will command a company, if they cannot lead an army, and in default of being honoured by great and important personages, are glad to receive the respect of the little and the insignificant; so covetous are they of honour in any shape.

Precisely so.

Then answer me yes or no to this: when we describe a man as having a longing for something, are we to assert that he longs after the whole class that the term includes, or only after one part to the exclusion of another?

He longs after the whole.

Then shall we not maintain that the philosopher, or the lover of wisdom, is one who longs for wisdom not partially, but wholly?

True.

So that if a person makes difficulties about his studies, especially while he is young and unable to discriminate between what is profitable and what is not, we shall pronounce him to be no lover of learning or of wisdom; just as when a man is nice about his eating, we deny that he is hungry or desirous of food, and instead of describing him as fond of eating, we call him a bad feeder.

Yes, and we shall be right in doing so.

On the other hand, when a man is ready and willing to taste every kind of knowledge, and addresses himself joyfully to his studies with an appetite which never can be satiated, we shall justly call such a person a philosopher, shall we not?

To which Glaucon replied, You will find your description includes a great number and a strange company. All the lovers of sights, I conclude, are philosophers, because they take pleasure in acquiring knowledge; and those who delight in hearing are a very singular set to reckon among philosophers — those, I mean, who will never, if they can help it, be present at a philosophical discussion, or any similar entertainment, but are unfailing attendants at every Dionysian festival, whether held in town or country, and run about as if they had let out their ears on hire to listen to all the choruses of the season. Are we then to give the title of philosophers to all these people, as well as to others who have a taste for any similar studies, and to the professors of small arts?

Certainly not, I replied: we must call them counterfeit philosophers.

And whom, he asked, do you call genuine philosophers?

Those who love to see truth, I answered.

In that, he said, you cannot be wrong: but will you explain what you mean?

That would be not at all easy, with a different questioner: but you, I imagine, will make me the admission I require.

What is it?

That since beauty is the opposite of deformity, they are two things.

Of course they are.

Then since they are two, each of them taken separately is one thing.

That also is true.

The same thing may be said likewise of justice and injustice, good and evil, and all general conceptions. Each of them in itself is one thing, but by the intermixture with actions and bodies and with one another, through which they are everywhere made visible, each appears to be many things.

You are right.

By the help of this principle, then, I draw a distinction between those whom you described just now as lovers of sights, lovers of arts, and practical persons, on the one hand, and on the other, those about whom we are now inquiring, to whom alone we can rightly give the name of philosophers.

Explain what you mean.

Why, I suppose that those who love seeing and hearing admire beautiful sounds and colours and forms, and all artistic products into which these enter; but the nature of beauty in itself their understanding is unable to behold and embrace.

Yes, it certainly is as you say.

But those who are capable of reaching to the independent contemplation of abstract beauty will be rare exceptions, will they not?

They will indeed.

Therefore if a man recognises the existence of beautiful things, but disbelieves in abstract beauty, and has not the power to follow should another lead the way to the knowledge of it, is his life, think you, a dreaming or a waking one? Just consider. Is it not dreaming when a person, whether asleep or awake, mistakes the likeness of anything for the real thing of which it is a likeness?

I confess I should say that a person in that predicament was dreaming.

Take again the opposite case, of one who acknowledges an abstract beauty, and has the power to discern both this essence and the objects into which it enters, and who never mistakes such objects for the essence, nor the essence for the objects; does such a person, think you, live a dreaming or a waking life?

A waking life, undoubtedly.

If so, shall we not be right in calling the mental process of the latter knowledge, because he really knows, and that of the former opinion, because he merely opines?

Yes, perfectly right.

Well then, should this person, whom we describe as opining but not knowing, grow wroth with us, and contend that what we say is not true, shall we be able to appease his indignation and gently convince him, disguising from him the fact that he is in an unsound state?

That were certainly desirable.

Come then, consider what we are to say to him. Would you like us to make certain inquiries of him, premising that if he really does know anything, we shall not in the least grudge him his knowledge? On the contrary, we shall be truly glad to find that it is so. But answer us this question, we shall say: When a man knows, does he know something or nothing? Be so good, Glaucon, as to make answer in his behalf.

My answer will be that he knows something.

Something that exists, or does not exist?

Something that exists: for how could a thing that does not exist be known?

Are we then quite sure of this fact, in whatever variety of ways we might examine it, that what completely exists may be completely known, whereas that which has no existence at all must be wholly unknown?

We are perfectly sure of it.

Good: now, if there be anything so constituted as at the same time to be and not to be, must it not lie somewhere between the purely existent and the absolutely nonexistent?

It must.

Well then, as knowledge is correlative to the existent, and the negation of knowledge necessarily to the non-existent, must we not try to find something intermediate between science and ignorance, if there is anything of the kind, to correspond to this that is intermediate between the existent and the non-existent?

Yes, by all means.

Do we speak of opinion as a something?

Undoubtedly we do.

Do we consider it a faculty distinct from science or identical with it?

Distinct from it.

Therefore opinion is appointed to one province and science to another, each acting according to its own peculiar power

Just so.

Is it not the nature of science, as correlative to the existent, to know how the existent exists? But first there is a distinction which I think it necessary to establish.

What is that?

We shall hold that faculties, as a certain general class, are the things whereby we, and every other thing, are able to do whatever we can do – for example, I call sight and hearing faculties, if you happen to understand the special conception which I wish to describe.

I do understand it.

Then let me tell you what view I take of them. In a faculty I do not see either colour, or form, or any of those qualities that I observe in many other things, by regarding which I can in many cases distinguish to myself between one thing and another. No, in a faculty I look only to its province and its function, and thus I am led to call it in each case by this name, pronouncing those faculties to be identical whose provinces and functions are identical, and those diverse whose provinces and functions are diverse. But pray, how do you proceed?

Just in the same way.

Now then, return with me, my excellent friend. Under what general term do you class science? Do you make it a faculty?

Yes I do; it is of all the faculties the most powerful.

Well, is opinion a faculty; or are we to refer it to some other denomination?

Not to any other: for that whereby we are able to opine can only be opinion.

Well, but a little while ago you admitted that science and opinion are not identical.

Why, how could a sensible man identify the fallible with the infallible?

Very good: so we are clearly agreed that opinion is a thing distinct from science?

It is.

If so, each of them has by its nature a different province and a different efficacy.

The inference is inevitable.

Science, I believe, has for its province to know the nature of the existent.

Yes.

And the province of opinion is, we say, to opine.

Yes.

Does opinion take cognisance of precisely that material which science knows? In other words, is the object-matter of opinion identical with that of science? Or is that impossible?

It is impossible, after the admissions we have made; that is, if it be granted that different faculties have different provinces, and that both opinion and science are faculties, and that the two are distinct – all which we affirm. These premises make it impossible to identify the object-matter of science and that of opinion.

Then if the existent is the object-matter of knowledge, that of opnion must be something other than the existent?

It must.

Well then, does opinion exercise itself upon the non-existent, or is it impossible to apprehend even in opinion that which does not exist? Consider – does not the person opining carry his thought towards something? Or is it possible to have an opinion, but an opinion about nothing?

It is impossible.

Then the person who opines has an opinion about some one thing?

Yes.

Well, but the non-existent could not be called some one thing; it might, on the contrary, with the greatest truth be styled nothing.

Just so.

But to the non-existent we were constrained to assign ignorance, and to the existent, knowledge.

And rightly.

Then neither the existent nor the non-existent is the object of opinion?

No.

Therefore opinion cannot be either ignorance or knowledge.

Apparently not.

Then does it lie beyond either of these, so as to surpass either knowledge in certainty or ignorance in uncertainty?

It does neither.

Then tell me, do you look upon opinion as something more dusky than knowledge, more luminous than ignorance?

Yes, it is strongly so distinguished from either.

And does it lie within these extremes?

Yes.

Then opinion must be something between the two.

Precisely so.

Now a little while back, did we not say that if anything could be found so constituted as at the same time to be and not to be, it must lie between the purely existent and the absolutely not existent, and must be the object neither of science nor yet of ignorance, but of a third faculty, which should be similarly discovered in the interval between science and ignorance?

We did.

But now we have discovered between these two a faculty which we call opinion.

We have.

It will remain then for us, apparently, to find what that is which partakes both of being and of not being, and which cannot be rightly said to be either of these absolutely; in order that, should it discover itself to us, we may justly proclaim it to be the object of opinion, thus assigning extremes to extremes, and means to means. Am I not right?

You are.

These positions then being laid down, I shall proceed to interrogate that worthy man who denies the existence of anything absolutely beautiful, or any form of abstract beauty, which forever continues the same and unchangeable, though he acknowledges a variety of beautiful objects – that lover of sights who cannot endure to be told that beauty is one, and justice one, and so on of the rest – My good sir, I shall say, of all these beautiful things, is there one which may not appear ugly? Of all these just things, is there one which may not appear unjust? Or of these holy things, one which may not appear unholy?

No, answered Glaucon: they must inevitably appear in a certain sense both fair and foul, both just and unjust, both holy and unholy.

Again, may not the many double things be considered halves just as well as doubles?

Just as well.

In the same way, have the things which we describe as great, small, light, heavy, any better claim to these titles than to their opposites?

No, they will always be equally entitled to either.

Would it be more correct, then, to predicate of those many objects, that each of them is, or is not, that which it is said to be?

You remind me of the conundrums with a contradiction in them, that are proposed at table, and of the children's riddle[9] about the eunuch who threw at the bat, hinting darkly with what he hit it, and on what it sat: for the things in question have the same ambiguous character, and one cannot positively conceive of them as either being or not being, or as both being and not being, or as neither.

Can you tell then, said I, what to do with them, or where they may be better put than in the interspace between being and not being? For I presume they will not appear either darker than the non-existent, and so more non-existent, or more luminous than the existent, and therefore more existent.

You are perfectly right.

Hence we have discovered, apparently, that the mass of notions, current among the mass of men, about beauty, justice and the rest, roam about between the confines of pure existence and pure non-existence.

We have.

And we before admitted that if anything of this kind should be brought to light, it ought to be described as the object of opinion, and not of knowledge – these intermediate rovers being caught by the intermediate faculty.

We did make this admission.

Therefore, when people have an eye for a multitude of beautiful objects, but can neither see beauty in itself, nor follow those who would lead them to it – when they behold a number of just things, but not justice in itself, and so in every instance, we shall say they have in every case an opinion, but no real knowledge of the things about which they opine.

It is a necessary inference.

But what, on the other hand, must we say of those who contemplate things as they are in themselves, and as they exist ever permanent and immutable? Shall we not speak of them as knowing, not opining?

That also is a necessary inference.

Then shall we not assert that such persons admire and love the objects of knowledge – the others, the objects of opinion? For we have not forgotten, have we, that we spoke of these latter as loving and looking upon beautiful sounds and colours and the like, while they will not hear of the existence of an abstract beauty?

We have not forgotten it.

Shall we commit any fault then, if we call these people philodoxical rather than philosophical, that is to say, lovers of opinion rather than lovers of wisdom? And will they be very much offended with us for telling them so?

No, not if they will take my advice: for it is wrong to be offended with the truth.

Those therefore that set their affections on that which in each case really exists, we must call not philodoxical, but philosophical?

Yes, by all means.

NOTES TO BOOK FIVE

1 χρυσοχοήσοντας. This passage has been explained by all previous commentators to signify, 'Have we come here to be disappointed in our expectations?' χρυσοχοεῖν, literally, 'to smelt gold', being taken to mean 'to embark in a bubble speculation'. But χρυσοχοεῖν, in its proverbial sense, appears to have meant 'to do anything rather than the matter in hand'. This may be gathered from a passage in the orator Deinarchus: 'He learnt under the instruction of Aeschines to smelt gold, and not to do or suffer what was set before him.' It would be useless to speculate as to what accident brought χρυσοχοεῖν into vogue in this sense, rather than any other word: but the reader will observe that an impetuous and strongly-coloured remark of this kind is put with ethical propriety into the mouth of Thrasymachus.

2 In allusion, probably, to the famous story of Arion; Herodotus i, 24.

3 The original is given by Stobaeus as a quotation from Pindar.

4 *Works and Days* 40.

5 *Iliad* vii, 321.

6 *Iliad* viii, 162.

7 *Works and Days* 121.

8 The word στάσις, here translated 'sedition', was the familiar term for the party warfare, generally between an aristocratic and a democratic faction, which raged with extreme violence in most Greek states. The reader is requested to understand the word 'sedition' in the sense of civil conflict, or the antagonism of domestic factions.

9 The riddle is thus given by the scholiast: 'A tale is told that a man and not a man, seeing and not seeing a bird and not a bird, seated on wood and not on wood, hit it and did not hit it with a stone and not a stone.' It is partly explained in the text, and we leave the further solution of it to the reader.

BOOK SIX

Thus, Glaucon, I said, after pursuing a lengthened inquiry we have not without difficulty discovered who are true philosophers and who are not.

Yes, he replied; probably it was not easy to abridge the inquiry.

Apparently not, I said. However that may be, I think, for my part, that the result would have been brought out still more clearly if we had to speak of this only, without discussing the many points that still await our notice if we wish to ascertain wherein the superiority of a righteous over an unrighteous life consists.

Then what are we to do next?

We have only to take the step next in order. Since those who are able to apprehend the eternal and immutable are philosophers, while those who are incapable of this and who wander in the region of change and multiformity are not philosophers, which of the two, tell me, ought to be governors of a state?

What must I reply, if I am to do justice to the question?

Ask yourself which of the two are to be thought capable of guarding the laws and customs of states, and let these be appointed guardians.

You are right.

Can there be any question as to whether a blind man or one with quick sight is the right person to guard and keep any thing?

There can be no question about it.

Then do you think that there is a particle of difference between the condition of blind persons and the state of those who are absolutely destitute of the knowledge of things as they really are, and who possess in their soul no distinct exemplar, and cannot, like painters, fix their eyes on perfect truth as a perpetual standard of reference, to be contemplated with the minutest care before they proceed to deal with earthly canons about things beautiful and just and good, laying them down where they are required, and where they already exist watching over their preservation?

No, indeed there is not much difference.

Shall we then appoint such persons to the office of guardians, in preference to those who not only have gained a knowledge of each thing in its reality, but in practical skill are not inferior to the former, and come behind them in no other department of excellence?

Why, if these latter are not wanting in the other qualifications, it would be perfectly absurd to choose any others. For just the point in which they are superior may be said to be the most important of all.

Then shall we proceed to explain how the same persons will be enabled to possess both qualifications?

By all means.

If so, we must begin by gaining a thorough insight into their proper character, as we said at the outset of this discussion. And I think, if we agree tolerably on that point, we shall also agree that the two qualifications may be united in the same persons, and that such characters, and no others, are the proper governors of states.

How so?

With regard to the philosophic nature, let us take for granted that its possessors are ever enamoured of all learning that will reveal to them somewhat of that real and permanent existence which is exempt from the vicissitudes of generation and decay.

Let it be granted.

Again, I said, let us also assume that they are enamoured of the whole of that real existence, and willingly resign no part of it, be it small or great, honoured or slighted; as we showed on a previous occasion in speaking of the ambitious and the amorous.

You are right.

Now then proceed to consider whether we ought not to find a third feature in the character of those who are to realise our description.

What feature do you mean?

I mean truthfulness; that is, a determination never to admit false-hood in any shape, if it can be helped, but to abhor it, and love the truth.

Yes, it is probable we shall find it.

Nay, my friend! It is not only probable, but absolutely inevitable, that one who is by nature prone to any passion should be well pleased with everything that is bound by the closest ties to the beloved object.

True, he said.

And can you find any thing allied to wisdom more closely than truth?

Certainly not.

And is it possible for the same nature to love wisdom, and at the same time love falsehood?

Unquestionably it is not.

Consequently, the genuine lover of knowledge must, from his youth up, strive intensely after all truth.

Yes, he must thoroughly.

Well, but we cannot doubt that when a person's desires set strongly in one direction, they run with corresponding feebleness in every other channel, like a stream whose waters have been diverted into another bed.

Undoubtedly they do.

So that when the current has set towards science and all its branches, a man's desires will, I fancy, hover around pleasures that are purely mental, abandoning those in which the body is instrumental – provided that the man's love of wisdom is real, not artificial.

It cannot be otherwise.

Again, such a person will be temperate and thoroughly uncovetous: for he is the last person in the world to value those objects which make men anxious for money at any cost.

True.

Once more, there is another point which you ought to take into consideration when you are endeavouring to distinguish a philosophic from an unphilosophic character.

What is that?

You must take care not to overlook any taint of meanness. For surely little-mindedness thwarts above everything the soul that is destined ever to aspire to grasp truth, both divine and human, in its integrity and universality.

That is most true.

And do you think that a spirit full of lofty thoughts, and privileged to contemplate all time and all existence, can possibly attach any great importance to this life?

No, it is impossible.

Then such a person will not regard death as a formidable thing, will he?

Certainly not.

So that a mean and cowardly character can have no part, as it seems, in true philosophy.

I think it cannot.

What then? Can the man whose mind is well-regulated, and free from covetousness, meanness, pretentiousness and cowardice, be by any possibility hard to deal with or unjust?

No, it is impossible.

Therefore, when you are noticing the indications of a philosophical or unphilosophical temper, you must also observe in early youth whether the mind is just and gentle, or unsociable and fierce.

Quite so.

There is still another point which I think you must certainly not omit.

What is that?

Whether the mind in question is quick or slow at learning. For you can never expect a person to take a decent delight in an occupation which he goes through with pain, and in which he makes small progress with great exertion?

No, it would be impossible.

Again, if he can remember nothing of what he has learned, can he fail, being thus full of forgetfulness, to be void of knowledge?

No, he cannot.

Then will not his fruitless toil, think you, compel him at last to hate both himself and such employment?

Doubtless it will.

Let us never, then, admit a forgetful mind into the ranks of those that are counted worthy of philosophy, but let us look out for a good memory as a requisite for such admission.

Yes, by all means.

Again, we should certainly say that the tendency of an unrefined and awkward nature is wholly towards disproportion.

Certainly.

And do you think that truth is akin to disproportion, or to proportion?

To proportion.

In addition, then, to our other acquirements, let us search for a mind naturally well-proportioned and graceful, whose native instincts will permit it to be easily led to apprehend the forms of things as they really are.

By all means.

What then? Do you think that the qualities which we have enumerated are in any way unnecessary or inconsistent with one another, provided the soul is to attain unto full and satisfactory possession of real existence?

On the contrary, they are most strictly necessary.

Then can you find any fault with an employment which requires of a man who would pursue it satisfactorily that nature shall have given him a retentive memory, and made him quick at learning, lofty-minded and graceful, the friend and brother of truth, justice, fortitude and temperance?

No, he replied; the very genius of criticism could find no fault with such an employment.

Well, can you hesitate to entrust such characters with the sole management of state affairs, when time and education have made them ripe for the task?

Here Adeimantus interposed and said; It is true, Socrates, that no one can dispute these conclusions; but still, every time that such theories are propounded by you, the hearers feel certain misgivings of the following kind. They fancy that, from want of practice in your method of question and answer, they are at each question led a little astray by the reasoning, until at the close of the discussion these little divergences are found to amount to a serious false step, which makes them contradict their original notions. And as unskilful draught-players are in the end hemmed into a corner by the skilful, till they cannot make a move, just in the same way your hearers conceive themselves to be at last hemmed in and reduced to silence by this novel kind of draughts played with words instead of counters. For they are not at all the more convinced that the conclusion to which they are brought is the true one. And in saying this, I have the present occasion before my eye. For at this moment a person will tell you that though at each question he cannot oppose you with words, yet in practice he sees that all the students of philosophy who have devoted themselves to it for any length of time, instead of taking it up for educational purposes and relinquishing it while still young, in most cases become exceedingly eccentric, not to say quite depraved,

while even those who appear the most respectable are notwithstanding so far the worse for the pursuit which you commend that they
become useless to their country.

When he had said this, I replied; Then do you think this objection
untrue?

I am not sure, he answered, but I should be glad to hear what you
think of it.

Let me tell you that I hold it to be a true objection.

How then can it be right to assert that the miseries of our cities will
find no relief until those philosophers who on our own admission are
useless to them, become their rulers?

You are asking a question, I replied, which I must answer by the
help of an illustration.

And you, I suppose, have not been in the habit of employing
illustrations.

Ah! You rally me, do you, now that you have got me upon a
subject in which demonstration is so difficult? However, listen to the
illustration, that you may see still better how stingy I am with the
work. So cruel is the position in which those respectable men are
placed, in reference to their states, that there is no single thing whose
position is analogous to theirs. Consequently I have to collect
materials from several quarters for the imaginary case which I am to
use in their defence, like painters when they paint goat-stags and
similar monsters.

Figure to yourself a fleet, or a single ship, in which the state of
affairs on board is as follows. The captain, you are to suppose, is
taller and stronger than any of the crew, but rather deaf and rather
short-sighted, and correspondingly deficient in nautical skill; and the
sailors are quarrelling together about the pilotage – each of them
thinking he has a right to steer the vessel, although up to that
moment he has never studied the art, and cannot name his
instructor, or the time when he served his apprenticeship; more than
this, they assert that it is a thing which positively cannot be taught,
and are even ready to tear in pieces the person who affirms that it
can: meanwhile they crowd incessantly round the person of the
captain, begging and beseeching him with every importunity to
entrust the helm to them, and occasionally, failing to persuade him,
while others succeed better, these disappointed candidates kill their
successful rivals or fling them overboard, and after binding the high-

spirited captain hand and foot with mandragora or strong drink, or disabling him by some other contrivance, they remain masters of the ship, and apply its contents to their own purposes, and pass their time at sea in drinking and feasting, as you might expect with such a crew; and besides all this, they compliment with the title of 'able seaman', 'excellent pilot', 'skilful navigator', any sailor that can second them cleverly in either persuading or forcing the captain into installing them in command of the ship, while they condemn as useless every one whose talents are of a different order – having no notion that the true pilot must devote his attention to the year and its seasons, to the sky and the stars and the winds, and all that concerns his art, if he intends to be really fit to command a ship; and thinking it impossible to acquire and practise, along with the pilot's art, the art of maintaining the pilot's authority whether some of the crew like it or not. Such being the state of things on board, do you not think that the pilot who is really master of his craft is sure to be called a useless, star-gazing babbler by the mariners who form the crews of ships so circumstanced?

Yes, that he will, replied Adeimantus.

Well, said I, I suppose you do not require to see my illustration passed in review, to remind you that it is a true picture of our cities in so far as their disposition towards philosophers is concerned; on the contrary, I think you understand my meaning.

Yes, quite.

That being the case, when a person expresses his astonishment that philosophers are not respected in our cities, begin by telling him our illustration, and endeavour to persuade him that it would be far more astonishing if they were respected.

Well, I will.

And go on to tell him that he is right in saying that the most respectable of the proficients in philosophy are of no use to the world; only recommend him to lay the fault of it not on these good people themselves, but upon those who decline their services. For it is not in the nature of things that a pilot should petition the sailors to submit to his authority, or that the wise should wait at the rich man's door. No, the author of that witticism was wrong: for the real truth is that just as a sick man, be he rich or poor, must attend at the physician's door, so all who require to be governed must attend at the gate of him who is able to govern – it being against nature that the ruler, supposing him to be really good for anything, should have to entreat his subjects to submit to his rule. In fact you will not be wrong if you compare the statesmen of our time to the sailors whom we were just now describing, and the useless visionary talkers, as they are called by our politicians, to the veritable pilots.

You are perfectly right.

Under these circumstances, and amongst men like these, it is not easy for that noblest of occupations to be in good repute with those to whose pursuits it is directly opposed. But far the most grievous and most obstinate misconstruction under which philosophy labours, is due to her professed followers, who are doubtless the persons meant by the accuser of philosophy, when he declares, as you tell us, that most of those who approach her are utterly depraved, while even her best pupils are useless – to the truth of which remark I assented, did I not?

Yes, you did.

We have explained the reason why the good are useless, have we not?

Certainly we have.

Would you have us proceed next to discuss the question why the majority are inevitably depraved, and to endeavour to show, if we can, that of this also philosophy is guiltless?

Yes, by all means.

Let us then speak and listen alternately, recurring to the point where we were describing what ought to be the natural character of one who is to turn out a perfectly accomplished and virtuous man. The first and leading feature in such a person's character was, if you recollect, truth, which he was bound to pursue with the most absolute devotion, at the risk, should he be found an impostor, of being denied all share in true philosophy.

Yes, we said so.

Well, does not this point, for one, run strongly counter to the received opinion upon the subject?

Certainly it does.

Then shall we not be making a reasonably good defence if we say that the natural tendency of the real lover of knowledge is to strain every nerve to reach real existence; and that far from resting at those multitudinous particular phenomena whose existence falls within the region of opinion, he presses on undiscouraged, and desists not from his passion till he has apprehended the nature of each thing as it really is with that part of his soul whose property it is to lay hold of such objects, in virtue of its affinity to them; and that having, by means of this, verily approached and held intercourse with that which verily exists, he begets[1] wisdom and truth; so that then, and not till then, he knows, enjoys true life and receives true nourishment, and is at length released from his travail-pangs?

The defence will be the best possible, he replied.

Well, will such a person be tinged with any love of falsehood? Will he not, on the contrary, be imbued with a positive hatred of it?

He will.

Now, if truth leads the way, we can never admit that a train of evils follows her steps.

Certainly not.

On the contrary, we shall assert that she is attended by a sound and just disposition, followed in its turn by sobriety.

True.

And surely we need not repeat our demonstrations, and marshal over again the remaining retinue of the philosophic character. For we found, as you doubtless remember, that the natural accompaniments of the preceding are manliness, loftiness of spirit, a quick apprehension and a good memory. Upon this you objected that though everyone will be compelled to assent to our conclusions, still when one comes to drop the argument and turn his eyes simply to the persons who are the subjects of it, he will assert his conviction that a few are merely useless, the majority totally depraved. We therefore inquired into the grounds of this prejudice, and have now arrived at the question, why are the majority depraved? And this was the reason why we took up again the character of the real philosophers, and found ourselves compelled to define it.

True.

We must therefore study the pernicious influences which destroy this character in many persons, and from which only a few escape, who, you tell me, are styled useless, though not depraved. And then we must take into consideration the natures which imitate the truly philosophical, and settle down into the same pursuits, showing what they are mentally, and how they enter upon a profession which is too good and too high for them, and commit such a variety of blunders that they have everywhere and with all the world attached to philosophy the reputation you describe.

But what, he asked, are the pernicious influences to which you refer?

I will try to describe them to you, if I can. Every one will agree with us in this, I think, that such a character, possessing all those qualities which we assigned to it just now as essential to a full capacity for philosophy, is of rare and uncommon growth amongst men. Or do you think otherwise?

No, indeed I do not.

Then consider how many fatal dangers beset these rare characters.

Pray, what are they?

The thing which sounds most marvellous is this, that every one of the qualities commended by us has a tendency to vitiate and distract from philosophy the soul which possesses it. I allude to manliness, temperance, and all the characteristics which we have discussed.

It does sound strange.

And then, in addition to this, all the reputed advantages of beauty, wealth, strength of body, powerful connections in a state, and all their accompaniments, exercise a corrupting and a distracting influence. Now I have given you an outline of my meaning.

You have; and I shall be glad to learn it more in detail.

Only grasp it as a whole aright, and it will present itself to you in a clear light, and my previous remarks will not appear so strange.

What do you tell me to do?

In the case of all seeds, and of everything that grows, whether vegetable or animal, we know that whatever fails to find its appropriate nourishment, season, and soil will lack its proper virtues – the more in proportion as it is more vigorous. For evil is, I presume, more opposed to what is good than to what is not good.

Certainly.

Hence I think we may reasonably conclude that the finest natures get more harm than those of an inferior sort, when exposed to an ungenial nutriment.

Yes, we may.

Then may we not assert, Adeimantus, that minds naturally of the highest order do in like manner, if they happen to be ill-trained, become peculiarly wicked? Or do you think that great crimes and unalloyed depravity spring not, as I suppose, from a splendid character ruined by improper treatment, but from a worthless one;

and that a feeble nature will ever produce anything great, whether good or evil?

No, I think with you.

Well then, the nature which we appropriated to the philosopher must, I think, provided it meets with proper instruction, grow and attain to all excellence, but if it be sown, planted, and nourished on an ungenial soil, it is sure to run into the very opposite vices, unless some deity should providentially interpose. Or do you hold, with the multitude, that there are certain individuals corrupted by sophists in their youth, and certain individual sophists who corrupt in a private capacity to any considerable extent? Do you not rather think that those who hold this language are themselves the greatest of sophists, training most elaborately, and finishing to their own liking, both young and old, men and women?

Pray, when?

Whenever they crowd to the popular assembly, the law-courts, the theatres, the camp, or any other public gathering of large bodies, and there sit in a dense and uproarious mass to censure some of the things said or done, and applaud others, always in excess; shouting and clapping till in addition to their own noise, the rocks and the place wherein they are echo back redoubled the uproar of their censure and applause. At such a moment, how is a young man, think you, to retain his self-possession? Can any private education that he has received hold out against such a torrent of censure and applause, and avoid being swept away down the stream, wherever it may lead, until he is brought to adopt the language of these men as to what is honourable and dishonourable, and to imitate all their practices, and to become their very counterpart?

It is the sure consequence, Socrates.

However, I proceeded, we have not yet mentioned the surest influence at work.

What is that? he asked.

It is one which these schoolmasters and sophists bring into actual practice, if their words fail of success. For you cannot be ignorant that they chastise the disobedient with disfranchisement and fines and death.

They do, most decidedly.

Then what other sophist, think you, or what private instructions of an opposite tenor, can prevail over these influences?

None can, I imagine.

No, they cannot, I said; nay, the very attempt would be mere folly. For there is not, has not been, and indeed there never can be, a character that will regard virtue with different feelings, if trained in close contact with the education which popular assemblies impart. I am speaking humanly, my friend; for by all means let us except Providence, as the proverb says. For you may be well assured, that you will not be wrong in asserting that whatever has been preserved, and made what it ought to be, while the constitution of states is what it is, has been preserved by a divine interposition.

I am quite of that opinion.

Then I would further have you add the following to the list of your opinions.

What is it?

That all those mercenary adventurers who, as we know, are called sophists by the multitude, and regarded as rivals, really teach nothing but the opinions of the majority to which expression is given when large masses are collected, and dignify them with the title of wisdom. As well might a person investigate the caprices and desires of some huge and powerful monster in his keeping, studying how it is to be approached and how handled – at what times and under what circumstances it becomes most dangerous or most gentle, on what occasions it is in the habit of uttering its various cries, and further, what sounds uttered by another person soothe or exasperate it – and when he has mastered all these particulars by long continued intercourse, as well might he call his results wisdom, systematise them into an art, and open a school, though in reality he is wholly ignorant which of these humours and desires is fair and which foul, which good and which evil, which just and which unjust; and therefore is content to affix all these names to the fancies of the huge animal, calling what it likes good, and what it dislikes evil, without being able to render any other account of them – nay, giving the titles of 'just' and 'fair' to things done under compulsion, because he has not discerned himself, and therefore cannot point out to others, that wide distinction which really holds between the nature of the compulsory and the good. Tell me, in heaven's name, do you not think that such a person would make a strange instructor?

Yes, I do think so.

And do you think that there is any difference between such a person and the man who makes wisdom consist in having studied the whim and pleasures of the assembled many-headed multitude, whether in painting, or in music, or finally in politics? For though it be true, that if a man mix with the many, and ask their judgment on some poem or other work of art, or service rendered to the state, thus putting himself in their power further than he is obliged, he finds himself[2] irresistibly compelled to do whatever they command; yet tell me if you have ever in your life heard any one of them offer an argument which was not ridiculous, to prove that what the multitude commands is really good and fair?

No, and I think I never shall.

Then if you have laid all this to heart, let me remind you of another point: will it be possible for the multitude to tolerate or believe in the existence of an essential beauty, as opposed to the multiplicity of beautiful objects; or in the existence of any essential form, as opposed to the variety of its particular manifestations?

Certainly not.

Then the multitude cannot be philosophical.

It cannot.

And consequently the professors of philosophy are sure to be condemned by it.

They are.

And of course by those private adventurers who associate with the mob, and desire to please it.

Clearly.

Such being the case, what salvation do you see for a philosophic character that will enable it to persist in its vocation till it has reached the goal? Take our previous conclusions into your consideration; we agreed, you know, that a quick apprehension, a good memory, a manly and a lofty spirit, are qualities of the philosophic character.

Yes, we did.

Then will not such a person from his childhood be first in everything; especially if his bodily are equal to his mental endowments?

To be sure he will.

Then I fancy his friends and fellow-citizens will wish, when he grows older, to use him for their own purposes.

Doubtless.

Consequently they will fall down at his feet with prayers and compliments, securing and flattering by anticipation his future power.

Yes, it is certainly a common case.

Then how do you expect such a person to behave under these circumstances – above all if he happen to be a rich and high-born member of a powerful state, and of a tall and goodly presence besides? Will he not be full of extravagant hopes, and conceive himself competent to direct the affairs of Greeks and foreigners, and make that an excuse for giving himself lofty airs, till he is swollen with self-importance and empty senseless conceit?

Undoubtedly he will.

While he is in this frame of mind, suppose someone approaches him gently, and tells him – what is quite true – that there is no real wisdom in him, and that he stands in need of it, and that without slaving for its acquisition it cannot be gained; do you think it an easy matter to gain his attention in the midst of such evil influences?

No, it is very far from easy.

If, however, I continued, thanks to an excellent nature and an inborn taste for philosophic inquiry, one such individual shall haply take heed, and allow himself to be bent and drawn towards philosophy, what do we think will be the behaviour of those who count upon losing his services and his companionship? Will they leave a word unsaid, or a deed undone, that can possibly prevent the pupil from yielding, or the master from succeeding in his persuasions – calling in private machinations and public prosecutions?

Of course that is what they will do, he replied.

Will it be possible, then, for such a person to be a student of philosophy?

Certainly not.

Thus you see, do you not, how right we were in saying that in fact the very ingredients of the philosophic character, when subjected to an injurious treatment, are in a manner the causes of a man's falling away from the pursuit of philosophy; to which result the reputed advantages of wealth, and all outward pomp and state, likewise contribute.

Yes, indeed, it was a true observation.

This, then, my excellent friend, is the ruin, such and so grievous is the corruption, of the finest character with reference to the noblest pursuit – a character too which is, besides, rarely to be met with, as we affirm. And in the ranks of this class, beyond a doubt, are to be found both those men who inflict the greatest injury on states and individuals, and also those who labour for their good, when the tide turns that way: whereas a little mind never influences in any great degree either individuals or states.

That is very true.

Thus it comes to pass that those who, as her nearest relatives, are most bound to espouse philosophy, fall away, and leave her desolate and inconsummate, and while for their part they live a life unsuited to them and unreal, philosophy, bereft as it were of relatives, is exposed to the advances of a different class of persons unworthy of her, who bring her to shame and fasten on her those reproaches with which you tell me she is loaded, to the effect that her associates are either worth nothing, or, as in the majority of cases, deserving of heavy punishment.

Why, certainly that is the common remark.

Yes, I said, and a natural remark. For other puny men, seeing this field open, albeit rich in grand names and showy titles, are only too thankful to desert their trades and rush into philosophy, like criminals who break out of prison and run for refuge to a temple, whenever they happen to show remarkable address in their own despicable profession. For though all this is come upon philosophy, nevertheless the rank and splendour which she still retains far transcend those of any other profession; and these are coveted by many whose natural talents were defective from the first, and whose souls have since been so grievously marred and enervated by their life of drudgery, as their bodies have been disfigured by their trades and crafts. Must not that be the case?

Certainly it must.

And does their appearance strike you as much better than that of a little bald-headed tinker who has made some money, has had his chains just knocked off, has been washed in a bath, dressed out in a new coat and got up as a bridegroom, in which character, owing to his master's poverty and destitution, he is on the point of marrying his daughter?

I see no difference at all between the two cases.

Then what may we expect the issue of such a match to be like? Will it not be a baseborn and worthless progeny?

It cannot be otherwise.

Well, and when those who are all unworthy of instruction draw near and hold intercourse with her beyond their deserts, how must we describe the character of those notions and opinions which are the issue of such a connection? May they not be called, with the utmost propriety, sophisms – a spurious brood without one trace of genuine insight?

Yes, precisely so.

Hence, Adeimantus, I continued, those who worthily associate with philosophy form a very small remainder, made up, I conceive, either of noble and well-trained characters condemned to exile, who in the absence of all pernicious influences have been true to their nature, and continued steadfast to philosophy; or of some large-minded men, bred in petty states, who have looked down with contempt upon the politics of their country. Possibly, too, a small section may have come to her from other professions, which natural gifts have justified them in despising. Moreover, the bridle which curbs our friend Theages may be equally efficacious in other instances. For Theages is kept in check by ill-health, which excludes him from a public life, though in all other respects he has every inducement to desert philosophy. I need not mention the super-natural sign which restrains me; for I fancy it has been granted to few, if any, before my time. Now he who has become a member of this little band, and has tasted how sweet and blessed his treasure is, and has watched the madness of the many, with the full assurance that there is scarcely a person who takes a single judicious step in his public life, and that there is no ally with whom he may safely march to the succour of the just, nay, that should he attempt it, he will be like a man that has fallen among wild beasts – unwilling to join in their iniquities, and unable singly to resist the fury of all, and therefore destined to perish before he can be of any service to his country or his friends, and do no good to himself or any one else – having, I say, weighed all this, such a man keeps quiet and confines himself to his own concerns, like one who takes shelter behind a wall on a stormy day, when the wind is driving before it a hurricane of dust and rain; and when from his retreat he sees the infection of lawlessness spreading over the rest of mankind, he is well content if he can in any way live his life here untainted in his own person by unrighteousness and unholy deeds, and when the time for his release arrives, take his departure amid bright hopes with cheerfulness and serenity.

Well, said Adeimantus, he will certainly have effected before his departure not the least important objects.

Nor yet, I rejoined, the most important, if he fail to find a political constitution suited to him, for under such a constitution he will not only himself reach a higher stage of growth, but he will also secure his country's welfare together with his own. Well then, I continued, the causes of the prejudice against philosophy, and the injustice of this prejudice, have in my opinion been satisfactorily disposed of, unless you have anything to add.

No, I have nothing more to say on this head: but which of the constitutions of our time is the one that you call suited to philosophy?

There is not one that I can call so: nay, what I complain of is precisely this, that no state, as now constituted, is a worthy sphere for a philosophic nature. Hence that nature becomes warped and deteriorated. For just as the seed of a rare exotic, when sown in a foreign soil, habitually becomes enfeebled and loses its essential character, and eventually passes into a common plant of the country, so this kind of character at the present day, failing to preserve its peculiar virtues, degenerates into tendencies that are not its own: but if it could only find the most perfect constitution, answering to itself as the most perfect of characters, it will then give proof that it is the true divine type, whereas all other kinds of character and of vocation are merely human. Now, I make no doubt you will proceed to ask me what this constitution is.

You are mistaken, he said; what I was going to ask was whether you were thinking of this constitution whose organisation we have discussed, or of another.

The same, I replied, in all points but one; and this one point was alluded to during the discussion, when we said that it would be necessary to have constantly present in the state some authority that should view the constitution in the very light in which you, the legislator, viewed it when you framed the laws.

True, it was alluded to.

But it was not sufficiently developed, because I was alarmed by your objections, which showed that the demonstration of it would be tedious and difficult: for it is by no means the easiest part of the discussion that is left.

What is that part?

To show in what way a state may handle philosophy without incurring utter destruction. For we know that all great things are hazardous, and, according to the proverb, beautiful things are indeed hard of attainment.

Nevertheless, he said, let this point be cleared up, in order that the demonstration may be complete.

The hindrance, if any, will arise not from want of will, but from want of power. My zeal, at any rate, you shall see with your own eyes. For observe at once with what reckless zeal I proceed to assert that a state ought to deal with the pursuit of philosophy on a plan the very reverse of that now in vogue.

How so?

At present, those who pursue philosophy at all are mere striplings just emerged from boyhood, who take it up in the intervals of house-keeping and business, and after just dipping into the most abstruse part of the study (by which I mean dialectic) abandon the pursuit altogether; and these are the most advanced philosophers; and ever afterwards, if on being invited they consent to listen to others whose attention is devoted to it, they think it a great condescension, because they imagine that philosophy ought to be made a mere secondary occupation; and on the approach of old age, all but a very few are extinguished far more effectually than the sun of Heracleitus,[3] inasmuch as they are not, like it, rekindled.

And pray what is the right plan? he asked.

Just the opposite. In youth and boyhood they ought to be put through a course of training in philosophy suited to their years; and while their bodies are growing up to manhood, especial attention should be paid to them, as a serviceable acquisition in the cause of philosophy. At the approach of that period during which the mind begins to attain its maturity, the mental exercises ought to be rendered more severe. Finally when their bodily powers begin to fail, and they are released from public duties and military service, from that time forward they ought to lead a dedicated life and consecrate themselves to this one pursuit, if they are to live happily on earth, and after death to crown the life they have led with a corresponding destiny in another world.

Well, indeed, Socrates, I do not doubt your zeal. But I expect most of your hearers, beginning with Thrasymachus, to oppose you with still greater zeal, and express their unqualified dissent.

Do not make a quarrel between me and Thrasymachus, when we have just become friends – though I do not mean to say that we were enemies before. I shall leave nothing untried until I have either won him over to my way of thinking, along with the rest, or have achieved something for their good in that future state, should they ever happen, in a second existence, to encounter similar discussions.

Truly a trifling adjournment! he exclaimed.

Rather speak of it as a nothing, compared with all time. However, it need not surprise us that most people disbelieve in my doctrines; for they have never yet seen our present theory realised. No, what is much more likely is that they have met with proposals somewhat resembling ours, but forced expressly into appearing of a piece with one another, instead of falling spontaneously into agreement, as in the present case. They have never yet seen, in either one or more instances, a man moulded into the most perfect possible conformity and likeness to virtue, both in words and in works, reigning in a state as perfect as himself. Or do you think they have?

No, indeed I do not.

And further, my dear friend, they have not listened often enough to discussions of an elevated and liberal tone confined to the strenuous investigation of truth by all possible means, simply for the sake of knowing it; and which therefore will, both in private disquisitions and in public trials, keep at a respectful distance from those subtleties and special pleadings whose sole aim it is to prolong debate and elicit applause.

You are right again.

It was for these reasons, and in anticipation of these results, that notwithstanding my fears I was constrained by the force of truth on a former occasion to assert that no state or constitution, or individual either, can ever become perfect until these few philosophers who are at present described as useless though not depraved, find themselves accidentally compelled, whether they like it or not, to accept the charge of a state, which in its turn finds itself compelled to be obedient to them; or until the present sovereigns and kings, or their sons, are divinely inspired with a genuine love of genuine philosophy. Now to assert the impossibility of both or either of these contingencies, I for my part pronounce irrational. If they are impossible, we may fairly be held up to derision as mere visionary theorists. Am I not right?

You are.

If then persons of first-rate philosophical attainments, either in the countless ages that are past have been, or in some foreign clime, far beyond the limits of our horizon, at the present moment are, or hereafter shall be, constrained by some fate to undertake the charge of a state, I am prepared to argue to the death in defence of this assertion, that the constitution described has existed, does exist, yea and will exist, wherever the Muse aforesaid has become mistress of a state. For its realisation is no impossibility, nor are our speculations impracticable; though their difficulty is even by us acknowledged.

I am of the same opinion, said he.

But are you prepared to say that the majority, on the contrary, entertain a different opinion?

Perhaps so.

My excellent friend, beware how you bring so heavy a charge against the multitude. No doubt they will change their minds if you avoid controversy, and endeavour with all gentleness to remove their prejudice against the love of learning, by showing them whom you understand by philosophers, and defining, as we have just done, their nature and cultivation, that they may not suppose you to mean such characters as are uppermost in their own thoughts. Or shall you venture to maintain that even if they look at them from your point of view, they will entertain a different opinion from yours, and return another sort of answer? In other words, do you think that an unmalicious and gentle person can quarrel with one who is not quarrelsome, or feel malice towards one who is not malicious? I will anticipate you with the declaration that in my opinion a disposition so perverse may be found in some few cases, but not in the majority of mankind.

I am myself entirely of your opinion, he replied.

Then are you not also of my opinion on just this point, that the ill-will which the multitude bear to philosophy is to be traced to those who have forced their way in, like tipsy men, where they had no concern, and who abuse one another and delight in picking quarrels, and are always discoursing about persons – conduct peculiarly unsuitable to philosophy?

Very unsuitable.

For surely, Adeimantus, he who has his thoughts truly set on the things that really exist, cannot even spare time to look down upon the occupations of men, and by disputing with them, catch the infection of malice and hostility. On the contrary, he devotes all his time to the contemplation of certain well-adjusted and changeless objects; and beholding how they neither wrong nor are wronged by each other, but are all obedient to order and in harmony with reason, he studies to imitate and resemble them as closely as he can. Or do you think it possible for a man to avoid imitating that with which he reverently associates?

No, it is impossible.

Hence the philosopher, by associating with what is godlike and orderly, becomes, as far as is permitted to man, orderly and godlike himself: though here, as everywhere, there is room for misconstruction.

Indeed, you are right.

So that if he ever finds himself compelled to study how he may introduce into the habits of men, both in public and in private life, the things that draw his notice in that higher region, and to mould others as well as himself, do you think that he will prove an indifferent artist in the production of temperance and justice and all public virtue?

Certainly not.

Well, but if the multitude are made sensible that our description is a correct one, will they really be angry with the philosophers, and will they discredit our assertion that a state can only attain to true happiness if it be delineated by painters who copy the divine original?

They will not be angry, if they are made sensible of the fact. But pray how do you mean them to sketch it?

They will take for their canvas, I replied, a state and the moral nature of mankind, and begin by making a clean surface; which is by no means an easy task. However you are aware that at the very outset they will differ from all other artists in this respect, that they will refuse to meddle with man or city, and hesitate to pencil laws, until they have either found a clear canvas, or made it clear by their own exertions.

Yes, and they are right.

In the next place, do you not suppose that they will sketch in outline the form of their constitution?

Doubtless they will.

Their next step, I fancy, will be to fill up this outline, and in doing this they will often turn their eyes to this side and to that, first to the ideal forms of justice, beauty, temperance and the like, and then to the notions current among mankind; and thus by mingling and combining the results of their studies, they will work in the true human complexion, guided by those realisations of it among men, which, if you remember, even Homer has described as godly and godlike.

You are right.

And I imagine they will go on rubbing out here and repainting there, until they have done all in their power to make the moral character of men as pleasing as may be in the eye of heaven.

Well, certainly their picture will be a very beautiful one.

Do we then, I continued, make any progress in persuading those assailants who by your account were marching stoutly to attack us, that such a painter of constitutions is to be found in the man whom we praised lately in their hearing, and who occasioned their displeasure, because we proposed to deliver up our cities into his hands? And do they feel rather less exasperation at being told the same thing now?

Yes, much less, if they are wise.

I think so too; for pray, how will they be able to dispute our position? Can they deny that philosophers are enamoured of real existence and of truth?

No, it would be indeed ridiculous to do that.

Well, can they maintain that their character, such as we have described it, is not intimately allied to perfection?

No, they cannot.

Once more, will they tell us that such a character, placed within reach of its appropriate studies, will fail to become as thoroughly good and philosophical as any character can become? Or will they give the preference to those whom we discarded?

Surely not.

Will they then persist in their anger, when I assert that till the class of philosophers be invested with the supreme authority in a state, such state and its citizens will find no deliverance from evil, and the fabulous constitution which we are describing will not be actually realised?

Probably they will grow less angry.

What do you say to our assuming, not merely that they are less angry, but that they are perfectly pacified and convinced, in order that we may shame them into acquiescence, if nothing else will do?

By all means assume it.

Well then, let us regard these persons as convinced so far. But in the next place, will anybody maintain that kings and sovereigns cannot by any possibility beget sons gifted with a philosophic nature?

No one in the world will maintain that.

And can any one assert that if born with such a nature, they must necessarily be corrupted? I grant that their preservation is a difficult matter; but I ask, is there any one who will maintain that in the whole course of time not one of all the number can ever be preserved from contamination?

Who could maintain that?

Well but, I continued, one such person, with a submissive state, has it in his power to realise all that is now discredited.

True, he has.

For surely if a ruler establishes the laws and customs which we have detailed, it is, I presume, not impossible for the citizens to consent to carry them out.

Certainly not.

And pray, would it be a miracle beyond the verge of possibility if what we think right were thought right by others also?

For my part I think not.

But I believe we have quite convinced ourselves, in the foregoing discussion, that our plan, if possible, is the best.

Yes, quite.

So that the conclusion, apparently, to which we are now brought with regard to our legislation is that what we propose is best, if it can be realised, and that to realise it is difficult, but certainly not impossible.

True, that is our conclusion, he said.

Well, then, this part of the subject having been laboriously completed, shall we proceed to discuss the questions still remaining – in what way, and by the help of what pursuits and studies, we shall secure the presence of a body of men capable of preserving the constitution unimpaired, and what must be the age at which these studies are severally undertaken?

Let us do so by all means.

I have gained nothing, I continued, by my old scheme of omitting the troublesome questions involved in the treatment of the women and children, and the appointment of the magistrates, which I was induced to leave out from knowing what odium the perfectly correct method would incur, and how difficult it would be to carry into effect. Notwithstanding all my precautions, the moment has now arrived when these points must be discussed. It is true the question of the women and children has been already settled, but the inquiry concerning the magistrates must be pursued quite afresh. In describing them we said, if you recollect, that in order to place their patriotism beyond the reach of suspicion, they must be tested by pleasure and by pain, and proved never to have deserted their principles in the midst of toil and danger and every vicissitude of fortune, on pain of forfeiting their position if their powers of endurance fail; and that whoever comes forth from the trial without a flaw, like gold tried in the fire, must be appointed to office, and receive, during life and after death, privileges and rewards. This was pretty nearly the drift of our language, which from fear of awakening the question now pending, turned aside and hid its face.

Your account is quite correct, he said; I remember perfectly.

Yes, my friend, I shrank from making assertions which I have since hazarded; but now let me venture upon this declaration, that we must make the most perfect philosophers guardians.

We hear you, he replied.

Now consider what a small supply of these men you will, in all probability, find. For the various members of that character which we described as essential to philosophers, will seldom grow incorporate: in most cases that character grows disjointed.

What do you mean?

You are aware that persons endowed with a quick comprehension, a good memory, sagacity, acuteness, and their attendant qualities, do not readily grow up to be at the same time so noble and lofty-minded as to consent to live a regular, calm and steady life: on the contrary, such persons are drifted by their acuteness hither and thither, and all steadiness vanishes from their life.

True.

On the other hand, those steady and invariable characters whose trustiness makes one anxious to employ them, and who in war are slow to take alarm, behave in the same way when pursuing their studies; that is to say, they are torpid and stupid, as if they were benumbed, and are constantly dozing and yawning, whenever they have to toil at anything of the kind.

That is true.

But we declare that unless a person possesses a pretty fair amount of both qualifications, he must be debarred all access to the strictest education, to honour and to government.

We are right.

Then do you not anticipate a scanty supply of such characters?

Most assuredly I do.

Hence we must not be content with testing their behaviour in the toils, dangers and pleasures which we mentioned before; but we must go on to try them in ways which we then omitted, exercising them in a variety of studies and observing whether their character will be able to support the highest subjects, or whether it will flinch from the trial, like those who flinch under other circumstances.

No doubt it is proper to examine them in this way. But pray, which do you mean by the highest subjects?

I presume you remember that after separating the soul into three specific parts, we deduced the several natures of justice, temperance, fortitude and wisdom?

Why, if I did not remember, I should deserve not to hear the rest of the discussion.

Do you also remember the remark which preceded that deduction?

Pray, what was it?

We remarked, I believe, that to obtain the best possible view of the question we should have to take a different and a longer route, which would bring us to a thorough insight into the subject: still that it would be possible to subjoin a demonstration of the question, flowing from our previous conclusions. Thereupon you said that such a demonstration would satisfy you; and then followed those investigations, which to my own mind were deficient in exactness; but you can tell me whether they contented you.

Well, to speak for myself, I thought them fair in point of measure; and certainly the rest of the party held the same opinion.

But, my friend, no measure of such a subject which falls perceptibly short of the truth can be said to be quite fair: for nothing imperfect is a measure of anything, though people sometimes fancy that enough has been done, and that there is no call for further investigation.

Yes, he said, that is a very common habit, and arises from indolence.

Yes, but it is a habit remarkably undesirable in the guardian of a state and its laws.

So I should suppose.

That being the case, my friend, such a person must go round by that longer route, and must labour as devotedly in his studies as in his bodily exercises. Otherwise, as we were saying just now, he will never reach the goal of that highest science which is most peculiarly his own.

What! he exclaimed. Are not these the highest? Is there still something higher than justice and those other things which we have discussed?

Even so, I replied: and here we must not contemplate a rude outline, as we have been doing: on the contrary, we must be satisfied with nothing short of the most complete elaboration. For would it not be ridiculous to exert oneself on other subjects of small value, taking all imaginable pains to bring them to the most exact and spotless perfection, and at the same time to ignore the claim of the highest subjects to a corresponding exactitude of the highest order?

The sentiment is a very just one. But do you suppose that anyone would let you go without asking what that science is which you call the highest, and of what it treats?

Certainly not, I replied; so put the question yourself. Assuredly you have heard the answer many a time, but at this moment either you have forgotten it, or else you intend to find me employment by raising objections. I incline to the latter opinion; for you have often been told that the essential form of the good is the highest object of science, and that this essence, by blending with just things and all other created objects, renders them useful and advantageous. And at this moment you can scarcely doubt that I am going to assert this, and to assert, besides, that we are not sufficiently acquainted with this essence. And if so – if, I say, we know everything else perfectly without knowing this – you are aware that it will profit us nothing, just as it would be equally profitless to possess everything without possessing what is good. Or do you imagine it would be a gain to possess all possessible things, with the single exception of things good, or to apprehend every conceivable object, without apprehending what is good – in other words, to be destitute of every good and beautiful conception?

Not I, believe me.

Moreover, you doubtless know besides that the chief good is supposed by the multitude to be pleasure – by the more enlightened, insight?[4]

Of course I know that.

And you are aware, my friend, that the advocates of this latter opinion are unable to explain what they mean by insight, and are compelled at last to explain it as insight into that which is good.

Yes, they are in a ludicrous difficulty.

They certainly are: since they reproach us with ignorance of that which is good, and then speak to us the next moment as if we knew what it was. For they tell us that the chief good is insight into good, assuming that we understand their meaning as soon as they have uttered the term 'good'.

It is perfectly true.

Again: are not those whose definition identifies pleasure with good just as much infected with error as the preceding? For they are forced to admit the existence of evil pleasures, are they not?

Certainly they are.

From which it follows, I should suppose, that they must admit the same thing to be both good and evil. Does it not?

Certainly it does.

Then is it not evident that this is a subject often and severely disputed?

Doubtless it is.

Once more: is it not evident, that though many persons would be ready to do and seem to do, or to possess and seem to possess, what seems just and beautiful without really being so, yet, when you come to things good, no one is content to acquire what only seems such? On the contrary, everybody seeks the reality, and semblances are here, if nowhere else, treated with universal contempt.

Yes, that is quite evident.

This good then, which every soul pursues as the end of all its actions, divining its existence, but perplexed and unable to apprehend satisfactorily its nature, or to enjoy that steady confidence in relation to it which it does enjoy in relation to other things, and therefore doomed to forfeit any advantage which it might have derived from those same things – are we to maintain that on a subject of such overwhelming importance, the blindness we have described is a desirable feature in the character of those best members of the state in whose hands everything is to be placed?

Most certainly not.

At any rate, if it be not known in what way just things and beautiful things come to be also good, I imagine that such things will not possess a very valuable guardian in the person of him who is ignorant on this point. And I surmise that none will know the just and the beautiful satisfactorily till he knows the good.

You are right in your surmises.

Then will not the arrangement of our constitution be perfect, provided it be overlooked by a guardian who is scientifically acquainted with these subjects?

Unquestionably it will. But pray, Socrates, do *you* assert the chief good to be science or pleasure or something different from either?

Ho, ho, my friend! I saw long ago that you would certainly not put up with the opinions of other people on these subjects.

Why, Socrates, it appears to me to be positively wrong in one who has devoted so much time to these questions, to be able to state the opinions of others without being able to state his own.

Well, I said, do you think it right to speak with an air of information on subjects on which one is not well-informed?

Certainly not with an air of information, but I think it right to be willing to state one's opinion for what it is worth.

Well, but have you not noticed that opinions divorced from science are all ill-favoured? At the best they are blind. Or do you conceive that those who, unaided by the pure reason, entertain a correct opinion, are at all superior to blind men who manage to keep the straight path?

Not at all superior, he replied.

Then is it your desire to contemplate objects that are ill-favoured, blind and crooked, when it is in your power to learn from other people about bright and beautiful things?

I implore you, Socrates, cried Glaucon, not to hang back, as if you had come to the end. We shall be content even if you only discuss the subject of the chief good in the style in which you discussed justice, temperance and the rest.

Yes, my friend, and I likewise should be thoroughly content. But I distrust my own powers, and I feel afraid that my awkward zeal will subject me to ridicule. No, my good sirs: let us put aside, for the present at any rate, all inquiry into the real nature of the chief good. For methinks it is beyond the measure of this our enterprise to find the way to what is, after all, only my present opinion on the subject. But I am willing to talk to you about that which appears to be an off-shoot of the chief good, and bears the strongest resemblance to it, provided it is also agreeable to you; but if it is not, I will let it alone.

Nay, tell us about it, he replied. You shall remain in our debt for an account of the parent.

I wish that *I* could pay, and you receive, the parent sum, instead of having to content ourselves with the interest springing from it. However, here I present you with the fruit and scion of the essential good. Only take care that I do not involuntarily impose upon you by handing in a forged account of this offspring.

We will take all the care we can; only proceed.

I will do so as soon as we have come to a settlement together, and you have been reminded of certain statements made in a previous part of our conversation, and renewed before now again and again.

Pray what statements?

In the course of the discussion we have distinctly maintained the existence of a multiplicity of things that are beautiful, and good, and so on.

True, we have.

And also the existence of an essential beauty, and an essential good, and so on; reducing all those things which before we regarded as manifold to a single form and a single entity in each case, and addressing each as an independent being.

Just so.

And we assert that the former address themselves to the eye, and not to the pure reason; whereas the forms address themselves to the reason and not to the eye.

Certainly.

Now with what part of ourselves do we see visible objects?

With the eye-sight.

In the same way we hear sounds with the hearing, and perceive everything sensible with the other senses, do we not?

Certainly.

Then have you noticed with what transcendent costliness the architect of the senses has wrought out the faculty of seeing and being seen?

Not exactly, he replied.

Well then, look at it in this light. Is there any other kind of thing which the ear and the voice require, to enable the one to hear and the other to be heard, in the absence of which third thing the one will not hear and the other will not be heard?

No, there is not.

And I believe that very few, if any, of the other senses require any such third thing. Can you mention one that does?

No, I cannot.

But do you not perceive that in the case of vision and visible objects there is a demand for something additional?

How so?

Why, granting that vision is seated in the eye, and that the owner of it is attempting to use it, and that colour is resident in the objects, still, unless there be present a third kind of thing, devoted to this especial purpose, you are aware that the eyesight will see nothing, and the colours will be invisible.

Pray what is the third thing to which you refer?

Of course I refer to what you call light.

You are right.

Hence it appears that of all the pairs aforesaid, the sense of sight, and the faculty of being seen, are coupled by the noblest link, whose nature is anything but insignificant – unless light is an ignoble thing.

No, indeed; it is very far from being ignoble.

To whom, then, of the gods in heaven, can you refer as the author and dispenser of this blessing? And whose light is it that enables our sight to see so excellently well, and makes visible objects appear?

There can be but one opinion on the subject, he replied: your question evidently alludes to the sun.

Then the relation subsisting between the eyesight and this deity is of the following nature, is it not?

Describe it.

Neither the sight itself, nor the eye, which is the seat of sight, can be identified with the sun.

Certainly not.

And yet of all the organs of sensation, the eye, methinks, bears the closest resemblance to the sun.

Yes, quite so.

Further, is not the faculty which the eye possesses dispensed to it from the sun, and held by it as something adventitious?

Certainly it is.

Then is it not also true that the sun, though not identical with sight, is nevertheless the cause of sight, and is moreover seen by its aid?

Yes, quite true.

Well then, I continued, believe that I meant the sun when I spoke of the offspring of the chief good, begotten by it in a certain resemblance to itself – that is to say, bearing the same relation in the visible world to sight and its objects, which the chief good bears in the intellectual world to pure reason and its objects.

How so? Be so good as to explain it to me more at length.

Are you aware that whenever a person makes an end of looking at objects upon which the light of day is shedding colour, and looks instead at objects coloured by the light of the moon and stars, his eyes grow dim and appear almost blind, as if they were not the seat of distinct vision?

I am fully aware of it.

But whenever the same person looks at objects on which the sun is shining, these very eyes, I believe, see clearly, and are evidently the seat of distinct vision?

Unquestionably it is so.

Just in the same way understand the condition of the soul to be as follows. Whenever it has fastened upon an object over which truth and real existence are shining, it seizes that object by an act of reason, and knows it, and thus proves itself to be possessed of reason: but whenever it has fixed upon objects that are blent with darkness – the world of birth and death – then it rests in opinion, and its sight grows dim as its opinions shift backwards and forwards, and it has the appearance of being destitute of reason.

True, it has.

Now this power, which supplies the objects of real knowledge with the truth that is in them, and which renders to him who knows them the faculty of knowing them, you must consider to be the essential form of good, and you must regard it as the origin of science and of truth so far as the latter comes within the range of knowledge: and though knowledge and truth are both very beautiful things, you will be right in looking upon good as something distinct from them, and even more beautiful. And just as in the analogous case it is right to regard light and vision as resembling the good, but wrong to identify them with the sun, so in the case of science and truth it is right to regard both of them as resembling good, but wrong to identify either of them with good; because, on the contrary, the quality of the good ought to have a still higher value set upon it.

That implies an inexpressible beauty, if it not only is the source of science and truth, but also surpasses them in beauty; for I presume you do not mean by it pleasure.

Hush! I exclaimed. Not a word of that. But you had better examine the illustration further, as follows.

Show me how.

I think you will admit that the sun ministers to visible objects not only the faculty of being seen, but also their vitality, growth and nutriment, though it is not itself equivalent to vitality.

Of course it is not.

Then admit that in like manner the objects of knowledge not only derive from the good the gift of being known, but are further endowed by it with a real and essential existence; though the good, far from being identical with real existence, actually transcends it in dignity and power.

Hereupon Glaucon exclaimed with a very amusing air, good heavens! What a miraculous superiority!

Well, I said, you are the person to blame, because you compel me to state my opinions on the subject.

Nay, let me entreat you not to stop, till you have at all events gone over again your similitude of the sun, if you are leaving anything out.

Well, to say the truth, I am leaving out a great deal.

Then pray do not omit even a trifle.

I fancy I shall leave much unsaid; however, if I can help it under the circumstances, I will not intentionally make any omission.

Pray do not.

Now understand that according to us there are two powers reigning, one over an intellectual and the other over a visible region and class of objects; if I were to use the term 'firmament'[5] you might think I was playing on the word. Well then, are you in possession of these as two kinds – one visible, the other intellectual?

Yes, I am.

Suppose you take a line divided into two unequal parts – one to represent the visible class of objects, the other the intellectual – and divide each part again into two segments on the same scale. Then, if you make the lengths of the segments represent degrees of distinctness or indistinctness, one of the two segments of the part which stands for the visible world will represent all images – meaning by images, first of all shadows, and in the next place, reflections in water and in close-grained, smooth, bright substances, and everything of the kind, if you understand me.

Yes, I do understand.

Let the other segment stand for the real objects corresponding to these images – namely the animals about us, and the whole world of nature and of art.

Very good.

Would you also consent to say that with reference to this class, there is, in point of truth and untruthfulness, the same distinction between the copy and the original that there is between what is matter of opinion and what is matter of knowledge?

Certainly I should.

Then let us proceed to consider how we must divide that part of the whole line which represents the intellectual world.

How must we do it?

Thus: one segment of it will represent what the soul is compelled to investigate by the aid of the segments of the other part, which it employs as images, starting from hypotheses and travelling not to a first principle, but to a conclusion. The other segment will represent the objects of the soul as it makes its way from an hypothesis to a first principle which is not hypothetical, unaided by those images which the former division employs, and shaping its journey by the sole help of real essential forms.

I have not understood your description so well as I could wish.

Then we will try again. You will understand me more easily when I have made some previous observations. I think you know that the students of subjects like geometry and calculation assume by way of materials, in each investigation, all odd and even numbers, figures, three kinds of angles, and other similar data. These things they are supposed to know, and having adopted them as hypotheses, they decline to give any account of them, either to themselves or to others, on the assumption that they are self-evident; and making these their starting point, they proceed to travel through the remainder of the subject, and arrive at last, with perfect unanimity, at that which they have proposed as the object of investigation.

I am perfectly aware of the fact, he replied.

Then you also know that they summon to their aid visible forms, and discourse about them, though their thoughts are busy not with these forms but with their originals, and though they discourse not with a view to the particular square and diameter which they draw, but with a view to the absolute square and the absolute diameter, and so on. For while they employ by way of images those figures and diagrams aforesaid, which again have their shadows and images in water, they are really endeavouring to behold those abstractions which a person can only see with the eye of thought.

True.

This, then, was the class of things which I called intellectual; but I said that the soul is constrained to employ hypotheses while engaged in the investigation of them – not travelling to a first principle (because it is unable to step out of, and mount above, its hypotheses) but using as images just the copies that are presented by things below – which copies, as compared with the originals, are vulgarly esteemed distinct and valued accordingly.

I understand you to be speaking of the subject-matter of the various branches of geometry and the kindred arts.

Again, by the second segment of the intellectual world understand me to mean all that the mere reasoning process apprehends by the force of dialectic, when it avails itself of hypotheses not as first principles, but as genuine hypotheses, that is to say as stepping-stones and impulses, whereby it may force its way up to something that is not hypothetical, and arrive at the first principle of everything and seize it in its grasp; which done, it turns round and takes hold of that which takes hold of this first principle, till at last it comes down to a conclusion, calling in the aid of no sensible object whatever, but simply employing abstract, self-subsisting forms, and terminating in the same.

I do not understand you so well as I could wish, for I believe you to be describing an arduous task, but at any rate I understand that you wish to declare distinctly that the field of real existence and pure intellect, as contemplated by the science of dialectic, is more certain than the field investigated by what are called the arts, in which hypotheses constitute first principles, which the students are compelled, it is true, to contemplate with the mind and not with the senses, but at the same time, as they do not come back, in the course of inquiry, to a first principle, but push on from hypothetical premises, you think that they do not exercise pure reason on the questions that engage them, although taken in connection with a first principle these questions come within the domain of the pure reason. And I believe you apply the term understanding, not pure reason, to the mental habit of such people as geometricians – regarding understanding as something intermediate between opinion and pure reason.

You have taken in my meaning most satisfactorily; and I beg you will accept these four mental states as corresponding to the four segments – namely pure reason corresponding to the highest, understanding to the second, belief to the third, and conjecture to the last; and pray arrange them in gradation, and believe them to partake of distinctness in a degree corresponding to the truth of their respective objects.

I understand you, said he. I quite agree with you, and will arrange them as you desire.

NOTES ON BOOK SIX

1 γεννήσας νοῦν καὶ ἀλήθειαν. We have here translated νοῦν 'wisdom'. For νοῦς is, according to Plato, sometimes the organ within us by which we apprehend the highest objects of knowledge, and sometimes, as here, the knowledge thus obtained. In the same way Coleridge, in *The Friend*, after defining reason as an organ bearing the same relation to spiritual objects – the universal, the eternal and the necessary – as the eye bears to material and contingent phenomena, goes on to say 'that it is an organ identical with its appropriate objects. Thus god, the soul, eternal truth, etc., are the objects of reason; but they are themselves reason. We name god the supreme reason; and Milton says,

> Whence the soul
> Reason receives, and reason is her being'

Elsewhere we have generally translated νοῦς 'reason' or 'pure reason'; and as Plato contrasts νοῦς and διάνοια, we have ventured to translate the latter by the word 'understanding', as the best equivalent in the nomenclature of modern philosophy since the time of Kant.

2 ἡ Διομήδεια ἀνάγκη. The origin of the proverb is uncertain.

3 Heracleitus is said to have believed that the sun was extinguished every evening and rekindled every morning.

4 φρόνησις: practical wisdom, or insight.

5 The play upon τὸ ὁρατόν, 'the visible', and οὐρανός, 'heaven', cannot be represented in English. The meaning apparently is: 'I do not use the term οὐρανός, lest you should suppose that I wish to connect it etymologically with ὁράω.'

BOOK SEVEN

Now then, I proceeded to say, go on to compare our natural condition, so far as education and ignorance are concerned, to a state of things like the following. Imagine a number of men living in an underground cavernous chamber, with an entrance open to the light extending along the entire length of the cavern, in which they have been confined, from their childhood, with their legs and necks so shackled that they are obliged to sit still and look straight forwards, because their chains render it impossible for them to turn their heads round: and imagine a bright fire burning some way off, above and behind them, and an elevated roadway passing between the fire and the prisoners, with a low wall built along it, like the screens which conjurors put up in front of their audience, and above which they exhibit their wonders.

I have it, he replied.

Also figure to yourself a number of persons walking behind this wall, and carrying with them statues of men and images of other animals, wrought in wood and stone and all kinds of materials, together with various other articles, which overtop the wall; and as you might expect, let some of the passers-by be talking, and others silent.

You are describing a strange scene, and strange prisoners.

They resemble us, I replied. For let me ask you, in the first place, whether persons so confined could have seen anything of themselves or of each other beyond the shadows thrown by the fire upon the part of the cavern facing them?

Certainly not, if you suppose them to have been compelled all their lifetime to keep their heads unmoved.

And is not their knowledge of the things carried past them equally limited?

Unquestionably it is.

And if they were able to converse with one another, do you not think that they would be in the habit of giving names to the objects which they saw before them?

Doubtless they would.

Again: if their prison-house returned an echo from the part facing them whenever one of the passers-by opened his lips, to what, let me ask you, could they refer the voice, if not to the shadow which was passing?

Unquestionably they would refer it to that.

Then surely such persons would hold the shadows of those manufactured articles to be the only realities.

Without a doubt they would.

Now consider what would happen if the course of nature brought them a release from their fetters, and a remedy for their foolishness, in the following manner. Let us suppose that one of them has been released, and compelled suddenly to stand up, and turn his neck round and walk with open eyes towards the light; and let us suppose that he goes through all these actions with pain, and that the dazzling splendour renders him incapable of discerning those objects of which he used formerly to see the shadows. What answer should you expect him to make if some one were to tell him that in those days he was watching foolish phantoms, but that now he is somewhat nearer to reality, and is turned towards things more real, and sees more correctly; above all, if he were to point out to him the several objects that are passing by, and question him, and compel him to answer what they are? Should you not expect him to be puzzled, and to regard his old visions as truer than the objects now forced upon his notice?

Yes, much truer.

And if he were further compelled to gaze at the light itself, would not his eyes, think you, be distressed, and would he not shrink and turn away to the things which he could see distinctly, and consider them to be really clearer than the things pointed out to him?

Just so.

And if some one were to drag him violently up the rough and steep ascent from the cavern, and refuse to let him go till he had drawn him out into the light of the sun, would he not, think you, be vexed and indignant at such treatment, and on reaching the light, would he not find his eyes so dazzled by the glare as to be incapable of making out so much as one of the objects that are now called true?

Yes, he would find it so at first.

Hence, I suppose, habit will be necessary to enable him to perceive objects in that upper world. At first he will be most successful in distinguishing shadows; then he will discern the reflections of men and other things in water, and afterwards the realities; and after this he will raise his eyes to encounter the light of the moon and stars, finding it less difficult to study the heavenly bodies and the heaven itself by night than the sun and the sun's light by day.

Doubtless.

Last of all, I imagine, he will be able to observe and contemplate the nature of the sun, not as it *appears* in water or on alien ground, but as it *is* in itself in its own territory.

Of course.

His next step will be to draw the conclusion that the sun is the author of the seasons and the years, and the guardian of all things in the visible world, and in a manner the cause of all those things which he and his companions used to see.

Obviously, this will be his next step.

What then? When he recalls to mind his first habitation, and the wisdom of the place, and his old fellow-prisoners, do you not think he will congratulate himself on the change, and pity them?

Assuredly he will.

And if it was their practice in those days to receive honour and commendations one from another, and to give prizes to him who had the keenest eye for a passing object, and who remembered best all that used to precede and follow and accompany it, and from these data divined most ably what was going to come next, do you fancy that he will covet these prizes, and envy those who receive honour and exercise authority among them? Do you not rather imagine that he will feel what Homer describes, and wish extremely

> To drudge on the lands of a master,
> Under a portionless wight,

and be ready to go through anything rather than entertain those opinions and live in that fashion?

For my own part, he replied, I am quite of that opinion. I believe he would consent to go through anything rather than live in that way.

And now consider what would happen if such a man were to descend again and seat himself on his old seat. Coming so suddenly out of the sun, would he not find his eyes blinded with the gloom of the place?

Certainly he would.

And if he were forced to deliver his opinion again, touching the shadows aforesaid, and to enter the lists against those who had always been prisoners, while his sight continued dim and his eyes unsteady – and if this process of initiation lasted a considerable time – would he not be made a laughing-stock, and would it not be said of him that he had gone up only to come back again with his eyesight destroyed, and that it was not worth while even to attempt the ascent? And if any one endeavoured to set them free and carry them to the light, would they not go so far as to put him to death, if they could only manage to get him into their power?

Yes, that they would.

Now this imaginary case, my dear Glaucon, you must apply in all its parts to our former statements, by comparing the region which the eye reveals to the prison-house, and the light of the fire therein to the power of the sun: and if by the upward ascent and the contemplation of the upper world you understand the mounting of the soul into the intellectual region, you will hit the tendency of my own surmises, since you desire to be told what they are, though indeed, god only knows whether they are correct. But be that as it may, the view which I take of the subject is to the following effect. In the world of knowledge, the essential form of good is the limit of our inquiries, and can barely be perceived, but when perceived, we cannot help concluding that it is in every case the source of all that is bright and beautiful – in the visible world giving birth to light and its master, and in the intellectual world dispensing, immediately and with full authority, truth and reason; and that whosoever would act wisely, either in private or in public, must set this form of good before his eyes.

To the best of my power, said he, I quite agree with you.

That being the case, I continued, pray agree with me on another point, and do not be surprised that those who have climbed so high are unwilling to take a part in the affairs of men, because their souls are ever loath to desert that upper region. For how could it be otherwise, if the preceding simile is indeed a correct representation of their case?

True, it could scarcely be otherwise.

Well, do you think it a marvellous thing that a person who has just quitted the contemplation of divine objects for the study of human infirmities, should betray awkwardness, and appear very ridiculous, when with his sight still dazed and before he has become sufficiently habituated to the darkness that reigns around, he finds himself compelled to contend in courts of law, or elsewhere, about the shadows of justice, or images which throw the shadows, and to enter the lists in questions involving the arbitrary suppositions entertained by those who have never yet had a glimpse of the essential features of justice?

No, it is anything but marvellous.

Right: for a sensible man will recollect that the eyes may be confused in two distinct ways and from two distinct causes – that is to say, by sudden transitions either from light to darkness or from darkness to light. And believing the same idea to be applicable to the soul, whenever such a person sees a case in which the mind is perplexed and unable to distinguish objects, he will not laugh irrationally, but he will examine whether it has just quitted a brighter life, and has been blinded by the novelty of darkness, or whether it has come from the depths of ignorance into a more brilliant life, and has been dazzled by the unusual splendour; and not till then will he congratulate the one upon its life and condition, and compassionate the other; and if he chooses to laugh at it, such laughter will be less ridiculous than that which is raised at the expense of the soul that has descended from the light of a higher region.

You speak with great judgment.

Hence, if this be true, we cannot avoid adopting the belief that the real nature of education is at variance with the account given of it by certain of its professors, who pretend, I believe, to infuse into the mind a knowledge of which it was destitute, just as sight might be instilled into blinded eyes.

True; such are their pretensions.

Whereas our present argument shows us that there is a faculty residing in the soul of each person, and an instrument enabling each of us to learn; and that just as we might suppose it to be impossible to turn the eye round from darkness to light without turning the whole body, so must this faculty, or this instrument, be wheeled round, in company with the entire soul, from the perishing world, until it be enabled to endure the contemplation of the real world and the brightest part thereof, which according to us is the form of good. Am I not right?

You are.

Hence, I continued, this very process of revolution must give rise to an art teaching in what way the change will most easily and most effectually be brought about. Its object will not be to generate in the person the power of seeing. On the contrary, it assumes that he possesses it, though he is turned in a wrong direction and does not look towards the right quarter; and its aim is to remedy this defect.

So it would appear.

Hence, while on the one hand the other so-called virtues of the soul seem to resemble those of the body, inasmuch as they really do not pre-exist in the soul, but are formed in it in the course of time by habit and exercise, the virtue of wisdom, on the other hand, does most certainly appertain, as it would appear, to a more divine substance which never loses its energy, but by change of position becomes useful and serviceable, or else remains useless and injurious. For you must, ere this, have noticed how keen-sighted are the puny souls of those who have the reputation of being clever but vicious, and how sharply they see through the things to which they are directed, thus proving that their powers of vision are by no means feeble, though they have been compelled to become the servants of wickedness, so that the more sharply they see, the more numerous are the evils which they work.

Yes, indeed it is the case.

But, I proceeded, if from earliest childhood these characters had been shorn and stripped of those leaden, earth-born weights which grow and cling to the pleasures of eating, and gluttonous enjoyments of a similar nature, and keep the eye of the soul turned upon the things below – if, I repeat, they had been released from these snares, and turned round to look at objects that are true, then these very same souls of these very same men would have had as keen an eye for such pursuits as they actually have for those in which they are now engaged.

Yes, probably it would be so.

Once more: is it not also probable, or rather is it not a necessary corollary to our previous remarks, that neither those who are uneducated and ignorant of truth, nor those who are suffered to linger over their education all their life, can ever be competent overseers of a state – the former because they have no single mark in life which they are to constitute the end and aim of all their conduct both in private and in public, the latter because they will not act without compulsion, fancying that while yet alive they have been translated to the islands of the blest.

That is true.

It is therefore our task, I continued, to constrain the noblest characters in our colony to arrive at that science which we formerly pronounced the highest, and to set eyes upon the good, and to mount that ascent we spoke of; and when they have mounted and looked long enough, we must take care to refuse them that liberty which is at present permitted them.

Pray what is that?

The liberty of staying where they are, and refusing to descend again to those prisoners, or partake of their toils and honours, be they mean or be they exalted.

Then are we to do them a wrong, and make them live a life that is worse than the one within their reach?

You have again forgotten, my friend, that law does not ask itself how some one class in a state is to live extraordinarily well. On the contrary, it tries to bring about this result in the entire state; for which purpose it links the citizens together by persuasion and by constraint, makes them share with one another the benefit which each individual can contribute to the common weal, and does actually create men of this exalted character in the state, not with the intention of letting them go each on his own way, but with the intention of turning them to account in its plans for the consolidation of the state.

True, he replied; I had forgotten.

Therefore reflect, Glaucon, that far from wronging the future philosophers of our state, we shall only be treating them with strict justice, if we put them under the additional obligation of watching over their fellow-citizens and taking care of them. We shall say; It is with good reason that your compeers elsewhere refuse to share in the labours of their respective states. For they take root in a city spontaneously, in defiance of the prevailing constitution; and it is but fair that a self-sown plant, which is indebted to no one for support, should have no inclination to pay to anybody wages for attendance. But in your case, it is we that have begotten you for the state as well as for yourselves, to be like leaders and kings of a hive – better and more perfectly trained than the rest, and more capable of playing a part in both modes of life. You must therefore descend by turns, and associate with the rest of the community, and you must habituate yourselves to the contemplation of these obscure objects. For when habituated, you will see a thousand times better than the residents, and you will recognise what each image is, and what is its original, because you have seen the realities of which beautiful and just and good things are copies. And in this way you and we shall find that the life of the state is a substance, and not a phantom like the life of our present states, which are mostly composed of men who fight among themselves for shadows, and are at feud for the administration of affairs, which they regard as a great boon. Whereas I conceive the truth stands thus: that city in which the destined rulers are least eager to rule will inevitably be governed in the best and least factious manner, and a contrary result will ensue if the rulers are of a contrary disposition.

You are perfectly right.

And do you imagine that our pupils, when addressed in this way, will disobey our commands, and refuse to toil with us in the state by turns, while they spend most of their time together in that bright region?

Impossible, he replied: for certainly it is a just command, and those who are to obey it are just men. No, doubtless each of them will enter upon his administration as an unavoidable duty – conduct the reverse of that pursued by the present rulers in each state.

True, my friend; the case stands thus. If you can invent for the destined rulers a life better than ruling, you may possibly realise a well-governed city: for only in such a city will the rulers be those who are really rich, not in gold, but in a wise and virtuous life, which is the wealth essential to a happy man. But if beggars, and persons who hunger after private advantages, take the reins of the state, with the idea that they are privileged to snatch advantage from their power, all goes wrong. For the post of magistrate is thus made an object of strife; and civil and intestine conflicts of this nature ruin not only the contending parties, but also the rest of the state.

That is most true.

And can you mention any life which contemns state-offices, except the life of true philosophy?

No indeed, I cannot.

Well, but the task of government must be undertaken by persons not enamoured of it: otherwise their rivals will dispute their claim.

Unquestionably it must.

Then what other persons will you compel to enter upon the duties of guardians of the state, if you discard those who understand most profoundly the means of attaining the highest excellence in the administration of a country, and who also possess honours of a different stamp, and a nobler life than that of a statesman?

I shall not discard them, he replied; I shall address myself only to them.

And now would you have us proceed to consider in what way such persons are to arise in the state, and how they are to be carried up to the light, like those heroes who are said to have ascended up to heaven from the nether world?

Certainly I would have you do so.

Apparently this is a question involving not the mere turning of a shell,[1] but the revolution of a soul, which is traversing a road leading from a kind of night-like day up to a true day of real existence; and this road we shall doubtless declare to be true philosophy.

Exactly so.

Then must we not consider what branch of study possesses the power required?

Certainly we must.

Then, Glaucon, can you tell me of a science which tends to draw the soul from the fleeting to the real? Whilst I speak, I bethink myself that we certainly said, did we not, that our pupils must be trained in their youth to war?

Yes, we did say so.

Then the science which we are in quest of must possess this feature as well as the former.

What feature?

That it can be turned to use by warlike men

That is certainly advisable, if it be practicable.

Now in the foregoing discussion we were for training our pupils through the agency of music and gymnastic.

True.

Gymnastic, I believe, is engaged upon the changeable and perishing; for it presides over the growth and waste of the body.

That is evident.

Hence gymnastic cannot be the study for which we are looking.

No, it cannot.

But what do you say to music, considered in the extent in which we previously discussed it?

Nay, he replied, music was only the counterpart of gymnastic, if you remember: for it trained our guardians by the influence of habit, and imparted to them, not science, but a kind of harmoniousness by means of harmony, and a kind of measuredness by means of measure, and in the subjects which it treated, whether fabulous or true, it presented another series of kindred characteristics: but it contained no branch of study tending to any advantage resembling the one of which you are now in quest.

Your memory is very exact, I made answer: for music really did possess nothing of the kind. But, my excellent Glaucon, where are we to find the thing we want? All the useful arts, I believe, we thought degrading.

Unquestionably we did: yet what other study is there still remaining, apart from music and gymnastic and the useful arts?

Come then, if we can find nothing beyond and independent of these, let us take one of those studies which are of universal application.

Pray, which?

That general one, for example, of which all arts, trains of thought, and sciences, avail themselves, and which is also one of the first things that everyone must learn.

Tell me the nature of it.

I allude to that common process of distinguishing the numbers one, two and three. And I call it briefly, number and calculation. For may it not be said of these that every art and science is compelled to crave a share in them?

Certainly it may.

And is not the science of war one of the number?

Beyond a doubt it is.

To take an example from tragedy, I proceeded, Palamedes on all occasions makes out that Agamemnon was a very ridiculous general. For you have remarked, have you not, that he claims by the invention of numbers to have marshalled the ranks of the army at Troy, and to have counted over the ships and every thing else — as if such things had been uncounted before his time, and as if Agamemnon had been even ignorant how many feet he had, which would naturally be the case if he did not know how to count? Yet what do you think of Agamemnon as a general?

He was a strange one in my opinion, if this story be true.

Then can we help concluding that to be able to calculate and count is a piece of knowledge indispensable to a warrior?

Yes, most indispensable, if he is to understand how to handle troops at all, or rather, if he is to be anything of a man.

And does your notion of this science coincide with mine?

Pray, what is your notion?

It seems to be by nature one of those studies leading to reflection, of which we are in quest; but no one appears to make the right use of it as a thing which tends wholly to draw us towards real existence.

Explain your meaning.

I will endeavour to make my own opinion clear to you. And you, on your side, must join me in studying those things which I distinguish in my own mind as conducive, or not, to the end in view, and express your assent or dissent, in order that we may see more clearly, in the next place, whether I am right in my surmises as to the nature of this science.

Pray go on with your distinctions.

I will. If you observe, some of the objects of our perceptions do not stimulate the reflection into exercise, because they appear thoroughly appreciated by the perception; whereas others urge the reflection strenuously to examine them, because the perception appears to produce an unsound result.

It is plain you are talking of objects seen at a distance, and painting in perspective.

You have not quite hit my meaning.

Then pray, what sort of objects do you mean?

I regard as non-stimulants all the objects which do not end by giving us at the same moment two contradictory perceptions. On the other hand, all the objects which do end in that way I consider stimulants – meaning those cases in which the perception, whether incident from a near or a distant object, communicates two equally vivid, but contradictory, impressions. You will understand my meaning more clearly thus: here you have three fingers, you say – the little finger, the middle and the third.

Very good.

Well, suppose me to be speaking of them as they appear on a close inspection. Now, here is the point which I wish you to examine with reference to them.

Pray, what is it?

It is evident that they are all equally fingers: and so far, it makes no difference whether the one we are looking at be in the middle or outside, whether it be white or black, thick or thin, and so on. For so long as we confine ourselves to these points, the mind seldom feels compelled to ask the reflection, what is a finger? Because in no instance has the sight informed the mind at the same moment that the finger is the opposite of a finger.

No, certainly not.

Then, naturally, such impressions cannot be stimulating or awakening to the reflection.

True.

But how is it, pray, with the relative sizes of the fingers? Does the sight distinguish them satisfactorily, and does it make no difference to it whether the position of one of them be in the middle or at the outside? And in like manner, does the touch estimate thickness and thinness, softness and hardness, satisfactorily? And is there no defect in the similar communications of the other senses? Or rather, do they not all proceed thus? To begin with the perception which takes cognisance of hard things: is it not constrained to take cognisance also of soft things, and does it not intimate to the mind that it feels the same thing to be both hard and soft?

It does.

In such cases, then, must not the mind be at a loss to know what this perception means by hard, since it declares the same thing to be also soft; and what the perception of weight means by light and heavy, when it informs the mind that the heavy is light, and the light heavy?

Why yes, he answered, such interpretations will be strange to the mind, and will require examination.

Hence it is natural for the mind in such circumstances to call in the aid of reasoning and reflection, and to endeavour to make out whether each announcement is single or double.

Undoubtedly.

Should it incline to the latter view, is it not evident that each part of every announcement has a unity and character of its own?

It is evident.

If then each is *one*, and both together make two, the mind will conclude that the two are separable. For if they were inseparable, it could only conclude that they are *one*, not *two*.

True.

Well; the sense of sight, we say, gave us an impression in which the sensations of great and small were confounded, instead of being separated. Am I not right?

You are.

But on the other hand reflection, reversing the process of the sight, was compelled, in order to make the sensible impression clear, to look at great and small as things distinct, not confounded.

True.

Then is it not some contradiction of this kind that first prompts us to ask, 'What then, after all, is greatness, and what smallness?'

No doubt it is.

And thus we are led to distinguish between objects of reflection and objects of sight.

Most rightly so.

This, then, was the meaning which I was just now attempting to convey, when I said that some objects tend to stimulate thought, while others have no bias towards awakening reflection – placing in the former category everything that strikes upon the senses in conjunction with its immediate opposite, and in the latter everything of which this cannot be said.

Now I understand you, he replied; and I agree with you.

Well, to which of the two classes do you think that number and unity belong?

I cannot make up my mind.

Indeed! Let our previous remarks help you to a conclusion. If unity, in and by itself, is thoroughly grasped by the sight or any other sense, like the finger we spoke of, it cannot possess the quality of drawing the mind towards real existence. But if some contradiction is always combined with it in all its manifestations, making it appear the opposite of unity quite as much as unity itself, in that case a critic will be immediately required, and the mind will be compelled to puzzle over the difficulty, and stir up the inward faculty of thought to the investigation, and put the question, 'What, after all, is unity in itself?' And thus the study of the unit will be one of the things which turn and lead us to the contemplation of real existence.

You are right, said he: the observation of the unit does certainly possess this property in no common degree: for the same thing presents at the same moment the appearance of one thing and an infinity of things.

Then if this is the case with the unit, is it not also the case with all numbers without exception?

Doubtless it is.

Well, but calculation and arithmetic treat of number exclusively.

Certainly they do.

And apparently they conduct us to truth.

Yes, in a manner quite extraordinary.

Hence it would appear that the science of numbers must be one of the studies of which we are in quest. For the military man finds a knowledge of it indispensable in drawing up his troops, and the philosopher must study it because he is bound to rise above the changing and cling to the real, on pain of never becoming a skilful reasoner.

True.

But our guardian, as it happens, is both soldier and philosopher.

Undoubtedly he is.

Therefore, Glaucon, it will be proper to enforce the study by legislative enactment, and to persuade those who are destined to take part in the weightiest affairs of state to study calculation and devote themselves to it, not like amateurs, but perseveringly, until by the aid of pure reason they have attained to the contemplation of the nature of numbers – not cultivating it with a view to buying and selling, as merchants or shopkeepers, but for purposes of war and to facilitate the conversion of the soul itself from the changeable to the true and the real.

What you say is admirable.

Indeed, I continued, talking of this science which treats of calculation, it has only just occurred to me how elegant it is, and how valuable it may be to us in many ways in carrying out our wishes, provided it be pursued for the sake of knowledge, and not for purposes of trade.

How so? he asked.

Because, as we were saying just now, it mightily draws the soul upwards, and compels it to reason about abstract numbers, steadily declining the discussion when any numbers are proposed which have bodies that can be seen and touched. For I presume you are aware that good mathematicians ridicule and disallow any attempt to part the unit in the course of argument; and if *you* divide it into pieces, like small change, *they* multiply it back again and take every precaution to prevent the unit from ever losing its unity and presenting an appearance of multiplicity.

That is quite true.

Now suppose, Glaucon, that someone were to ask them the following question – My excellent friends, what kind of numbers are you discussing? Where are the numbers in which the unit realises your description of it, which is that every unit is equal, each to each, without the smallest difference, and contains within itself no parts? What answer should you expect them to make?

If you ask me, I should expect them to say that the numbers about which they talk are only capable of being conceived in thought, and cannot be dealt with in any other way.

Then, my friend, do you see that this science is, in all likelihood, absolutely necessary to us, since it evidently obliges the mind to employ the pure intelligence in the pursuit of pure truth?

It certainly possesses this quality in an eminent degree.

Again, have you ever noticed that those who have a turn for arithmetic are, with scarcely an exception, naturally quick at all sciences; and that men of slow intellect, if they be trained and exercised in this study, even supposing they derive no other benefit from it, at any rate progress so far as to become invariably quicker than they were before?

That is true.

And I am pretty sure also that you will not easily find many sciences that give the learner and student so much trouble and toil as arithmetic.

No, certainly you will not.

Then on all these accounts, so far from rejecting this science, we must employ it in the education of the finest characters.

I agree with you, said he.

Then let us consider this as one point settled. In the second place, let us inquire whether we ought to concern ourselves about the science which borders on arithmetic.

What is that? Do you mean geometry?

Even so, I replied.

It is obvious, he continued, that all that part of it which bears upon strategy does concern us. For in encamping, in occupying positions, in closing up and deploying troops, and in executing all the other manoeuvres of an army in the field of battle or on the march, it will make every difference to a military man whether he is a good geometrician, or not.

Nevertheless, I replied, a trifling knowledge of geometry and calculation will suffice for these purposes. The question is whether the larger and more advanced part of the study tends at all to facilitate our contemplation of the essential form of good. Now according to us, this is the tendency of everything that compels the soul to transfer itself to that region in which is contained the most blissful part of that real existence which it is of the highest importance for it to behold.

You are right.

Consequently if geometry compels the soul to contemplate real existence, it does concern us; but if it only forces the changeful and perishing upon our notice, it does not concern us.

Yes, so we affirm.

Well then, on one point at any rate we shall encounter no opposition from those who are even slightly acquainted with geometry – when we assert that this science holds a position which flatly contradicts the language employed by those who handle it.

How so?

They talk, I believe, in a very ridiculous and poverty-stricken style. For they speak invariably of squaring, and producing, and adding, and so on, as if they were engaged in some business, and as if all their propositions had a practical end in view: whereas in reality I conceive that the science is pursued wholly for the sake of knowledge.

Assuredly it is.

There is still a point about which we must be agreed, is there not?

What is it?

That the science is pursued for the sake of the knowledge of what eternally exists, and not of what comes for a moment into existence, and then perishes.

We shall soon be agreed about that. Geometry, no doubt, is a knowledge of what eternally exists.

If that be so, my excellent friend, geometry must tend to draw the soul towards truth, and to give the finishing stroke to the philosophic spirit – thus contributing to raise up what at present we so wrongly keep down.

Yes, it will do so most forcibly.

Then you must, in the most forcible manner, direct the citizens of your beautiful city on no account to fail to apply themselves to geometry. For even its secondary advantages are not trifling.

Pray, what are they?

Not to mention those which you specified as bearing upon the conduct of war, I would insist particularly upon the fact, of which we are assured – that where a ready reception of any kind of learning is an object, it will make all and every difference whether the pupil has applied himself to geometry or not.

Yes, undoubtedly it will.

Shall we, then, impose this, as a secondary study, upon our young men?

Yes, let us do so, he replied.

Again: shall we make astronomy a third study? Or do you disapprove?

I quite approve of it, said he. For to have an intimate acquaintance with seasons and months and years is an advantage not only to the agriculturist and the navigator, but also, in an equal degree, to the general.

You amuse me by your evident alarm lest the multitude should think that you insist upon useless studies. Yet indeed it *is* no easy matter, but on the contrary a very difficult one, to believe that in the midst of these studies an organ of our souls is being purged from the blindness, and quickened from the deadness, occasioned by other pursuits – an organ whose preservation is of more importance than a thousand eyes; because only by it can truth be seen. Consequently those who think with us will bestow unqualified approbation on the studies you prescribe, while those who have no inkling at all of this doctrine will think them valueless, because they see no considerable advantage to be gained from them beyond their practical applications. Therefore consider at once with which of the two parties you are conversing: or else, if you are carrying on the discussion chiefly on your own account, without any reference to either party, you surely will not grudge another man any advantage which he may derive from the conversation.

I prefer the latter course: I mean to speak, put my questions, and give my answers, chiefly on my own account.

Then take a step backwards, I continued. We were wrong a moment ago in what we took as the science next in order to geometry.

What did we take?

Why, after considering plane surfaces, we proceeded to take solids in a state of revolution, before considering solids in themselves. Whereas the correct way is, proceed from two dimensions to three; which brings us, I believe, to cubical dimensions and figures into which thickness enters.

True, Socrates; but these subjects, I think, have not yet been explored.

They have not, I replied; and for two reasons. In the first place, they are difficult problems, and but feebly investigated, because no state holds them in estimation: and in the second place, those who do investigate them stand in need of a superintendent, without whom they will make no discoveries. Now, to find such a person is a hard task to begin with; and then, supposing one were found, as matters stand now the pride of those who are inquisitive about the subject would prevent their listening to his suggestions. But if a state, in its corporate capacity, were to pay honour to the study, and constitute itself superintendent thereof, these students would yield obedience, and the real nature of the subject, thus continuously and vigorously investigated, would be brought to light. For even now, slighted and curtailed as it is not only by the many, but also by professed inquirers who can give no account of the extent of its usefulness, it nevertheless makes progress, in spite of all these obstacles, by its inherent elegance; and I should not be at all surprised if its difficulties were cleared up.

There certainly is a peculiar fascination about it. But pray explain more clearly what you were saying just now. I think you defined geometry as the investigation of plane surfaces.

I did.

You then proceeded to place astronomy next to geometry, though afterwards you drew back.

Yes, I said, the more I haste to travel over the ground, the worse I speed. The investigation of space of three dimensions succeeds to plane geometry; but because it is studied absurdly, I passed it over, and spoke of astronomy, which implies motion of solid bodies, as the next step after geometry.

You are right.

Then let us assign the fourth place in our studies to astronomy, regarding the existence of the science now omitted as only waiting for the time when a state shall take it up.

It is a reasonable idea, Socrates. And to return to the rebuke which you gave me a little while ago for my vulgar commendation of astronomy, I can now praise the plan on which you pursue it. For I suppose it is clear to every one that astronomy at all events compels the soul to look upwards, and draws it from the things of this world to the other.

It is not clear to me, I replied, though perhaps it may be to everyone else: for that is not my opinion.

Then what is your opinion?

It seems to me that astronomy, as now handled by those who embark on philosophy, positively makes the soul look downwards.

How so?

I think you have betrayed no want of intrepidity in the conception you have formed of the true nature of that learning which deals with the things above. For probably, if a person were to throw his head back and learn something from the contemplation of a carved ceiling, you would suppose him to be contemplating it, not with his eyes, but with his reason. Now, perhaps your notion is right, and mine foolish. For my own part, I cannot conceive that any science makes the soul look upwards unless it has to do with the real and invisible. It makes no difference whether a person stares stupidly at the sky, or looks with half-shut eyes upon the ground; so long as he is trying to study any sensible object, I deny that he can ever be said to have learned anything, because no objects of sense admit of scientific treatment; and I maintain that his soul is looking downwards, not upwards, though he may be lying on his back, like a swimmer, to study, either in the sea or on dry land.

I am rightly punished, he rejoined, for I deserved your rebuke. But pray, what did you mean by saying that astronomy ought to be studied on a system very different from the present one, if it is to be studied profitably for the purposes that we have in view?

I will tell you. Since this fretted sky is still a part of the visible world, we are bound to regard it, though the most beautiful and perfect of visible things, as far inferior nevertheless to those true revolutions which real velocity, and real slowness, existing in true number and in all true forms, accomplish relatively to each other, carrying with them all that they contain: which are verily apprehensible by reason and thought, but not by sight. Or do you think differently?

No, indeed, he replied.

Therefore we must employ that fretted sky as a pattern or plan to forward the study which aims at those higher objects, just as we might employ diagrams which fell in our way, curiously drawn and elaborated by Daedalus or some other artist or draughtsman. For I imagine a person acquainted with geometry, on seeing such diagrams, would think them most beautifully finished, but would hold it ridiculous to study them seriously in the hope of detecting thereby the truths of equality, or duplicity, or any other ratio.

No doubt it would be ridiculous.

And do you not think that the genuine astronomer will view with the same feelings the motions of the stars? That is to say, will he not regard the heaven itself, and the bodies which it contains, as framed by the heavenly architect with the utmost beauty of which such works are susceptible? But as to the proportion which the day bears to the night, both to the month, the month to the year, and the other stars to the sun and moon and to one another – will he not, think you, look down upon the man who believes such corporeal and visible objects to be changeless and exempt from all perturbations? And will he not hold it absurd to bestow extraordinary pains on the endeavour to apprehend their true condition?

Yes, I quite think so, now that I hear you suggest it.

Hence we shall pursue astronomy with the help of problems, just as we pursue geometry: but we shall let the heavenly bodies alone, if it is our design to become really acquainted with astronomy, and by that means to convert the natural intelligence of the soul from a useless into a useful possession.

The plan which you prescribe, said he, is, I am confident, many times more laborious than the present mode of studying astronomy.

Yes, I replied; and I imagine we shall prescribe everything else on the same scale, if we are to be of any use as legislators. But to proceed: what other science in point can you suggest?

I cannot suggest any, on such short notice.

Well, motion, if I am not mistaken, admits of certainly more than one variety: a perfect enumeration of these varieties may perhaps be supplied by some learned philosopher. Those which are manifest to people like us are two in number.

Pray, what are they?

We have already described one; the other is its counterpart.

What is that?

It would seem, I replied, that our ears were intended to detect harmonious movements, just as our eyes were intended to detect the motions of the heavenly bodies; and that these constitute in a manner two sister sciences, as the Pythagoreans assert, and as we, Glaucon, are ready to grant. If not, what other course do we take?

We take the course you mentioned first: we grant the fact.

Then, as the business promises to be a long one, we will consult the Pythagoreans upon this question, and perhaps upon some other questions too – maintaining, meanwhile, our own principle intact.

What principle do you mean?

Never to let our pupils attempt to study any imperfect branch of these sciences, or anything that ever fails to arrive ultimately at that point which all things ought to reach, as we said just now in treating of astronomy. For you can scarcely be ignorant that harmony also is treated just like astronomy in this – that its professors, like the astronomers, are content to measure the notes and concords distinguished by the ear, one against another, and therefore toil without result.

Yes indeed, and they make themselves quite ridiculous. They talk about 'repetitions', and apply their ears closely, as if they were bent on extracting a note from their neighbours: and then one party asserts that an intermediate sound can still be detected, which is the smallest interval and ought to be the unit of measure, while the other party contends that now the sounds are identical – both alike postponing their reason to their ears.

I see you are alluding to those good men who tease and torture the chords, and rack them upon the pegs. But not to make the metaphor too long by enlarging upon the blows given by the plectrum, and the peevishness, reserve and forwardness of the strings, I here abandon this style, and tell you that I do not mean these persons, but those whom we resolved but now to consult on the subject of harmony. For they act just like the astronomers; that is, they investigate the numerical relations subsisting between these audible concords, but they refuse to apply themselves to problems, with the object of examining what numbers are, and what numbers are not, consonant, and what is the reason of the difference.

Why, the work you describe would require faculties more than human.

Call it rather a work useful in the search after the beautiful and the good, though useless if pursued with other ends.

Yes, that is not unlikely.

In addition to this, I continued, if the study of all these sciences which we have enumerated should ever bring us to their mutual association and relationship, and teach us the nature of the ties which bind them together, I believe that the diligent treatment of them will forward the objects which we have in view, and that the labour, which otherwise would be fruitless, will be well bestowed.

I have the same presentiment, Socrates. But the work you speak of is a very great one.

Do you allude to the prelude? I replied: or to what? Surely we do not require to be reminded that all this is but the prelude to the actual hymn which we have to learn? For I presume you do not look upon the proficients in these studies as dialecticians.

No, indeed I do not, barring a very few exceptions that have fallen in my way.

But of course you do not suppose that persons unable to take a part in the discussion of first principles can be said to *know* a particle of the things which we affirm they ought to know.

No, that again is not my opinion.

Then, Glaucon, have we not here the actual hymn, of which dialectical reasoning is the consummation? This hymn, falling as it does within the domain of the intellect, can only be imitated by the faculty of sight, which as we said strives to look steadily, first at material animals, then at the stars themselves, and last of all at the very sun itself. In the same way, whenever a person strives, by the help of dialectic, to start in pursuit of every reality by a simple process of reason, independent of all sensuous information – never flinching until by an act of the pure intelligence he has grasped the real nature of good – he arrives at the very end of the intellectual world, just as the last-mentioned person arrived at the end of the visible world.

Unquestionably.

And this course you name dialectic, do you not?

Certainly I do.

On the other hand, the release of the prisoners from their chains, and their transition from the shadows of the images to the images themselves and to the light, and their ascent from the cavern into the sunshine; and when there, the fact of their being able to look, not at the animals and vegetables and the sun's light, but still only at their reflections in water, which are indeed divine and shadows of things real, instead of being shadows of images thrown by a light which may itself be called an image, when compared with the sun; these points, I say, find their counterpart in all this pursuit of the above-mentioned arts, which possesses this power of elevating the noblest part of the soul, and advancing it towards the contemplation of that which is most excellent in the things that really exist, just as in the other case the clearest organ of the body was furthered to the contemplation of that which is brightest in the corporeal and visible region.

For myself, he replied, I accept this statement. And yet I must confess that I find it hard to accept, though at the same time, looking at it in another way, I find it hard to deny. However, as the discussion of it need not be confined to the present occasion, but may be repeated on many future occasions, let us assume the truth of your present theory, and so proceed to the hymn itself, and discuss it as we have discussed the prelude. Tell us, therefore, what is the general character of the faculty of dialectic, and into what specific parts it is divided, and lastly what are its methods. For these methods will in all likelihood be the roads that lead to the very spot where we are to close our march, and rest from our journey.

My dear Glaucon, I replied, you would not be able to follow me further, though on *my* part there should be no lack of willingness. You would no longer be looking at the similitude of that whereof we speak, but at the truth itself in the shape in which it appears to me. Whether I am right or not, I dare not go so far as to decide positively: but I suppose I am warranted in affirming that we are not far wrong.

Undoubtedly you are.

And may I not also affirm that the faculty of dialectic can alone reveal the truth to one who is master of the sciences which we have just enumerated, and that in no other way is such knowledge possible?

Yes, on that point also you are warranted in speaking positively.

At any rate, I continued, no one will contradict us when we assert that there is no other method which attempts systematically to form a conception of the real nature of each individual thing. On the contrary, all the arts, with a few exceptions, are wholly addressed to the opinions and wants of men, or else concern themselves about the production and composition of bodies, or the treatment of things which grow and are compounded. And as for these few exceptions, such as geometry and its accompanying sciences, which according to us in some small degree apprehend what is real – we find that though they may dream about real existence, they cannot behold it in a waking state, so long as they use hypotheses which they leave unexamined, and of which they can give no account. For when a person assumes a first principle which he does not know, on which unknown first principle depends the web of intermediate propositions and the final conclusion – by what possibility can such mere admissions ever constitute science?

It is indeed impossible.

Hence the dialectic method, and that alone, adopts the following course. It carries back its hypotheses to the very first principle of all, in order to establish them firmly; and finding the eye of the soul absolutely buried in a swamp of barbarous ignorance, it gently draws and raises it upwards, employing as handmaids in this work of revolution the arts which we have discussed. These we have often called sciences, because it is customary to do so, but they require another name, betokening greater clearness than opinion, but less distinctness than science. On some former occasion we fixed upon the term understanding to express this mental process. But it appears to me to be no part of our business to dispute about a name, when we have proposed to ourselves the consideration of such important subjects.

You are quite right, said he: we only want a name which when applied to a mental state shall indicate clearly what phenomena it describes.

Indeed I am content, I proceeded, to call as before the first division science, the second understanding, the third belief, and the fourth conjecture – the two latter jointly constituting opinion, and the two former intelligence. Opinion deals with the changing, intelligence with the real; and as the real is to the changing, so is intelligence to opinion; and as intelligence is to opinion, so is science to belief, and understanding to conjecture. But the analogy between the objects of these mental acts, and the twofold division of the provinces of opinion and of intelligence, we had better omit, Glaucon, to prevent burdening ourselves with discussions far outnumbering all the former.

Well, I certainly agree with you upon those other points, so far as I can follow you.

Do you also give the title of dialectician to the person who takes thoughtful account of the essence of each thing? And will you admit that so far as a person has no such account to give to himself and to others, so far he fails to exercise pure reason upon the subject?

Yes. I cannot doubt it, he replied.

Then shall you not also hold the same language concerning the good? Unless a person can strictly define by a process of thought the essential form of the good, abstracted from everything else, and unless he can fight his way as it were through all objections, studying to disprove them not by the rules of opinion, but by those of real existence, and unless in all these conflicts he travels to his conclusion without making one false step in his train of thought – unless he does all this, shall you not assert that he knows neither the essence of good, nor any other good thing; and that any phantom of it which he may chance to apprehend is the fruit of opinion and not of science; and that he dreams and sleeps away his present life, and never wakes on this side of that future world in which he is doomed to sleep for ever?

Yes, he said; I shall most decidedly assert all this.

Then certainly, if you ever had the actual training of those children of yours, whose nature and education you are theoretically super-intending, I cannot suppose that you would allow them to be magistrates in the state, with authority to decide the weightiest matters, while they are as irrational as the strokes of a pen.

No, indeed I should not.

You will pass a law, no doubt, ordering them to apply themselves especially to that education which will enable them to use the weapons of the dialectician most scientifically?

I shall, with your help.

Then does it not seem to you that dialectic lies, like a coping-stone, upon the top of the sciences, and that it would be wrong to place any other science above it, because the series is now complete?

Yes, I believe you are right, he replied.

Hence, I continued, it only remains for you to fix upon the persons to whom we are to assign these studies, and the principle of their distribution.

That is evidently the case.

Do you remember what kind of persons we selected, when we were choosing the magistrates some time ago?

Of course I do.

Well, I would have you regard the qualities we mentioned as so far entitling their owners to be selected: that is to say, we are bound to prefer the most steady, the most manful, and as far as we can, the most comely. But in addition to this, besides requiring in them a noble and resolute moral nature, they must also possess such qualifications as are favourable to this system of education.

Pray, which do you determine these to be?

They must bring with them a piercing eye for their studies, my excellent friend, and they must learn with ease. For assuredly severe studies try the mettle of the mind much more than bodily exercises, because the labour comes more home to it in the former case, as it is limited to the mind instead of being shared by the body.

True.

Then we must include in the objects of our search a good memory, a dauntless demeanour, and a thorough love of work. Else, how can you expect to induce a man to go through with his bodily labours, and to learn and practise so much besides?

No, we can hold out no inducement to a man who does not possess talents of the highest order.

At any rate, I continued, it is certain that the false view of philosophy which at present prevails, and the disrepute into which she has fallen, may be traced, as I said before, to the fact that people apply themselves to philosophy without any regard to their own demerits: whereas the study of her is the privilege of her genuine sons, to the exclusion of the baseborn.

What do you mean by genuine?

In the first place, he that would study her must not halt in his love of work. He must not be half-laborious, and half-indolent, which is the case when a man loves exercise and the chase, and all bodily toil, but dislikes study and feels an aversion for listening and inquiring, and in fact hates all intellectual labour. On the other hand, those people are equally halt whose love of work has taken the opposite form.

What you say is perfectly true.

In the same way, may we not affirm that a soul is crippled with reference to truth if, while it hates voluntary falsehood, and cannot endure it in itself, and is exceedingly indignant when other people are guilty of an untruth, it nevertheless calmly accepts involuntary false-hood, and instead of being distressed when its lack of knowledge is detected, is fain to wallow in ignorance with the complacency of a brutal hog?

No doubt you are right.

Above all, I proceeded, we must watch the genuine and the base-born on the side of temperance, fortitude, loftiness of mind and all the separate virtues. For whenever states or private persons have no eye for qualities like these, they unwittingly employ, as magistrates or as friends, men who are halt and illegitimate in one or other of these respects.

Unquestionably it is so.

Hence we on our side must take every precaution in all matters of this description. For if we can procure persons sound in limb and sound in mind, and train them up under the influence of these lofty studies and severe discipline, justice herself will find no fault with us, and we shall preserve our state and constitution; whereas if we select pupils of a different stamp, our success will be turned into failure, and we shall draw down upon philosophy a still heavier storm of ridicule.

That would be indeed a disgrace.

It certainly would. But very likely I made myself ridiculous just this minute.

How so? he asked.

I forgot, replied I, that we were not serious, and spoke too earnestly. For as I spoke, I looked towards philosophy, and seeing her assailed with unmerited contumely, I was so indignant, and so angry with those who are responsible for it, that I believe I expressed myself too seriously.

No, indeed you did not: at least, in listening I did not think so.

Well, in speaking, it struck me that I did. But, to proceed, let us not forget that it will be impossible in this instance to select persons advanced in years, as we did in the former. For we must not be persuaded by Solon into thinking that a man, as he grows old, can learn many things. On the contrary, an old man can sooner run than learn; and the wide range of severe labours must fall wholly on the young.

Unquestionably so.

Arithmetic, therefore, and geometry, and all the branches of that preliminary education which is to pave the way for dialectic, must be taught our pupils in their childhood, care being taken to convey instruction in such a shape as not to make it compulsory upon them to learn.

Why so?

Because, I replied, no trace of slavery ought to mix with the studies of the freeborn man. For the constrained performance of bodily labours does, it is true, exert no evil influence upon the body, but in the case of the mind, no study pursued under compulsion remains rooted in the memory.

That is true.

Hence, my excellent friend, you must train the children to their studies in a playful manner, and without any air of constraint, with the further object of discerning more readily the natural bent of their respective characters.

Your advice is reasonable.

Do you remember our saying that the children must also be taken on horseback within sight of actual war; and that on any safe occasion they must be brought into the field and made to taste blood, like young hounds?

I do remember it, he replied.

Accordingly we must make a select list, including everyone who has displayed remarkable self-possession in the midst of all these labours, studies and dangers.

At what age must that be done?

As soon as they are released from the necessary bodily exercises, during which, whether they last two or three years, nothing else can be done. For weariness and sleep are enemies to study. And besides, the behaviour of each in his exercises is one of the tests of character, and a very important one too.

Doubtless it is.

After this period, I continued, these choice characters selected from the ranks of the young men of twenty must receive higher honours than the rest, and the detached sciences in which they were educated as children must be brought within the compass of a single survey, to show the co-relation which exists between them and the nature of real existence.

Certainly this is the only kind of instruction which will be found abiding, when it has once effected an entrance.

Yes, and it is also a most powerful criterion of the dialectic character. For according as a man can survey a subject as a whole or not, he is, or is not, a dialectician.

I agree with you.

Hence it will be your duty to have an eye to those who show the greatest ability in these questions, and the greatest firmness, not only in study, but also in war and the other branches of discipline: and when they are thirty years old and upwards, you must select them out of the ranks of your picked men, and raise them to greater honours, and try them by the test of dialectic ability, in order to see who is able to divest himself of his eyes and his other senses, and advance in company with truth towards real existence. And here it is, my friend that great caution is required.

For what special reason? he inquired.

Do you not perceive, I said, what an immense evil at present accompanies dialectic?

Pray what is it?

Insubordination, I replied, with which I believe dialecticians to be tainted.

Indeed you are right.

Are you at all surprised at the fact, and do you make no allowance for the persons in question?

Pray explain yourself.

By way of parallel case, figure to yourself a supposititious child, brought up in the midst of great wealth, and extensive connections of high family, and surrounded by flatterers; and suppose him, on arriving at manhood, to learn that his alleged parents are not his real parents, though he cannot discover the latter. Can you guess what would be his behaviour towards his flatterers and towards his spurious parents, first while he was ignorant of the fact of his substitution, and secondly when he became aware of it? Or would you like to listen to my own conjectures?

I should, he replied.

Well, I suspect that so long as he is ignorant of the truth, he will honour his father and his mother and his other apparent relations more than his flatterers, and that he will not allow the former to want anything so quickly as the latter, and that he will be more likely to be guilty of insubordination in word or deed and of disobedience in important things towards his flatterers than towards his supposed parents.

Probably he will.

On the other hand, I suspect that after he has learned the truth, his esteem and regard for his parents will be diminished, while his respect for his flatterers will be heightened, to whom he will now listen very much more than before, and proceed to live as they would have him live, associating with them undisguisedly and wholly abandoning all concern for that fictitious father, and those pretended relations, unless his disposition is remarkably good.

Your description is perfectly true to nature. But how does this comparison bear upon those who apply themselves to dialectic?

I will tell you. We have, I believe, from childhood decided opinions about things just and beautiful, and we have been bred up to obey and honour these opinions, just as we have grown up in submission to our parents.

True.

Now these opinions are combated by certain pleasurable pursuits, which flatter our soul and try to draw it over to their side, though they fail to persuade us, if we are at all virtuous; in which case, we honour those ancestral opinions and continue loyal to them.

True.

Well, but when such a person is met by the question, what is beauty? – and having given the answer which he used to hear from the legislator, is confuted by the dialectic process; and when frequent and various defeats have forced him to believe that there is as much deformity as beauty in what he calls beauty, and that justice, goodness, and all the things which he used to honour most, are in the like predicament – how do you think he will behave thenceforth towards his old opinions, so far as respect and obedience are concerned?

Of course he will not pay them the same respect or the same obedience as before.

And so long as he neither honours nor acknowledges his former belief, as he used to do, while at the same time he fails to discover the true principles, is not that flattering life the only one to which he will be likely to attach himself?

It is.

In other words, he will appear, I suppose, to have abandoned his loyalty, and to have become lawless.

There cannot be a doubt of it.

Well now, is not this condition of the students of dialectic a natural one, and as I said just now, does it not deserve to be treated with great forbearance?

Yes, and with pity too, he replied.

Then in order that you may not have to feel this pity for those men of thirty, must you not use every precaution in introducing them to dialectic?

Certainly.

And will it not be one great precaution to forbid their meddling with it while young? For I suppose you have noticed that whenever boys taste dialectic for the first time, they pervert it into an amusement, and always employ it for purposes of contradiction, and imitate in their own persons the artifices of those who study refutation – delighting, like puppies, in pulling and tearing to pieces with logic anyone who comes near them.

They do, to an extravagant extent.

Hence, when they have experienced many triumphs and many defeats, they fall, quickly and vehemently, into an utter disbelief of their former sentiments: and thereby both they and the whole cause of philosophy have been prejudiced in the eyes of the world.

That is perfectly true.

The man of more advanced years, on the contrary, will not suffer himself to be led away by such madness, but will imitate those who are resolved to discuss and examine truth, rather than those who play at contradiction for amusement, and as a consequence of his superior discretion, will increase, instead of diminishing, the general respect for the pursuit.

You are right.

Again; were we not studying precaution throughout, when we said some time back that the characters which are to be initiated into dialectic must be stable and orderly, in opposition to the present system, which allows anybody, however unfit, to enter the field?

Certainly we were.

Would it suffice, then, for the acquisition of dialectic, that a man should continue constantly and strenuously devoted to the study – resigning every other pursuit for it, just as, in its turn, he resigned everything for gymnastic – during a period twice as long as that which he bestowed on his bodily exercises?

Do you mean six years, or four?

It does not matter much, I replied. Say five. After this you will have to send them down again into the cavern we described, and compel them to take commands in war, and to hold such offices as befit young men, that they may also keep up with their neighbours in practical address. And here again you must put them to the test, to see whether they will continue steadfast notwithstanding every seduction, or whether possibly they may be a little shaken.

And how long a time do you assign for this?

Fifteen years, I replied. Then, as soon as they are fifty years old, those who have passed safely through all temptations, and who have won every distinction in every branch whether of action or of science, must be forthwith introduced to their final task, and must be constrained to lift up the eye of the soul and fix it upon that which gives light to all things; and having surveyed the essence of good, they must take it as a pattern to be copied in that work of regulating their country and their fellow-citizens and themselves, which is to occupy each in turn during the rest of life; and though they are to pass most of their time in philosophical pursuits, yet each, when his turn comes, is to devote himself to the hard duties of public life, and hold office for their country's sake – not as a desirable, but as an unavoidable occupation; and thus having trained up a constant supply of others like themselves to fill their place as guardians of the state, they will depart and take up their abode in the islands of the blessed. And the state will put up monuments to their memory at the public expense, and offer sacrifices to them as demigods, if the Pythian oracle will authorise it, or at least as highly-favoured and godlike men.

Like a sculptor, Socrates, you have finished off the leading men in a style of faultless beauty.

Say leading women too, Glaucon. For do not suppose that my remarks were intended to apply at all more to men than to women, so long as we can find women whose talents are equal to the situation.

You are right, he said, if they are to share with the men in everything on a footing of equality, according to our account.

Well then, do you agree that our theory of the state and constitution is not a mere aspiration, but though full of difficulties, capable of realisation in one way, and only one, which as we have said, requires that one, if not more, of the true philosophers shall be invested with full authority in a state, and contemn the honours of the present day, in the belief that they are mean and worthless; and that, deeply impressed with the supreme importance of right and of the honours to be derived from it, and regarding justice as the highest and most binding of all obligations, he shall, as the special servant and admirer of justice, carry out a thorough reform in his own state.

How is that to be done?

All who are above ten years old in the city must be despatched into the country, and their children must be taken and bred up beyond the influence of that common character, which their parents among others possess, in the manners and laws of the true philosophers, the nature of which we have described above; and tell me, will not this be the quickest and easiest way to enable a state and a constitution such as we have represented to establish itself and prosper, and at the same time be a blessing to the nation in which it has taken root?

Yes, quite so, he replied: and I believe, Socrates, you have stated correctly the means that would be employed, if such a constitution were ever realised.

And have we not by this time discussed to satiety this state and the individual that resembles it? For I presume it is also clear what sort of person we shall expect him to be.

It is clear, he replied; and the present inquiry is, I believe, concluded.

NOTES TO BOOK SEVEN

1 The allusion is to a game played with shells.

BOOK EIGHT

Very well; then we agree, Glaucon, upon these points – namely that if the constitution of a state is to be carried to perfection, it must recognise a community of women, a community of children and of education in all its branches, and in like manner, a community of pursuits in war and in peace; and that its kings must be those who have shown the greatest ability in philosophy and the greatest aptitude for war.

Yes, we agree so far.

In addition to this, we also admitted that as soon as the rulers have established their position, they are to take the soldiers, and settle them in dwelling-places of a certain description; in which, by our direction, no private rights are admitted, but which are the common property of all. And besides determining the nature of their dwellings, we also determined, if you recollect, how far they were to be permitted to have anything which they could call their own.

Yes, he replied, I recollect that we pronounced against their holding any such property as is commonly held at the present day, and decided that in their capacity of trained soldiers and guardians they ought to receive in return for their guardianship year by year from the other citizens the maintenance required by their position, and devote their attention to the whole state including themselves.

You are right. But now that we have concluded this subject, let us recall to mind the point from which we diverged, in order that we may resume our old route.

That will not be difficult, he replied. You were talking pretty much as you are now doing – giving us to understand that you had finished the discussion of the commonwealth, and saying that you applied the term 'good' to such a state as you had then described, and to the man who resembled it; though as it would seem, you had it in your power to tell us of a still more excellent state, and of a still more excellent man. At the same time you declared that if your state were right, all others must be wrong. Of the remaining constitutions I remember you mentioned four principal varieties which you said it might be worth while to consider – noticing their faults and observing in their turn the men who resemble them in order that, after viewing them all and agreeing as to the best and the worst man, we might examine whether or not the best is happiest and the worst most wretched. And on my asking you to specify the four constitutions to which you alluded, we were interrupted by Polemarchus and Adeimantus; and thereupon you took up the discussion which has brought you to this point.

Your memory is perfectly correct.

Then allow me to grapple with you, like a wrestler, in my old attitude; and when I repeat my former question, exert yourself to give me the answer which was then upon your lips.

I will do my best, I replied.

Well, it is my particular desire to be told what are the four constitutions to which you referred.

I shall find no difficulty in answering your question. The constitutions to which I allude, and to which in fact special names have been given, are the following. First, we have the constitution of Crete and Sparta, which has the general voice in its favour. Second in order, as in estimation, stands oligarchy, as it is called, a commonwealth fraught with many evils. Then comes democracy, which is the adversary and successor of oligarchy; and finally, that glorious thing, despotism, which differs from all the preceding, and constitutes the fourth and worst disease of a state. I suppose you cannot tell me of any other form of polity which stands conspicuously by itself in kind? For I believe we may regard as minor links in the series just given all principalities and purchased sovereignties and similar constitutions, which are to be found fully as often among the barbarians as among the Greeks.

Yes, we certainly hear of many strange instances of them.

Now, are you aware that the varieties of human character and the varieties of existing constitutions must be exactly equal in point of number? Or do you imagine that constitutions grow upon a tree or rock, instead of springing out of the moral dispositions of the members of each state, according as this or that disposition turns the scale as it were, and drags everything else in its wake?

I believe the latter to be their sole origin.

Consequently, if there are five varieties of commonwealth, there must be also five varieties of mental constitution among individuals.

Certainly.

We have already discussed the man who resembles aristocracy, whom we rightly affirm to be both good and just.

We have.

Then must we proceed to describe those inferior men, to wit, the contentious and ambitious man, answering to the Spartan constitution; and likewise the oligarchical, and the democratical, and the despotic man, in order that we may get a view of the most unjust man, and contrast him with the most just, and so may complete our inquiry into the respective merits of pure justice and pure injustice, so far as the happiness or misery of their possessors is concerned: in order that we may either listen to Thrasymachus and pursue injustice, or yield to the argument which is coming into view, and follow after justice?

We ought by all means so to do.

Well then, as our practice from the first has been to examine moral characteristics in the state prior to doing so in the individual, because such a method conduces to greater clearness, so, if you please, we will begin on the present occasion by examining the ambitious constitution – I do not know of any other name in use; we must call it timocracy, or timarchy – and with this in sight, we will proceed to examine the ambitious man, and then go on to oligarchy and the oligarchical man; and next, after looking at democracy, we will contemplate the democratical man; and lastly, we will enter into a city which is governed by a despot and observe it, and then look into the soul which is its counterpart, and so endeavour to become competent judges of the question proposed.

There would at least be sound reason in such a method of observing and deciding.

Come then, I proceeded, let us endeavour to describe how timocracy will grow out of aristocracy. May we not lay down the rule that changes in any constitution originate, without exception, in the governing body, and only when that body becomes the seat of dissensions? For so long as it continues unanimous, it cannot be shaken, though it be very insignificant in point of numbers.

Yes, that is true.

Then pray, Glaucon, how will our state be shaken, and in what way will divisions arise either between the auxiliaries and the magistrates, or in these bodies themselves? Would you have us pray to the Muses, like Homer, to tell us 'how first division entered'; and would you have us describe them as talking in tragic, high-flown style, playing with us as children, and jesting while they pretend to speak seriously?

What will their answer be?

Something to this effect – It is indeed difficult for a state, thus constituted, to be shaken. But since everything that has come into being must one day perish, even a system like ours will not endure for all time, but must suffer dissolution. The dissolution will be as follows: not only the vegetable, but also the animal kingdom, is liable to alternations of fertility and barrenness, mental and bodily; and these alternations are coincident with certain cyclical revolutions, which vary in each case in length according to the length of life of the particular thing. Now, as touching the fruitfulness and barrenness of your own race, though the persons whom you have trained to be governors of the state are men of wisdom, yet in despite of all observation and calculation they will miss the propitious time. It will give them the slip, and they will beget children on wrong occasions. Now the cycle of a divine race is contained in a perfect number;[1] but the cycle of a human race is expressed by a geometrical number, on which depends the good or bad quality of the births. And when your guardians, from ignorance of this, arrange unseasonable marriages, the children of such marriages will not be well-endowed or fortunate. The best of them will be established in power by their predecessors, but nevertheless they will be unworthy of it, and having entered upon the functions of their fathers, they will first of all begin to slight us, in defiance of their duties as guardians, and underrate music first, and then gymnastic. Thus your young men will grow up worse educated, and in consequence of this, magistrates will take office who will fail in their duty of discriminating Hesiod's races and yours, that is to say the golden and silver and brazen and iron. And this mixture of iron with silver and of brass with gold will breed inequality and incongruous irregularity; and wherever these take root, their growth always produces enmity and war. So that we may positively assert that the rise of such a generation will invariably be marked by divisions.

Yes, and we shall allow that the answer of the Muses is the right one.

How could it be otherwise, when the Muses speak?

And what do the Muses say next? he asked.

As soon as a division had arisen, the two parties would be likely to diverge rapidly – the races of iron and brass inclining to money-making and the acquisition of land and houses, of silver and gold, while the other two richly-endowed races would, in the absence of all poverty, turn their minds to virtue and the ancient constitution of things. But the violence of their mutual contentions would induce the two parties to come to an agreement, on the understanding that they should divide and appropriate the land and houses, and enslave their formerly free wards, friends and maintainers, from thenceforth to be held as an inferior tribe and as servants, and apply themselves to war and their own protection.

I believe you have described correctly the passage to timocracy.

Then will not this constitution be a kind of mean between aristocracy and oligarchy?

Assuredly it will.

Such being the passage, how will the state in question conduct itself after the change? Is it not obvious that being a mean between its former constitution and oligarchy, it will imitate partly the one, and partly the other, besides having some peculiarities of its own?

Precisely so.

Then in the respect which the warrior class will pay to the magistrates, and in the abstinence of that class from agriculture, handicrafts, and all other pursuits of gain, and in the establishment of public messes, and devotion to gymnastic and the training which war requires – in all such points it will imitate the former constitution, will it not?

It will

But in its fear of installing the wise in office, because the wise men in its possession are no longer men of sufficiently simple and sterling stuff, but of compound nature, and in its degenerate inclination towards men of spirit and of a narrower character, with a greater turn for war than for peace, and in the value which it set upon the arts and stratagems which war calls out, and in the incessant hostilities which it carries on – in most of these points it will have a character of its own, will it not?

It will.

Again, I continued, such persons will, like the members of oligarchies, be covetous of wealth, and will have a passionate but concealed regard for gold and silver, from the fact of their owning storehouses and private treasuries in which they can deposit and secrete their riches, and also walled houses, which are verily private nests wherein they may spend with a lavish hand on wives or any other object that may please them.

Most true, he said.

Hence, while their covetous nature makes them prodigal of other people's money, they will at the same time be parsimonious of their own, because they value it and have to conceal the possession of it; and they will enjoy their pleasures in secret, shunning the law as boys shun their father, because they have been trained not by persuasion but by force, inasmuch as they have slighted the true muse that goes hand in hand with profound philosophical inquiry, and have honoured gymnastic above music.

You are certainly describing a constitution which is a compound of good and evil.

Yes, it is a compound, I replied: but owing to the preponderance of the spirited element, there is one thing in particular which it exhibits in the clearest colours, and that is party-spirit and the love of distinction.

Yes, decidely it does.

Such, then, will be the origin, and such or nearly such the character of this constitution, if we are satisfied to sketch a theoretical outline of its form, without perfectly elaborating it; which we need not do, because we can distinguish sufficiently even from such a sketch the most just and the most unjust man, and because it is a work of hopeless length to discuss without any omission every constitution and every character.

You are right, he said.

Who then is the man that answers to this constitution? What is his origin, and what his character?

I imagine, said Adeimantus, that as a man of party-spirit, he must rather closely resemble our friend Glaucon.

Perhaps so, I replied, as a party-man; but in the following points I do not think that his nature and Glaucon's correspond.

What are these points?

He must be more self-willed than Glaucon, and rather less fond of literature: still he must be studious and fond of listening, but no speaker. A person of this character will not despise slaves, like the perfectly educated man, though he will behave harshly to them and at the same time gently to the free-born. He will also be exceedingly obedient to the magistrates, with a passion for distinction and command, to which he lays claim not on the ground of oratory or anything of the kind, but on the ground of deeds of arms and exploits congenial to war, devoted as he is to bodily exercise and field-sports.

True, this is the character of the corresponding commonwealth.

In addition to this, will not such a person in his younger days despise wealth? But as he grows older, will he not be always paying it more respect, because he has a touch of the nature of the money-lover, and because his virtue is not free from blemish, owing to his having parted from the best guardian?

Who is that guardian? asked Adeimantus.

Rational inquiry, I replied, blended with music; for this alone by its presence and indwelling can preserve its owner in the possession of life-long virtue.

It is well said.

Such we find to be the character of the timocratic young man, who resembles the timocratic state.

Very true.

Again, his origin, I proceeded, may be traced as follows. He is the youthful son of an excellent father, who living, as is not uncommon, in a city where the constitution is defective, avoids honours and offices and litigation and all similar marks of a restless spirit, and is willing to suffer loss rather than get into trouble.

Pray describe the formation of such a character.

It dates from the time when the son listens to his mother's complaint, who is looked down upon by the other women because her husband is not a member of the government, and who also sees that he does not concern himself much about money, and will not fight and rail as a litigant in the law-courts or in the public assemblies, to all which things he exhibits great indifference; and who further perceives that he is always inwardly reflecting, and that he pays no great respect to herself, though he offers her no disrespect: for all which reasons she is vexed, and tells her son that his father is nothing of a man and culpably inactive, not to mention all the other choice expressions which women are in the habit of lavishing on such men.

Ay, said Adeimantus, they have indeed plenty to say that is quite in keeping with their own character.

And no doubt you are aware, I continued, that the servants also of such persons – servants who seem to have their masters' interests at heart – do sometimes privately make similar observations to the sons, and that if they see a man in debt to the father, or wronging him in any other way, and no proceedings taken against him, they exhort the son, when he is grown up, to take revenge on all such people, and be more of a man than his father. Likewise when the son goes abroad, he hears and sees other instances of the same thing. He hears the quiet and unmeddlesome called simpletons in the city, and sees that they are held in small esteem, while the busybodies are honoured and commended. Thereupon the young man, hearing and seeing all this, and on the other hand listening to his father's conversation and narrowly examining his pursuits side by side with those of other men, is pulled two ways by two influences. On the one hand his father is watering and nursing the rational element in his soul, and on the other hand everyone else is watering and nursing the appetitive and the spirited element of his nature; and because, though his disposition is not that of a bad man, he nevertheless has mixed in the bad society of others, he is drawn by these combined influences into a middle ground, where he delivers up the government of himself to that middle element which is hot-tempered and contentious, and turns out a high-spirited, ambitious man.

It appears to me, said he, that you have exactly described the production of such a character.

Then we are in possession of the second constitution, and the second man.

We are.

Must we not then, to use the words of Aeschylus, proceed to describe

Another man matched with another state?

Or rather, according to our plan, must we not begin with the state?

By all means, he replied.

Well, I think that the constitution which comes next in order will be oligarchy.

Pray, what kind of constitution do you mean by an oligarchy?

A constitution grounded upon a property qualification, I replied, in which the wealthy rule, while the poor have no part in the government.

I understand.

Ought we not to describe the first steps in the transition from timarchy to oligarchy?

We ought.

Well, no doubt even a blind man could find out how the transition is brought about.

How?

It is the influx of gold into those private treasuries that ruins the constitution just described. For the first result of this is that the owners invent ways of spending their money, and pervert the laws with that intent, and disobey them in their own persons and in the persons of their wives.

It would be strange if they did not.

They then proceed, if I am not mistaken, to eye one another with jealous looks, and to enter upon a course of rivalry which stamps the same character on the general body of which they are members.

It is what we might expect.

And thenceforth they press forward on the path of money-getting, losing their esteem for virtue in proportion as the esteem for wealth grows upon them. For can you deny that there is such a gulf between wealth and virtue, that when weighed as it were in the two scales of a balance, one of the two always falls as the other rises?

That is quite true.

Consequently when wealth and the wealthy are honoured in a state, virtue and the virtuous sink in estimation.

Obviously.

And what is honoured at any time is practised, and what is dishonoured is neglected.

True.

Hence instead of being contentious and ambitious, such persons end by becoming lovers of gain and covetous; and while they commend and admire and confer office upon the wealthy, they despise the poor.

Assuredly they do.

So that at length they pass a law, which is the essence of an oligarchical constitution, by which they agree upon a certain sum, which is larger or smaller according to the strength of the oligarchical principle, and forbid any share in the government to those who have not property up to the stipulated amount. And they bring about these measures by violence, with arms in their hands, if they have not previously succeeded in establishing the proposed constitution by the alarm which they have inspired. Or am I wrong?

No, you are right.

And this, in a word, is the establishment of oligarchy.

True: but pray, what is the character of the constitution, and what are the faults which we attributed to it?

Its first fault, I answered, lies in the very nature of its essential law. For consider what would be the result if we elected our pilots on this principle of a property qualification – refusing the post to the poor man, though he were a better pilot.

We should make sad work with the voyage, he replied.

Does not this apply to any management of anything else whatever?

Yes, I think so.

Do you except a state? I asked; or do you include it?

I include it most especially, he replied, in consideration of the superior difficulty and importance of its management.

Then here is one of the faults of oligarchy, and that a grievous one.

Evidently.

Again: is the following fault at all less grievous than the first?

What is it?

Why, that such a city must necessarily lose its unity and become two cities, one comprising the rich and the other the poor; who reside together on the same ground, and are always plotting against one another.

Why, this fault, I am sure, is quite as bad as the former.

Once again, it is certainly not a commendable thing that they should be incapable (as they probably will be) of waging any war; the fact being that if they arm and employ the populace, they cannot help dreading them more than the enemy, whereas if they hesitate to employ them, they must appear veritable oligarchs in the actual battle; to which we must add that their love of money renders them unwilling to pay war-taxes.

You are right.

Again, to return to a point against which we were inveighing some time ago, do you think it right that the same persons should be engaged at the same time in the various occupations of agriculture, trade and war – which is the case under such a constitution?

No, there is nothing to be said for it.

Now, consider whether the following evil, which is greater than all the others, is not admitted by this constitution, and by none of the preceding.

What is it?

I allude to the practice of allowing one person to sell all his property, and another to acquire it – the former owner living in the city without being a recognised portion of the state either as trader, artisan, trooper or foot-soldier; but described as a destitute man and a pauper.

None of the preceding constitutions admitted such a practice.

To say the least, such a casualty is not prohibited in cities whose constitution is oligarchical. Otherwise it would be impossible for some persons to be extravagantly rich while others are utter paupers.

True.

Let me ask you to examine another point. At the time when such a man was spending money in his wealthy days, was he one whit more useful to the state for the purposes which we were just now specifying? Or was it the case that though he seemed to be one of the government, he was really neither governor nor servant of the state, but only a consumer of its resources?

The latter is the true account, he replied. He seemed what you say, but he was really only a consumer.

Then would you have us assert that as the drone grows up in the hive to be the plague of the bees, so also does such a man grow up as a drone in his house, to be the plague of the state?

Undoubtedly, Socrates, he does.

And is it not true, Adeimantus, that though god has provided none of the flying drones with stings, he has made only *some* of these walking drones stingless, while to some he has given formidable stings? And that while the stingless ones end in an old age of beggary, the stinging drones, on the contrary, furnish out of their ranks all who bear the name of criminals?

It is most true.

It is quite clear then, that whenever you see beggars in a city, you may be certain that in the same place lurk thieves, cut-purses, temple-robbers and the instruments of all similar crimes.

True.

Well, and in oligarchical states do you not see beggars?

Yes, he said; almost all are beggars except the governors.

Then is it, or is it not, our opinion that there are also many evil-doers in such states, armed with stings, whom the magistrates are careful to keep down by main force?

Certainly it is our opinion.

Then shall we not assert that the cause which produces such persons therein is want of education and bad training, and a bad condition of the commonwealth?

Yes, we shall.

Well then, this, or something like it, will be the character of a state governed by an oligarchy; and it will contain quite as many evils, if not more.

You are near the mark, he said.

Then let us close our account here of this commonwealth which is called oligarchy, and which takes its governors by a property qualification; and let us proceed to examine how the man who resembles it grows up, and what he is when he has grown up.

By all means let us do so.

Tell me then, is the transition from the timocratic man whom we have described to the oligarchical, effected thus, or nearly thus?

How?

The timocratic man has a son, who at first emulates his father and follows his steps, and then suddenly sees him founder on the state as on a sunken rock, and his property and his person thrown over-board – sees him, after commanding his country's armies or holding some other high office, brought to trial, damaged by lying informers, and either put to death or banished or disfranchised, and all his substance taken from him.

All this might very well happen, he replied.

Well, my friend, the instant the son has seen and felt this, and lost his property, he becomes alarmed, I suppose, and thrusts ambition and that high-spirited element head-foremost from the throne of his heart, and being humbled by poverty he turns to money-getting, makes mean and petty savings, and by working hard accumulates wealth. Do you not think that such a person does then instal on that throne the appetitive and covetous element, and make of it an eastern monarch within himself, adorning it with diadem and collar, and girding the scimitar by its side?

I do, he answered.

But the rational and the high-spirited elements, I think, he sets down on the ground below it, on this side and on that, as subjects and slaves – forbidding the former to investigate or reason about anything, save how to multiply riches, and forbidding the latter to admire or esteem anything save wealth and the wealthy, or to be ambitious after a single object save the acquisition of riches and whatever else may conduce to this.

There can be no other transformation of an ambitious into a covetous young man so speedy and so thorough.

Then tell me, is such a person oligarchical?

Well, at any rate the man from whom he is by transformation derived, resembled the constitution which was the antecedent of oligarchy.

Let us examine whether he will resemble oligarchy.

Yes, let us.

Well then, first of all, will he not resemble oligarchy in setting the highest value on riches?

Assuredly he will.

And also in the fact that he is parsimonious and hard-working, satisfying only his necessary appetites, and refusing himself all other expenses, and subjugating his other desires as idle.

Exactly so.

In other words, he is a sordid man, making a profit out of everything, and given to hoarding: one of those persons who are positively commended by the great body of men. Or am I wrong in supposing that such will be the man who resembles the constitution we have just described?

If you ask me, I think you are right. At any rate, the oligarchical state, as well as the person under discussion, values money above everything.

The reason being, I believe, that such a man has taken no pains with his education.

I fancy he has not: else he would not have appointed, nor would he so highly honour, a blind leader of the chorus.

Very true. And now let me ask you to consider whether we must not assert that drone-like appetites, which are either beggarly or criminal, grow up in him owing to his want of education, and that these appetites are forcibly held down by other prudential considerations.

Certainly we must assert it.

And do you know where you must look in order to see their evil deeds?

Where?

You must look to occasions where they are guardians of orphans, and to any similar accidents which put it completely in their power to act unjustly.

True.

Then is it not clear from this that in his other contracts, in which his apparent justice secures him a good name, such a person is holding down by a kind of constrained moderation a class of evil appetites that are within him, which he does not tame by reason, or convince that it would be wrong to gratify them, but which circumstances and his own apprehensions teach him to suppress, because he trembles for the rest of his substance?

Yes, it is quite clear.

Indeed, my friend, I am quite sure that when these people have to spend what is not their own, you will find that most of them possess the appetites akin to the drone.

Most decidedly they do.

Hence such a person, far from being at peace within himself, will be a double-minded, not a single-minded, man, though he will generally find his lower appetites vanquished by his higher.

True.

And for these reasons, I think, such a person will present a better outside than many; but the genuine virtue of a soul attuned to concord and harmony will fly somewhere far away from him.

So I think.

And no doubt the parsimonious man makes a miserable rival as a private citizen, when a prize or any other honourable distinction is contested, for he will not spend money to win himself renown in such matches, from fear of exciting his expensive appetites by inviting them to share in the struggle and the rivalry; so that in fact he follows the practice of an oligarchy in employing only some few parts of himself in his wars, and in most cases spares his purse and submits to defeat.

Exactly so.

Then are we still incredulous, I asked, as to the similarity and correspondence subsisting between the oligarchical state and the parsimonious money-hunter?

Not at all, he answered.

And now we must proceed, I should suppose, to examine in what way democracy arises, and what is its character when it has arisen, in order that once again we may discover the character of the corresponding man, and place him by our side for judgment.

Yes, if we would act consistently, we must take that course.

Is not the transition from oligarchy to democracy brought about by an intemperate craving for extravagant wealth, which is publicly acknowledged to be the greatest of blessings, and the attainment of which is considered a duty – the transition itself taking the following form?

Pray describe it.

Since the power of the rulers in an oligarchical state is, I believe, wholly due to their great wealth, they are unwilling to put the licentious young men of their time under restraint to the extent of rendering it illegal for them to run through their property, because they hope, by purchasing the possessions of such persons, and by lending money to them, to make themselves still richer and more honoured.

Most unquestionably.

And is it not manifest by this time that it is impossible for the citizens of a state to honour wealth and at the same time acquire a proper amount of temperance, because they cannot avoid neglecting either the one or the other?

It is pretty well manifest, he replied.

Hence the rulers in such states, by their reckless admission of unrestrained licence, not unfrequently compel men of noble birth to become poor.

Yes, that they do.

And the persons thus impoverished lurk, I should suppose, in the city, harnessed and armed with stings – some owing debts, and others disfranchised, and others labouring under both misfortunes – hating and plotting against the new owners of their property and against all who are better off than themselves, and enamoured of revolution.

True.

These capitalists, on the other hand, keep prying after their own interests, and apparently do not see their enemies; and whenever one of the remainder yields them opportunity, they wound him by infusing their poisonous money, and then recover interest many times as great as the parent sum, and thus make the drone and the beggar multiply in the state.

Yes, that they do.

And they cannot make up their minds to extinguish this great evil, either by that cauterising operation of prohibiting people from disposing of their property at their own pleasure, or by employing another method which provides by a different law for the removal of such dangers.

Pray, what law do you mean?

I mean one which is next best to the former, and which constrains the citizens to apply themselves to virtue. For if it be enacted that voluntary contracts be as a general rule entered into at the proper risk of the contractor, people will be less shameless in their money-dealings in the city, and such evils as we have just now described will be of less common growth therein.

Yes, much less common.

But as it is, the various inducements I have mentioned encourage the governing body in the state to handle their subjects in this ungentle way. On the other hand, if we look at the rulers themselves and their children, do we not see that the young men are made luxurious and indolent both in body and mind, and so idle and effeminate that they cannot resist pleasure and encounter pain?

Unquestionably they are.

And that their seniors are indifferent to everything except making money, and as careless about virtue as the poor themselves?

Certainly they are.

In this state of things, when the rulers and their subjects encounter one another either in travelling or in some other common occupation, whether it be a pilgrimage or a military expedition, in which they are fellow-sailors or fellow soldiers; or when they are witnesses of one another's behaviour in moments of danger, in which the poor can by no possibility be despised by the rich, because it often happens that a rich man, nursed in luxury and surfeited with abundance, finds himself posted in battle by the side of some lean and sunburnt poor man, to whom by his laboured breathing he betrays his sore distress; when, I repeat, all this takes place, do you imagine that these poor men can avoid thinking that it is through their own cowardice that such incapable people are wealthy, or that they can refrain from repeating to one another, when they meet in private, 'Our governors are naught'?

Nay, I am quite sure that they do so.

Now just as a sickly body requires but a small additional impulse from without to bring on an attack of illness, and sometimes even without any external provocation is divided against itself, so in the same way, does not this city, whose condition is identical with that of a diseased body, require only the slight excuse of an external alliance introduced by the one party from an oligarchical city, or by the other from a democratical, to bring on an acute disease and an inward battle? And is it not sometimes, even without such external influences, distracted by factions?

Most decidedly it is.

Democracy then, I think, arises whenever the poor win the day, killing some of the opposite party, expelling others, and admitting the remainder to an equal participation in civic rights and offices; and most commonly the offices in such a state are given by lot.

Yes, you have described correctly the establishment of democracy, whether it be effected by an actual appeal to arms, or by the terrified withdrawal of the other party.

And now tell me, I continued, in what style these persons administer the state, and what is the character of this third constitution. For obviously we shall find the corresponding man marked, to a certain extent, with the same features.

True, said he.

First of all, are they not free, and does not liberty of act and speech abound in the city, and has not a man licence therein to do what he will?

Yes, so we are told.

And clearly, where such licence is permitted, every citizen will arrange his own manner of life as suits his pleasure.

Clearly he will.

Hence I should suppose that in this commonwealth there will be the greatest diversity of character.

Unquestionably there will.

Possibly, I proceeded, this constitution may be the most beautiful of all. Embroidered as it is with every kind of character, it may be thought as beautiful as a coloured dress embroidered with every kind of flower. And perhaps, I added, as children and women admire dresses of many colours, so many persons will decide in favour of this commonwealth, as the most beautiful.

No doubt many will.

Yes, my excellent friend, and it would be a good plan to explore it, if we were in search of a commonwealth.

Why, pray?

Because it contains every kind of commonwealth in consequence of that licence of which I spoke, and perhaps a person wishing to found a state, as we were just now doing, ought to go into a democratical city, as a bazaar of commonwealths, and choose out the character that takes his fancy, and then found his state according to the choice he has made.

We may safely say that he is not likely to be at a loss for patterns.

Again, consider that in this state you are not obliged to hold office, though your talents may be equal to the task; and that you need not submit to government, if you dislike it, or go to war when your fellow-citizens are at war, or keep peace when they are doing so, if you do not want peace; and again, consider that though a law forbids your holding office or sitting on a jury, you may nevertheless do both the one and the other, should it occur to you to do so: and now tell me, is not such a course of life divinely pleasant for the moment?

Yes, perhaps it is, he replied, for the moment.

Once more, is not the meekness of some of those who have been tried in a court of law exquisite? Or have you failed to notice in such a commonwealth how men who have been condemned to death or exile stay all the same, and walk about the streets, and parade like heroes, as if no one saw or cared?

I have seen many instances of it, he replied.

And is there not something splendid in the forbearance of such a commonwealth, and in its entire superiority to petty considerations? Nay, it positively scorns the doctrine which, when we were founding our state, we laid down with an air of importance, to the effect that no one who is not endowed with an extraordinary nature can ever become a good man, unless from his earliest childhood he plays among beautiful objects and studies all beautiful things. How magnificently it tramples all this underfoot, without troubling itself in the least about the previous pursuits of those who enter on a political course, whom it raises to honour if they only assert that they wish well to the people.

Yes, he said, it behaves very grandly.

These, then, will be some of the features of democracy, to which we might add others of the same family; and it will be, in all likelihood, an agreeable, lawless, parti-coloured commonwealth, dealing with all alike on a footing of equality, whether they be really equal or not.

The facts you mention are notorious.

And now let me ask you to examine the character of the corresponding individual. Or must we begin, as in the case of the commonwealth, by investigating his origin?

Yes, he replied.

Then am I not right in supposing that he will be the son of the parsimonious and oligarchical man, bred up under his father's eye and in his father's character?

Doubtless he will.

And this son, like the father, will put a violent constraint upon those pleasures within him that tend to extravagance and not to money-getting; which, you know, are called unnecessary pleasures.

Clearly he will.

Now, that we may not talk in the dark, would you like us first to define the necessary and unnecessary appetites?

I should.

May we not justly apply the term necessary to those appetites which we cannot get rid of, and to those whose satisfaction does us good? For our nature cannot help feeling both these classes of desires, can it?

Certainly it cannot.

Then we shall be justified in predicating necessity of them.

We shall.

Again, shall we not be right if we assert all those appetites to be unnecessary, which we can put away from us by early training, and the presence of which, besides, never does us any good and in some cases does positive harm?

Yes, we shall be right.

Would it not be as well to select an example of the existing appetites of each kind, in order that we may gain a general idea of them?

Decidedly it would.

Will not the appetite for food (that is to say, simple bread and meat), within the bounds of health and a good habit of body, be a necessary appetite?

I think so.

The appetite for bread at least is surely necessary by a double claim, as being not only beneficial but also indispensable to the support of life.

Yes.

On the other hand, the appetite for meat is necessary so far as it may contribute advantageously to a good habit of body.

Certainly.

Again, the appetite for other viands of a less simple kind, of which by early correction and training most people can rid themselves, and which is hurtful to the body and hurtful to the soul, in its endeavours after wisdom and temperance, may be rightly styled an unnecessary appetite, may it not?

Yes, most rightly.

And must we not assert that the appetites of this second class are also expensive, whereas the others contribute to money-making, because they are a help towards production?

Undoubtedly

Can we say the same of the passion of love and the other appetites?

Yes.

Now did we not describe the man to whom we lately gave the name of 'drone' as one burdened with those expensive pleasures and desires, and governed by the unnecessary appetites, while we described the man who is governed by the necessary as parsimonious and oligarchical?

Undoubtedly we did.

Let us now return, I continued, and explain how the oligarchical man is transformed into the democratical.

How is it?

I would have you suppose that the commencement of a young man's transition from inward oligarchy to democracy dates from the moment when, after being brought up, as we were saying just now, in ignorance and parsimony, he has tasted the honey of the drones, and made acquaintance with fiery and terrible wild beasts, who are able to procure him all kinds of pleasures, of a varied and manifold nature.

It cannot be otherwise.

And may we say that just as the state was transformed by the assistance afforded by a foreign alliance to one of the two parties, in virtue of a common character, so in the same way the young man is transformed by the analogous assistance from without, afforded by a certain species of appetites to one of the two parties present with him, in virtue of a real affinity and similarity?

Assuredly we may.

And should the oligarchical element within him be supported by some counter-alliance, derived perhaps from his father, or perhaps from his other relations, who rebuke and reproach him, then I imagine there ensues a genuine struggle of parties and an inward battling with himself.

Undoubtedly.

And occasionally, I fancy, the democratical interest yields to the oligarchical, and certain of the appetites are either cut to pieces or expelled, owing to the presence of a sense of shame in the young man's mind, and order is once more restored.

Yes, this does take place sometimes.

But some new appetites, I conclude, akin to those expelled, are privily nursed up, and owing to the lack of science in his father's training, become numerous and strong.

Yes, this is generally the case.

And these appetites, of course, draw him to his old associates, and by their secret communications engender in him a multitude of others.

Undoubtedly.

And finally, I imagine, they seize upon the citadel of the young man's heart, because they perceive it to be destitute of sound knowledge and beautiful studies and true theories, which verily keep the best watch and ward in the minds of men who are the favourites of heaven.

Yes, quite the best.

And to supply their place, I fancy, false and presumptuous theories and opinions start up in the man, and secure this post aforesaid.

That they do.

Does he not, in consequence, return to those lotus-eaters, and dwell with them without disguise; and if his relatives send any assistance to the parsimonious element of his soul, do not those presumptuous theories close the gates of the royal fortress within him, and not only refuse an entrance to the actual auxiliary force, but even decline to admit an embassy of individuals in the shape of admonitions from elder persons; and do they not fight in person and gain the day; and stigmatising the sense of shame as folly, do they not thrust it out to an ignominious exile, and expel temperance with insults under the name of cowardice; and do they not prove, by the aid of many useless appetites, that moderation and orderly expenditure are boorish and illiberal, and banish them as such beyond the border?

Most certainly they do.

And no doubt, when by the discharge of these virtues they have purified the soul of him who is now in their power, and is being initiated by them into the great mysteries, they proceed at once to restore insolence, and disorder, and licentiousness and shamelessness, in great splendour, accompanied by a numerous retinue and with crowns on their heads, extolling them and calling them by soft names, describing insolence as good breeding, and disorder as freedom, and licentiousness as magnificence, and shamelessness as bravery. Is not this, I asked, pretty much the way in which the man who is brought up in the gratification only of necessary appetites alters so far in his youth as to liberate from servitude and control the unnecessary and injurious pleasures?

Yes, very evidently it is, he replied.

From that day forward a man of this description spends, I should suppose, just as much money and labour and time on unnecessary as upon necessary pleasures. But should he be so fortunate as to set a limit to his wildness, and as he grows older, when the tumult of passion has mostly gone by, should he go so far as to readmit to a certain extent portions of the banished, and not surrender himself wholly to the invaders, in that case it is the habit of his life to make no distinction between his pleasures, but to suffer himself to be led by the passing pleasure which chance as it were throws in his way, and to turn to another when the first is satisfied – scorning none, but fostering all alike.

Exactly so.

Yes, I proceeded, and whenever he is told that though some

pleasures belong to the appetites which are good and honourable, others belong to the evil appetites, and that the former ought to be practised and respected, but the latter chastised and enslaved, he does not receive this true doctrine, or admit it into his castle. On the contrary, at all these assertions he shakes his head, and maintains that all appetites are alike, and ought to be equally respected.

Yes, this is precisely his condition and his behaviour.

Hence, I continued, he lives from day to day to the end in the gratification of the casual appetite, now drinking himself drunk to the sound of music, and presently putting himself under training, sometimes idling and neglecting everything, and then living like a student of philosophy. And often he takes a part in public affairs, and starting up, speaks and acts according to the impulse of the moment. Now he follows eagerly in the steps of certain great generals, because he covets their distinctions; and anon he takes to trade, because he envies the successful trader. And there is no order or constraining rule in his life, but he calls this life of his pleasant and liberal and happy, and follows it out to the end.

Well, said he, you have certainly described a life that might be led by a man whose motto is Liberty and Equality.

Yes, I replied; and I conceive it to be also a multitudinous life, replete with very many characters; and I imagine that this is the man who by the beautiful variety of his nature answers to the city which we described – a man whose life many men and many women would envy, and who contains within him very many exemplars of commonwealths and characters.

True.

What then? May we place this man opposite democracy, in the belief that he may be rightly addressed as democratical?

Be it so, he replied.

It only remains for us, I continued, to describe the most beautiful of all commonwealths, and the most beautiful of all men – that is to say, despotism and the despot.

You are quite right.

Come then, my dear friend, tell me in what way despotism arises. That it is a transformation of democracy is all but obvious.

It is.

Then does democracy give birth to despotism precisely in the way in which oligarchy gave birth to democracy?

Explain this.

The thing which oligarchy professed to regard as supremely good, and which was instrumental in establishing it, was excessive wealth, was it not?

It was.

Well, it was the insatiable craving for wealth, and the disregard of everything else for the sake of money-making, that destroyed oligarchy.

True, it was

Then may we say that democracy, like oligarchy, is destroyed by its insatiable craving for the object which it defines to be supremely good?

And what, according to you, is that object?

Freedom, I replied. For I imagine that in a democratical city you will be told that it has, in freedom, the most beautiful of possessions, and that therefore such a city is the only fit abode for the man who is a freeman by nature.

Why, certainly such language is very much in fashion.

To return, then, to the remark which I was trying to make a moment ago: am I right in saying that the insatiable craving for a single object and the disregard of all else transform democracy as well as oligarchy, and pave the way, as a matter of course, for despotism?

How so?

Whenever a democratical city which is thirsting for freedom has fallen under the presidency of a set of wicked toastmasters, and has quaffed the wine of liberty untempered far beyond the due measure, it proceeds, I should imagine, to arraign its rulers as accursed oligarchs, and chastises them on that plea, unless they become very submissive and supply it with freedom in copious draughts.

Yes, that is what is done.

And likewise it insults those who are obedient to the rulers with the titles of willing slaves and worthless fellows, while the rulers who carry themselves like subjects, and the subjects who carry themselves like rulers, it does, both privately and publicly, commend and honour. Must it not follow that in such a city freedom goes all lengths?

Of course it must.

Yes, my friend, and does not the prevailing anarchy steal into private houses, and spread on every side, till at last it takes root even among the brute creation?

What are we to understand by this?

I mean, for example, that a father accustoms himself to behave like a child, and stands in awe of his sons, and that a son behaves himself like a father, and ceases to respect or fear his parents, with the professed object of proving his freedom. And I mean that citizens and resident aliens and foreigners are all perfectly equal.

You are right as to the results of such a state of things.

I have told you some of the results. Let me tell you a few more trifles of the kind. The schoolmaster, in these circumstances, fears and flatters his scholars, and the scholars despise their masters and also their tutors. And speaking generally, the young copy their elders, and enter the lists with them both in talking and in acting; and the old men condescend so far as to abound in wit and pleasantry, in imitation of the young, in order, by their own account, to avoid the imputation of being morose or domineering.

Exactly so.

But the extreme limit, my friend, to which the freedom of the populace grows in such a commonwealth is only attained when the purchased slaves of both sexes are just as free as the purchasers. Also I had almost forgotten to mention to what extent this liberty and equality is carried in the mutual relations subsisting between men and women

Then in the words of Aeschylus, said he, shall we not give utterance to that which is already on our lips?

By all means, I replied. I, for one, am doing so when I tell you that no one could believe, without positive experience, how much more free the domestic animals are under this government than any other. For verily the hound, according to the proverb, is like the mistress of the house; and truly even horses and asses adopt a gait expressive of remarkable freedom and dignity, and run at any body who meets them in the streets, if he does not get out of their way: and all the other animals become in the same way gorged with freedom.

It is my own dream that you are repeating to me. This often happens to me when I walk into the country.

Now putting all these things together, I proceeded, do you perceive that they amount to this, that the soul of the citizens is rendered so sensitive as to be indignant and impatient at the smallest symptom of slavery? For surely you are aware that they end by making light of the laws themselves, whether statute or customary, in order that, as they say, they may not have the shadow of a master.

I am very well aware of it.

This then, my friend, if I am not mistaken, is the beginning, so fair and headstrong, out of which despotism grows.

Headstrong indeed! But what is the next step?

That very disease, I replied, which broke out in oligarchy and ruined it, appears in democracy also with increased strength and virulence, aggravated by the licence of the place, and occasions its enslavement. Indeed, to do anything in excess seldom fails to provoke a violent reaction to the opposite extreme, not only in the seasons of the year and in the animal and vegetable kingdoms, but also especially in commonwealths.

This is only natural.

Thus excessive freedom is unlikely to pass into anything but excessive slavery, in the case of states as well as of individuals.

It is.

Hence in all likelihood democracy, and only democracy, lays the foundation of despotism; that is to say, the most intense freedom lays the foundation for the heaviest and the fiercest slavery.

Yes, it is a reasonable statement.

However, this, I think, was not your question: you were asking, what is this disease which fastens upon democracy as well as upon oligarchy, and reduces the former to bondage.

That was my question.

Well then, I alluded to that class of idle and extravagant men, in which the bravest lead and the more cowardly follow. We compared them, if you recollect, to stinging and stingless drones, respectively.

Yes, and rightly so.

Now the presence of these two classes, like phlegm and bile in the body, breeds in every commonwealth disturbance. Therefore a skilful physician and legislator, just like a cunning bee-keeper, must take measures in advance, if possible, to prevent their presence; but should they make their appearance, he must have them cut out, as quickly as possible, along with the combs themselves.

That must he, without a doubt.

Then let us handle the matter thus, in order that we may see more distinctly what we wish to see.

How?

Let us suppose a democratic state to be divided, as is really the case, into three parts. The class of people we have described constitutes, I believe, one of these divisions, and is generated by licence in a democratical as abundantly as in an oligarchical state.

True.

But it is much more keen in the former than in the latter.

How so?

In the latter it is despised and excluded from office, and therefore proves untrained and feeble. But in democracy it is, I conceive, with a few exceptions, the sole presiding body; and its keenest members speak and act, while the residue sit on the benches round, and hum applause, and will not brook any opposite statement: so that all the concerns of such a commonwealth are, with some trifling exceptions, in the hands of this body.

Certainly.

In addition to this, a second body is being constantly severed from the mass.

What is it like?

If all are occupied in amassing riches, I presume that those who are most orderly by nature generally become wealthiest.

It is likely to be so.

Hence I conclude that out of these persons the readiest and most copious supply of honey is squeezed for the drones.

To be sure: how could honey be squeezed out of the poor?

And they are called wealthy, which means, I suppose, that they are the provender of the drones.

Pretty nearly so.

The third class will consist of those members of the people who work with their own hands, and do not meddle with politics, and are not very well off. And this class is, in a democracy, the most numerous and the most important of all, when collected.

True, but it will seldom collect, unless it receives a share of the honey.

And therefore it always does receive a share; with this proviso, that its leaders, while depriving the moneyed class of their substance, and making division of it among the people, manage, if possible, to keep the largest share for themselves.

Undoubtedly, with that proviso, it does get a share.

Now these despoiled persons are compelled, I imagine, to defend themselves by speaking before the people and acting to the best of their ability.

Of course they are.

And for this behaviour, even if they do not desire a revolution, they are accused by the opposite party of plotting against the people, and of being oligarchs.

Undoubtedly.

Therefore in the end, when they see that from want of information and in consequence of the artful misrepresentations of their calumniators the people are unwittingly bent on wronging them, from that moment forward, whether they wish it or not, they become, as a matter of course, veritable oligarchs. For this evil, amongst others, is engendered in them by the sting of that drone of which we spoke.

Yes, precisely so.

Hence arise impeachments, prosecutions and trials, directed by each party against the other.

Certainly.

And is it not always the practice of the people to select a special champion of their cause, whom they maintain and exalt to greatness?

Yes, it is their practice.

Then, obviously, whenever a despot grows up, his origin may be traced wholly to this championship, which is the stem from which he shoots.

That is quite obvious.

And what are the first steps in the transformation of the champion into a tyrant? Can we doubt that the change dates from the time when the champion has begun to act like the man in that legend which is current in reference to the temple of Lycaean Zeus in Arcadia?

What legend?

According to it, the worshipper who tasted the one human entrail, which was minced up with the other entrails of other victims, was inevitably metamorphosed into a wolf. Have you never heard the story?

Yes, I have.

In like manner, should the people's champion find the populace so very compliant that he need make no scruple of shedding kindred blood – should he with unrighteous charges, as is the wont of such persons, prosecute his victims and render himself blood-guilty, making away with human life and tasting the blood of his fellows with unholy tongue and lips – should he banish and kill, and give the signal for cancelling debts and redistributing the land; is it not from thenceforth the inevitable destiny of such a man either to be destroyed by his enemies, or to become a tyrant, and be metamorphosed from a man into a wolf?

There is no escape from the alternative.

Such is the fate of the man who is at feud with the moneyed class.

It is.

And if he is banished, and afterwards restored in despite of his enemies, does he not return a finished tyrant?

Obviously he does.

And if his enemies find themselves unable to expel him, or to put him to death, by accusing him to the state, in that case they take measures to remove him secretly by a violent end.

Yes, that is the usual expedient.

In order to prevent this, those who have gone so far always adopt that notorious device of the tyrant, which consists in asking the people for a bodyguard, in order that the people's friend may not be lost to them.

Just so.

And the people, I imagine, grant the request; for they are alarmed on his account, while they are confident on their own.

Just so.

Consequently, when this is observed by a man who has wealth, and with his wealth the character of being a hater of democracy, forthwith, in accordance with the oracle given to Croesus,

> By the pebbly bed of the Hermus,
> Flies he, and halts no more, nor shuns the reproach of a coward.

Why, he would not have the chance of shunning it a second time.

And those that are arrested are given up to death, I imagine.

Of course they are.

But as for that champion himself, it is quite clear that far from being laid with 'his huge form hugely prostrate', he has overthrown many another man, and stands in the chariot of the state, metamorphosed from a champion into a consummate tyrant.

Yes, there is no help for it.

Pray, I continued, are we to discuss the happiness both of the man himself and of the city in which such a mortal resides?

By all means let us do so, he replied.

Well, in his early days, and at the beginning of his despotism, has he not a smile and a greeting for everybody that he meets, and does he not repudiate the idea of his being a tyrant, and promise largely both in public and in private; and is it not his practice to remit debts, and make grants of land to the people and to his own partisans, while he pretends to be mild and gracious to all?

It cannot be otherwise.

But as soon as he has relieved himself of his exiled enemies, by becoming reconciled to some and by destroying others, his first measure is, I imagine, to be constantly exciting wars, in order that the people may stand in need of a leader.

It is his natural course.

Is it not further his intention so to impoverish his subjects by war-taxes as to constrain them to devote themselves to the requirements of the day, and thus render them less likely to plot against himself?

Manifestly it is.

And am I not right in supposing that should he suspect any persons of harbouring a spirit of freedom that will not suffer him to reign in peace, it is his intention to throw them in the way of the enemy, and so get rid of them without suspicion? For all these reasons must not a tyrant be always stirring up war?

He must.

Then is it not the obvious result of such a course that he gets more and more detested by the citizens?

Of course it is.

And does it not follow that a few of the boldest of his influential partisans speak their mind fearlessly to him and to one another, and find fault with his policy?

So one would expect.

Now, if the tyrant is to keep up his authority, he must put all these people quietly out of the way, until he has left himself not a friend nor an enemy who is worth anything.

Certainly he must.

Then he must keenly notice who is manly, who high-minded, who prudent, who wealthy. And in such a happy condition is he, that whether he wishes it or not, he is compelled to be the enemy of all these, and to plot against them, till he has purged them out of the city.

What a glorious purification!

Yes, said I, it runs directly counter to the process by which the physician purges the body. For the physician removes what is bad, and leaves what is good, but the tyrant removes the good, and leaves the bad.

Why, apparently it is his only course, if he wishes to reign.

In fact he is bound in the chains of a delightful necessity, which orders him either to live amongst persons the majority of whom are good for nothing, and to live hated by them, or else to cease to exist.

That is the alternative.

Hence, in proportion as he grows more and more detested by the citizens for such conduct, he will require a more numerous and a more trusty bodyguard, will he not?

Of course he will.

And pray, whom can he trust? And from whence will he procure faithful retainers?

Oh, they will come in flocks spontaneously, if he pays them their wages.

By my word, I believe you are thinking of another miscellaneous swarm of foreign drones.

You are not mistaken.

But would he hesitate to enlist recruits on the spot?

By what process?

By taking their slaves from the citizens, emancipating them, and enrolling them in his own body-guard.

Most decidedly he would not hesitate: for indeed such persons are really his most trusty adherents.

A tyrant is, indeed, a divinely happy creature, according to your account, if he adopts such men as friends and faithful adherents, after he has destroyed those former ones.

Well, he certainly *does* take this course.

And do not these comrades of his admire him highly, and do not the young citizens associate with him, while the good hate and shun him?

How can it be otherwise?

It is not without reason, said I, that people regard tragedy on the whole as wise, and Euripides as a master therein.

Pray why?

Because, among other remarks, he has made the following, which shows a thoughtful mind: 'tyrants are wise by converse with the wise.' And he clearly meant by the 'wise' those with whom the tyrant associates.

Yes, and as one of its numerous merits, tyranny is extolled as something godlike, by the other poets as well as by Euripides.

This being the case, the writers of tragedy, like wise men as they are, will excuse us, and those who copy our commonwealth, for refusing them admittance into the state because they are panegyrists of tyranny.

I imagine that at any rate all polite tragedians will excuse us.

At the same time, I believe, they will make the round of the other states, gather together the populace, hire fine, loud, persuasive voices, and so draw over the commonwealths to tyranny and democracy.

To be sure they will.

And for these services they are, moreover, paid and honoured, by tyrants chiefly, as we should expect, and to a smaller extent by democracy. But in proportion as they advance higher up the hill of commonwealths, their honour flags more and more, as if it were prevented from mounting by loss of breath.

Exactly so.

However, this is a digression. Let us return to the inquiry, how that army of the tyrant, that goodly, large, diversified and ever-changing army, is to be supported.

It is clear, he replied, that, if there be sacred property in the city, the tyrant will expend it; and that to whatever extent the produce of such sales from time to time can be made available, the war-taxes which the people are compelled to pay will be proportionally diminished.

But what is he to do when this resource fails?

Evidently he will draw on his parent's estate for the maintenance of himself and his boon-companions, his messmates and his mistresses.

I understand you. You mean that the people, that begat the tyrant, will maintain him and his companions.

It cannot avoid doing so.

But pray explain yourself, I proceeded. Suppose the people resent this notion, and assert that it is unjust for a father to have to maintain a grown-up son, since on the contrary, the son ought to maintain the father; and that they had begotten and installed him not with the intent that when he was grown big, they should be made the slaves of their own slaves, and maintain him and them with a mob of others, but with the intent that under his championship they should be emancipated from the rich men of the state, and the gentlemen, as they are called; and suppose they now bid him depart out of the city, together with his friends, like a father expelling a son from home along with some riotous boon-companions? What then?

Why the people will then at length most certainly discover how feeble they are in comparison with the nursling which they have begotten and cherished and exalted, and that in ejecting him, they are the weaker expelling the stronger.

What! I exclaimed. Will the tyrant venture to lay violent hands on his father, and beat him if he refuses to comply with his wishes?

Yes, that he will, *when* he has taken away his father's weapons.

You make out that a tyrant is a parricide, and a hardhearted nurse of old age; and apparently the government will henceforth be an open and avowed tyranny; and according to the proverb, the people, flying from the frying-pan of the service of free men, will have fallen into the fire of a despotism exercised by slaves; in other words, they will have exchanged that vast and unseasonable liberty for the new dress of the harshest and bitterest of all slaveries.

No doubt that is the course of events.

Well then, will any one be disposed to disagree with us if we assert that we have discussed satisfactorily the transition from democracy to tyranny, and the character of the latter when established?

We have done so quite satisfactorily, he replied.

NOTES ON BOOK EIGHT

1 We have not attempted to translate the mathematical passage that follows, because we found it wholly impossible to do so. The solutions proposed do not seem satisfactory. We venture to suggest the following partial solutions as probable: αὐξήσεις δυνάμεναί τε καὶ δυναστευόμεναι, 'The product of the root multiplied by its square', or $2 \times 2^2 = 8$, $3 \times 3^2 = 27$. τρεῖς ἀποστάσεις δὲ ὅρους λαβοῦσαι, 'Having received three times the middle terms, and four times the extremes'. Thus, 2, 8, 3, 27 are the extremes; 4 and 9 are the middle terms. Therefore we have $8 + 32 + 12 + 108 = 160$, and $12 + 27 = 39$. Adding 8 and 27 from above, $160 + 39 + 27 + 8 = 234$. ὧν ἐπίτριτος πύθμην = ⁴/₃ $\times 234 = 312$. πεμπάδι συζυγείς, $312 + 5 = 317$: τρὶς αὐξηθείς, $317 \times 3 = 951$. The 'two harmonies' are represented by a square, (τὴν μὲν ἴσην ἰσάκις) 9, which multiplied by 100 (ἕκατον τοσαυτάκις) gives 900; and by a rectangular parallelogram, of which one side is represented by 3 (ἰσομήκη μὲν τῇ), the other by 17 (προμήκη), because $3 \times 17 = 51$. The meaning of the remainder we cannot even guess at.

BOOK NINE

It only remains for us, I proceeded, to inquire how the democratical man is transformed into the tyrannical, and what is the character of the latter after the change, and whether his manner of living is happy or the reverse.

True, this case is still remaining, he said.

Then do you know, I asked, what I am still desiderating?

What is it?

I think that the number and nature of the appetites has not been satisfactorily defined: and while this deficiency continues, the inquiry upon which we are entering will be wrapped in obscurity.

It is not too late to supply the deficiency, is it?

Certainly it is not. Observe the peculiarity which I wish to notice in the case before us. It is this. Some of the unnecessary pleasures and appetites are, if I mistake not, unlawful, and these would appear to form an original part of every man, though in the case of some persons, under the correction of the laws and the higher appetites aided by reason, they either wholly disappear, or only a few weak ones remain, while in the case of others they continue strong and numerous.

And pray, what are the appetites to which you refer?

I refer to those appetites which bestir themselves in sleep; when, during the slumbers of that other part of the soul, which is rational and tamed and master of the former, the wild animal part, sated with meat or drink, becomes rampant, and pushing sleep away endeavours to set out after the gratification of its own proper character. You know that in such moments there is nothing that it dares not do, released and delivered as it is from any sense of shame and reflection. It does not shrink from attempting in fancy unholy intercourse with a mother, or with any man or deity or animal whatever; and it does not hesitate to commit the foulest murder, or to indulge itself in the most defiling meats. In one word, there is no limit either to its folly or its audacity.

Your description is perfectly true.

But I imagine, whenever a man's personal habit is healthful and temperate, and when before betaking himself to rest he has stimulated the rational part of him, and feasted it on beautiful discussions and high inquiries, by means of close and inward reflection, while on the other hand he has neither stinted nor gorged the appetitive part in order that it may sleep instead of troubling with its joys or its griefs that highest part, which may thus be permitted to pursue its studies in purity and independence, and to strain forward till it perceives something till then unknown, either past, present or future; and when in like manner he has calmed the spirited element by avoiding every burst of passion which would send him to sleep with his spirit stirred – when, I say, he proceeds to rest, with two elements out of the three quieted, and the third, wherein wisdom resides, aroused, you are aware that at such moments he is best able to apprehend truth, and that the visions which present themselves in his dreams are then anything but unlawful.

I perfectly coincide in your opinion.

Well, we have been carried too far out of our way in order to make these remarks. What we wish to recognise is that apparently a terrible species of wild and lawless appetites resides in every one of us, even when in some cases we have the appearance of being perfectly self-restrained. And this fact, it seems, becomes evident in sleep. Pray consider whether you think me right and agree with me.

Yes, I do agree.

Remember then the character which we ascribed to the man of the people. The history of his origin was, I believe, that he had been trained up from early years under the eye of a parsimonious father, who respected only the money-making appetites, and despised those unnecessary appetites which have for their object amusement and display. Am I not right?

You are.

By intercourse with more fashionable men, replete with those appetites which we just now discussed, he had run, like them, into utter riot, in detestation of his father's parsimony, but as he possessed a better disposition than his corrupters, he was drawn in two directions, and ended by adopting an intermediate character; and while enjoying every pleasure in perfect moderation, as he imagined, he lived a life which was neither illiberal nor unlawful, and was thus transformed from an oligarchical into a democratical man.

Yes, this was and is our opinion touching such a person.

Well then, I continued, figure to yourself that this man has grown old in his turn, and that a young son is being bred up again in his habits.

Very good.

Imagine further, that he takes to the same courses that his father did – that he is seduced into an utter violation of law, or to use the language of his seducers, into perfect freedom, and that his father and his other relations bring support to these intermediate appetites, which is met by counter support on the other side; and when these terrible sorcerers and tyrant-makers have despaired of securing the young man by other spells, imagine that they contrive to engender in him some passion, to champion those idle appetites which divide among themselves all that offers for distribution – and this passion you may describe as a kind of huge, winged drone: for how else can you describe the passion entertained by such men?

I cannot describe it otherwise.

This done, the other appetites, fraught with incense and perfumes and garlands and wines and the loose pleasures which form part of such convivialities, begin to buzz around this drone, and exalt and nurse him to the uttermost, till they have engendered in him the sting of desire, and from that moment forward this champion of the soul, with frenzy for his bodyguard, is goaded on to madness: and if he detects within himself any opinions or appetites which are regarded as good, and which still feel a sense of shame, he destroys them or thrusts them from his presence, until he has purged out temperance, and filled himself with alien frenzy.

You exactly describe the generation of a tyrannical man.

Is not this the reason why love has of old been called a tyrant?

Probably it is.

Also, my friend, does not a drunken man possess what may be called a tyrannical spirit?

He does.

And we know that an insane or deranged person expects to be able to lord it not only over men, but even over gods, and attempts to do so.

Certainly he does.

So, my excellent friend, a man becomes strictly tyrannical when-ever by nature, or by habit, or by both together, he has fallen under the dominion of wine, or love, or insanity.

Yes, precisely so.

Such is his origin, apparently, and such his nature: but pray, how does he live?

As they say in the game, he replied, *you* must tell *me* that.

Be it so, said I. Well, if I am not mistaken, from henceforth feasts and revels and banquets and mistresses and every thing of the kind become the order of the day with persons whose minds are wholly under the pilotage of an indwelling tyrant passion.

It must be so.

And do not many frightful appetites, that abound in wants, shoot up by their side every day and every night?

Yes, many indeed.

So that all existing revenues are soon spent.

Of course they are.

Then follow schemes for raising money, and consequent loss of property.

Undoubtedly.

And when every resource has failed, must not those violent appetites, which have nestled thickly within, lift up their voices? And goaded on, as these people are, by their appetites, and specially by that ruling passion under which all the rest serve as bodyguard, must they not, in a frenzy of rage, look out for some man of substance whom they may rob by fraud or violence?

Yes, indeed, they must.

So that if they cannot pillage in every quarter, they are constrained to suffer grievous throes and pangs.

They are.

Now, just as the inward pleasures of later growth overreached the original pleasures and took away what belonged to them – in the same way will not the man himself determine to overreach his father and mother, though he is younger than they, and to help himself at their expense out of his father's property, if he has expended his own share?

Undoubtedly he will.

And if his parents oppose his designs, will he not attempt in the first instance to cheat and outwit them?

Assuredly he will.

And whenever that is impossible, will he proceed to robbery and violence?

I think so.

Then if his aged father and mother hold out against him and offer resistance, will he be so scrupulous as to shrink from playing the tyrant?

I am not altogether without my fears for the parents of such a man.

Nay but, Adeimantus, I beseech you to consider that his attachment to his unnecessary and unconnected mistress is new, while his love for his very own indispensable mother is old, and that his affection for his unnecessary and unconnected friend who is in the bloom of youth, is of recent date compared with that for his very own father, his oldest friend, faded and aged as he is; and this being the case, can you believe that he would beat his mother and father for the sake of his mistress and his friend, and that he would make the former the slaves of the latter, if he brought them into the same house?

Upon my word I believe he would, he replied.

Then to all appearance it is a most delightful thing to be the parents of a tyrannical son.

Yes, that it is.

Well, but when the property of his father and mother begins to fail the son, while at the same time the swarm of pleasures has mustered thick within him, will not his first exploit be to break into a house or strip some benighted traveller of his clothes, and will he not afterwards proceed to sweep off the contents of some temple? And in the meantime those old and, in common estimation, just opinions, which he held from childhood on the subject of base and noble actions, will be defeated by those opinions which have been just emancipated from slavery, aided by that ruling passion whose bodyguard they form – opinions which so long as he was subject to the laws and to his father, and while his inward constitution was democratical, used to be emancipated only in the dreams of sleep. But now that this passion has become his absolute lord and master, that character which used to be his only in dreams, and at rare intervals, has become his constant waking state. There is not a dire murder, a forbidden meat or an unholy act, from which he will restrain himself; but this passion that lives and reigns within him, in the midst of utter disrule and lawlessness, will by virtue of its sole supremacy seduce its possessor, as in the case of a state, into unbounded recklessness, to procure means for the maintenance of itself and its attendant rout, which has partly made entrance from without as a result of wicked companionship, and partly been liberated and released from restraint within by the adoption of similar habits and by the agency of the passion itself. Or am I wrong in my description of the life of such a man?

No, you are right, he replied.

And if, I proceeded, a city contains only a few such characters, the rest of the population being sober-minded, these people quit the place and enlist in the bodyguard of some other tyrant, or else serve as mercenaries in any war that may be going on. But if they live in a time of peace and quiet, they commit many small mischiefs on the spot in the city.

Such as what, pray?

Such as theft, burglary, cutting purses, stealing clothes, sacrilege, kidnapping; and sometimes they turn informers, if they have a talent for speaking, and perjure themselves and take bribes.

True, these are small mischiefs, if the perpetrators are few in number.

Things that are small, I replied, are small comparatively: and assuredly all these mischiefs, in their bearings on the corruption and misery of a state, do not, as the proverb says, nearly come up to the mark of a tyrant. For whenever such persons, and others, their close retainers, become numerous in a state, and perceive their own numbers, then assisted by the folly of the people, these men prove the parents of the tyrant, who is simply that one of their number whose own soul contains the mightiest and hugest tyrant.

So one might expect, because such a person must have most of the tyrant about him.

Consequently if the citizens yield willing obedience, all goes smoothly. But should the state prove refractory, the tyrant will chastise, if he can, his fatherland, just as in the former case he chastised his mother and father, and to do this, he will summon to his assistance youthful comrades, under whose imperious authority he will hold and keep his once-loved mother-country, as the Cretans call it, or father-land. And this will be the consummation of the appetite of such a person.

Assuredly it will.

And do not these persons display the same character in private, even before they attain to power? In the first place, in their intercourse with others, is it not the case either that all their associates are their flatterers and creatures, or that if they want anything from anybody, they go down on their knees for it, and do not blush to assume all the appearances of intimate friendship, whereas when they have gained their point they become distant and estranged?

Precisely so.

Thus all their life long they live friendless, and always either masters or slaves, for a tyrant nature can never taste real freedom and friendship.

Certainly it cannot.

Then shall we not be right if we call such persons faithless?

Undoubtedly we shall.

And not only faithless, but also supremely unjust, if we were right in our former conclusions as to the nature of justice.

And certainly we were right.

Then let us describe summarily the most wicked man. He is one whose real and waking state is the very counterpart of the ideal and dreamlike description which we have given.

Exactly so.

Such is the end of the man, who with a nature profoundly tyrannical gains absolute power, and the longer his life of tyranny lasts, the more exactly does he answer to our description.

That is unquestionably true, said Glaucon, taking up the reply.

That being the case, I continued, will not the man who shall be proved to be most vicious be thereby proved to be also most miserable? And will it not be apparent that the man whose tyranny has lasted longest in the intensest form, has really been for the longest time most intensely vicious and miserable, notwithstanding the variety of opinions entertained by the mass of people?

Yes, that much is certain, he replied.

And can we help regarding the tyrannical man as the counterpart and representative of the state which is under the sway of a tyrant, the democratical man of the democratical state, and so on?

Unquestionably we cannot.

Hence, as city is to city in point of virtue and happiness, so also is man to man: is it not so?

Undoubtedly it is.

Then in point of virtue, how does a city under a tyrant stand as compared with a city under such a kingly government as we at first described?

They are the very opposite of one another, he replied: one is supremely virtuous, and the other supremely wicked.

I shall not ask you which is which, because that is obvious. But do you decide the question of happiness and misery in the same way, or not? And here let us not be dazzled by looking only at the tyrant, who is merely a unit in the mass, or at a few of his immediate retainers; but as it is our duty to enter and survey the state as a whole, let us, before giving our opinion, creep into every part of it and look about.

Well, your proposal is a just one: indeed it is clear to everybody that a city governed by a tyrant is the most miserable of cities, whereas a city under kingly rule is the happiest of cities.

Then shall I not do right, if in discussing the corresponding men, I make the same proposal, and recognise only *his* verdict, who can in thought penetrate into a man's character, and look through it, and who does not, like a child, scrutinise the exterior till he is dazzled by the artificial glitter which the tyrannical man carries on the outside, but on the contrary sees through it all thoroughly? Suppose I give it as my opinion that we are all bound to listen to the judge who is not only capable of passing sentence, but has also lived in the same place with the person in question, and has been an eye-witness of his goings on at home and of his bearing towards the several members of his family – wherein he will be most thoroughly stripped of the theatrical garb – and also of his behaviour in public perils, and suppose we bid him take all these particulars into consideration, and then pronounce how, on the score of happiness and misery, the tyrant stands as compared with the other men?

This proposal, he replied, would be also a most just one.

Then in order that we may have some person who will reply to our questions, should you wish us to claim a place among those who, besides being competent to deliver judgment, have before now encountered people of this description?

Yes, I should.

Come then, let me beg you to consider the question in the following light. Bearing in mind the similarity that subsists between the state and the man, examine them singly in turn, and tell me the circumstances in which each is placed.

To what circumstances do you refer?

To begin with the state, do you predicate freedom or slavery of one which is under the dominion of a tyrant?

Consummate slavery.

And yet you see it contains masters and freemen.

True, it does contain a few such persons; but the mass of the inhabitants, I might say, and the best of them, are reduced to an ignominious and miserable servitude.

Now, since the man resembles the state, must not the same order of things exist in him also, and must not his soul be freighted with abundance of slavery and servility, those parts of it which were the best being enslaved, while a small part, and that the most corrupt and insane, is dominant?

It must be so.

If so, will such a soul, by your account, be bond or free?

I should certainly say the former.

To return, is not the city which is enslaved to a tyrant utterly precluded from acting as it likes?

Yes, quite so.

Then the soul also which is the seat of a tyranny, considered as a whole, will be very far from doing whatever it wishes. On the contrary, it will be always dragged by the brute force of passionate desire, and will be filled with confusion and remorse.

Beyond a doubt.

And must the city which is the seat of a tyranny be rich or poor?

It must be poor.

Then the tyrannical soul also must be always poverty-stricken and craving.

Just so.

Again: must not such a city and such a man be, as a matter of course, a prey to fear?

Yes, indeed.

Do you expect to find in any other city more weeping and wailing and lamentation and grief?

Certainly not.

And to return to the individual, do you imagine such things to exist in any one so abundantly as in this tyrannical man, who is maddened by appetites and longings?

Why, how could they?

Looking then, I suppose, at all these facts, and others like them, you have decided that the city is the most miserable of cities.

And am I not right?

You are very right. But once more, looking at the same facts, what account do you give of the tyrannical man?

I should say that he is quite the most miserable of all men.

There you are no longer right.

How so?

I believe that this person is still not the most miserable of all.

Then who is?

You will perhaps think the following person even more miserable.

Describe him.

I refer to the man who, being tyrannical, is prevented from living a private life because he is so unfortunate as to have the post of tyrant, by some mischance, procured for him.

I infer from the previous remarks that you are right.

Yes, I said; but you must not be content with surmises here: on the contrary, you must examine the subject thoroughly by such a process of reasoning as we are pursuing. For surely the point under investigation is of the highest moment, being as it is the choice between a good and an evil life.

That is perfectly true.

Observe, then, whether I am right. It appears to me that in examining the question, we ought to begin our inquiry with the following considerations.

What are they?

We must begin by considering the individual case of those private members of cities who are wealthy and possess many slaves. For they have this point in common with the tyrant, that they rule over many persons. The difference lies in the greater number of his subjects.

Yes it does.

And now, are you aware that such persons are confident and do not fear their servants?

Yes; what should make them fear them?

Nothing, but do you understand the reason of it?

Yes, it is because all the city supports each individual.

You are right. Well, but if some deity were to lift out of the city a single individual, possessed of fifty slaves or more, and were to plant him with his wife and children in some desert along with the rest of his substance and his servants, where none of the freemen would be likely to help him, would he not be seized, think you, with an indescribable terror lest he and his wife and children should be murdered by his servants?

Yes, with utter terror, I think.

And would he not be compelled from that time forward to coax some of his very slaves, and to promise largely, and emancipate them without any excuse for it? In fact, would he not appear in the light of an abject flatterer of his attendants?

He is doomed to death if he fails to do so.

But what if heaven had surrounded him with a multitude of other neighbours who would not endure that one person should claim the rights of a master over another, but punished with the utmost severity any such person whom they caught?

In that case he would be, I imagine, involved still further in an utterly evil plight, because he is hemmed in by a ring of warders, all of whom are his enemies.

And is not the tyrant a prisoner in a similar prison? For if his nature is such as we have described, he is replete with multitudinous terrors and longings of every kind; and though he has a greedy and inquisitive soul, is he not the only citizen who is precluded from travelling or setting eyes upon all those objects which every free man desires to see? Does he not bury himself in his house, and live for the most part the life of a woman, while he positively envies all other citizens who travel abroad and see grand sights?

Yes, assuredly he does.

Such being his evil condition, I continued, a larger harvest of misery is reaped by that person, who, with an evil inward constitution like that of the tyrannical man, to whom you just now ascribed consummate wretchedness, is forced out of private life, and constrained by some accident to assume despotic power – thus undertaking to rule others when he cannot govern himself, just like a person who with a diseased and incontinent body is compelled to pass his life, not in retirement, but in wrestling and contending with other persons.

Undoubtedly, Socrates, the cases are very similar, and your account is very true.

Then, my dear Glaucon, is not the condition of the tyrant utterly wretched, and does he not live a life which is even more intolerable than that of the man who, by your verdict, lives most intolerably?

Unquestionably, he replied.

So whatever may be thought, a very tyrant is in real truth a very slave in the most abject and intense shape, and a flatterer of the most vicious: and so far from satisfying his cravings in the smallest degree, he stands in utmost need of numberless things, and is in good truth a pauper in the eyes of one who knows how to contemplate the soul as a whole; and all his life long he is loaded with terrors, and full of convulsions and pangs, if he resembles the disposition of the state over which he rules: and he does resemble it, does he not?

Certainly he does.

Then we shall also, in addition to this, ascribe to the man what we stated before – namely, that he cannot help being, and in virtue of his power becoming, more and more envious, faithless, unjust, friendless, impure, and the host and nurse of every vice; and in consequence of all this he must in the first place be unhappy in himself, and in the next place he must make those who are near him as unhappy as himself.

No sensible man will contradict you.

Then pray go on, I proceeded, and like the judge who passes sentence after going through the whole case, declare forthwith who is first, in your opinion, in point of happiness, and who second, and so on – arranging all the five men in order: the kingly, the timocratical, the oligarchical, the democratical, the tyrannical.

Well, he said, the decision is an easy one. I arrange them, like choruses, in the order of their entrance – in point of virtue and vice, happiness and misery.

Shall we, then, hire a herald, or shall I make proclamation in person – that the son of Ariston has given his sentence to the effect that he is the happiest man who is best and justest – that is, who is most kingly, and who rules over himself royally; whereas he is the most wretched man who is worst and most unjust – that is, who is most tyrannical, and who plays the tyrant to the greatest perfection both over himself and over a city?

Let such be your proclamation, he replied.

And am I to add to my proclamation that it makes no difference whether or not all men and gods find out their characters?

Do so.

Very well, I proceeded, this will make one demonstration for us. The following must make a second, if it shall be approved.

What is it?

Since the soul of each individual has been divided into three parts corresponding to the three classes in the state, our position will admit, I think, of a second demonstration.

What is it?

It is the following. As there are three parts, so there appear to me to be three pleasures, one appropriate to each part; and similarly three appetites and governing principles.

Explain yourself.

According to us, one part was the organ whereby a man learns, and another that whereby he shows spirit. The third was so multiform that we were unable to address it by a single appropriate name; so we named it after that which is its most important and strongest characteristic. We called it appetitive, on account of the violence of the appetites of hunger, thirst and sex, and all their accompaniments; and we called it peculiarly money-loving, because money is the chief agent in the gratification of such appetites.

Yes, we were right.

Then if we were to assert that the pleasure and the affection of this third part have gain for their object, would not this be the best summary of the facts upon which we should be likely to settle by force of argument, as a means of conveying a clear idea to our minds, whenever we spoke of this part of the soul? And shall we not be right in calling it money-loving and gain-loving?

I confess I think so, he replied.

Again, do we not maintain that the spirited part is wholly bent on winning power and victory and celebrity?

Certainly we do.

Then would the title of strife-loving and honour-loving be appropriate to it?

Yes, most appropriate.

Well, but with regard to the part by which we learn, it is obvious to every one that its entire and constant aim is to know how the truth stands, and that this of all the elements of our nature feels the least concern about wealth and reputation.

Yes, quite the least.

Then shall we not do well to call it knowledge-loving and wisdom-loving?

Of course we shall.

Does not this last reign in the souls of some persons, while in the souls of other people one or other of the two former, according to circumstances, is dominant?

You are right.

And for these reasons may we assert that men may be primarily classed under the three heads of lovers of wisdom, of strife, and of gain?

Yes, certainly.

And that there are three kinds of pleasures, respectively underlying the three classes?

Exactly so.

Now are you aware, I continued, that if you choose to ask three such men each in his turn, which of these lives is pleasantest, each will extol his own beyond the others? Thus the money-making man will tell you that compared with the pleasures of gain, the pleasures of being honoured or of acquiring knowledge are worthless, except in so far as they can produce money.

True.

But what of the honour-loving man? Does he not look upon the pleasure derived from money as a vulgar one, while on the other hand he regards the pleasure derived from learning as a mere vapour and absurdity, unless honour be the fruit of it?

That is precisely the case.

And must we not suppose that the lover of wisdom regards all the other pleasures as, by comparison, very far inferior to the pleasure of knowing how the truth stands, and of being constantly occupied with this pursuit of knowledge; and that he calls those other pleasures strictly necessary, because if they were not necessary, he would feel no desire for them?

We may be certain that it is so, he replied.

Then whenever a dispute is raised as to the pleasures of each kind and the life itself of each class, not in reference to degrees of beauty and deformity, of morality and immorality, but in reference merely to their position in the scale of pleasure and freedom from pain – how can we know which of the three men speaks most truly?

I am not quite prepared to answer.

Well, look at the question in this light. What must be the instrument employed in passing a judgment, in order that such a judgment may be correct? Must it not be experience, wisdom and reasoning? Or can one find a better organ of judging than these?

Of course we cannot.

Then observe. Of the three men, which is the best acquainted by experience with all the pleasures which we have mentioned? Does the lover of gain study the nature of real truth to such an extent as to be, in your opinion, acquainted with the pleasure of knowledge better than the lover of wisdom is acquainted with the pleasure of gain?

There is a great difference, he replied. The lover of wisdom is compelled to taste the pleasures of gain from his childhood, whereas the lover of gain is not compelled to study the nature of the things that really exist, and thus to taste the sweetness of this pleasure and become acquainted with it: rather I should say, it is not easy for him to do this, even if he has the inclination.

Hence, I proceeded, the lover of wisdom is far superior to the lover of gain in practical acquaintance with both the pleasures.

He is indeed.

But what of the lover of honour? Is he acquainted with the pleasure of wisdom as thoroughly as the lover of wisdom is acquainted with the pleasure of honour?

Nay, said he; honour waits upon them all if each works out the object of his pursuit. For the rich man is honoured by many people, as well as the courageous and the wise; so that all are acquanted with the nature of the pleasure to be derived from the fact of being honoured. But the nature of the pleasure to be found in the contemplation of truth, none can have tasted, except the lover of wisdom.

Then, as far as practical acquaintance goes, the lover of wisdom is the best judge of the three.

Quite so.

Also we know that he alone can lay claim to wisdom as well as experience.

Undoubtedly.

Once more; the organ by which judgment is passed is an organ belonging, not to the lover of gain or of honour, but to the lover of wisdom.

What is that organ?

We stated, I believe, that judgment must be passed by means of reasoning. Did we not?

We did.

And reasoning is, in an especial degree, the organ of the lover of wisdom.

Certainly.

Consequently, if wealth and gain were the best instruments for deciding questions as they arise, the praise and the censure of the lover of gain would necessarily be most true.

Quite so.

And if honour, victory and courage were the best instruments for the purpose, the sentence of the lover of honour and of strife would be most true, would it not?

Obviously it would.

But since experience, wisdom and reasoning are the best instruments – what then?

Why of course, he replied, the praise of the lover of wisdom and of reasoning is the truest.

Then if the pleasures are three in number, will the pleasure of this part of the soul by which we learn be pleasantest? And will the life of that man amongst us in whom this part is dominant be also most pleasant?

Unquestionably it will; at any rate, the man of wisdom is fully authorised to praise his own life.

And what life, I asked, does the judge pronounce second, and what pleasure second?

Obviously, the pleasure of the warlike and honour-loving man. For it approaches the first more nearly than the pleasure of the money-making man does.

Then the pleasure of the lover of gain is to be placed last, as it appears.

Undoubtedly, he replied.

Thus will the unjust man be twice in succession foiled, and twice conquered by the just. And now for the third and last time, address yourself, like a combatant in the great games, to Olympian Zeus the Preserver, and observe that in the pleasure of all but the wise man there is some thing positively unreal and ungenuine, and slight as the rude outline of a picture, as I think I have been told by some learned man. And let me say that a fall in this bout will be the heaviest and most decisive of all.

Quite so: but explain yourself.

I shall find what we want, I replied, if you will respond while I prosecute the inquiry.

Put your questions by all means.

Tell me then, I proceeded, do we not assert that pain is the opposite of pleasure?

Assuredly we do.

And also that there is such a thing as a simultaneous absence both of pleasure and of pain?

Certainly there is.

In other words, you admit that there is a point midway between the two at which the mind reposes from both. Is not that your meaning?

It is.

Have you forgotten the language which people hold when they are ill?

Give me a specimen of it.

They tell us that nothing is pleasanter than health, but that before they were ill, they had not found out its supreme pleasantness.

I remember.

Do you not also hear persons who are in excessive pain say that nothing is so pleasant as relief from pain?

I do.

And I think you find that on many other similar occasions persons, when they are uneasy, extol as supremely pleasant, not positive joy, but the absence of, and repose from, uneasiness.

True, he replied; and perhaps the reason is that at such times this relief does become positively pleasant and delightful.

In the same way we might expect that when a person's joy has ceased, the repose from pleasure will be painful.

Perhaps so.

Thus the repose which we described just now as midway between pleasure and pain must be now one, now the other.

So it would seem.

Can that which is neither pleasure nor pain become both?

I think not.

Again, pleasure and pain, when present in the mind, are both of them emotions, are they not?

They are.

But was not the simultaneous absence of pleasure and of pain shown just now to indicate a state of undoubted repose, midway between the two?

It was.

Then how can it be right to regard the absence of pain as pleasant, or the absence of pleasure as painful?

It cannot be right.

Hence the repose felt at the times we speak of is not really, but only appears to be, pleasant by the side of what is painful, and painful by the side of what is pleasant; and these representations will in no instance stand the test of comparison with veritable pleasure, because they are only a species of enchantment.

I confess that the argument points to that conclusion.

In the next place, turn your eyes to pleasures which do not grow out of pains, to prevent your imagining, as perhaps at the present moment you might do, that it is a law of nature that pleasure should be a cessation of pain, and pain a cessation of pleasure.

Pray where am I to look, and what pleasures do you mean?

Among many others, I replied, you may, if you will, take as the best example for your consideration the pleasures of smell, which without the existence of any previous uneasiness, spring up suddenly in extraordinary intensity, and when they are over leave no pain behind.

That is quite true.

Then do not let us be persuaded that genuine pleasure consists in the release from pain, or that genuine pain consists in the release from pleasure.

No.

But it is certain that speaking roughly, most of the so-called pleasures which reach the mind through the body, and the keenest of them, belong to this species – that is to say, they are a kind of release from pain.

They are.

Does not the same remark apply to those pleasures and pains of anticipation which precede them?

It does.

Now, are you aware what the character of these pleasures is, and what they most resemble?

What?

Do you believe that there is in the nature of things a real above, and below, and an intermediate?

Yes, I do.

And do you imagine that a person, carried from below to that intermediate position, could help fancying that he is being carried above? And when he is stationary in that situation, and looks to the place from whence he has been carried, do you imagine that he can help supposing his position to be above, if he has not seen the real above?

For my own part, he replied, I assure you I cannot imagine how such a person is to think differently.

Well, supposing him to be carried to his old place, would he think that he is being carried below, and would he be right in so thinking?

Of course he would.

And will not all this happen to him because he is not acquainted with the real above, and between, and below?

Obviously it will.

Then can you wonder that persons unacquainted with truth, besides holding a multitude of other unsound opinions, stand to pleasure and pain and their intermediate in such a position that though when they are carried to what is painful, they form a correct opinion of their condition, and are really in pain, yet when they are carried from pain to the middle point between pain and pleasure, they obstinately imagine that they have arrived at fullness of pleasure – which they have never experienced – and consequently are deceived by contrasting pain with the absence of pain, like persons who not knowing white, contrast grey with black, and take it for white?

No, indeed, I cannot wonder at it; nay, I should wonder much more if it were not so.

Well, consider the question in another light. Are not hunger and thirst, and similar sensations, a kind of emptiness of the bodily constitution?

Undoubtedly.

Similarly, are not ignorance and folly an emptiness of the mental constitution?

Yes, certainly.

Will not the man who eats, and the man who gets understanding, be filled?

Of course.

And will fullness, induced by a real substance, be more true or less true than that induced by a less real substance?

Obviously, the more real the substance, the more true is the fullness.

Then do you think that pure being enters more largely into the constitution of the class of substances like bread and meat and drink, and food generally, than into the constitution of that species of things which includes true opinion and science and understanding, and in a word, all virtue? In forming your judgment look at the matter thus. Do you believe that real existence is essentially the attribute of that which is closely connected with the unchanging and immortal and with truth, and which is itself unchanging and immortal, and appears in substances like itself, or is it rather the attribute of that which is closely connected with the changeful and mortal, and which is itself changeful and mortal, and appears in things of kindred mould?

It is the attribute of the former in a very superior degree, he replied.

And does science enter at all less largely than real existence into the substance of the unchanging?

Certainly not.

Well, does truth enter less largely?

No.

That is to say, if truth enters less largely, real existence enters less largely also?

Necessarily so.

Speaking universally, does not the cultivation of the body in all its branches contain truth and real existence in a less degree than the cultivation of the soul in all its branches?

Yes, in a much less degree.

And do you not regard the body itself as less true and real than the soul?

I do.

And is not that which is filled with substances more real, and which is itself more real, really more filled than that which is filled with things less real, and which is itself less real?

Undoubtedly it is.

Hence, as it is pleasant to a subject to be filled with the things that are naturally appropriate to it, that subject which is really more filled, and filled with real substances, will in a more real and true sense be productive of true pleasure, whereas that subject which partakes of things less real will be less really and less securely filled, and will participate in a less true and less trustworthy pleasure.

The conclusion is absolutely inevitable, he replied.

Those, therefore, who are unacquainted with wisdom and virtue, and who spend their time in perpetual banqueting and similar indulgences, are carried down, as it appears, and back again only as far as the midway point on the upward road; and between these limits they roam their life long, without ever overstepping them so as to look up towards, or be carried to, the true above: and they have never been really filled with what is real, or tasted sure and unmingled pleasure; but like cattle, they are always looking downwards, and hanging their heads to the ground, and poking them into their dining-tables, while they graze and get fat and propagate their species; and to satiate their greedy desire for these enjoyments, they kick and butt with hoofs and horns of iron, till they kill one another under the influence of ravenous appetites, because they fill with things unreal the unreal and incontinent part of their nature.

Certainly, Socrates, said Glaucon, you describe like an oracle the life of the majority of persons.

And does it not follow that they consort with pleasures mingled with pain, which are mere phantoms and rude outlines of the true pleasure, and which are so coloured by simple juxtaposition to pain that they appear in each case to be extravagantly great, and beget a frantic passion for themselves in the breasts of the foolish people, and are made subjects of contention, like that phantom of Helen for which, according to Stesichorus, the combatants at Troy fought, in ignorance of the true Helen?

Such a state of things, he replied, follows as a matter of course.

And now to come to the spirited element. Must not the consequences be exactly similar, whenever a man labours for the gratification of this part of his nature, either in the shape of jealousy from motives of ambition, or in the shape of violence from love of strife, or in the shape of anger out of discontent, while he pursues after honour and victory and anger to his own satisfaction, without reflection and without sound sense?

The consequences in this case also must necessarily be similar.

And what is the inference? May we assert confidently that of all the appetites with which the gain-loving and honour-loving elements are conversant, those which follow the leading of science and reason, and along with them pursue the pleasures which wisdom directs, till they find them, will find not only the truest pleasures that they can possibly find, in consequence of their devotion to truth, but also the pleasures appropriate to them, since what is best for each is also most appropriate?

Yes, no doubt it is most appropriate

Hence so long as the whole soul follows the guidance of the wisdom-loving element without any dissension, each part can not only do its own proper work in all respects – or in other words, be just – but, moreover it can enjoy its own proper pleasures in the best and truest shape possible.

Yes, precisely so.

On the other hand, whenever either of the two other elements has gained the mastery, it is fated not only to miss the discovery of its own pleasure, but also to constrain the other principles to pursue an alien and untrue pleasure.

Just so.

Well, the further a thing is removed from philosophy and reason, the more likely will it be to produce such evil effects, will it not?

Yes, much more likely.

And that is furthest removed from reason which is furthest removed from law and order, is it not?

Quite obviously.

And have not the passionate or tyrannical appetites been proved to be furthest removed from law and order?

Yes, quite the furthest.

Whereas the kingly and regular appetites stand nearest to law and order, do they not?

They do.

Hence, if I am not mistaken, the tyrant will be furthest from, and the king nearest to, true and specially appropriate pleasure.

It is undeniable.

And therefore the tyrant will live most unpleasantly, and the king most pleasantly.

It is quite undeniable.

And pray, are you aware of the extent to which the discomfort of the tyrant's life exceeds that of the king's?

I wait for you to tell me.

There are three pleasures, it appears – one genuine and two spurious. Now the tyrant has trespassed beyond these last, has fled from law and reason, and lives with a bodyguard of slavish pleasures: and the extent of his inferiority is hard indeed to state, unless perhaps it may be stated thus.

How?

Reckoning from the oligarchical man, the tyrant stands third, I believe, in the descending line; for the democratical man stood between.

Yes.

Then if our former remarks were true, must not the pleasure with which he consorts be, so far as truth is concerned, a copy of a copy, the original of which is in the possession of the oligarchical man?

Just so.

Again, reckoning from the kingly man, the oligarchical in his turn stands third in the descending line, supposing us to identify the aristocratical and the kingly?

True, he does.

Therefore the tyrant is thrice three times[1] removed from true pleasure.

Apparently so.

Then it seems that tyrannical pleasure may be represented geometrically by a square number, 9.

Exactly so.

And by squaring and cubing, it is made quite clear to what a great distance the tyrant is removed.

Yes, to an arithmetician it is.

Conversely, if you wish to state the distance at which the king stands from the tyrant in point of reality of pleasure, by working out the multiplication you will find that the former lives 729 times more pleasantly than the latter, or that the latter lives more painfully than the former in the same proportion.

You have brought out an extraordinary result in calculating the difference between the just man and the unjust on the score of pleasure and pain.

Well, I replied, I am sure that the number is correct, and applicable to human life, if days and nights and months and years are applicable thereto.

And no doubt they are.

Then if the good and just man so far surpasses the wicked and unjust in point of pleasure, will he not surpass him incalculably more in gracefulness of life, in beauty and in virtue?

Yes, indeed he will, incalculably.

Well, then, I continued, now that we have arrived at this stage of the argument, let us resume that first discussion which brought us hither. It was stated, I believe, that injustice is profitable to the man who is consummately unjust while he is reputed to be just. Or am I wrong about the statement?

No, you are right.

This is the moment for arguing with the author of this remark, now that we have come to an agreement as to the respective effects of a course of injustice and a course of justice.

How must we proceed?

We must mould in fancy a representation of the soul, in order that the speaker may perceive what his remark amounts to.

What kind of representation is it to be?

We must represent to ourselves, I replied, a creature like one of those which according to the legend existed in old times, such as Chimera, and Scylla, and Cerberus, not to mention a host of other monsters, in the case of which we are told that several generic forms have grown together and coalesced into one.

True, we do hear such stories.

Well, mould in the first place the form of a motley many-headed monster, furnished with a ring of heads of tame and wild animals, which he can produce by turns in every instance out of himself.

It requires a cunning modeller to do so; nevertheless, since fancy is more plastic than wax and substances as pliable as wax, suppose it done.

Now proceed, secondly, to mould the form of a lion, and thirdly, the form of a man. But let the first be much the greatest of the three, and the second next to it.

That is easier: it is done.

Now combine the three into one, so as to make them grow together to a certain extent.

I have done so.

Lastly, invest them externally with the form of one of the three, namely, the man, so that the person who cannot see inside, and only notices the outside skin, may fancy that it is one single animal – to wit, a man.

I have done it.

And now to the person who asserts that it is profitable for this creature man to be unrighteous, and that it is not for his interest to do justice, let us reply that his assertion amounts to this, that it is profitable for him to feast and strengthen the multifarious monster and the lion and its members, and to starve and enfeeble the man to such an extent as to leave him at the mercy of the guidance of either of the other two, without making any attempt to habituate or reconcile them to one another, but leaving them together to bite and struggle and devour each other.

True, he replied, the person who praises injustice will certainly in effect say this.

On the other hand, will not the advocate of the profitableness of justice assert that actions and words ought to be such as will enable the inward man to have the firmest control over the entire man, and with the lion for his ally, to cultivate, like a husbandman, the many-headed beast – nursing and rearing the tame parts of it, and checking the growth of the wild; and thus to pursue his training on the principle of concerning himself for all jointly, and reconciling them to one another and to himself?

Yes, these again are precisely the assertions of the person who praises justice.

Then in every way the panegyrist of justice will speak the truth, while the panegyrist of injustice will lie. For whether you look at pleasure, reputation or advantage, the panegyrist of the righteous man speaks truth, whereas all the criticisms of his enemy are unsound and ignorant.

I am thoroughly of that opinion, said he.

Let us therefore try to win him over mildly (for his error is involuntary), and let us put this question to him; My good friend, may we not assert that the practices which are held to be fair and foul are fair or foul according as they either subjugate the brutal parts of our nature to the man – perhaps I should rather say, to the divine part – or make the tame part the servant and slave of the wild? Will he say yes? Or how will he reply?

He will say yes, if he will take my advice.

Then according to this argument, I proceeded, can it be profitable for any one to take gold unjustly, since the consequence is that in the moment of taking the gold he is enslaving the best part of him to the most vile? Or, it being admitted that, had he taken gold to sell a son or a daughter into slavery, and a slavery among wild and wicked masters, it could have done him no good to receive even an immense sum for such a purpose, will it be argued that if he ruthlessly enslaves the divinest part of himself to the most ungodly and accursed, he is *not* a miserable man and is not being bribed to a far more awful destruction than Eriphyle, when she took the necklace as the price of her husband's life?

I will reply in his behalf, said Glaucon: it is indeed much more awful.

And do you not think that intemperance, again, has been censured time out of mind for the reason that during its outbreaks that great and multiform beast, which is so terrible, receives more liberty than it ought to have?

Obviously, you are right.

And are not the terms self-will and discontent used to convey a reproof, whenever the lion-like and serpentine creature is exalted and enhanced out of all harmony?

Exactly so.

Again, are not luxury and effeminacy censured because they relax and unnerve this same creature, by begetting cowardice in him?

Undoubtedly they are.

And are not the reproachful names of flattery and servility bestowed whenever a person subjugates this same spirited animal to the turbulent monster, and to gratify the latter's insatiable craving for money, trains the former from the first, by a long course of insult, to become an ape instead of a lion?

Certainly you are right.

And why, let me ask you, are coarseness and vulgarity considered discreditable? May we not assert that these terms imply that the most excellent element in the person to whom they are attributed is naturally weak, so that instead of being able to govern the creatures within him, he pays them court, and can only learn how to flatter them?

Apparently so, he replied.

Then in order that such a person may be governed by an authority similar to that by which the best man is governed, do we not maintain that he ought to be made the servant of that best man, in whom the divine element is supreme? We do not indeed imagine that the servant ought to be governed to his own detriment, which Thrasymachus held to be the lot of the subject: on the contrary, we believe it to be better for every one to be governed by a wise and divine power, which ought if possible to be seated in the man's own heart – the only alternative being to impose it from without, in order that we may be all alike, so far as nature permits, and mutual friends from the fact of being steered by the same pilot.

Yes, that is quite right.

And this, I continued, is plainly the intention of law – that common friend of all the members of a state – and also of the government of children, which consists in withholding their freedom until the time when we have formed a constitution in them, as we should in a city; and until by cultivating the noblest principle of their nature we have established in their hearts a guardian and a sovereign, the very counterpart of our own, from which time forward we suffer them to go free.

Yes, that is plain.

Then pray, Glaucon, on what principle, and by what line of argument, can we maintain that it is profitable for a man to be unjust or intemperate, or to commit any disgraceful act which will sink him deeper in vice, though he may increase his wealth thereby, or acquire additional power?

We cannot maintain that doctrine on any ground.

And by what argument can we uphold the advantages of disguising the commission of injustice, and escaping the penalties of it? Am I not right in supposing that the man who thus escapes detection grows still more vicious than before, whereas if he is found out and punished, the brute part of him is quenched and tamed, and the tame part is liberated, and the whole soul is moulded to the loftiest disposition; and thus, through the acquisition of temperance and justice combined with wisdom, attains to a condition which is more precious than that attained by a body endowed with strength and beauty and health, in the exact proportion in which the soul is more precious than the body?

Yes, indeed, you are right.

Hence, I conclude, the man of understanding will direct all his energies through life to this one object, his plan being in the first place to honour those studies which will impress this high character upon his soul, while at the same time he slights all others.

Obviously.

And as for his bodily habit and bodily support, in the second place, far from living devoted to the indulgence of brute irrational pleasure, he will show that even health is not an object with him, and that he does not attach preeminent importance to the acquisition of strength or health or beauty unless they are likely to make him temperate, because in keeping the harmony of the body in tune, his constant aim is to preserve the symphony which resides in the soul.

Yes, no doubt it is, if he intends to be a genuine votary of music.

Will he not also show how strictly he upholds that system and concord which ought to be maintained in the acquisition of wealth? And will he not avoid being dazzled by the congratulations of the crowd into multiplying infinitely the bulk of his wealth, which would bring him endless trouble?

I think he will.

On the contrary, an anxious reference to his inward constitution, and a watchful care that none of its parts be pushed from their propriety owing to a superabundance or scantiness of substance, will be the principles by which, to the best of his ability, he will steer his course in adding to, or spending out of, his property.

Precisely so.

And, once more, in reference to honours – with the same standard constantly before his eyes, he will be glad to taste and partake of those which he thinks will make him a better man, whereas he will shun, in private and in public, those which he thinks likely to break up his existing condition.

If that is his chief concern, I suppose he will not consent to interfere with politics.

By my faith, you are wrong, I replied; for he certainly will – at least in his own city, though perhaps not in his native land, unless some providential accident should occur.

I understand, he replied. He will do so, you mean, in the city whose organisation we have now completed, and which is confined to the region of speculation; for I do not believe it is to be found anywhere on earth.

Well, said I, perhaps in heaven there is laid up a pattern of it for him who wishes to behold it, and beholding, to organise himself accordingly. And the question of its present or future existence on earth is quite unimportant. For in any case he will adopt the practices of such a city, to the exclusion of those of every other.

Probably he will, he replied.

NOTES TO BOOK NINE

1 Let A = kingly pleasure, B = oligarchical pleasure, C = tyrannical pleasure. If A be represented by 1, B will be represented by 3. But A : B :: B : C. Therefore A : C :: 1 : 9. And, cubing, A : C :: 1: 729. The whole passage is obviously playful.

BOOK TEN

Well, I continued, I must say that while I am led by a variety of considerations to believe that we were unquestionably right in our plans for organising the state, I feel this conviction most strongly when I think of our regulations about poetry.

What was the nature of them?

They were to the effect that we ought on no account to admit that branch of poetry which is imitative. And now that the specific parts of the soul have been each separately defined, the conviction that such poetry must be unhesitatingly refused admittance is to my mind even clearer than it was before.

Explain what you mean.

I am quite sure that you will not denounce me to the tragedians, and the whole company of imitative poets, and therefore I do not mind saying to you that all imitative poetry would seem to be detrimental to the understanding of those hearers who do not possess the antidote in a knowledge of its real nature.

Pray, what is the purport of your remarks?

I must speak my mind, although I confess I am checked by a kind of affectionate respect for Homer, of which I have been conscious since I was a child. For of all those beautiful tragic poets he seems to have been the original master and guide. But it would be wrong to honour a man at the expense of truth, and therefore I must, as I said, speak out.

By all means do so.

Listen then, or rather reply.

Put your questions.

Can you give me any account of the nature of imitation generally? For I assure you I am at a loss myself to understand its real meaning.

And so you expect *me* to understand it.

It would not be extraordinary if you did, for it often happens that short-sighted people make out objects sooner than quick-sighted.

True; but in your presence, if I did make a discovery, I should not have the courage to mention it; therefore look yourself.

Well, is it your wish that we should pursue our usual course in the outset of our investigation? We have, I believe, been in the habit of assuming the existence, in each instance, of some one form which includes the numerous particular things to which we apply the same name. Do you understand, or not?

I do understand.

Then let us, on the present occasion, take any one of those numerous things that suits your pleasure. For example, if this instance suits you, there are of course many beds and many tables.

Certainly.

But of forms in connection with these articles, there are, I believe, only two — one the form of a bed, and one that of a table.

Yes.

Have we not also been accustomed to say that the manufacturer of each of these articles is looking at the form while he is constructing the beds or the tables which we employ, or whatever it may be? For of course, no manufacturer constructs the form itself, because that is impossible.

Certainly it is.

But pray consider how you will describe the following workman.

To whom do you allude?

I allude to the workman who constructs all the articles which come within the province of the whole class of artisans.

You are talking of a marvellously clever man.

Wait a little, and you will have better reasons for saying so. Besides being able to construct all manufactured articles, the same artisan produces everything that grows out of the ground, and creates all living things, himself among others; and in addition to this, heaven and earth and the gods and all the heavenly bodies and all the beings of the nether world are his workmanship.

What an extraordinarily ingenious person you are describing!

You are incredulous, are you? Then tell me, do you think that the existence of such an architect is a complete impossibility? Or do you believe that in one way there could, and in another way there could not, be a manufacturer of such a variety of things? Do you not perceive that in a kind of way even you yourself could construct this multiplicity of objects?

Pray, what is this way? he asked.

Far from being difficult, I replied, it is a rapid method, and admits of many variations. Perhaps the most rapid way of all would be to take a mirror, and turn it round in every direction. You will not be long in making the sun and the heavenly bodies, nor in making the earth, nor in making yourself and every other living thing, and all inanimate objects and plants, and everything that we mentioned just now.

Yes, we can produce so many appearances, but assuredly not truly existing things.

Right, and your observation is just to the point. Now in my opinion the painter also belongs to this class of architects, does he not?

Certainly he does.

But I suppose you will say that all his creations are unreal. And yet the painter too, in a kind of way, constructs a bed. Or am I wrong?

Yes, the painter too constructs a bed in appearance.

But what of the manufacturer of beds? Did you not certainly say a minute ago that he did not construct the form, which, according to our doctrine constitutes the reality of a bed, but only a particular bed?

Yes, I did say so.

Consequently, if he does not construct what really exists, must we not say that he does not construct a real thing, but only something like the reality, but still unreal? And if any one were to describe the work of the bedwright, or of any other artisan, as perfectly real, his account of the matter would be in all probability untrue, would it not?

Yes, in the opinion of those who are versed in such discussions as these.

Then let us not be at all surprised at finding that things as substantial as a bed are shadowy objects when contrasted with reality.

True.

Should you like us to employ these illustrations in our inquiry into the real nature of an imitator?

If you please, he replied.

Well, here we have three sorts of beds, of which one exists in the nature of things; and this we shall attribute, if I am not mistaken, to the workmanship of god. If not, to whom can we attribute it?

We can only attribute it to him, I think.

The second is made by the upholsterer.

Yes.

And the third is the production of the painter, is it not?

Be it so.

Thus we have three kinds of beds, and three superintendents of their manufacture – the painter, the upholsterer, god.

Yes, three.

Now whether it was that god did not choose to make more than one bed, or that by a species of necessity he was precluded from making more than one in the universe, he has at any rate made only one, which is the absolute essential bed. But two, or more than two, such beds have not been created by god, and never will be.

How so?

Because, if god had made only two, a single bed would again have made its appearance, whose form would enter into the other two in their turn; and *this* would be the absolute essential bed, and not the two.

You are right.

Knowing this, I should suppose, and wishing to be the real maker of the really existing bed, and not a certain indefinite manufacturer of a certain indefinite bed, god created a single such bed.

It seems so.

Then are you in favour of our addressing him as the creator, for example, of this object?

Yes, he replied, it is but just to do so, seeing that by creation he has made both this and everything else.

And what of the upholsterer? Must we not style him the artificer of a bed?

Yes.

May we go on to call the painter the artificer and maker of this same article?

Certainly not.

Then, by your account, what is he with reference to a bed?

In my opinion he might most justly be styled the imitator of that of which the other two are artificers.

Well, then, do you call the author of that which is twice removed from the thing as it was created an imitator?

Yes, exactly so.

Hence, since the tragedian is an imitator, we may predicate of him likewise, that he, along with all the other imitators, is the third in descent from the sovereign and from truth.

So it would appear.

Then we are unanimous as to the nature of the imitator. But answer me one question about the painter. Do you suppose that a painter attempts to imitate the originally created object, or the productions of the artificer?

The latter, he replied.

As they really exist, or as they appear? Define this further.

What do you mean?

I mean this: when you look at a bed sideways, or in front, or from any other position whatever, does it alter its identity at all, or does it continue really the same, though it appears changed? And so of everything else?

The latter is the true account: it appears different, but it is not really changed.

Now, this is the point which I wish you to consider. To which of the two is painting, in every instance, directed? Does it study to imitate the real nature of real objects, or the apparent nature of appearances? In other words, is it an imitation of a phantasm, or of truth?

Of the former, he replied.

The imitative art then, is, I conceive, completely divorced from truth, and apparently it is enabled to effect so much because it only seizes upon an object in a small part of its extent, and that small part is unsubstantial. For example, we say the painter will paint us a shoemaker, a carpenter or any other craftsman without knowing anything about their trades; and notwithstanding this ignorance on his part, let him be but a good painter, and if he paints a carpenter and displays his picture at a distance, he will deceive children and silly people by making them think that it really is a carpenter.

No doubt he will.

Be that as it may, I will tell you, my friend, how I think we ought to feel in all such cases. Whenever a person tells us that he has fallen in with a man who is acquainted with all the crafts, and who sums up in his own person all the knowledge possessed by other people singly, to a degree of accuracy which no one can surpass – we must reply to our informant that he is a silly fellow, and has apparently fallen in with a juggler and mimic, whom he has been deceived into thinking omniscient because he was himself incapable of discriminating between science, and ignorance, and imitation.

That is most true.

And now, I continued, we must proceed to consider the case of tragedy and its leader, Homer; because we are told by some persons that dramatic poets are acquainted not only with all arts, but with all things human which bear upon virtue and vice, and also with things divine. For to write well, a good poet must, they say, possess a knowledge of his subject, or else he could not write at all. Hence we must inquire whether the poets whom these people have encountered are mere imitators, who have so far imposed upon the spectators that when they behold their performances, they fail to perceive that these productions are twice removed from reality, and easily worked out by a person unacquainted with the truth, because they are phantoms and not realities; or whether our informants are so far right, that good poets do really know the subjects about which they seem to the multitude to speak well.

Yes, we must by all means investigate the matter.

Well then, do you think that if a man could produce both the original and the representation, he would give himself up seriously to the manufacture of the representations, and make this the object of his life, under the idea that he professes a most noble purpose?

I do not think so.

On the contrary, if he were truly instructed as to the nature of the things which he imitates, he would, I imagine, bestow far more industry upon real actions than upon the imitations, and he would endeavour to leave behind him a number of excellent works as memorials of himself, and would be more anxious to be the panegyrised than the panegyrist.

I agree with you, said he; for the honour and the profit are much greater in the one case than in the other.

Now on ordinary subjects, let us not demand an explanation from Homer or any other poet, by asking why, if any of the ancient or modern poets were adepts in the healing art and not mere imitators of the physician's language, they have not the credit of having effected any cures, like Asclepius, or of having left behind them a body of scholars in physic, as Asclepius left his descendants; neither let us question them concerning the other arts, which may be dismissed from the discussion. But concerning those grandest and most beautiful subjects which Homer undertakes to treat, such as war, and the conduct of campaigns, and the administration of cities, and the education of man, it is surely just to institute an inquiry, and ask the question, thus: 'My dear Homer, if you are really only once removed from the truth, with reference to virtue, instead of being twice removed and the manufacturer of a phantom, according to our definition of an imitator, and if you used to be able to distinguish between the pursuits which make men better or worse, in private and in public, tell us what city owes a better constitution to you, as Lacedaemon owes hers to Lycurgus, and as many cities, great and small, owe theirs to many other legislators? What state attributes to you the benefits derived from a good code of laws? Italy and Sicily recognise Charondas in this capacity, and we Solon. But what state recognises you?' Will he be able to mention any?

I think not, replied Glaucon: at least we are not told any tale of the kind even by the very poets who claim him as their ancestor.

Well then, does the story go that any war in Homer's time was brought to a happy termination under his command, or by his advice?

No, not one.

Well, is he said to have been, like Thales the Milesian and Anacharsis the Scythian, the author of a number of ingenious inventions bearing upon the useful arts or other practical matters, which would convey the impression of his having been a man of wisdom in the active duties of life?

No, certainly nothing of the sort is said of him.

Well then, is it reported of Homer that though not a public man, he nevertheless in his lifetime personally conducted, in private, the education of certain disciples who used to delight in his society, and handed down to posterity an Homeric way of living; just as Pythagoras was in an extraordinary degree beloved personally as a companion, not to mention that his successors, who to this day call their mode of living by his name, are considered to a certain extent conspicuous in the world?

No, Socrates; nothing of this kind either is reported of him. Indeed, if the stories about Homer are true, the education of his friend Creophylus might possibly be thought even more ridiculous than his name. For we are told that even Creophylus[1] neglected Homer singularly in his lifetime.

No doubt that is the story. But do you suppose, Glaucon, that if Homer had been really able to educate men and make them better, from the fact of being capable not merely of imitating but of knowing the subjects in question, he could have failed to attract to his side a multitude of companions who would have loved and honoured him? For so long as Protagoras of Abdera, and Prodicus of Ceos, and a host of other persons can, as we see, persuade the men of their day by private intercourse that they will be incapable of managing their own house and city, unless *they* superintend their education; and so long as the wisdom implied in this insures to these teachers an affection so unbounded that they are almost carried about on the shoulders of their companions, is it conceivable that if Homer and Hesiod were really capable of improving men in virtue, they should have been suffered by their contemporaries to travel about reciting? Is it not more likely that they would have been hugged more closely than gold, and constrained to stay at home with their countrymen? Or else, if this favour were refused, that they would have been escorted in their wanderings till their disciples had received a satisfactory education?

I believe you are unquestionably right, Socrates.

Then must we not conclude that all writers of poetry, beginning with Homer, copy unsubstantial images of every subject about which they write, including virtue, and do not grasp the truth? In fact, as we were saying just now, will not the painter, without understanding anything about shoemaking, paint what will be taken for a shoemaker by those who are as ignorant on the subject as himself, and who judge by the colours and forms?

Yes certainly he will.

And just in the same way, I fancy, we shall assert that the poet as well as the painter lays on a species of colours, in the shape of verbs and nouns, to represent the several professions, of which he only understands enough to be able to imitate them, so that if he writes in metre, rhythm and harmony about shoemaking, or about general-ship, or about any subject whatever, people who are as ignorant as himself, and who judge merely by the form of expression, look upon his poetry as very excellent, so powerful is the charm which these musical appliances naturally possess. For I suppose you know what a poor appearance the works of poets present, when they have been stripped of their musical colouring, and are rehearsed in their proper nakedness. Doubtless you have observed the fact.

Yes, I have, he replied.

Does it not remind one of the withered appearance presented by the countenances of those who have once been blooming without being beautiful, whenever their bloom has deserted them?

Precisely so.

Now let me ask you to examine the following point. According to us, the maker of the image, that is, the imitator, understands only the appearance and not the reality. Is it not so?

Yes.

Do not let us leave the matter half-explained, but let us examine it satisfactorily.

Proceed.

A painter, by our account, will paint a bit and bridle, will he not?

Yes.

But the bridle and bit will be made by the saddler and the smith, will they not?

Certainly.

Then does the painter understand how the bit and bridle ought to be shaped? Or is it the case that even the makers, the smith and the saddler, are ignorant on this subject, which is only understood by the rider, who knows how to use the things in question?

That is the true state of the case.

Then may we not assert that all things are in the same predicament?

What do you mean?

May we not assert that each single thing involves three particular arts – the province of the first being to use the thing, of the second to produce it, of the third to imitate it?

Yes, we may.

Are not the excellence, beauty and correctness of every manufactured article, or living creature, or action, to be tried only by a reference to the purpose intended in their construction, or in their natural constitution?

True, they are.

Hence the man who makes use of a thing must necessarily be best acquainted with it, and must in the course of using it keep the maker informed as to the success or failure of its performances. For example, a fluteplayer no doubt informs a flutemaker about the flutes which he employs in the exercise of his art, and will direct him how they ought to be made; and the flutemaker will submit to his directions.

Of course.

The one has a thorough acquaintance with good and bad flutes, and conveys information upon which the other relies, and will make accordingly: is not that the case?

Yes, it is.

Hence the maker of the instrument will entertain a correct belief with regard to its beauty or badness, by holding communication with the person who has a thorough acquaintance with the subject, and by being compelled to listen to his instructions, whereas the user of the same instrument will possess science on these points.

Exactly so.

But which of the two will the imitator possess? Will he, by actually using the things he describes, know scientifically whether his productions are beautiful and right or not, or will he entertain correct opinion, from being compelled to put himself in communication with the man of real knowledge, and to submit to his directions as to the style in which he ought to work?

Neither.

That is to say, the imitator will neither know scientifically, nor entertain correct opinions, with reference to the beauty or badness of the things which he imitates.

It seems not.

The poetical imitator will be charmingly wise upon the subjects which he treats.

Not exactly.

However, he will go on imitating, notwithstanding his being thoroughly ignorant as to what constitutes a thing good or bad. Nay, apparently he will copy the vague notions of beauty which prevail among the uninformed multitude.

Yes, what else can he copy?

Then to all appearance, we are pretty well agreed so far as this, that the imitative person knows nothing of importance about the things which he imitates, and that therefore imitation is an amusement and not a serious business, and that those who cultivate tragic poetry in iambic or in epic verse are without exception in the highest possible degree imitators.

Exactly so.

Then in the name of heaven, I continued, does not this process of imitation deal with something twice removed from the truth? Answer me.

It does.

But pray, how do you describe that part of human nature on which it exercises the power which it possesses?

Explain what part you mean.

I will. Objects of the same size, I believe, appear to us to vary in magnitude according to their distance from our eyes.

They do.

And things which look bent under water appear straight when taken out of the water; and the same objects look either concave or convex, owing to mistakes of another kind about colours to which the eye is liable: and clearly there exists in the soul a kind of utter confusion of this sort. And it is just this natural infirmity of ours which is assailed with every species of witchcraft by the art of drawing, as well as by jugglery and the numerous other inventions of the same sort.

True.

And have not the processes of measuring and counting and weighing made their appearance most agreeably to aid us in dispelling these tricks of fancy, and to overthrow within us the power of vague notions of degrees of magnitude, quantity and weight, and establish the control of the principle which has calculated or measured or weighed?

Undoubtedly.

And surely this must be the work of the rational element in the soul.

Yes, certainly it must.

But when this element, after frequent measuring, informs us that one thing is greater or less than, or equal to, another thing, it is contradicted at the same moment by the appearance which the same things present.

Yes.

Did we not assert the impossibility of entertaining, at the same time and with the same part of us, contradictory opinions with reference to the same things?

Yes, and we were right in asserting it.

Then that part of the soul whose opinion runs counter to the measurements cannot be identical with that part which agrees with them.

Certainly not.

But surely that part which relies on measurement and calculation must be the best part of the soul.

Doubtless it must.

Hence that which contradicts this part must be one of the inferior elements of our nature.

Necessarily so.

This was the point which I wished to settle between us, when I said that painting, or to speak generally the whole art of imitation, is busy about a work which is far removed from truth, and that it associates moreover with that part of us which is far removed from wisdom, and is its mistress and friend for no wholesome or true purpose.

Unquestionably.

Thus the art of imitation is the worthless mistress of a worthless friend, and the parent of a worthless progeny.

So it seems.

Does this apply only to the imitation which addresses itself to the eye? Or may we extend it to that which addresses itself to the ear, which I believe we name poetry?

Probably we may.

Well, I proceeded, do not let us rely only on the probable evidence derived from painting, but let us prosecute further inquiries into that very part of the intellect with which the imitative art of poetry associates, and let us examine whether it is worthless or good.

Yes, we ought to do so.

Let us state the case thus. The imitative art, if we are right, imitates men who are engaged in voluntary or involuntary actions and who according to the result of their actions, think themselves well off or the reverse, and who in the midst of all these circumstances are conscious either of joy or of grief. Is there anything to be added to this?

No, nothing.

Now, in this variety of circumstances, is a man's state one of unanimity? Or is he at feud and war with himself in his actions, just as he was at feud and entertained contradictory opinions at the same moment about the same subjects, where his sight was concerned? But I remember that on this subject we need not come to an agreement now, for we settled all this satisfactorily in the past conversations, in which we admitted that our soul is fraught with an infinite number of these simultaneous contradictions.

We were right.

Yes, we were, I continued. But there was something then omitted, which I think it is now necessary to discuss.

What was that?

We said, I believe, at the time, that a good man, if he meet with a misfortune, like that of losing a son or anything else that he values most highly, will bear it more easily than any one else.

Certainly he will.

But now, let us further examine whether he will feel no sorrow at all, or whether, this being impossible, he will observe some kind of moderation in grief.

The latter is the truer account.

Now let me ask you a question about him. Do you think he will fight against his grief, and resist it most, when the eyes of his equals are upon him, or when he is alone by himself in solitude?

He will do so much more, I imagine, when he is observed.

But when he is alone, I fancy, he will venture to say much which he would be ashamed to say in the hearing of another person; and he will do much, which he would not like any one to see him doing.

Just so.

Now that which urges him to resist his grief is reason and law, is it not? While that which prompts him to indulge it is the affliction itself?

True.

But when there are two opposite attractions in a man at the same time in reference to the same thing, he must, according to our doctrine, be a double man.

Of course he must.

Is not one part of him prepared to obey the directions of law?

What are they?

Law, I believe, tells him that it is best to keep as quiet as possible in misfortunes, and check all feelings of discontent, because we cannot estimate the amount of good and evil contained in these visitations, and at the same time impatience does not help us forwards, and because none of the affairs of this life deserve very serious anxiety, while grief stands in the way of that behaviour which we ought to adopt in our troubles without a moment's delay.

To what do you allude?

It is our duty to think over the event that has taken place, and to arrange our affairs to meet the emergency in the way which reason pronounces best, like the player who moves his pieces according to the dice which he has thrown; and instead of hugging the wounded part, like children after a fall, and continuing to roar, we ought ever to habituate the soul to turn with all speed to the task of healing and righting the fallen and diseased part, thus putting a stop to lamentation by the aid of medicine.

Certainly that would be the best behaviour under misfortune.

Then the better part of us, we say, consents to be led by such reasoning.

Obviously it does.

On the other hand, shall we not maintain that the element which prompts us to think of, and grieve over, our misfortune, and which has an insatiable appetite for lamentations, is irrational and idle, and the friend of cowardice?

Certainly we shall.

This being the case, the peevish temper furnishes an infinite variety of materials for imitation, whereas the temper which is wise and calm is so constantly uniform and unchanging that it is not easily imitated; and when imitated, it is not easily understood, especially by a general gathering of all sorts of persons collected in a theatre. For these people witness the imitation of a state which if I am not mistaken, is far from being their own.

It is, unquestionably.

Hence it is clear that the imitative poet has, in the nature of things, nothing to do with this calm temper of soul, and that his wisdom is not set on pleasing it, if he is intended to gain a reputation in the world; but his business is with the peevish and changeful temper, because it is easily imitated.

That is clear.

Then we shall be justified now in laying hands on him, and placing him on a level with the painter. For he resembles the painter in producing things that are worthless when tried by the standard of truth; and he resembles him also in this, that he holds intercourse with a part of the soul which is like himself, and not with the best part. And this being the case, we shall henceforth be justified in refusing to admit him into a state that would fain enjoy a good constitution, because he excites and feeds and strengthens this worthless part of the soul, and thus destroys the rational part, like a person who should strengthen the hands of the dissolute members of a state and raise them to supreme power, and at the same time bring the educated class to destruction. Precisely in the same way we shall assert that the imitative poet likewise implants an evil constitution in the soul of each individual, by gratifying that senseless part which, instead of distinguishing the greater from the less, regards the same things now as great and now as small, and manufactures fantastic phantoms that are very widely removed from truth.

Exactly so.

But still, I continued, we have not yet brought forward the heaviest count in our indictment. For that poetry should be able to damage the great majority even of good men is, I conceive, a crime of the deepest dye.

Undoubtedly it is, if the indictment can be sustained.

Attend, and then judge. The best of us, I believe, while listening to the passages in which Homer or one of the tragedians represents some suffering hero who spins out a long speech in his lamentations, or perhaps some persons engaged in beating their breasts and bemoaning themselves in song, are delighted, as you know, and give ourselves up to be led along, and sympathise with the sufferer, and earnestly praise as a good poet the writer who can bring us as much as possible into this frame of mind.

I know it, of course.

But on the other hand, whenever sorrow comes home to one of us, you are aware that we pride ourselves upon the opposite conduct; that is, we glory in being able to endure with calmness, because in our estimation this behaviour is manly, while the other which we praised before is womanish.

I am aware of it, he said.

Then is this praise rightly bestowed? I mean, is it right to feel pleasure and bestow praise, instead of being disgusted, when one sees a man behaving as one would scorn and blush to behave oneself?

No, indeed, he replied, this does not seem reasonable.

It does not, said I, if you look at it in another light.

In what light?

If you consider that the part which is forcibly held down when those calamities of our own occur, and which has hungered for the privilege of weeping and bewailing itself fully and without stint, because it is its nature to covet this satisfaction, is the very part that is fed to satiety by the poets, and delights in those descriptions: and that meanwhile, that part of us which is naturally the noblest from not having been sufficiently trained by reason and by habit, relaxes in its watch over this querulous part, because it is surveying the afflictions of others, and because it is not discreditable to itself to praise and compassionate another man, who professes to be good, though his grief is ill-timed. In fact, it looks upon the pleasure as so much clear gain, and will not allow itself to be deprived of it by a contempt for the whole poem. For it is given, I think, only to a few to reflect that the conduct of other people must necessarily influence our own, and that it is no easy matter, after feeding the strength of the principle of pity upon the sufferings of others, to keep it under restraint when we suffer ourselves.

That is most true.

Does not the same reasoning apply also to jokes which you would yourself be ashamed to make, but which in comic representations, or even in private life, you will be very well pleased to hear, and will not hate as immoral – acting in this just as you acted in your pity? For on such occasions you give the rein to that element which in your own case you check by reason, when it would fain create laughter, because you dread the reputation of a buffoon; and having thus given it strength and spirit, you have often in your own conduct been unconsciously seduced into adopting the character of a comic poet.

Very true.

And in the case of love, and anger, and all the mental sensations of desire, grief and pleasure, which as we hold accompany all our actions, is it not true that poetic imitation works upon us similar effects? For it waters and cherishes these emotions, which ought to wither with drought, and constitutes them our rulers when they ought to be our subjects, if we wish to become better and happier instead of worse and more miserable.

I cannot deny it.

Then, Glaucon, whenever you meet with eulogists of Homer, who tell you that he has educated Greece, and that he deserves to be taken up and studied with an eye to the administration and guidance of human affairs, and that a man ought to regulate the tenor of his whole life by this poet's directions, it will be your duty to greet them affectionately as excellent men to the best of their ability, and to admit that Homer is first and greatest among tragic poets; but you must not forget that with the single exception of hymns to the gods and panegyrics on the good, no poetry ought to be admitted into a state. For if you determine to admit the highly-seasoned muse of lyric or epic poetry, pleasure and pain will have sovereign power in your state, instead of law and those principles which, by the general consent of all time, are most conformable to reason.

That is perfectly true.

Having recurred to the subject of poetry, I continued, let this defence serve to show the reasonableness of our former judgment in banishing from our state a pursuit which has the tendencies we have described: for in doing so we were yielding to reason. But that poetry may not charge us with being, to a certain extent, harsh and rough, let us address her, and say that there is a quarrel of long standing between philosophy and poetry. For those lines,

> That yelping cur, which at its master barks,

and

> Mighty he is in the vain talk of fools,

and

> The lordly mob of godwise folks,

and

> Poor are those subtle thinkers,

and a thousand others, are marks of an old antagonism between the two. But nevertheless let us admit that if the poetry whose end is to please, and imitation, can give any reasons to show that they ought to exist in a well-constituted state, we for our part will gladly welcome them home again. For we are conscious of being enchanted by such poetry ourselves, though it would be a sin to betray what seems to us the cause of truth. Am I not right in supposing that you, my friend, are enchanted by poetry, especially when you contemplate it under Homer's guidance?

Yes, I am, powerfully.

Then is it not just that the sentence of exile should remain in force against poetry until she has made her defence either in lyrical or in some other measure?

Certainly it is.

And I suppose we shall also allow those of her patrons who are lovers of poetry without being poets to advocate her cause in prose by maintaining that poetry is not only pleasurable, but also profitable in its bearings upon governments and upon human life: and we shall listen favourably. For we shall be gainers, I presume, if poetry can be proved to be profitable as well as pleasurable.

Undoubtedly we shall be gainers.

But if not, why in that case, my dear friend, we must take a lesson from those persons who after becoming enamoured of an object, deny their passion at any cost, if they think it injurious: for though the love of such poetry which has grown up in us under the training of our admirable constitutions, will make us cordially desirous that it should appear perfectly excellent and true, still, so long as it is unable to make good its defence we shall protect ourselves, as we listen, by inwardly repeating, like a charm, the argument which we have just brought to a close; and we shall be on our guard against falling anew into that childish passion which most people acknowledge. At any rate, we have learned that we must not make a serious pursuit of such poetry, in the belief that it grasps truth and is good: on the contrary, the listener, apprehending danger to the constitution within him, is bound to be on his guard against it, and to adopt the opinion which we have expressed on the subject.

I thoroughly agree with you.

Indeed, my dear Glaucon, the choice between becoming a good or a bad man involves a great stake – yes, a greater stake than people suppose. Therefore it is wrong to be heedless of justice and the rest of virtue, under the excitement of honour, or wealth, or power, or even of poetry.

I agree with you, he replied, at the conclusion of our inquiry; and I fancy every one else will do the same.

And yet, I continued, we have not discussed the principal wages of virtue, and the greatest of the prizes that are held out to it.

If there are others greater than those already mentioned, they must be of extraordinary magnitude.

But how, I replied, can anything great be compressed into a brief space of time? And the whole interval between childhood and old age is brief, I conceive, compared to eternity.

Rather describe it as nothing.

What then? Do you think that it is the duty of an immortal thing to trouble itself about this insignificant interval, and not about eternity?

I think it ought to concern itself about eternity: but what do you mean by this?

Have you not learned, I asked, that our soul is immortal, and never dies?

He looked at me, and said in amazement, No, really, *I* have not, but can *you* maintain this doctrine?

Yes, as I am an honest man, I replied: and I think you could also. It is quite easy to do it.

Not to me, he said: at the same time I should be glad to hear from you what by your account is so easy.

Be so good as to listen.

Proceed, by all means.

Do you call one thing good and another evil?

I do.

And do we hold the same opinion as to the meaning of the two terms?

What opinion do you hold?

I hold that the term evil comprises everything that destroys and corrupts, and the term good everything that preserves and benefits.

So do I.

Again: do you maintain that everything has its evil, and its good? Do you say, for example, that the eyes are liable to the evil of ophthalmia, the entire body to disease, corn to mildew, timber to rot, copper and iron to rust – or in other words, that almost everything is liable to some connatural evil and malady?

I do.

And is it not the case that whenever an object is attacked by one of these maladies, it is impaired and, in the end, completely broken up and destroyed by it?

Doubtless it is so.

Hence everything is destroyed by its own connatural evil and vice; otherwise, if it be not destroyed by this, there is nothing else that can corrupt it. For that which is good will never destroy anything, nor yet that which is neither good nor evil.

Of course not.

If then we can find among existing things one which is liable to a particular evil, which can indeed mar it, but cannot break it up or destroy it, shall we not be at once certain that a thing so constituted can never perish?

That would be a reasonable conclusion.

Well, then, is not the soul liable to a malady which renders it evil?

Certainly it is; all those things which we were lately discussing – injustice, intemperance, cowardice and ignorance – produce that result.

That being the case, does any one of these things bring about the dissolution and destruction of the soul? Turn it over well in your mind, that we may not be misled by supposing that when the crimes of the unjust and foolish man are found out, he is destroyed by his injustice, which is a depraved state of the soul. No, consider the case thus. The depravity of the body, that is to say disease, wastes and destroys the body, and reduces it to a state in which it ceases to be a body; and all the things which we named just now are brought by their own proper vice, which corrupts them by its adhesion or indwelling, to a state in which they cease to exist. I am right, am I not?

Yes.

Then proceed to examine the soul on the same method. Is it true that when injustice and other vices reside in the soul, they corrupt and wither it by contact or indwelling, until they have brought it to death, and severed it from the body?

Certainly, they do not produce that effect.

Well, but on the other hand it is irrational to suppose that a thing can be destroyed by the depravity of another thing, though it cannot be destroyed by its own.

True, it is irrational.

Yes it is, Glaucon; for you must remember that we do not imagine that a body is to be destroyed by the proper depravity of its food, whatever that may be, whether mouldiness or rottenness or anything else. But if the depravity of the food itself produces in the body a disorder proper to the body, we shall assert that the body has been destroyed by its food remotely, but by its own proper vice or disease, immediately: and we shall always disclaim the notion that the body can be corrupted by the depravity of its food, which is a different thing from the body – that is to say, the notion that the body can be corrupted by an alien evil, without the introduction of its own native evil.

You are perfectly correct.

Then according to the same reasoning, I continued, unless depravity of body introduces into the soul depravity of soul, let us never suppose that the soul can be destroyed by an alien evil without the presence of its own peculiar disease; for that would be to suppose that one thing can be destroyed by the evil of another thing.

That is a reasonable statement.

Well then, let us either refute this doctrine and point out our mistake, or else, so long as it remains unrefuted, let us never assert that a fever, or any other disease, or fatal violence, or even the act of cutting up the entire body into the smallest possible pieces, can have any tendency to destroy the soul, until it has been demonstrated that in consequence of this treatment of the body, the soul itself becomes more unjust and more unholy. For so long as a thing is exempt from its own proper evil, while an evil foreign to it appears in another subject, let us not allow it to be said that this thing, whether it be a soul or anything else, is in danger of being destroyed.

Well, certainly no one will ever prove that the souls of the dying become more unjust in consequence of death.

But in case any one should venture to encounter the argument, and to assert that the dying man becomes more depraved and unjust, in order to save himself from being compelled to admit that the soul is immortal, I suppose we shall infer that if the objector is right, injustice is as fatal as a disease to its possessor; and we shall expect those who catch this essentially deadly disorder to die by its agency, quickly or slowly according to the violence of the attack, instead of finding, as we do at present, that the unjust are put to death in consequence of their injustice, by the agency of other people who punish them for their crimes.

Then really, said he, injustice cannot be thought such a very dreadful thing, if it is to be fatal to its owner; because in that case it will be a release from evils. But I am inclined to think that on the contrary, we shall find that it kills other people if it can, while it endows its possessor with peculiar vitality, and with sleeplessness as well as vitality. So widely and permanently is it removed, to all appearance, from any tendency to destroy its owner.

You say well, I replied. For surely when the soul cannot be killed and destroyed by its own depravity and its own evil, hardly will the evil which is charged with the destruction of another thing, destroy a soul or anything else, beyond its own appropriate object.

Yes, hardly. At least that is the natural inference.

Hence, as it is destroyed by no evil at all, whether foreign to it or its own, it is clear that the soul must be always existing, and therefore immortal.

It must.

Well then, I continued, let us consider this proved. And if so, you understand that the souls that exist must be always the same. For if none be destroyed, they cannot become fewer. Nor yet can they become more numerous, because if any class of things immortal became more numerous, you know that something mortal must have contributed to swell its numbers; in which case, everything would finally be immortal.

True

But reason will forbid our entertaining this opinion, which we must therefore disavow. On the other hand, do not let us imagine that the soul in its essential nature, and viewed by itself, can possibly be fraught with abundance of variety, unlikeness and disagreement.

What do you mean?

A thing cannot easily be eternal, as we have just proved the soul to be, if it is compounded of many parts, and if the mode of composition employed is not the very best.

Probably it cannot.

Now, the immortality of the soul has been established beyond the reach of doubt by our recent argument, to which other demonstrations might be added: but to understand its real nature, we must look at it not, as we are now doing, after it has been marred by its association with the body, and by other evils; but we must carefully contemplate it by the aid of reasoning, when it appears in unsullied purity; and then its surpassing beauty will be discovered, and the nature of justice and injustice, along with all the questions which we have now discussed, will be far more clearly discerned. As it is, we have given a true account of the soul in its present appearance. But we have looked at it in a state like that of the sea god Glaucus, whose original nature can no longer be readily discerned by the eye, because the old members of his body have been either broken off, or crushed and in every way marred by the action of the waves, and because extraneous substances, like shellfish and seaweed and stones, have grown to him, so that he bears a closer resemblance to any wild beast whatever than to his natural self. The soul, as we are contemplating it, has been reduced to a similar state by a thousand evils. But we ought to fix our attention on one part of it exclusively, Glaucon.

On what part?

On its love of wisdom, that we may learn to what it clings, and with what it desires to have intercourse, in virtue of its close connection with the divine, the immortal and the eternal; and what it would become if it invariably pursued the divine, and were, by the impulse thence derived, lifted out of the sea in which it now is, and disencumbered of the stones and shellfish and that uncouth multitude of earthy and rocky substances with which, because earth has been its food, it is now overgrown in consequence of those banquetings which are called felicitous. And then we should see whether it is essentially multiform or uniform, or otherwise constituted, and how. But at present we have, if I am not mistaken, discussed pretty thoroughly its affections and manifestations in human life.

Yes, undoubtedly we have.

And have we not, I continued, divested ourselves of all secondary considerations in the course of the argument; and without introducing the rewards and the reputation which justice confers, as you said that Homer and Hesiod do, have we not found that justice, taken by itself, is best for the soul, also taken by itself, and that the soul is bound to practise just actions, whether it possess the ring of Gyges, and in addition to this ring the helmet of Hades, or not?

It is most true that we have done so.

Then may we now, Glaucon, proceed without offence to take into account those great and abundant rewards which justice, along with the rest of virtue, wins to the soul from gods and men, not only during a man's lifetime, but also after his death?

Yes he replied, undoubtedly we may.

Will you repay me what you borrowed in the course of the argument?

Pray, what did I borrow?

I granted to you that the just man should have the reputation of being unjust, and the unjust man the reputation of being just. For you were of opinion that even if it were impossible that the true state of the case should be concealed both from men and gods, still this ought to be granted for the sake of the argument, in order that pure justice might be weighed against pure injustice. You remember, do you not?

Indeed, I should be in fault if I did not.

But now that judgment has been passed upon them, I in my turn demand in behalf of justice, that we should admit the estimation in which she is held to be what it really is, both among gods and among men, in order that she may receive the prizes of victory which she earns by her outward appearance and bestows upon those who possess her – now that it has been proved that the blessings derived from really being just are given by her, without any deception, to those who truly receive her.

Your demand is a just one.

Then will you not first restore to me this admission, that the gods at least are not mistaken as to the real character of the just and the unjust man?

We will.

That being the case, the one will be dear to the gods, and the other hateful in their sight, as we also agreed originally.

True.

And shall we not agree that all things which come from the gods, come in the best possible shape to the man whom they love, unless some past sin has already doomed him to a certain amount of suffering?

Certainly they do.

Hence in the case of the just man, we must assume that whether poverty be his lot, or sickness, or any other reputed evil, all will work for his final advantage, either in this life or in the next. For unquestionably, the gods can never neglect a man who determines to strive earnestly to become just, and by the practice of virtue to grow as much like god as man is permitted to do.

No, such a man is not likely to be neglected by one whom he resembles.

But in the case of the unjust man, must we not entertain the opposite opinion?

Certainly we must.

Then these will be the prizes bestowed by the gods upon the just man.

So it seems to me, at all events.

But what, I continued, do men bestow on him? Does not the case stand thus, if we are to set down the truth? Do not those clever unjust men behave like runners who run well from the starting-place to the turning post, but flag from thence to the goal? They start off briskly, but end by making themselves ridiculous, and slink away crestfallen and uncrowned. But the really good runners receive the prize at the end of the course, and are crowned. Is not this also generally the case with the just? Towards the close of every action, every social relation, and life itself, do they not gain a good name, and win the prizes from the hands of their fellow-men?

Certainly they do.

Then will you suffer me to say of them what you said of the unjust? For I shall not hesitate to declare that the just, when they are advanced in years, hold office, if they like, in their own city, and marry into what families they please, and wed their daughters to whomsoever they choose. In a word, I now say of the just all that you said of the unjust. On the other hand, I likewise affirm of the unjust that the greater part of them, even if they escape detection in their youth, are found out and turned into ridicule at the end of their course; and that as they grow old, they are insulted in their misery by strangers as well as by their fellow-citizens, and forced to submit to the scourge, and finally to the rack and the heated iron, which you rightly described as barbarous treatment. Imagine yourself to have been told by me that they undergo all those inflictions. And now, as I said, consider whether you will suffer me to speak in this way.

Undoubtedly I shall, he replied; for your statement is just.

Such then, I continued, will be the prizes, the rewards and the gifts which are bestowed on the just man, in his lifetime, by gods and by men, in addition to those good things which justice of itself placed in his possession.

Yes, he replied, and they are very magnificent as well as very certain.

These, however, are nothing, in number or in magnitude, compared with the lot that awaits the just and the unjust after death. And this must be described, in order that we may award to each the complement of recompense, which the argument is bound to set forth.

Speak on; there are few things that I would more gladly hear.

Well, I will tell you a tale, not like that of Odysseus to Alcinous,[2] but of what once happened to a brave man, Er the son of Armenius, a native of Pamphylia, who according to story was killed in battle. When the bodies of the slain were taken up ten days afterwards for burial in a state of decomposition, Er's body was found to be still fresh. He was carried home, and was on the point of being interred, when on the twelfth day after his death, as he lay on the funeral-pyre, he came to life again, and then proceeded to describe what he had seen in the other world. His story was that when the soul had gone out of him, it travelled in company with many others till they came to a mysterious place in which were two gaps, adjoining one another, in the earth, and exactly opposite them two gaps above in the heaven. Between these gaps sat judges who after passing sentence commanded the just to take the road to the right upwards through the heaven, and fastened in front of them some symbol of the judgment that had been given; while the unjust were ordered to take the road downwards to the left, and also carried behind them evidence of all their evil deeds. When he came to the place himself, he was told that he would have to carry to men a report of the proceedings of that other world; and he was admonished to listen, and watch everything that went on there. So he looked, and beheld the souls on one side taking their departure at one of the gaps in the heaven and the corresponding gap in the earth, after judgment had been passed upon them; while at the two other gaps he saw them arriving, squalid and dusty or pure and bright, according as they ascended from earth or descended from heaven. Each soul, as it arrived, wore a travel-stained appearance, and gladly went away into the meadow and there took up quarters, as people do when some great festival is pending. Greetings passed between all that were known to one another; and those who had descended from heaven were questioned about heaven by those who had risen out of the earth; while the latter were questioned by the former about earth. Those who were come from earth told their tale with lamentations and tears, as they bethought them of all the dreadful things that they had seen and suffered in their subterranean journey, which they said had lasted a thousand years: while those who were come from heaven described enjoyments and sights of marvellous beauty. It would take a long time, Glaucon, to repeat at length the many particulars of their stories, but according to Er, the main points were the following. For every one of all the crimes, and all the personal injuries, committed by them, they suffered tenfold retribution when the turn for it came. The cycle of punishment recommenced every century, because the length of human life was estimated at a hundred years – the object being to make them pay the penalty for each offence ten times over. Thus all who had been guilty of a number of murders, or had betrayed and enslaved cities and armies, or had been accomplices in any other villainy, were intended to undergo tenfold sufferings for all and each of their offences; while on the other hand, those who had done any charitable acts, and had shown themselves just and holy, were meant to receive on the same principle their due reward. With regard to those whose death followed close upon their birth, he gave some particulars which need not be recorded. But according to his narrative, the punishment for impiety, disobedience to parents, and the murder of near relations, was unusually severe; and the reward for piety and obedience unusually great. For he was within hearing, he said, when one of the spirits asked another where Ardiaeus the Great was. Now this Ardiaeus had been sovereign in a city of Pamphylia, a thousand years before that time, and was said to have put his aged father and elder brother to death, besides committing a number of other wicked actions. The spirit to whom the question was addressed replied, 'He is not come, and is not likely to come hither. For this, you must know, was one of the terrible sights that we beheld. When we were close to the aperture, and were on the point of ascending, after having undergone all our other sufferings, we suddenly came in sight of Ardiaeus and others, of whom the greater part, I think I may say, had been despots, though it is true there were also a few private persons who had once been reckoned among enormous criminals. These people, when they thought themselves sure of ascending immediately, were repulsed by the aperture, which bellowed whenever one of these incurable sinners, or anybody who had not fully expiated his offences, attempted to ascend. Thereupon certain fierce and fiery-looking men who were in attendance and understood the meaning of the sound, seized some of them by the waist and carried them off; but Ardiaeus and others were bound hand and foot and head, and thrown down, and flayed with scourges, and dragged out by the wayside, and carded, like wool, upon thorn-bushes; and those who were passing by at the time were informed why they were put to this torture, and that they were being carried away in order to be flung into Tartarus. We had already gone through a great variety of alarms, but none of them were equal to the terror that then seized us, lest that sound should be uttered when any of us tried to go up; and most glad we all were to ascend, when it was not heard.' This will convey an idea of the penalties and the tortures, while the rewards were precisely the opposite. When seven days had elapsed since the arrival of the spirits in the meadow, they were compelled to leave the place, when their time came, and set out on the eighth day, and travel three days, till they arrived on the fourth at a place from whence they looked down upon a straight pillar of light, stretching across the whole heaven and earth, more like the rainbow than anything else, only brighter and clearer. This they reached, when they had gone forward a day's journey; and arriving at the centre of the light, they saw that its extremities were fastened by chains to the sky. For this light binds the sky together, like the hawser that strengthens a trireme,[3] and thus holds together the whole revolving universe. To the extremities is fastened the distaff of Necessity, by means of which all the revolutions of the universe are kept up. The shaft and hook of this distaff are made of steel, the whorl is a compound of steel and other materials. The nature of the whorl may be thus described. In shape it is like an ordinary whorl, but from Er's account we must picture it to ourselves under the form of a large hollow whorl, scooped out right through, into which a similar, but smaller, whorl is nicely inserted, like those boxes which fit into one another. In the same way a third whorl is inserted within the second, a fourth within the third, and so on to four more. For in all there are eight whorls, inserted into one another – each concentric circle showing its rim above the next outer, and all together forming one solid whorl embracing the shaft, which is passed right through the centre of the eighth. The first and outermost whorl has the broadest rim; the sixth has the next broadest; then comes the fourth; then the eighth; then the seventh; then the fifth; then the third; and the second has the narrowest rim. The rim of the greatest whorl exhibits a variety of colours; that of the seventh is most brilliant; that of the eighth derives its colour from the reflected light of the seventh; that of the second and that of the fifth are similar, but of a deeper colour than the others; the third has the palest colour; the fourth is rather red; and the sixth is almost as pale as the third. Now the distaff as a whole spins round with uniform velocity; but while the whole revolves, the seven inner circles travel slowly round in the opposite direction, and of them the eighth moves quickest, and after it the seventh, sixth and fifth, which revolve together: the fourth, as it appeared to them, completes its revolution with a velocity inferior to the last mentioned; the third ranks fourth in speed; and the second, fifth. The distaff spins round upon the knees of Necessity. Upon each of its circles stands a siren, who travels round with the circle, uttering one note in one tone; and from all the eight notes there results a single harmony. At equal distances around sit three other personages, each on a throne. These are the daughters of Necessity, the Fates, Lachesis, Clotho and Atropos; who clothed in white robes, with garlands on their heads, chant to the music of the sirens – Lachesis the events of the past, Clotho those of the present, Atropos those of the future. Clotho with her right hand takes hold of the outermost rim of the distaff, and twirls it altogether, at intervals; and Atropos with her left hand twirls the inner circles in like manner; while Lachesis takes hold of each in turn with either hand. Now the souls, immediately on their arrival, were required to go to Lachesis. An interpreter first of all marshalled them in order, and then having taken from the lap of Lachesis a number of lots and plans of life, mounted a high pulpit, and spoke as follows: 'Thus saith the maiden Lachesis, the daughter of Necessity. Ye short-lived souls, a new generation of men shall here begin the cycle of its mortal existence. Your destiny shall not be allotted to you, but you shall choose it for yourselves. Let him who draws the first lot be the first to choose a life, which shall be his irrevocably. Virtue owns no master: he who honours her shall have more of her, and he who slights her, less. The responsibility lies with the chooser. Heaven is guiltless.' Having said this, he threw the lots down upon the crowd; and each spirit took up the one which fell by his side, except Er himself, who was forbidden to do so. Each, as he took up his lot, saw what number he had drawn. This done, the plans of life, which far outnumbered the souls that were present, were laid before them on the ground. They were of every kind. There were lives of all living things, and among them every sort of human life. They included sovereignties, of which some were permanent and others were abruptly terminated and ended in poverty and exile and beggary. There were also lives of famous men, renowned either for beauty of person and feature, for bodily strength and skill in games, or else for high birth and the merits of ancestors; and in the same way there were lives of undistinguished men, and likewise lives of celebrated and uncelebrated women. But no settled character of soul was included in them, because with the change of life the soul inevitably becomes changed itself. But in every other respect the materials were very variously combined – wealth appearing here, and poverty there; disease here, and health there; and here again a mean between these extremes. This, my dear Glaucon, is apparently the moment when everything is at stake with a man; and for this reason, above all others, it is the duty of each of us diligently to investigate and study, to the neglect of every other subject, that science which may haply enable a man to learn and discover who will render him so instructed as to be able to discriminate between a good and an evil life, and according to his means to choose, always and everywhere, that better life, by carefully calculating the influence which the things just mentioned, in combination or in separation, have upon real excellence of life; and who will teach him to understand what evil or good is wrought by beauty tempered with poverty or wealth, and how the result is affected by the state of soul which enters into the combination; and what is the consequence of blending together such ingredients as high or humble birth, private or public life, bodily strength or weakness, readiness or slowness of apprehension, and everything else of the kind, whether naturally belonging to the soul or accidentally acquired by it; so as to be able to form a judgment from all these data combined, and with an eye steadily fixed on the nature of the soul, to choose between the good and the evil life, giving the name of evil to the life which will draw the soul into becoming more unjust, and the name of good to the life which will lead it to become more just, and bidding farewell to every other consideration. For we have seen that in life and in death it is best to choose thus. With iron resolution must he hold fast this opinion when he enters the future world, in order that there as well as here he may escape being dazzled by wealth and similar evils; and may not plunge into usurpations or other corresponding courses of action to the inevitable detriment of others, and to his own still heavier affliction; but may know how to select that life which always steers a middle course between such extremes, and to shun excess on either side to the best of his power, not only in this life, but also in that which is to come. For by acting thus, he is sure to become a most happy man.

To return; the messenger from the other world reported that on the same occasion the interpreter spoke to this effect: 'Even the last comer, if he chooses with discretion and lives strenuously, will find in

store for him a life that is anything but bad, with which he may well
be content. Let not the first choose carelessly, or the last despond.' As
soon as he had said these words, the one who had drawn the first lot
advanced, and chose the most absolute despotism he could find; but
so thoughtless was he and greedy, that he had not carefully examined
every point before making his choice; so that he failed to remark that
he was fated therein, amongst other calamities, to devour his own
children. Therefore, when he had studied it at his leisure, he began to
beat his breast and bewail his choice; and disregarding the previous
admonitions of the interpreter, he laid the blame of his misfortune
not upon himself, but upon fortune and destiny, and upon anybody
sooner than himself. He was one of those who had come from
heaven, and had lived during his former life under a well-ordered
constitution, and hence a measure of virtue had fallen to his share
through the influence of habit, unaided by philosophy. Indeed,
according to his account, more than half the persons similarly deluded
had come from heaven; which is to be explained by the fact of their
never having felt the discipline of trouble. For the majority of those
who came from the earth did not make their choice in this careless
manner, because they had known affliction themselves and had seen
it in others. On this account, and also through the chances of the lot,
most of the souls exchanged an evil destiny for a good, or a good
destiny for an evil. But if a man were always to study wisdom
soundly, whenever he entered upon his career on earth, and if it fell
to his lot to choose anywhere but among the very last, there is every
probability, to judge by the account brought from the other world,
that he would not only be happy while on earth, but also that he
would travel from this world to the other and back again, not along a
rough and subterranean, but along a smooth and heavenly, road. It
was a truly wonderful sight, he said, to watch how each soul selected
its life – a sight at once melancholy and ludicrous and strange. The
experience of their former life generally guided the choice. Thus he
saw the soul which had once been that of Orpheus choosing the life
of a swan, because from having been put to death by women, he
detested the whole race so much that he would not consent to be
conceived and born of a woman. And he saw the soul of Thamyras
choosing the life of a nightingale. He saw also a swan changing its
nature, and selecting the life of a man; and its example was followed
by other musical animals. The soul that drew the twentieth lot chose

a lion's life. It was the soul of Ajax the son of Telamon, who shrunk from becoming a man because he recollected the decision respecting the arms of Achilles. He was followed by the soul of Agamemnon, who had been also taught by his sufferings to hate mankind so bitterly that he adopted in exchange an eagle's life. The soul of Atalanta, which had drawn one of the middle lots, beholding the great honours attached to the life of an athlete, could not resist the temptation to take it up. Then he saw the soul of Epeus the son of Panopeus, assuming the nature of a skilful work-woman. And in the distance, among the last, he saw the soul of the buffoon Thersites putting on the exterior of an ape. It so happened that the soul of Odysseus had drawn the last lot of all. When he came up to choose, the memory of his former sufferings had so abated his ambition that he went about a long time looking for a quiet retired life, which with great trouble he discovered lying about, and thrown contemptuously aside by the others. As soon as he saw it, he chose it gladly, and said that he would have done the same if he had even drawn the first lot. In like manner some of the other animals passed into men, and into one another – the unjust passing into the wild, and the just into the tame: and every kind of mixture ensued.

Now when all the souls had chosen their lives in the order of the lots, they advanced in their turn to Lachesis, who dispatched with each of them the destiny he had selected, to guard his life and satisfy his choice. This destiny first led the soul to Clotho in such a way as to pass beneath her hand and the whirling motion of the distaff, and thus ratified the fate which each had chosen in the order of precedence. After touching her, the same destiny led the soul next to the spinning of Atropos, and thus rendered the doom of Clotho irreversible. From thence the souls passed straightforward under the throne of Necessity. When the rest had passed through it, Er himself also passed through, and they all travelled into the plain of Forgetfulness, through dreadful suffocating heat, the ground being destitute of trees and of all vegetation. As the evening came on, they took up their quarters by the bank of the river of Indifference, whose water cannot be held in any vessel. All persons are compelled to drink a certain quantity of the water; but those who are not preserved by prudence drink more than the quantity: and each, as he drinks, forgets everything. When they had gone to rest, and it was now midnight, there was a clap of thunder and an earthquake, and in a moment the souls were carried up to their birth, this way and that, like shooting stars. Er himself was prevented from drinking any of the water; but how and by what road he reached his body, he knew not: only he knew that he suddenly opened his eyes at dawn, and found himself laid out upon the funeral-pyre.

And thus, Glaucon, the tale was preserved and did not perish; and it may also preserve us, if we will listen to its warnings; in which case we shall pass prosperously across the river of Lethe, and not defile our souls. Indeed, if we follow my advice, believing the soul to be immortal and to possess the power of entertaining all evil, as well as all good, we shall ever hold fast the upward road, and devotedly cultivate justice combined with wisdom, in order that we may be loved by one another and by the gods, not only during our stay on earth, but also when, like conquerors in the games collecting the presents of their admirers, we receive the prizes of virtue, and in order that both in this life and during the journey of a thousand years which we have described, we may never cease to prosper.

NOTES TO BOOK TEN

1 The drift of the whole passage is this – what a bad educator must Homer have been, if even his intimate friend Creophylus could neglect him. The joke about the name of Creophylus is not very obvious, because the reading is uncertain.

2 That is, according to the commentators, not a long story.

3 οἷον τὰ ὑποζώματα τῶν τριήρων. We must remember that in Greek astronomy, the sky was regarded as a solid transparent vault in which the stars were fixed. The sides of this vault, according to the account in the text, are held together by a straight horizontal belt of light 'the ends of whose chains are fastened to the sky', that is to say, 'whose ends are chained to the sky'. But what is the meaning of οἷον τὰ ὑποζώματα τῶν τριήρων? Some commentators take τὰ ὑποζώματα to mean the rowers' benches, which would of course help to hold the sides of a vessel together. But there is not sufficient authority for this interpretation. On the other hand, how can 'a *straight* pillar of light' be compared to a rope passed round the hull of a ship in order to hold its timbers together, which is another interpretation of ὑπόζωμα? If this interpretation be correct, the point of comparison is not the appearance presented, but only the effects produced by this process of 'undergirding' or 'frapping'. At any rate it seems certain, from a passage in the *Laws* (945c), that the word ὑποζώματα means some kind of rope; and perhaps Schneider is right in explaining it as a large rope, or hawser, passed from stem to stern in order to strengthen a vessel. Still this is not satisfactory, though we are unable to propose any better explanation.

In what follows, a rough description of the first observed phenomena of astronomy is conveyed. The motion of the whole distaff represents the apparent diurnal revolution of the heaven round the earth as centre of the system. The seven innermost whorls, with their independent motions, represent the orbits of Saturn, Jupiter, Mars, Venus, Mercury, the Sun and the Moon. The outermost whorl with its 'variety of colours' represents the fixed stars.

ANALYSIS OF THE REPUBLIC

Socrates and Glaucon, having gone down to the Piraeus to witness the first celebration of a festival lately introduced from Thrace, fall in with Polemarchus, Adeimantus, Niceratus and some other friends, who persuade them to proceed to the house of Cephalus, the father of Polemarchus. A conversation upon the subject of old age, its faults and its trials, carried on between Cephalus and Socrates, introduces the question – what is justice? Cephalus then retires, leaving Polemarchus to continue the discussion with Socrates.

Polemarchus begins by propounding a definition of justice given by Simonides, who makes it consist in restoring to everybody what is due to him.

The question, then, is, what did Simonides mean by the term 'due'? Apparently he meant little more than 'appropriate'; for, according to him, the nature of the debt depends upon the nature of the relation subsisting between the two parties; so that in reality he makes justice consist in doing good to our friends and harm to our enemies.

Socrates then asks Polemarchus to define the term 'friends'; and when the latter replies that our friends are those whom we regard as good and honest men, Socrates shows that as we are constantly liable to misjudge the characters of people, we must maintain either that it is just to injure the good, which is an immoral doctrine; or else that it is occasionally just to injure our friends, which directly contradicts the doctrine of Simonides.

To escape from this dilemma, Polemarchus shifts his ground, and states the theory of Simonides thus: it is just to help our friends if they are good men, and to injure our enemies if they are bad men.

In reply to this Socrates, arguing from analogy, shows that to injure a man is tantamount to making him less virtuous, and therefore less just. But how can a just man, by the exercise of his justice, render the character of another less just than it was? The idea is preposterous.

Therefore the definition of Simonides, as amended by Polemarchus, is again proved to be incorrect.

Hereupon Thrasymachus thrusts himself into the discussion, and after some hesitation, defines justice as 'the interest of the stronger'. He supports his definition by the following argument. In every state it is considered unjust to violate the laws: the laws are framed to serve the interests of the government: and the government is stronger than its subjects: therefore, universally, justice is the interest of the stronger, or, might is right.

But, urges Socrates, a government often makes mistakes, and enacts laws which are detrimental to its own interests: and according to Thrasymachus, justice requires the subject in every instance to obey the laws of the land: consequently, it is often just for the subject to do what is prejudicial to the interests of the government – that is, what is *not* for the interest of the stronger. Therefore justice cannot be defined as the interest of the stronger.

To avoid this conclusion, Thrasymachus retracts his previous admission, and explains that properly speaking, a governor, in so far as he is a governor, cannot be said to make mistakes; and that therefore the government, speaking strictly, always legislates to its own advantage, while justice commands the subject to obey.

Socrates, in reply, demonstrates that every art, and therefore the art of government among others, consults the interests not of the artist or superior, but of the subject or inferior.

Upon this, Thrasymachus abruptly turns the discourse by declaring that a governor treats his subjects just like the shepherd who fattens his flock for his own private advantage; and that really injustice, practised on an extensive scale, is by far the best and most lucrative course that a man can adopt.

Socrates first corrects the assertion that the shepherd fattens his flock for his own private advantage, because it follows from the rule laid down by Thrasymachus himself, that properly speaking, the shepherd, in so far as he is a shepherd, considers simply the good of his sheep. Further, how can we account for the fact that a governor expects to be paid for his work except on the supposition that the benefits of government accrue not to the governor, but to the subject? Indeed, strictly speaking, every artist is remunerated, mediately by his art, but immediately by what Socrates calls 'the art of wages', which generally accompanies the others.

Secondly, he turns to the position that perfect injustice is more profitable than perfect justice, and elicits from Thrasymachus the assertion that justice is mere good nature, whereas injustice is genuine good policy, and therefore wise and good and powerful. By a display of verbal ingenuity he forces him to admit, (1) that the unjust man tries to go beyond or overreach both the just and the unjust, while the just man only tries to overreach the unjust: (2) that everyone who is skilful in an art, and therefore wise, and therefore good, endeavours to go beyond or outdo, not the skilful, but the unskilled: (3) that therefore the good and wise do not try to go beyond those who are like themselves, but only those who are unlike themselves: whence we may infer that the just man is wise and good, and that the unjust man is evil and ignorant. He then proceeds to show that injustice tends to produce strife and division, while justice induces harmony and concord; and that injustice destroys all capacity for joint action both in states and in individuals, and is therefore an element of weakness, not of strength.

Finally, Socrates endeavours to show that the soul, like the eye and the ear and every other thing, has a work or function to perform, and possesses a virtue by which alone it can be enabled to perform that work. This virtue of the soul is justice; and therefore without justice the soul's work cannot be well done, and the soul itself cannot live happily. Hence the just man is happy, and the unjust man is miserable; and therefore injustice can never be more profitable than justice. Still, Socrates admits that these arguments are not conclusive to his own mind, because he has not yet discovered the real nature of justice.

BOOK II

In the beginning of the second book, Glaucon and Adeimantus resume the ground which Thrasymachus has resigned. They would gladly believe that a just life is really preferable to an unjust life, but they cannot help seeing that too much stress has been laid by the eulogists of justice upon its accidental advantages, to the neglect of its intrinsic qualities. Would not a person be quite ready to commit injustice, if he could be sure of never suffering from the injustice of other men? Is not justice a kind of compromise, brought about by the necessities of social life? Do the poets ever praise it in, and for, itself? And assuming the existence of the gods, how do they regard the just and the unjust man? May not the sins of the latter be expiated by sacrifice; and in that case, will he not be as happy as the just man in the next world, and is he not much happier than the just in the present life?

Socrates acknowledges the difficulty of the question, and proposes to examine the nature of justice and injustice in a wider field, and on a larger scale. May not justice be predicated of a state, as well as of an individual? And if so, will it not be more fully developed, and therefore more intelligible, in the former than in the latter? Let us trace the rise of a state, and then we shall be able also to trace the rise of justice and injustice.

Man, isolated from his fellow-men, is not self-sufficient. Hence the origin of society, and of the state, which requires the concurrence of four or five men at least, who establish the first elements of a division of labour, which becomes more minute as the members of the community increase. Thus the society comprises at first only husbandmen, builders, clothiers, shoemakers. To these are soon added carpenters, smiths, shepherds, graziers. Gradually a foreign trade arises, which necessitates increased production at home, in order to pay for the imported goods. Production carried out on so large a scale will call into existence a class of distributors, shops and a currency. Thus the state requires merchants, sailors, shop-keepers and hired labourers.

A state thus constituted will be well supplied with the necessaries of life, if its members do not multiply too rapidly for its resources. But if it is to be supplied with the luxuries, as well as with the necessaries, of life, it must contain in addition cooks, confectioners, barbers, actors, dancers, poets, physicians, etc. It will therefore require a larger territory, and this want may involve it in a war with its neighbours. But war implies soldiers, and soldiers must be carefully trained to their profession. Hence the state must possess a standing army, or class of guardians.

How are these guardians to be selected, and what qualities must they possess? They must be strong, swift and brave, high-spirited but gentle, and endowed with a taste for philosophy.

But how must they be educated? In the first place, we must be very scrupulous about the *substance* of the stories which they are taught in their childhood. Nothing derogatory to the dignity of the gods must be admitted in these tales. They must not be taught that the gods wage war against one another, or that they break treaties, or that they afflict men with misfortunes, or that they appear in a variety of shapes on earth, or that they mislead us by falsehood. Neither must they be encouraged to fear death, by being told that the future life is a gloomy one: nor must the characters of great men be represented to them in an unworthy, or ludicrous, or sensual light. On the contrary, truth, courage and self-control must be inculcated by all the stories that are employed in their education.

BOOK III

In the second place, the *form* in which the stories are conveyed will greatly affect the nature of their influence. Poetry may be either purely imitative, as in the drama; or purely narrative, as in the dithyramb; or a compound of both, as in the epic. Now the same person cannot do, or imitate, a great number of things successfully. Hence, if the guardians are to study imitation at all, they must only be allowed to imitate men of high and exalted character. The style in which such men speak and write is always simple and severe, and very sparingly interspersed with imitation. Such, therefore, must be the style in which the guardians are to be permitted to speak themselves, and in which the poets who superintend their education must be compelled to write.

Again: strict regulations must be enforced with reference to songs, harmonies and musical instruments. No soft and enervating music is to be admitted into the perfect state. All musical instruments must be excluded, with the exception of the lyre, the guitar and the pipe. Similarly, all complex rhythms are to be prohibited, and only the simple ones retained. And the object of all these regulations is to foster and develop in the minds of the pupils a sense of beauty, harmony and proportion, which will influence their whole character and all their intercourse with one another.

Having thus discussed music, in the Greek sense of the term, Socrates proceeds in the next place to discuss gymnastic. The diet of the guardians must be simple and moderate, and therefore healthy. This will make them independent of the physician's advice, except under peculiar circumstances. And here we must remember that it is a mistake to regard gymnastic as simply bearing the same relation to the body that music does to the mind. Rather we ought to say that gymnastic develops the spirited element of our nature, just as music develops the philosophic: and the great object of all education is to temper and blend these two elements together in just and harmonious proportion.

So much for the education and discipline of the guardians. Now obviously, the magistrates of the state must be chosen out of this superior class. They must, indeed, be the oldest, the most prudent, the ablest, and above all the most patriotic and unselfish members of the body. These are the true guardians of the state; the remainder are to be called auxiliaries. And in order to convince the citizens of the wisdom and justice of this order of things, we must tell them a story to the effect that they were all originally fashioned in the bowels of the earth, their common mother; and that it pleased the gods to mix gold in the composition of some of them, silver in that of others, iron and copper in that of others. The first are to be guardians, the second auxiliaries, the third husbandmen and craftsmen; and this rule must be most carefully observed and perpetuated, otherwise the state will most certainly perish.

Finally, we must select a camp within the city for this army of guardians and auxiliaries, in which they are to live a hardy, frugal life, quartered in tents, not in houses, supported by the contributions of the other citizens, and above all, possessed of nothing which they can call their own: otherwise they are almost sure to become wolves instead of watch-dogs.

BOOK IV

Hereupon Adeimantus objects that the life of this select body of guardians will be anything but a happy one.

Perhaps so, replies Socrates; but that is not the question. The object of the true legislator is to make the entire state, with its three classes of guardians, auxiliaries and producers, a happy one. And this leads him to consider the duties of the Guardians. In the first place, they must endeavour to remove any tendency to excessive wealth or excessive poverty in the other members of the state. In the second place, they must be on their guard against a too rapid increase of territory. In the third place, all innovations in music and gymnastic must be strenuously put down. All minor regulations may be safely left to the discretion of the magistrates for the time being; and the religious rites and ceremonies must be referred to the decision of the Delphian Apollo.

And now, having traced the rise of a state from first to last, Socrates returns to the question – what is justice? And in what part of the state are we to look for it?

The state, if it has been rightly organised, must be perfectly good. If perfectly good, it must be wise, brave, temperate and just. Hence, regarding the virtue of the state as a given quantity, made up of wisdom, courage, temperance and justice, if we can find three of these, we shall by that very process have discovered the nature of the fourth.

The wisdom of the state obviously resides in the small class of guardians or magistrates. The courage of the state, also obviously, resides in the auxiliaries, and consists essentially in ever maintaining a right estimate of what is, or is not, really formidable.

The essence of temperance is restraint. The essence of political temperance lies in recognising the right of the governing body to the allegiance and obedience of the governed. It does not reside in one particular class, like wisdom and courage, but is diffused throughout the entire state in the form of a common consent, or harmony, upon this subject. Thus we have found the three: where, then, is the fourth?

After eliminating wisdom, courage and temperance, there still remains a something which enables the other three to take root in the state, and preserves them intact therein. This something must therefore be justice. It may be defined as that which teaches everybody to attend to his own business without meddling in that of other people – which fuses together the three classes in the state and keeps each in its proper place. Conversely, the essence of political injustice lies in a meddling, restless spirit pervading the three classes, and leading each to meddle with the offices, tools and duties of the other two.

Let us apply these results to the individual man.

What is found in the state must be also found in the individual. For how could it enter the state except through the individual members of the state? Hence we should expect to find in the individual man three principles, corresponding to the three classes of the state. Let us see whether this expectation is well grounded.

Two contradictory impulses, co-existing in the mind, cannot proceed from the same source. A thirsty man is often unwilling to drink. Hence there must be two principles within him – one prompting him, the other forbidding him, to drink. The former proceeds from appetite or desire, the latter from reason. Hence we have at least two distinct elements in the soul – one rational, the other irrational, appetitive or concupiscent.

In the same way we find ourselves obliged to distinguish a third element, which is the seat of anger, spirit and resentment, and may be called the spirited or passionate or irascible element. When there is any division between the rational and the irrational principles, this third principle always arrays itself on the side of the former. Thus we have the rational, the spirited and the concupiscent element in the individual, corresponding to the guardians, the auxiliaries and the productive class in the state. Hence the individual is wise in virtue of the wisdom of the rational element; courageous in virtue of the courage of the spirited element; temperate when the rational element governs with the full consent of the other two; and, finally, just when each of the three performs its own proper work without meddling with that of the others. And will not this inward harmony of the mind show itself outwardly in the performance of all those acts which are ordinarily considered just, and in the studied avoidance of everything unjust?

Injustice, on the other hand, disturbs and confounds the functions of the three principles; and this destruction of their concord and harmony shows itself externally in a variety of criminal acts. Justice, then, is a kind of natural harmony and healthy habit of mind, while injustice is a kind of unnatural discord and disease. And if so, surely it is superfluous to inquire which of the two is the more profitable to the possessor.

BOOK V

Having arrived at this point, Socrates is proceeding to describe the principal varieties of mental constitution and political organisation, when he is interrupted by Polemarchus and Adeimantus, who with the concurrence of the rest of the party beg him to explain in detail the community of women and children, to which he had before briefly alluded. With great reluctance he complies with their request.

The women, then, according to Socrates, are to be trained and educated exactly like the men. For the woman is just as capable of music and gymnastic as the man; and like him, she displays marked ability for a variety of pursuits – the only difference being one of degree, not of kind, caused by the fact that the woman is weaker than the man. Those women who give evidence of a turn for philosophy or war are to be associated with the guardians or auxiliaries, are to share their duties and become their wives. The connections thus formed are to be placed entirely under the control of the magistrates, and sanctified by religious solemnities; and the children are to be separated from their parents, and brought up in a state-establishment. In this way, and only in this way, is it possible for the guardians and auxiliaries to lose all sense of private property, and thus become conscious of a perfect unity of interest, which will preserve an unbroken harmony between these two bodies themselves, and between the individual members of them.

Socrates then proceeds to lay down rules for the early initiation of the children into the art of war; for the treatment of the cowards and of the brave; for the plundering of the dead, and the erection of trophies.

Hereupon Adeimantus, while admitting that such a community of women and children is in many ways highly desirable, calls upon Socrates to show whether, and how far, such a state of things is practicable.

To this Socrates replies by reminding Adeimantus that his object throughout has been to sketch a perfect commonwealth, in the full expectation of discovering thereby the nature of justice. The possibility of realising such a commonwealth in actual practice is quite a secondary consideration, which does not in the least affect the soundness of the method or the truth of the results. All that can fairly be demanded of him is to show how the imperfect polities at present existing may be brought most nearly into harmony with the perfect state which has just been described.

To bring about this great result, one fundamental change is necessary, and only one. The highest political power must, by some means or other, be vested in philosophers. To obviate the opposition which this paradox is likely to encounter, let us inquire into the nature of the true philosopher.

In the first place, the true philosopher is devotedly fond of wisdom in all its branches. And here we must carefully distinguish between the genuine and the counterfeit lover of wisdom. The point of the distinction lies in this, that the latter contents himself, for example, with the study of the variety of beautiful objects with which we are surrounded, whereas the former is never satisfied till he has penetrated to the essence of beauty in itself. The intellectual state of the former may be described as opinion, that of the latter as real knowledge, or science. For we have two extremes: (1) real existence, apprehended by science, and (2) the negation of existence, or nonexistence, which is to the negation of knowledge, or ignorance, what real existence is to science. Intermediate between real existence and nonexistence stands phenomenal existence; and intermediate between science and ignorance stands opinion. Hence we conclude that opinion takes cognisance of phenomenal existence. Those who study real existence must be called lovers of wisdom, or philosophers; those who study phenomenal existence must be called lovers of opinion, not philosophers.

BOOK VI

Thus we have learned to distinguish between genuine and counterfeit philosophers; and obviously the former, if any, are to be made the guardians of a state. Now let us enumerate the characteristics of the true philosophic disposition. They are: (1) an eager desire for the knowledge of all real existence; (2) hatred of falsehood, and devoted love of truth; (3) contempt for the pleasures of the body; (4) indifference to money; (5) highmindedness and liberality; (6) justice and gentleness; (7) a quick apprehension and a good memory; (8) a musical, regular and harmonious disposition.

Here Adeimantus objects that though he cannot deny the force of the arguments of Socrates, still in practice he finds that the devoted students of philosophy always become eccentric and useless, if not entirely depraved.

That is very true, replies Socrates; but on whom are we to lay the blame of such a state of things? Not on philosophy, but on the degraded condition of the politics and the politicians of the day. For in the present state of things, the genuine philosophic disposition is liable to be corrupted by a variety of adverse influences; and when those who might have proved genuine philosophers have been drawn away from the pursuit of philosophy, their place is supplied by bands of worthless and incompetent students, who by their sophistry and absurdities bring philosophy into general disrepute. The few who continue steadfast in their allegiance to philosophy resign politics in disgust, and are well content if they can escape the corrupting effect of contact with the world.

How is this evil to be remedied? The state itself must regulate the study of philosophy, and must take care that the students pursue it on right principles, and at a right age. And now, surely, we may expect to be believed when we assert that if a state is to prosper, it must be governed by philosophers. If such a contingency should ever take place (and why should it not?), our ideal state will undoubtedly be realised. So that, upon the whole, we come to this conclusion: the constitution just described is the best, if it can be realised; and to realise it is difficult, but not impossible.

The inference, then, is clear: these true philosophers are the genuine guardians of the ideal state. And thus Socrates is led to resume the question of the education of the guardians. He had before mentioned a number of tests to which they were to be submitted, previous to their being invested with authority as magistrates. He now goes on to say that they must be exercised, besides, in a variety of studies, ascending gradually from the lowest to the highest, in order to test still further their intellectual and moral qualities.

But what are these highest studies? The highest of all is the study of 'the good', whose possession is blindly coveted by all men, though none can give a clear account of its nature. Is it not obvious, then, that the guardians of the state must study this good? For without it, how can they perform the duties of their station?

What is this good? asks Adeimantus. Socrates confesses that he cannot answer the question definitely. He can only convey his notion of it by an analogy. In the world of sense we have the sun, the eye, visible objects: answering to which we have, in the intellectual world, the good, reason, the forms or archetypes of visi-objects, or in the language of Socrates, ideas. Or we may represent the same conception to ourselves more precisely thus. There are two worlds, one visible – that is, apprehended by the eye – the other intellectual – that is, apprehended by the pure intelligence. Each world comprises two subdivisions, which proceeding from the most uncertain to the most certain, are: (A) in the visible world, (1) images, i.e. shadows, reflections, &c.; (2) objects, i.e. all material things, whether animate or inanimate: (B) in the intellectual world, (1) knowledge attained by the aid of assumed premises on which all the conclusions depend, and employing by way of illustration the second class of (A), e.g. geometry; (2) knowledge in the investigation of which no material objects, but only the essential forms, are admitted, and in which hypotheses are used simply as a means of arriving at an absolute first principle from which unerring conclusions may be deduced.

Corresponding to these four classes, we have four mental states which, again proceeding from the most uncertain, are (a) conjecture, (b) belief, (c) understanding, (d) reason.

BOOK VII

And now, Socrates proceeds, to understand the real import of such an education as we have described, let us figure to ourselves a number of persons chained from their birth in a subterranean cavern, with their backs to the entrance of the cavern and a fire burning behind them, between which and the prisoners runs a roadway flanked by a wall high enough to conceal the persons who pass along the road, while it allows the shadows of things which they carry upon their heads to be thrown by the fire upon the wall of the cavern facing the prisoners, to whom these shadows will appear the only realities. Now suppose that one of them has been unbound, and taken up to the light of day, and gradually habituated to the objects around him, till he has learned really to appreciate them. Such a man is to the prisoners what the rightly-educated philosopher is to the mass of half-educated men. If he returns to the cavern, and resumes his old seat and occupations, he will at first be the laughing-stock of the place, just as the philosopher is the laughing-stock of the multitude. But once rehabituated to the cavern, his knowledge of the objects which throw the shadows will enable him to surpass the prisoners on their own ground. In the same way the philosopher, when once habituated to intercourse with the world, will surpass his worldly antagonists in the use of their own weapons. This we must compel our guardians to do.

To carry out the analogy still further, just as the whole body of the released prisoner was turned round in order to bring his eye to look in the right direction, so the purpose of education is to turn the whole soul round, in order that the eye of the soul, or reason, may be directed to the right quarter. Education does not generate or infuse a new principle; it only guides and directs a principle already in existence.

How is this revolution of the soul to be brought about? – By the agency of studies which tend to draw the mind from the sensuous to the real – from the visible to the invisible and eternal: and all pursuits which excite the mind to reflect upon the essential nature of things will produce this result. The series of studies of which this may be predicated comprises: (1) arithmetic; (2) plane geometry; (3) geometry of three dimensions; (4) astronomy pursued abstractly as a science of motion; (5) the science of harmonics; (6) dialectic, or the science of real existence.

Having finished the discussion of the nature of right education, Socrates proceeds to lay down a few general rules for the selection of the persons on whom such an education is to be bestowed, and for the time of life at which each branch of it is to be taken up. Above all, the study of dialectic must not be begun too early; otherwise it will certainly be perverted to a bad use. And here the discussion of the perfect state, and of the perfect man, terminates.

BOOK VIII

At the beginning of the eighth book Socrates resumes the subject which he had just commenced at the end of the fourth book, when he was interrupted by Adeimantus and Polemarchus, namely the principal varieties of mental constitution and political organisation.

All conceivable polities may be reduced to five great classes, represented by aristocracy, timocracy, oligarchy, democracy, and despotism or tyranny. Hence there are also five great classes of individual character, corresponding to the five kinds of common-wealth. For (urges Socrates) the state is the product of its individual citizens, and therefore the character of the former is to be traced in the character of the latter.

The perfect state and the perfect man, i.e. aristocracy and the aristocratical man, have already been discussed. It remains to trace the origin, and describe the character, of the four inferior men and states.

Everything that has had a beginning is liable to decay. Hence in the course of time divisions will arise between the three classes of the perfect commonwealth, and between the members of the classes themselves. The result will probably be an accommodation between the factions of the two higher classes, on the understanding that they shall divide the property of the other citizens, and reduce the third class to the condition of slaves or serfs. The distinguishing feature of such a state will be the preponderance of the spirited element, shown in a warlike, restless and ambitious spirit; whence Socrates calls it timocracy or timarchy, the government of honour.

Corresponding to this state, we have the timocratical man, in whom the spirited element and the love of honour are also predominant, and whom we may represent to ourselves as the son of the aristocratical man, partially seduced by evil influences from the pursuit of his father's example.

The love of wealth which entered with timocracy grows till it transforms timocracy into oligarchy, the essence of which consists in making political power depend upon a property qualification. This is its grand vice, and one consequence of it is that in such a commonwealth the extremes of wealth and poverty are found side by side. The city is divided into two sections, the rich and the poor, who hate and plot against one another.

Similarly, we may represent the oligarchical man to ourselves as the son of a timocratical man, whose career of ambition has been suddenly cut short, and whose son has consequently been deterred from the pursuit of honour, and become devoted to the pursuit of gain. Like the oligarchical state, he is a prey to inward divisions, though he keeps up appearances for the sake of improving his prospects of success in the acquisition of wealth.

The extravagant love of riches which pervades the governing body in an oligarchy gradually produces a dangerous class of poverty-stricken men, who at length appeal to arms, expel the rich, and establish an equality of civic rights. This is democracy. Liberty, degenerating into licence, is the chief feature of such a state.

In the same way, the democratical man is one in whom the licentious and extravagant desires have expelled the moderate appetites and the love of decorum which he inherited from his oligarchical father. Such a man lives a life of enjoyment from day to day, guided by no regulating principle, but turning from one pleasure to another, just as the fancy takes him. All pleasures are in his eyes equally good, and equally deserving of cultivation. In short, his motto is 'Liberty and Equality'.

The extravagant love of liberty which marks democracy prepares the way, by a natural reaction, for tyranny. The future tyrant is at first the select champion of the people in the contest with the oligarchical faction. Gradually he becomes more and more powerful, and if he is banished, soon returns with an accession of influence: next he obtains a bodyguard under specious pretences, and finally turns out a consummate tyrant.

BOOK IX

Lastly we come to the tyrannical man. He is the true child of the democratical man – one in whom a single absorbing passion has gradually become predominant, which takes under its protection all the lower appetites and desires, and ministers to their gratification. He is full of all kinds of cravings, which he is ready to satisfy at the expense of the violation of every natural tie. Faithless, unjust, unholy, this tyrannical man is the destined tyrant of the tyrannical state.

Now, as state is to state in point of happiness or misery, so is man to man. The aristocratical state is obviously the most virtuous and the happiest; the tyrannical state is confessedly the most wicked and miserable. Therefore the aristocratical man is the most virtuous and happy; the tyrannical despot, the most wicked and wretched.

Again: the soul of man contains, as we have found, three specific principles, the rational or wisdom-loving, the spirited or honour-loving, and the appetitive or gain-loving. There are likewise three species of pleasure, corresponding to these three principles. Now the philosopher extols wisdom as the source of greatest pleasure; the ambitious man, honour; the lover of gain, wealth. Which of the three is right? Which of the three can judge most correctly? Obviously the philosopher, because not only is he alone acquainted practically with all the three classes of pleasure, but also the organ employed in passing judgment is eminently his. Therefore we conclude that the pleasures of wisdom occupy the first rank; of honour, the second; of riches, the third. Therefore, once again we find that wisdom, virtue and happiness are inseparable.

Again: who can tell what pleasure really is, or know it in its essence, except the philosopher, who alone is conversant with realities? Hence we are justified in asserting that true pleasure can only be *then* attained, when the soul is attuned to harmony under the governance of the wisdom-loving or rational principle. Hence the more reasonable is a desire, the more pleasurable is its gratification. That which is most orderly and lawful is also most reasonable. Now, the desires of the aristocratical man are the most orderly and lawful, and therefore their gratification is attended with the most real pleasure. On the other hand, the desires of the tyrannical man are most remote from law and order, and therefore their gratification is attended with a very inferior amount of pleasure. Hence we find again that the aristocratical man is happier than the tyrannical.

And now we are in a position to criticise the doctrine advanced by Thrasymachus, that it is for a man's advantage to be thoroughly unjust, so long as he can evade the penalties of his crimes by keeping up the appearance of justice. We may figure to ourselves the human soul under the picture of a man, a lion, and a many-headed serpentine monster, combined together under a human form. This done, we may say to the man who declares that it is expedient to commit injustice, that in effect he maintains that it is expedient to starve and enfeeble the man, and to feast and strengthen the lion and the serpent. But this is, unquestionably, a monstrous hypothesis. So that all things considered, we conclude that it is best for everybody to be governed by a just and divine principle, which ought, if possible, to reside in a man's own soul; but if not, it must be imposed from without, in order that harmony may prevail in our social relations, from the fact of our acknowledging universally the authority of one master. To maintain this inward and outward harmony will be the single object of the just man, who will model himself on the pattern of this perfect commonwealth, which doubtless exists in heaven, if not upon earth.

BOOK X

In the tenth book, Socrates resumes the subject of poetry, and imitation generally. What, he inquires, is imitative art?

Take, by way of example, a bed or a table. We have: (1) the form or archetype of a bed, created by god, (2) the bed itself, made by the manufacturer, (3) the bed as represented by the painter, which is a copy of the second, which again is a copy of the first.

In the same way the poet imitates, not the forms, which are the only realities, but simply the phenomena of daily life and the opinions prevalent among the half-educated.

Or, again, look at it thus. Every manufactured article, e.g. a bridle, gives occasion to three separate arts; of which one teaches how to use the thing, another how to make it, the third how to imitate it. The user alone possesses a scientific acquaintance with the thing, and instructs the maker how to make it; the latter, therefore, possesses correct opinion. On the other hand, the imitator cannot be said to possess either science or correct opinion, but only vague notions, about the things which he imitates.

Again: to what part of the mind does imitative art address itself?

Certainly not to the rational element, which is the noblest part of our nature, but to some inferior element, which is always ready to give way under the pressure of calamity, and is full of change and perturbation, and which therefore offers, in return, the widest field for imitation. For a tranquil and sober temper presents small attraction to the imitative poet, and will not repay the trouble of imitation, or be appreciated by those to whom the poet is wont to address himself.

But worst of all, poetry weakens the mind by leading us to sympathise too deeply with the afflictions of others, and thus rendering us unfit to bear up under our own troubles. Therefore we are compelled, much against our will, to lay down the rule that only hymns in honour of the gods, and eulogies of great men and noble actions, are to be admitted into the perfect state. For it is no easy task to become a good man, and everything which opposes our progress in virtue must be scrupulously avoided.

This subject concluded, Socrates proceeds to discuss the rewards of virtue, which are infinitely enhanced by the consideration of the immortality of the soul, of which he here subjoins a short proof.

To everything there is a special vice or infirmity attached, by which, and which alone, that thing can be destroyed. Thus blindness destroys the eyesight, mildew destroys corn, and rot destroys timber. The peculiar infirmities attached to the soul are injustice, intemperance, cowardice, ignorance. Can these bring about the dissolution of the soul? No, certainly not: for they cannot destroy the soul immediately, as a disease destroys the body. though they may be, mediately, the cause of a man's being put to death by other people, which is quite a different thing. But if wickedness cannot destroy the soul, nothing else can; therefore the soul is immortal.

And now, having satisfied ourselves that justice is, in itself, the just man's best reward, we may fairly take into account the honours and emoluments which gods and men bestow upon him. For we cannot doubt that he is loved by the gods, and that all the dispensations of providence are designed for his good, even when they seem most adverse. And even men are sure to love and honour him, towards the close of his life, if not before. Still, all these rewards are as nothing when compared with those which after death await the just. To illustrate this, Socrates narrates the fable of Er the son of Armenius; and with this story the *Republic* closes.